About the author

Ifi Amadiume is an award-winning poet and a political activist as well as an academic. She has lived in Nigeria and the UK and is currently associate professor at Dartmouth College, Hanover. There, she teaches in both the Department of Religion and the African-American Studies Programme. Professor Amadiume is author of the influential *Male Daughters, Female Husbands* (Zed Books, 1988) which won the Choice Outstanding Academic Book of the Year award in 1989.

Daughters of the Goddess, Daughters of Imperialism: African women struggle for culture, power and democracy

Ifi Amadiume

Zed Books Ltd
LONDON • NEW YORK

Daughters of the Goddess, Daughters of Imperialism: African women struggle for culture, power and democracy was first published by Zed Books, 7 Cynthia Street, London N1 9JF, UK and Room 400, 175 Fifth Avenue, New York, NY 10010, USA in 2000

Distributed in the USA exclusively by St Martin's Press, Inc., 175 Fifth Avenue, New York, NY 10010, USA.

Cover designed by Andrew Corbett
Set in Monotype Ehrhardt and Univers by Ewan Smith
Printed and bound in the United Kingdom by Biddles Ltd, Guildford and King's Lynn

A catalogue record for this book is available from the British Library

ISBN 1 85649 805 0 cased
ISBN 1 85649 806 9 limp

Contents

This book is dedicated to the friends I made in Nigeria – courageous journalists, activist students and lecturers, committed trade unionists and unstoppable daughters of the Goddess – all of whom demonstrated to me the true meaning of commitment in the pursuit of social justice as they risked their lives in struggle under impossible conditions.

It is also dedicated to those African children and daughters of the Goddess betrayed and humiliated in refugee camps – more especially to the memory of the two Guinean children, Yaguine Koita, aged 15, and Fode Tounkara, aged 14, who died on 2 August 1999 in the landing gear of an aeroplane to Europe, on a suicidal mission to beg European leaders to save Africa.

Preface

After completing *Male Daughters, Female Husbands*, which involved intensive field work in rural Nnobi, I knew that I wanted to continue research on gender, women's organizations and power, but this time focusing more on contemporary history. The problem was how to make the shift from a methodology applied to work on a given Igbo society, although contextualized in a wider Igbo social history, to the study of gender, class and women's organizations in a broader national context.

When this research began in Nigeria in 1986, my experiences of work with local women and women's groups in the London Borough of Camden influenced my initial decision to document women's campaign issues and areas of abuse of children and women in Nigeria. It was not difficult to collect that kind of data: in the mid-1980s the Nigerian press was quite advanced, extremely vocal and a forum for debate and civil discourse. Women's groups were also making good use of the media to publicize issues. I was, however, soon dissatisfied with the laundry-list approach to women's issues. Between the end of 1985 and early 1987, when I was employed in the Institute for Development Studies, University of Nigeria, Enugu Campus, I revisited Nnobi and conducted local research and interviews. The gathering of data became more meaningful as a result of belonging, participating, observing and analysing. The importance of contextualized issues, particularly in relation to other social categories of persons or groups involved, redirected my interest to the question of structures and social institutions; hence the emphasis placed on local authorities as connecting institutions and platforms of contestation for resources and power between various classes of women.

This re-emphasis on structures and institutions enabled me to make the historical, spatial and cultural transitions necessary to connect the powerful titled women leaders of traditional African societies featured in *Male Daughters, Female Husbands* with the working concept 'daughters of the Goddess', applied in this study, in contrast to contemporary African women leaders empowered by European imperialism in Africa. By doing so, I know that I am laying myself open to criticism, and it is my intention to invite open debate on our contemporary failings in African women's movements.

My stay in Nigeria, 1985–87, coincided with great transformative events such as the 1985 IMF debate, the theme of which was 'to take or not to take?' Public opinion was against taking an IMF loan. In 1986, Nigerian public debate resulted in a proposal for a new political dispensation. In that same year, however, the military government went ahead and accepted an IMF loan and its required Structural Adjustment Programme (SAP). Its disintegrating effect on the economy was immediate and social conditions worsened. The military regime became even more brutal and fascist, and corruption spread. My choice of contrasting pre-SAP and post-SAP political discourses is therefore informed by history.

The scope of study widened when I returned to Britain in 1987, and again when I moved to the USA in 1993. Events, such as post-apartheid South Africa and the Fourth World Conference on Women in Beijing, in 1995, unfolded and fitted into my analysis. They gave me an opportunity to expand my comparative study of the gender and class politics of women's activities and the structures of relationships at local, national and international levels.

Critical as I am of how international women's conferences have become formalizing instruments of class reproduction, I am very much in favour of national and local conferences. In this, I am in agreement with Tabitha Kanongo[1] who stresses the importance of the body of 'knowledge' emerging from these debates as significant for academic analysis. This is specifically in its portrayal of the dynamism of the contemporary social situations where opinions are voiced and countered in open dialogue and debate, both verbally and in the popular presses. A researcher has direct access to social actors and social commentaries and ideas when attending these conferences and debates, and then reading the reports and interpretations in the local papers. For this work local sources of data include interviews, observed events, government reports, local press publications and opinions expressed in local newspapers.

I have avoided as much as possible the rhetoric of marginality and otherness, which I believe unfortunately shifts the focus from social actors as subjects to social actors as constructed objects of colonizing cultures. That kind of focus shows little knowledge of grassroots or folk-rich cultures and deep histories, nor does it reveal the exciting varieties in styles of oratory, argumentation and philosophizing, and people's expressions of their struggles against dominance.

Where possible, I have allowed social actors to speak for themselves. I have included many names of contemporary women in order that their contributions do not go unrecorded in history. This is a book full of local voices. So many women inspired me by the spirit of their commitment to activism that I promised to include as many names as I could. I hope I have not let them down.

By criticizing others, I have also criticized myself. As someone of privilege, I am saying all is not well: let us enter the twenty-first century with self-examination and, better still, argument, debate and resistance, in order to move forward in the struggle – empowering others, not just reinventing ourselves.

Ifi Amadiume
Dartmouth College, USA

Note

1. Tabitha Kanongo, 'Perceiving Women in Kenya's History', *Africa World Review*, May–October 1992.

Acknowledgements

In my immediate family, thanks to my children Kemdi and Amadi for simply being with me at all times! Thanks too to my dad, and my brothers and sisters, Ikem, Chinelo, Chidi, Ngozi and Ego for their love and patience. I still cry for my dead mum! Thanks to my people in Nnobi.

Staff at IDS, Enugu, thank you for a fellowship at your institute which gave me a chance to learn about rural development. CODESRIA and the friends that I made through your organization, I thank you for giving me the opportunity to be revitalized by several visits to Africa. Co-ordinators of CODESRIA social movements national network, thanks for your intellectual stimulation, and for asking me hard questions about gender and social movements. I am still researching them!

The London crowd, particularly friends at Finsbury Park, thanks for all your support. Nana and Uncle Commy, thanks for having the kids on Sundays. Laura, thanks for sitting and chatting even when I am typing away and seem distant! Little Jamie, thanks for liking my cooking! Thanks too to the twins, Soul and Joseph, who competed to ride pickaback on my back!

Deborah Hodges, administrative assistant in the Anthropology Department at Dartmouth College, scanned and retyped the manuscript brought from England into a computer, which made continued work on this book much easier for me. I thank you and other friends in the USA and Dartmouth College. Thanks to Malaika Omowale, my student research assistant, for references on reproductive health. I want also to acknowledge the useful comments of the late Professor Claude Ake and all those who attended the 1995 CASS conference in Lagos, Nigeria, on the health and rights of women.

I would like it to be known that I did not receive any funding for this research or to write this book, since African scholars, especially women, continue to receive little academic grant support.

I thank Louise Murray and Zed for finally agreeing to publish this book, and Ewan Smith for its production.

Nigeria: Statistics, Chronology, Human Rights

The nation-state known as Nigeria was created by British colonialists. Today, Nigeria has the highest population in Africa and occupies an area of 357,000 square miles (924,000 square kilometres). Its economy now ranks fourth in size after South Africa, Algeria and Egypt. Average GNP is estimated at US$310. The official census, which may be unreliable, in 1991 estimated the population at 88.5 million. In reality it is over 100 million. Over 80 per cent of people live in the rural areas. In October 1991, there were 30 states and 589 Local Government Areas (LGAs) whose population ranged between 150,000 and 800,000; in 1996, the Abacha regime increased them to 36 states and 772 LGAs.

Ethnic and religious mix

There is great diversity in language and ethnicity, yet at the same time there are shared traditions, values, behaviour patterns and beliefs.

Languages

There are 395 languages and about 250 ethnic groups divided into about 90,000 named communities. There are three regionally dominant language groups: Hausa-Fulani in the north, Yoruba in the southwest, and Igbo in the southeast.

Religions

The north is predominantly Islamic with pockets of pre-Islamic African religions. In the south, Christian missions have had a greater impact.

Politics

The politics of tribalism/ethnicity and regionalism/statism were introduced during the colonial period. Before, identification was not with tribes but with smaller units such as villages and clan groups.

State creation politics

1963 The Mid-West was carved out of the Western Region
1967 Colonel Yakubu Gowon created twelve states, supposedly to allay the fears of ethnic minorities
1976 Major-General Murtala Mohammed created 19 states
1987 General Babangida created 30 states, plus Abuja, the new federal capital of Nigeria (= 31 states)
1996 General Sani Abacha added six more states

Traditional economies

- mainly agricultural, artisanship craft, highly skilled in trade and commerce
- 1970–76: diversified economic sectors contributing to the GDP; agriculture, livestock, forestry and fishing declining from 48.8 per cent of the GDP in 1970–71 to 27.3 in 1976–77 as economy moved to dependency on oil
- also rapid decline in volumes of principal agricultural exports of cocoa beans, groundnuts, groundnut oil, palm kernel, palm oil, rubber, raw cotton, timber (logs and sawn)
- 1970–71: mining and quarrying increased from 10.2 per cent of GDP to 29.3 in 1976–77
- 1977: GDP per head $420
- 1995: $250 per head

Until the 1960s, Nigeria was the world's largest exporter of groundnut oil and palm produce, and the second largest exporter of cocoa. The three commodities made up 70 per cent of exports. The country was therefore dependent on agricultural exports until the growth in petroleum exports starting in 1969.

Farmers were frustrated by taxation, monopolies and price-fixing by marketing boards and, later, national boards for the various commodities. In the 1980s large-scale farming and development projects involved state intervention and huge borrowings from the World Bank. The Land Use Decree of March 1978 encouraged private sector involvement in large-scale farming. This translated into land appropriation from the peasantry.

Industries and occupations

Agriculture, livestock, forestry and fishing; mining and quarrying; manufacturing and crafts; electricity and water supply; building and construction; distribution; transport and communications; general government; education; health; other services.

Value of naira to US dollar (1980–94)

	1980	1981	1982	1983	1984	1985	1986	1987	1988	1989	1990	1991	1992	1993	1994
Official	0.55	0.61	0.67	0.72	0.77	0.89	2.02	4.02	4.54	7.39	8.04	9.91	17.03	22.05	21.89
Parallel	0.90	0.93	1.14	1.82	3.25	3.79	4.17	5.55	6.05	10.55	9.61	13.40	20.30	36.20	56.95
Inflation rate (%)	9.9	21	7.6	23.2	39.6	5.5	5.4	10.2	56.1	50.5	7.5	12.9	44.6	57.4	57

(*Source:* Central Bank of Nigeria, *Bullion,* Vol. 19, No. 4, October/December, 1995.)

Exchange rate of the naira in the black market rose steadily to between 80 and 100 or more to US dollar.

National economy

This has been troubled by corruption, mismanagement, low productivity and over-dependence on a single resource: oil from the Niger Delta area in the southeast (95 per cent of exports). The oil boom of the 1970s (as a result of 1973 Middle East war) expanded the economy. It contracted as the price of oil fell in the 1980s. This was disastrous because the economy had not diversified. Vast oil riches are enjoyed by a few who flaunt and squander their wealth.

- 1993: crude oil revenue accounted for more than 80 per cent of official revenue
- 1993: Nigeria accounted for 6.9 per cent of OPEC output
- 1994: Nigeria accounted for 7.1 per cent of OPEC output
- Nigerian crude oil export stands at around 1.9 million barrels per day (bpd) at about $14.50 per barrel
- oil companies include Shell-BP, Gulf, Safrap (Elf), Total plc, Mobil Oil plc, National Oil, African Petroleum plc, Texaco Nig. plc, UNI-PETROL Nig. plc, AGIP Nig. plc.
- Public utilities such as National Electrical Power plc, the Nigerian National Telecommunication, the Nigerian Railway, and the Nigerian National Petroleum Corporation perform poorly.

Literacy rate

Adult literacy in 1990 was 50.7 per cent.

Chronology of key dates in history and governance of political regimes

Of the eleven governments since independence, eight have been military and three civilian.

1914　Amalgamation of three separate colonial entities: the Northern and Southern Protectorates and the Colony of Lagos

1922, 1948, 1951　Various constitutions introduce principles of electoral politics. Party formations tend to be along regional–ethnic lines:

- NPC (Northern Peoples Congress) control the Northern Region government
- AG (Action Group) control the Western Region government
- NCNC (National Council of Nigeria and the Cameroons) control the Eastern Region government

1957   The Eastern and Western Regions become self-governing, while the north, fearing southern domination, delays independence

1959   Nigeria becomes self-governing

1060   1 October: Independence Day for a united Nigeria with three regions, including half of Cameroon which voted to remain with Nigeria, while Southern Cameroon voted to leave

1963   1 October: Nigeria becomes a republic with four regions plus the Mid-West

1966   15 January: So-called pro-Igbo coup kills Prime Minister Tafawa Balewa; General J. T. U. Ironsi proclaims military government

      May and September–October: Igbo pogrom

      July: Ironsi overthrown in anti-Igbo coup which installs Colonel Yakubu Gowon; a crisis of confidence follows

1967   27 May: Abolition of four regions in favour of twelve states

      30 May: Secession by Eastern Region and birth of the state of Biafra

      6 July: Start of civil war lasting two and a half years

      November: OPEC terms effective in petroleum industry

1970   12 January: Federal government wins

1971   Nigerian National Oil Corporation established

1975   Gowon government overthrown by General Murtala Mohammed in bloodless coup

1976   February: Murtala Mohammed assassinated; government passes peacefully to General Olusegun Obasanjo

1979   1 October: After thirteen years of military rule, electoral politics for Second Republic NPN – Shehu Shagari, UPN – Awolowo, NPP – Azikiwe, PRP – Aminu Kano, GNPP – Waziri Ibrahim, civilian rule restored

      Alhaji Shehu Shagari elected executive president; oil crash

1983   August: Shagari re-elected for Third Republic

      31 December: coup under General Muhammadu Buhari

1985   27 August: coup under General Ibrahim Babangida

1986   26 September: Nigeria takes IMF loan and imposes SAP

1988   Nigeria's debt is greater than GNP

1993 Elections contested between Bashorun M. K. O. Abiola and Alhaji Bashir Tofa for Fourth Republic which never comes into being; announcement of election results cancelled by Babangida after M. K. O. Abiola wins, gaining 58.4 per cent of the popular vote and a majority in twenty out of thirty states, plus the federal capital, Abuja, thus meeting the constitutional requirements that the winner obtains one-third of the votes in two-thirds of the states

26 August: Babangida forced to resign by a popular civilian opposition movement; hands over power to a nominated interim national government headed by Chief Ernest Shonekan

17 November: General Sani Abacha grabs power from the Shonekan interim government and declares himself head of state, nominating a provisional ruling council

1994 15 May: National Democratic Coalition (NADECO) formed; demands the actualization of 12 June mandate and that M. K. O. Abiola should form a national government by 31 May

31 May: NADECO declared illegal; crackdown on pro-democracy activists

11 June: M. K. O. Abiola declares himself president at Epetedo, Lagos Island; Nigeria locked in a political impasse

5 July: Beginning of oil workers' strike, demanding the installation of Abiola as president

6 July: Abiola charged with treason; imprisoned by General Abacha

8 August: Wole Soyinka, Nobel laureate and pro-democracy activist, goes to court to have the Abacha government declared illegal

12 September: Olu Onagoruwa sacked as attorney-general and minister of justice for disowning eight decrees promulgated by the government

5 November: Abacha launches his wife Maryam's family support programme

29 November: Constitutional Conference sitting in Abuja approves for establishment a national tribunal to identify all corrupt public officers since January 1984 and recover all properties illegitimately acquired by them at public expense

6 December: Constitutional Conference fixes termination of Abacha's government for 1 January 1996

1995 March: Abacha announces foiling a coup plot – over forty people arrested, including former head of state General Olusegun Obasanjo and retired Major-General Musa Yar'Adua, who later dies in gaol of undisclosed causes (8 December 1997)

1 October: Abacha extends his tenure by announcing a three-year transition programme and a handover to a civilian government on 1 October 1998

1996 4 June: Wife of Abiola, Kudirat Abiola, who fought for the release of her husband, is gunned down in broad daylight; her daughter Hafisat Abiola takes up her mother's work

1997 21 December: Supposed second coup against Abacha regime foiled and Lieutenant-General Oladipo Diya, deputy head of state, arrested with eleven others

1998 25 April: After a week of ethnic protests, rioting and bombing that saw nine people killed, parliamentary elections held as a first step of transition to civilian rule; pro-democracy groups tell Nigerians to boycott elections since all five government-sanctioned political parties have adopted Abacha as their presidential candidate; Nigerians register their opposition by refusing to vote; less than 10 per cent turn out

1 May: May Day protests against Abacha; seven people shot dead in Ibadan

8 June: Sudden death of General Abacha from a heart attack at fifty-four, leaving behind a disintegrated nation, impoverished and ethnically divided; news of his death greeted with cheers and street celebrations

9 June: General Abdulsalam Abubakar installed as president; promises to free political prisoners, including General Obasanjo, and to move to a transition to civilian and democratic rule by 29 May 1999 (this brings the total of promised dates of military exit to eight in twenty-two years, only one of which was met by Obasanjo)

7 July: Sudden and suspicious death of Chief Abiola in custody while meeting a high-powered delegation of senior US diplomats including Thomas R. Pickering, the Under-Secretary of State for Political Affairs, and Susan E. Rice, the Assistant Secretary for African Affairs. Widespread ethnic riots follow news of his death

1999 20 February: Vote for 360-member House of Representatives and 109 senators

27 February: Presidential election based more on ethnic alliances than ideological differences. Obasanjo wins nomination of Igbo-dominated People's Democratic Party over Alex Ekwueme, a former vice-president, who had built the party into a national party. The northern-dominated All People's Party goes into alliance with the Yoruba Party, the Alliance for Democracy Party, fielding Olu Falae as presidential candidate.

Seemingly gaining from the slogans of 'power shift' and 'June 12 issue', resulting in a consensus to allow the election of a southern president, Olusegun Obasanjo.

29 May Nigeria's Fourth Republic. General Abubakar becomes the second military ruler to hand over power to a democratically elected civilian government. Obasanjo is sworn in as the first civilian president of Nigeria in sixteen years. Obasanjo, for the first time in contemporary African history, appoints a woman, Dupe Adelaja, as Minister of State in the Ministry of Defence.

Nigerian human rights record

1. The country has suffered chronic political instability due to the failure of both the military and the politicians. The same familiar politicians and retired military have been banned and unbanned from politics. There has always been the same forum for the formation of political parties, e.g. Babangida's National Constitutional Assembly charged with ratifying a constitution for civil government, and under General Sani Abacha, the National Constitutional Conference charged with drawing up a programme for the restoration of democracy.

2. There has been consistent suppression of all forms of opposition.

3. There has been widespread corruption and draining of the economy by both the military and the politicians. In January 1978, Nigeria began borrowing heavily in the Eurocurrency market, resulting in internal and external indebtedness.

4. Spiralling inflation resulted from the SAP. General Babangida put together a Medium Term Economic Programme (MTEP) with the IMF and the World Bank early in 1993 to renegotiate external debt in order to win debt relief and the release of foreign aid for the stimulation of growth and employment. Babangida's government had hoped to gain access to IMF's Enhanced Structural Adjustment Programme (ESAP). General Abacha's short-term economic management strategies moved Nigeria away from IMF-backed free market reforms, fixed the exchange rate at 22 naira to the dollar and outlawed the free market where the dollar fetched twice as much, setting a 21 per cent ceiling on interest rates, arguing that it should be left alone to pursue its own policies and seek its own solutions. The World Bank claimed that Nigeria was not being managed and was out of control. In December 1993 Nigeria's total foreign debt stock was $28.7 billion. In June 1994 it was $29.8 billion, with debt arrears of $5.5 billion. Manufacturers faced difficulties obtaining foreign exchange to pay for imported inputs. Importers demanded a total of $17.7 billion in the first half of 1994 and got only $1.3 billion. In July–August

1994 the economy was at a standstill due to mass protests and strikes. In the first half of 1994 federally collected revenue stood at 95.87 billion naira. Federal government estimated expenditure was 90.7 billion naira, debt service payment accounted for 29.77 billion naira and extra-budgetary expenditure 27.19 billion naira.

5. The country experienced a lack of infrastructural facilities, with poor earnings, health, housing, sanitation, and access to water and electricity.

6. Health and education services collapsed.

7. The Nigerian government has collaborated with oil companies in environmental terrorism and repression: e.g. the plight of the Ogoni People of Rivers state in their conflict with Shell Oil and the imprisonment of Ken Saro-Wiwa, President, Movement for the Survival of Ogoni People (MOSOP) and eight other Ogoni activists. (Local environmental awareness led to the formation of MOSOP in 1992 to demand environmental and social rights.) There was widespread demand for the immediate release of Ken Saro-Wiwa, and for an independent full assessment of environmental and human rights abuses in the region. On 24 May 1994 Amnesty International declared Ken Saro-Wiwa a prisoner of conscience. On 10 November 1995 Ken Saro-Wiwa and eight other activists were hanged.

Introduction

This book critically examines tensions in a genealogy of transformations in women's organizations through a comparative study of the different contexts in which gender, class and race are dynamic factors. I analyse contradictions in rhetoric and practice as these factors shape women's issues and gender equality work in local and global contexts in Nigeria, Africa and Britain. I look at various women's groups and organizations and at the differences in their articulation of women's needs and rights; the formalized nature of the internationally informed language of rights; the laundry-list approach to women's issues in the women and development rhetoric; and the more volatile, combative and subversive language of civil discourse on social justice at the local level. The study then shifts to a structural and institutional perspective that moves beyond formalized rhetoric to contextual contestations of right, thus focusing on concrete situations of women's daily lives and struggles for social justice and the internal fractures and contradictions in the context of western cultural and economic imperialism. This book is therefore about gender, class and race relations under the present state system and the contemporary nature of power between different classes of women locally, nationally and globally.

Gender and the state

Marxist theorization on the state and class considers the state to be an instrument of the ruling class. More recently, using a gender perspective, Robert Fatton, Jr (1989) has applied this theory to the relationship between women, class and the state in Africa. According to Fatton, 'The existence of a ruling class requires the existence of a state whose role is to preserve and reproduce the social, political, and economic structures of the ruling class's dominance' (p. 47). He goes on to state, quite categorically: 'In Africa, class power is state power, the two are fused and inseparable. State power, however, is conspicuously male power, and this in turn implies that African women have been marginalized' (p. 48). This suggests that history has known only one type of state and that in all places at all times state power has been male. I agree with Fatton only to an extent, but argue for specificity and historization (Amadiume 1995).

Fatton argues that the patriarchal character of the state in Africa has meant that men and women of the same class are not equal, not even in the Afro-Marxist socialist states. The critique of the state in Africa has also been extended to the violent character of the neo-colonial state against specific classes of its citizens, especially women, students, the youth and the peasantry. Goran Hyden (1980) has argued that the 'weak' or 'soft' characteristic of this state accounts for its inability to impose its authority on all sectors of society, particularly the peasantry. Fatton rejects this thesis, pointing out the violent and repressive nature of the contemporary state which indicates hardness rather than softness.

It is on the basis of lack of integration that Hyden describes the state as weak. Rather than hardness or weakness, I would like to attribute the problems of the state in Africa to questions of legitimacy and contestation which have a historical explanation. I am going to call the contemporary African state a pseudo-state. The tendency of this state has been to rule through lies, dictatorship and violence. I am therefore in agreement with Fatton on the repressive character of this state, but disagree with him on the question of class and the marginalization of women, for in spite of his stated gender perspective in his analysis of the state, the actual use of gender is still limited to biological gender divisions. Fatton's notion of marginalization is still only in terms of women not having the same access to state power, state facilities and benefits as men. Fatton can therefore reaffirm the primacy of class:

> I contend that while class and state power are manifestly male power and thus contribute to the political underrepresentation and economic marginalization of women, they nonetheless fragment female unity. Indeed, class appurtenance and class interests divide women and overcome the solidarity generated by their common experience of suffering patriarchal abuses. Let me thus join in the old-fashioned pleas for the analytical primacy of class in analyzing society, state, and gender. (Fatton 1989: 64)

I take the position that it is not a question of either class or gender, but how these factors are interrelated in shifting political situations, hence the analytical notions of 'male daughters', 'female husbands' (Amadiume 1987) and 'daughters of the establishment' (Amadiume 1996) which I applied in my study of gender and class dynamic in different social systems which also relate to the state differently, to show how different categories of women wielded power on the basis of gender or class.

This analysis is further developed in the notions of 'daughters of the Goddess' and 'daughters of imperialism' as contrasting and dichotomous working analytical tools which I am going to use in this book to compare the politics and moral values of community-oriented African women leaders working with traditional African matriarchal models of power described in *Male Daughters, Female Husbands* and those women in partnership with the contemporary state and the global model of power. In reality, I accept that in plural systems, given the facts of multiculturalism, things are not quite as clear-cut as that and accept this potential criticism. However, I hope to show that in the competition for scarce social and economic resources, interest groups are manipulating multiple cultures and identities and the 'daughters of imperialism' are getting away with this more than the geographically and morally restricted 'daughters of the Goddess'. First, though, I wish to re-examine the topic of women and class which I have discussed with reference to Robert Fatton, Jr by looking critically at Pat Caplan's work on women and class in India to see what lessons can be drawn from this for a comparative study, as I hold Caplan in high regard and admire her work.

Women and class power

Pat Caplan (1985), in her study of women's organizations in India, applies a class and gender perspective, but seems to have reached a different conclusion from Robert Fatton Jr. She does not see all Indian women as having a common experience of patriarchal abuse, but as quite fundamentally divided by class, with ruling-class women actively involved in the business of class reproduction and the neutralization of the revolutionary potentialities of lower-class women. To what extent are some of the class cultural activities and aspirations which Caplan attributes to Indian women Indian or European? Their social welfare activities seem to me to reflect clearly a European lifestyle. According to Caplan: 'they choose activities that help create the culture specific to a particular class, and for this reason baking a cake, learning to conduct a conversation in English, or giving to and organising charity are important symbolic statements about class' (Caplan 1985: 167).

Caplan's theory of ruling-class Indian women as agents of class reproduction in India or as agents of the state is based on the assumption of a social class as a homogeneous, solid mass. This assumption neglects the fact that in a colonial situation of violent imperialism, the invading ruling class was external to the society. In order to retain control, it had systematically to reproduce something of itself. This it did by creating a new class in its own culture and ideology. In Africa, this was done on an individual basis through religion and mission education. A new space (geographical and cultural) was created in new city centres, new states, new state bureaucracies and other parastatals. The process in India, with its highly developed rigid class and caste system was obviously different. Yet the fact remains that aspects of European culture were imposed on Indians. In other words, India was subjected to European cultural imperialism. In reality, its class cultural expressions are therefore multicultural.

What was the role of European upper-class women and colonial wives in this cultural imperialism in India? Comparing the development of social welfare in Victorian England and modern India, Caplan concludes, 'there are trends in social welfare, and particularly in the association between women and welfare, which both countries have in common. This suggests that even while there are important cultural differences, the development of social welfare is a historically specific process in the growth of capitalism' (p. 217).

This was not the case in the British colonies, where even under non-capitalist economic conditions, colonial policy forcibly transformed natives from farmers to waged labourers and landless peasants. Colonial wives and missionaries at the same time found a relevance as philanthropists, and charity workers, teaching native women to reject their local organizations and form European-style women's organizations to do charity work. The colonial system introduced structures of charity and dependency.

It was European upper-class morality that was reproduced in India. This morality saw women's role in the public sector as limited to welfare activities, and welfare as an extension of women's domestic role. Consequently, the adjectives which upper- and middle-class Indian women apply to lower-class Indian women, such as 'poor', 'suffering', 'helpless', 'backward', 'ignorant' (Caplan pp. 202, 106–7), echo those used by the missionaries and colonial civilizers, as, for example, 'uplift', 'reform', 'rehabilitation', 'guidance', 'enlightenment'. The class rhetoric of the neo-missionaries in the ex-colonies is a familiar one. With a historical perspective which I hope to apply in this study, I am able to show its source, who taught it, when, where, how, and even the names of those who first learnt it willingly or under duress.

It seems therefore that a point of difference between the 'daughters of independence' and those of the colonizers is how to interpret history and how far back to remember. It is really a political question of who did what in history that is most relevant as a critique of continuing imperialism, which embodies a rejection of cultural imperialism. It is in the sense of this rejection of western cultural imperialism that Indian women re-evaluate and reinvent their history, looking back to what they consider the glorious age of women's high status, that is, the Vedic age, the period before the successive Moghul and British foreign invasions.

Such reinvented grand narratives contest imperialism. It is immaterial whether they are true or false; the context of their use is what matters. Non-invasion symbolizes autonomy and self-pride, while invasion signifies defeat and conquest, and therefore loss of self-esteem and autonomy. This I believe explains an equally growing interest in ancient African glories in certain tendencies of the Afrocentric movement. To invade is to violate and reproduce violence as the hunted becomes a hunter, a necessary condition of dominance (Bloch 1991). It is this violation that has determined or generated the gender character of contemporary class systems (Diop 1991; Amadiume 1997), since class power means privilege and unlimited access. Unlimited access means the breaking of boundaries, appropriation and exploitation, which are all characteristics of the contemporary state and the capitalist push for globalization. Yet, imperialism is not without opposition from the bottom up. I examine the counter-formalization opposition tendencies of grassroots people by using the term 'class chaos' which I prefer to the term transition, that has become the fashion these days for describing contemporary political upheavals in Africa.

Chaos in class

One of the most debated topics in the social sciences is the character and role of ritual in society, that is, how do the ruling classes rule? What is the basis of their power? How do they maintain hegemony over the masses? In this debate, there is a general agreement on the important role that ritual or formalized language plays in politics. For some, it is a means of achieving cohesion, while, for others, it fragments as it serves power (Bloch 1974; 1991). There are also differences in how people act in a ritual context. Does the controlled character of ritual or formal language rule out disagreement and opposition? Are people able to act rationally in a ritual context? Marxists have written a lot about the transformation of people's consciousness by the imposition of the ideology of the ruling classes through the educational system. Absolute truth and the right order are so constructed, they argue, that they rule out the possibility of contradiction.

What I am referring to as class chaos in the African situation would disprove this notion of class homogeneity and equilibrium. Because our received European culture was violently enforced and taught, the ability of Africans not to contradict themselves often depended on how well they grasped the English language. It is conceivable, as Frantz Fanon (1967) pointed out, that an alien ritual as an instrument of rule and power imposed a performance syndrome on Africans, whereby one had to learn to copy or to imitate the foreign rulers and their foreign culture. There was therefore a conscious awareness of the alien, meaning that participants could dissent, criticize, opt out or even laugh at themselves or others performing, thus suggesting rationality in cultural performance.

The strangeness of the whole situation also meant that participants could be dishonest and opportunistic, manipulating symbols and norms from the different moral systems at the same time, both African and European. The result is that our own class cultures and systems are therefore very volatile. It is more like an amazing theatre of life drama than an already scripted piece of performance. We see defiance, opposition, challenges and outright rejection. We see creativity in political puns as grassroots people often ridicule those in power, or as the youth and local women challenge the state.

A few recent examples from Nigeria in which popular language imposes its own counter-meaning on formal abbreviations as a form of criticism of power and corruption in government include: the former Nigerian military ruler General Olusegun Obasanjo's so-called 'agricultural revolution' officially known as Operation Feed the Nation, OFN, which became derided as Operation Finish the Naira and Operation Fool the Nation. Even Obasanjo's name was changed to the Igbo word *ogbasanjo*, meaning 'one who spreads evil or badness'. Under the brutal dictatorship of General Babangida, his assertive wife became Mamangida (Hausa term for mother of the house, but used here to mean horribly domineering) and their youngest daughter's name Safiatu was changed to Sapiatu, the Sap a pun, echoing people's suffering under SAP (the Structural Adjustment Programme) which I shall discuss in detail in Chapter 1. In these creative inventions, we see the lies of the ruling elites challenged and exposed.

The idea of uncritical and unopposed total class reproduction is also contradicted by the African situation where there is a decolonization movement, and where colonial rule and European culture did not eradicate completely all African traditional systems, and where settler colonialism could not reproduce an unchallenged solid monocultural elite. Thanks to continued European racism, its closed system and colour boundary, Africans have been exposing the 'false-consciousness' of aspirant African Europeans: the 'Uncle Toms' in African American parlance, the 'white coconuts', black outside, white inside, in South African parlance, '*onye ocha nna ya di oji*', white person whose father is black, in Igbo parlance, 'black skin, white masks', in Frantz Fanon's parlance. I do not believe this to mean that Africans are anti-progress and social mobility. It is a moral criticism of subservience, ruthlessness and treachery, often articulated by nonconformist Africans who have not been the 'darling' of European attention.

The ingratitude of Africans (read African opposition to imperialism) was continuously berated by the colonialists and missionaries. So also do African dictatorships use the same rhetoric *vis-à-vis* youths, women and grassroots opposition who become 'savages', 'thugs', 'hoodlums', 'undesirable elements' and so on. The degree to which Africans are demystified means that their rulers can never be certain of their loyalty, let alone their love. In this bizarre and alien system imposed through force, everybody is 'performing', indicating the depth of alienation and corruption.

Of all social categories, perhaps it is with African women that the theory of cultural reproduction appears to fall on its head, as African women of the elite classes oscillate between systems. Caplan reveals the lack of traditional organizations by European women. The only organizations which European women experienced beyond family life were church-based organizations, which meant that their lives rotated round domestic and charity work.

It is this same type of lifestyle that European women tried to reproduced in the colonies. This is why I am arguing that in the African situation, it is not the development of capitalism that has led to the development of voluntary social welfare organizations as Caplan claims in the Indian experience; it is the teachings of European women and their churches and schools. Historically, African women had already generated structures of challenging patriarchy. These institutions were subverted through the direct act of European women's efforts to reproduce their own home conditions in Africa. Through imperialism and violent abuse of African women, they produced elite women whom they taught not to challenge patriarchy, as I demonstrate in Chapter 2. Even so, a plural situation exists with professional and national elite women, whom I characterize as 'daughters of imperialism', and grassroots women, whom I call 'daughters of the Goddess', operating different moral systems.

I will use two contemporary Nigerian women to illustrate this point about multiple identities and systems that African elite women can manoeuvre, and how in spite of individual and class self-interest, in regions of old matriarchal institutions, old symbols could yet come into effect in new organizational forms. This is the case in the link between women, cash and market. It is not therefore surprising that Uyo, of the old palm-oil economy and the 1929 anti-colonial Women's War, would be the first state to produce a women's bank. As publicized in *Newswatch*: 'On the 7th of November, 1992, Akwa Ibom State Better Life Programme made history when it commissioned the first ever bank in Nigeria sponsored by women. The bank is called Uforo Community Bank.'[1] Even though this achievement resulted from collective community effort, the credit was given to, let us say, 'Her excellency' Mrs Establishment, who did not owe her position to local women's organizations but to the wife of the head of state. Consequently, the sanctions of accountability to organized local forces are eroded.

In this case, there are questions about a leadership which is not organic but dictatorial. Yet old ideologies are used in explanation, as the new leadership appropriates local women's efforts while representing these grassroots women as technologically ignorant and unskilful. This construction can be seen in this statement:

> One fact that reaffirmed Mrs Establishment's resolve to establish a financial institution with women in focus is that the Akwa Ibom woman is very hardworking, intelligent, enduring and resilient. While there is abundant labour and natural resources in the State, the Akwa Ibom woman lacks the financial resources and technological know-how to combine her attributes with the abundant resources to produce wealth for herself, her family and the greater society.

In this way, the language of 'developmentalism' can be used to solicit development funds or, as in this case, manage women's wealth and finances.

These women's long history of organization and economic achievements is thus denied in order to construct a missionary relevance for Mrs Establishment, an agent of the neo-colonial state system. We are therefore not surprised to learn that Mrs Establishment 'was encouraged by one of the key recommendations of the National Conference on the Implementations of the Geneva Declaration for the Advancement of Women, which emphasized the facilitation of credit/grants to women to enable them actively to participate in national development'. The 'mission' of the Community Bank is stated as follows:

a. To be the best-managed Community Bank in the country: employing well trained, highly motivated and seasoned bankers with wide experience in the industry.
b. To provide excellent bankng services to our numerous customers and promote the establishment of cottage/small-scale industries within our community.
c. To actualise the Akwa Ibom state government's policy on individual enterprise and rural industrialisation.

We shall see how this pattern of language will recur time and time again in claims by local elites, development advisers and workers, donor agencies, and global women's conferences to give relevance and legitimacy to leadership over rural and peasant women. I refer to this as developmentalism.

Even though Mrs Establishment claimed to be working for women, a man was appointed chief executive/manager of this Uforo Community

Bank. Another man was appointed as the loan officer. Mrs Establishment herself was reported to have had thirteen years' experience in banking as general manager. She resigned her job in order to join her husband. 'This facility is geared to ginger the interest of women in taking calculated business risk,' and, we are told, 'the establishment of Uforo Community Bank has opened a new chapter in the search for a new image for the women of Nigeria'. Of course, the commissioning was by her husband, the state governor, from whom we learn that the shareholdings of the bank are broad-based. In reality, this is a case of loss of autonomy by traditional women's organizations which had their own *esusu* system, an indigenous banking system in which women controlled their own cash and distributed trade capital among themselves.

We can compare Mrs Establishment with thirty-four-year-old Chief Mrs Adetayo Adunni Bankole, a former journalist who branched into trade.[2] Mrs Bankole also hails from a region of traditional trade matriarchs. She has traded in many things, including wholesale provisions, but ended up in textiles, and owns a company called Sublim Fabrics. She is structurally located in Yoruba women's traditional organizations in two states through title-taking. In 1990 she became Iyameso of Oke-Obaland, in Ogun state. In 1992 she became Otun Balogun Iyalaje of Ibadanland, Oyo state, deputy or right-hand person to the Balogun Iyalaje who is the mother of trades. In terms of structural and institutional women's representation and accountability, Chief Bankole is therefore in a different position to Mrs Establishment. In my working concepts, Chief Bankole is a daughter of the Goddess and Mrs Establishment is a daughter of imperialism.

The contrast between these two women *vis-à-vis* local women's organizations and concerns leads me to the national and global contexts of class and gender dynamics in women's struggles. What are the global structures and rhetorics that generated the contradiction that I find in Mrs Establishment's claims of concern for women's development and empowerment?

African women's voices and demands from Nairobi to Beijing

Since this long global march to women's equality and power began with the first UN Women's Conference held in Mexico City in 1975, women's issues have steadily got onto the agenda of UN conferences. References to these conferences now stand as a kind of genealogical authority-giving chain, and their resolutions have grown into a formalized text, generating a formalized language echoed the world over. These conferences include the UN Conference on Environment and Development, known as the

Earth Summit, in Rio, 1992; the International Conference on Population and Development, Cairo, September 1994; and the World Summit for Social Development, Copenhagen, March 1994. To this list can now be added the Fourth UN World Conference on Women, Beijing, 1995, which through its Platform for Action document has the unique achievement of pressing policy-makers to take action on women's issues and forcing governments seriously to address women's issues that have been spelt out for them. The Platform for Action with its 362-paragraph report signed by 189 countries denoted a dozen main areas of concern for the advancement of women. They include issues of women in poverty, global economics, women's human rights, armed conflict, violence against women, political and economic participation, power-sharing, institutional mechanisms, media, access to health care and education, environment and practices harmful to girl children.

Presented in this abstract manner of a laundry-list approach to women's issues, one can see how easy it is for European women to return from Beijing with an illusion of a truly global process and a harmonious global sisterhood, with all women saying the same thing in spite of diversity. I even heard a few bourgeois women saying that women's differences have finally been resolved and that women are now the same everywhere. One white woman even recounted to me how an African woman came crying to her for help, saying how there was nothing in Africa, and begged not to be forgotten. The white woman told me how she herself had tears in her eyes as she promised to help. Really, what the white woman was after was setting up a project in Africa. I leave the rest to the imagination.

Gertrude Mongella, secretary-general to the 1995 World Conference on Women, set the tone for a false sense of unity when she told African women in the women's newsletter *Femmeline*, 'We have to recognise that there is no women's agenda as such. There is just one national, one global agenda. But women will put different emphasis and different priorities on the issues based on where they want to go ... The problems of women are not different from country to country or region to region. They only differ in intensity.'[3]

Unity was again the focus of Mongella's speech of 24 August 1995. She gave two main reasons for the exceptionally high level of interest in the conference: that people were involved in the process, and that the issues of women are becoming more crucial, and more focused in international discussions. This suggests that the intensity of interaction has led to participants almost speaking the same language as opposed to the creative dissent and tensions of Nairobi '85. Then, the African women who went were truly non-privileged and anti-imperialist in thinking.

It is not surprising, therefore, to hear that women were interested not in text but in action. African women in Nairobi were suspicious of what was written down or what was claimed as agreed. Mongella said: 'Women keep asking me, "What are the actions?" They are not interested in the placement of a comma in the document. They are interested in what we are going to do to follow up to fight violence against women. Women want to hear what governments are going to do to stop discrimination against women in all parts of life.' Mongella declared that the 1995 conference would be different from previous women's conferences because there is now a very strong, built-in constituency of women. Women, she said, can no longer be ignored and that 'even if a government doesn't implement the Beijing Platform, they cannot ignore women's issues any more'. Her message for the conference: 'Forget what you are and what you do, and focus on the issues of women. We must all be united. Even though there are women from many different backgrounds coming to Beijing, their agenda is the same. The agenda is women.'

When Irene Santiago, executive director of the NGO Forum on Women '95, was interviewed by the same Dupe Adesioye, we can see from the following that the answers had already been agreed, for in spite of pointing out glaring regional economic, political and cultural differences between women, Santiago too spoke of common threads:

DAILY TIMES: As someone versed in women's issues, from what you have seen in the regional preparations, would you say women the world over have the same priorities? What would you say is the common focal point?

SANTIAGO: Let me tell you briefly what some of the other regions have developed as their own priorities. In Asia and the Pacific, it was clear that they wanted a new development model in spite of the fact that the region is the most progressive in the sense of economic growth, but it was an uneven growth. In Latin America and the Caribbean, they were interested in issues of violence against women, political participation as well as structural adjustment as they are most hard hit. In Europe and America, the interest is in human rights, the economy as well as political participation. Western Asian Arab women have the peace process, health, opportunities for education and employment. So you can see that there are many common threads linking all together, although, some are more emphasized than others.[4]

At the Nigerian national meeting, attended by representatives of fifty women's NGOs in preparation for the pre-conference regional meeting in Dakar, you could see differences between the contributions made by independent women and those professional women who had official positions in the network organization for Beijing '95. Nigerian women were concerned with contextual nitty-gritty details on issues of health, disability, land rights, poverty, work, environmental racism, oil pollution and environmental refugees.[5] Chief Mrs Fola Akintunde-Ighodalo, the first woman permanent secretary in Nigeria, talked in her keynote address about differences in the political commitment of three generations of Nigerian women, using the analogy of a relay race to show how the younger generation have lost the race or are about to lose the race because they are inactive and materialistic.

I like to think that these three generations represent, first, the traditional African resistance-matriarchs who fought the anti-colonial struggle; then, the daughters of the Goddess who fought the nationalist and liberation struggles for independence; and, finally, the daughters of imperialism who inherited the post-independence successor state and are partners in corruption. In the opinion of this daughter of the Goddess, even the National Council of Women's Societies (the umbrella organization for Nigerian women) has lost sight of its traditional objective of mass mobilization of women, to become 'a glorified reception committee for those in power'.[6] In Chief Akintunde-Ighodalo's opinion, women should aspire to positions through merit and should not accept any offers that come their way. The priority for Nigerian women in Beijing should be the eradication of poverty. In any case, poverty in Africa is the result of the embezzlement and looting of the public treasury. All that money is hidden in other countries and should be returned. Chief Akintunde-Ighodalo told Nigerian delegates to go and lobby 'those hiding our money, so that they can bring them back'.

In the Nigerian interview, Santiago said that simplification was necessary in order for the Commission on the Status of Women to 'be able to develop a global lobbying document for the NGOs much more easily'.[7] Part of this process of simplification was the use of the slogan, 'Women's rights are human rights'. Well, bourgeois women's rights are not human rights – they are rights of class privilege at the expense of human rights. When we hear it said in Washington that 'it takes a village' to do certain things, we get angry at this degree of appropriation of words and things that belong only to poor rural people these days, because we know that the White House, Washington and New York are not villages. We also know the histories of slavery, colonialism, developmentalism and refugeeism which destroyed and are still destroying villages and traditional village cultures in the southern hemisphere. In this book I talk about state lies and lies that daughters of imperialism tell as they look unflinchingly into the camera.

Well-meaning as these global concerns are, they should continue to be assessed in the context of Western economic, political and cultural imperialism. This is the reason for criticisms of the Platform for Action by indigenous women's groups. Dissenting voices from representatives of Women Empowering Women of Indian Nations, who were official observers to the United Nations Women's Conference, prepared a platform statement and position papers concerning Native American women addressing issues of the conference. In their opinion, the United States Platform addresses issues of the dominant female society but does not accurately reflect the concerns and viewpoints of Native American women, because of the difference in culture and language. For instance, out of 553 federally recognized Indian 'tribes' in the United States, 125 'tribes' have women as their 'tribal' elected leaders.

In their culture, Native American women, in general, play a role in their 'tribal' communities very different from that played by other American women in their own respective communities. To Native women, economic development does not necessarily mean more women on the board of directors of large corporations but may mean, locally, more jobs and less intrusion into the personal lives of the workers on the part of the employer. Traditional lifestyles and family values are of paramount importance and should be treated as sacred, especially in the economic sector.

The Platform was also criticized by women of colour coalitions, such as the International Network of Women of Colour and various Third World women's groups, as being Eurocentric and privileged, especially on issues such as abortion, sexuality, marriage, motherhood and reproductive rights. So also did some Islamic women's groups criticize the Platform for Action for trying to force Western European notions of modernity on Islamic countries, ignoring the role of religion and the importance of the integration of moral and spiritual values in all aspects of life in these cultures and societies where religion, or opposition to it, is at the very core of people's social identity. The less privileged sisters were on the other hand concerned with issues of women at the bottom, such as the evils of Structural Adjustment Programmes (SAPs), global economics, basic needs like right to land, citizenship, clean water, food and shelter, education and primary health care.

Where do African women stand in all this? In Nairobi 1985 the tension among African women was between the defensive government officials and women activists pushing for recognition and visibility of women's issues as well as for structural status in the sense of women's ministries or committees. It was clear that discourse recognized the right to national sovereignty and the need to persuade, criticize or even force own governments to see women and take women's issues seriously. During that period, African women had insisted on recognition of their different positions and their prioritization of issues of basic needs, not wants and rights. They also bracketed in their men as partners in their pursuit of social justice, progress and development.

What changed at Beijing? At Beijing 1995, the concern was not so much 'requests and demands for change', but monitoring of change as the official reports from regional meetings to discuss plans for Beijing by women from sub-Saharan Africa suggest. Conference genealogies were invoked for legitimation, and resolution texts guaranteed a reproduction of a global formalized language. In the African women's conferences, the reaffirmation of a genealogical tree of global and regional strategies on women usually begins with the UN Convention on the Elimination of All Forms of Discrimination Against Women (1979); then on to the Lagos Plan of Action and Final Act of Lagos (1980); the Kilimanjaro Programme of Action on Population and Self-Reliant Development (1984); the Arusha Strategies for the Advancement of Women Beyond the United Nations Decade (1984); the Nairobi Forward-Looking Strategies for the Advancement of Women (1985); the African Charter on Human and Peoples' Rights (1987); the Abuja Declaration on Participatory Development: The Role of Women in Africa in the 1990s (1989); the Arusha Declaration on Popular Participation (1990); and the Abuja Treaty establishing the African Economic Community (1991); the Universal Declaration of Human Rights covenants, and the various ILO labour standards. It is conceivable that there are African women who have made a career out of attending all these conferences. No doubt knowledge of the formalized language of these conferences has given elite women an advantaged leadership and access to donor agency funding.

In this new confidence in the importance of the leadership of elite women, Zimbabwe is usually cited as an example of strong leadership from better financed professional women's organizations, such as teachers, lawyers, doctors, women in the media, and so on. The belief is that these professional women with wider networks and alliances beyond national borders and better access to communications networks, through which they can copy what goes on elsewhere, are better able to lobby and to put pressure on local officials, and also able to monitor 'successes'.

All this gives the impression that the activists have become experts running projects and are therefore in a position to supervise and monitor implementation and change. Central to all this, however, is the impression given of a missing sense of national sovereignty, replaced by location in a global conglomerate. But who features in it? Whose concerns are addressed? What are the implications?

With this shift from a community or grassroots-articulated focus to professional leadership imposed from above, issues and goals have become repetitive in a fixed global language, and discourse is controlled by paid UN and other donor advisers, consultants and workers who commonly reiterate issues and goals as:

1. economic empowerment for women,
2. legal reform to benefit them, and
3. access to health services, particularly reproductive and sexual health.

Islamic women's organizations on their part raise issues such as:

1. marriage and polygamy, generally demanding increase in the marriage age for girls from fifteen to eighteen years
2. discriminatory criminal laws
3. divorce laws (e.g. in some Islamic countries, a man can divorce his wife without consulting her and pays alimony for one year only; if a woman remarries, her ex-husband automatically receives child custody)
4. passport restrictions for women whereby in many countries married women cannot leave the country or apply for a passport without their husband's permission
5. honour killing which allows men to kill females who bring shame to their families (Islamic feminists claim that this law often becomes a cover-up for child, sister, and wife abuse within the family, and very frequently it is the abuser that is protected and not the victim)

From these reports, the demands by grassroots women themselves based on needs are usually contextualized, less abstract and quite practical. They generally ask for favourable government policies to enable women to secure better jobs. They have demanded access to credit for income generation, such as credit to start a business or purchase a house or acquire land. Sometimes rural women have formed co-operatives or a women's bank in order to rotate business or trading capital. All in all, these are articulations of what grassroots women want to do themselves in order simply to live their lives; they do not constitute a plan to impose ideas or a lifestyle on anyone else.

Grassroots African women from different countries articulate common problems – the main one is poverty – and they are need-directed, often deciding to shun processed goods and relatively expensive machinery, reverting to their own technological resourcefulness and using what is easily available (for example, they will use local, traditional technology rather than buy costly machines for processing food).

In summary, a close look at demands by grassroots women shows that they would resort to self-reliance and self-sufficiency under their traditional organizational structures if left to these decisions. They thus compound Mrs Establishment's claim that they lack technological skills and need her budget management. It is only by looking at women as structurally located locally that we are able to see the tensions and contradictions between competing interest groups over all these resources. Certainly, conference reports and statistical reports give us some idea about women's advancement, some present realities, but not a contextualized and fuller picture that would reveal gender, class and race conflicts over power-sharing, which is what this study hopes to achieve.

Chapter 1 gives a general overview of the place of women in African development. From recent statistical reports and the work of some international agencies and human rights organizations, I try to establish factually the discriminations and injustices against women in various countries, proposing possible solutions to specific issues. The chapter uses the laundry-list approach to women's issues, much to my dissatisfaction. My method of analysis shifts from Chapter 2 up to Chapter 11 – my major case study, Nigeria – in which I apply a more comprehensive structural and institutional approach to look at external factors in the making of classes of women in Nigeria, the character of national women's organizations and tensions between these organizations as a result of differences in ideological orientations. I examine their competition as they vie for control over the masses of Nigerian women, particularly grassroots and rural women, even through the use of violence and state lies, thus reproducing the violence of the colonizers.

In Chapter 3 to Chapter 8, I look at how the different women's organizations and the Nigerian public in general are engaged in civil political discourses of rights and social justice over several women's issues. A major question is posed in Chapter 3 and echoed in subsequent chapters, i.e. Is the mobilization of women and gender equality work better done through formal state institutions, such as a women's committee in a strong and effective local government system, or by informal national women's organizations, or by labour-oriented women's organizations, or by umbrella women's organizations, or by First Lady cults of wives of African heads of state? Looking at formal and informal approaches to women's issues, I revisit Nnobi of *Male Daughters, Female Husbands* in Chapter 9 in which I examine the history of local government in Nigeria and the role of women in development in Nnobi.

Squarely on the side of the argument for women's mobilization and empowerment through the institution of a well-funded and accountable women's committee in a strong and effective local authority system, in Chapter 12 I examine the working of such a system in Britain and draw lessons for civil participation and democratization in multiethnic Nigeria, Africa, and particularly multiracial and multiethnic post-apartheid South Africa.

In the Conclusion, I return to the destructive effects of IMF-imposed SAPs and its associated capitalism on poor women and the general masses. I examine the United Nations Development Programme's (UNDP) long-term strategic thinking and planning in African countries in the form of the National Long-Term Perspective Studies (NLTPSs), the current UN Special Initiative on Africa and the effect that these plans would have on African women. Critiquing the imperialism of 'developmentalism', I revisit the pre-IMF/SAPs progressive civil political discourse of the 1970s in Africa which was informed by notions of self-reliant development and empowerment in sovereign African states or a sovereign federated pan-African state. This view is compared with the uncreative post-IMF/SAPs growth accounting and budget management mentality of the modern-ization tendency which has weakened the state in Africa. I argue that the language of revolution taught by the daughters of the Goddess and the progressive thinkers and activists of the 1960s and 1970s had a radicalizing influence on African feminists and radical women's groups who believed in another development, as opposed to contemporary development entre-preneurs and donor-empowered daughters of imperialism. I conclude by returning to the question of the character of an effective and inclusive state and the ideological implications of different forms of state, centralized or decentralized, on the issues of gender, race and class, and the question of rights and social justice.

The study concludes with a ten-point summary of recommendations for gender equity and social justice derived from the text.

Notes

1. *Newswatch*, 21 December 1992.

2. 'Women of Our Time', *Quality*, 29 December 1992.

3. Cited by Dupe Adesioye in her report on the Fifth African Regional Con-ference on Women, NGO Forum (Dakar, Senegal, November 1994), *Daily Times*, 14 February 1995.

4. Dupe Adesioye, interview with Irene Santiago, *Daily Times*, 23 February 1995.

5. 'Towards a Beijing Platform of Action', Daily Times, 18 April 1994; 'Women Prepare for Beijing', *Guardian on Sunday*, 13 March 1994.

6. 'Women Plan for World Conference', *Daily Times*, 23 March 1994.

7. 'We Now Look at Global Issues from Women's Perspective', *Daily Times*, 23 February 1995.

Bibliography

Amadiume, Ifi, 1987, *Male Daughters, Female Husbands: Gender and Sex in an African Society*. London and New Jersey: Zed Books.

— 1995, 'Gender, Political Systems and Social Movements: A West African Experience', in Mahmood Mamdani and E. Wamba-dia-Wamba (eds), *African Studies in Social Movements and Democracy*. Dakar, Senegal: CODESRIA Publications.

— 1996, 'Beyond Cultural Performance: Women, Culture and the State in Contemporary Nigerian Politics', in David Parkin, Lionel Caplan and Humphrey Fisher (eds), *The Politics of Cultural Performance*. Berghahn Books.

— 1997, *Reinventing Africa: Matriarchy, Religion and Culture*. London and New York: Zed Books.

Bloch, Maurice, 1974, 'Symbols, Song, Dance and Features of Articulation: Is Religion an Extreme Form of Traditional Authority?', in Maurice Bloch, 1989, *Ritual, History, and Power: Selected Papers in Anthropology*, Monographs on Social Anthropology, no. 58, London and Atlantic Highlands, NJ: Athlone Press. Also in *European Journal of Sociology* 15 (1974).

— 1991, *Prey into Hunter: The Politics of Religious Experience*. Cambridge: Cambridge University Press.

Caplan, Patricia, 1985, *Class and Gender in India: Women and Their Organizations in a South Indian City*. London and New York: Tavistock Publications.

Diop, Cheikh Anta, 1991, *Civilization or Barbarism: An Authentic Anthropology*. New York: Lawrence Hill Books.

Fanon, Frantz, 1970, *Black Skin, White Masks*. London: Paladin.

— 1967, *The Wretched of the Earth*, London: Penguin Books.

Fatton, Robert, Jr, 1989, 'Gender, Class and States in Africa', in Jane L. Parpart and Kathleen A. Staudt (eds), *Women and the State in Africa*. Boulder, CO and London: Lynne Rienner.

Hyden, Goran, 1980, *Beyond Ujamaa: Underdevelopment and an Uncaptured Peasantry*. Los Angeles: University of California Press.

Fourth World Conference on Women documents

Kampala Action Plan, Regional Conference on Women and Peace, 22–25 November 1993, Kampala, Uganda (endorsed by UN Economic Commission for Africa (UN-ECA) and the Organization of African Unity (OAU)).

The NGO Forum, statement by Layashi Yaker, United Nations Under-Secretary-General, Executive Secretary of the Economic Commission for Africa, 13–15 November 1994, United Nations Economic Commission for Africa.

Fifth African Regional Conference on Women, 16–23 November 1994, Dakar, Senegal. *Volume 2: Conference Papers on Priority Issues:*

Part I: *Women in the Peace Process*, United Nations Economic Commission for Africa, African Centre for Women, E/ECA/ACW/RC.V/EXP.2.

Part II A: *Women's Rights: A Critical Issue of Equality and Sustainable Development with Examples from Africa*, United Nations Economic Commission For Africa, African Centre for Women, E/ECA/ACW/RC.V/EXP/WP.3A.

Part II B: *Education, Health and Social Issues*, United Nations Economic Commission for Africa, African Centre for Women, E/ECA/ACW/RC.V/EXP/WP.3B.

Part III: *Economic Empowerment of Women*, United Nations Economic Commission for Africa, African Centre for Women, E/ECA/ACW/RC.V/EXP/WP.4A.

Part IV: *Political Empowerment of Women*, United Nations Economic Commission for Africa, African Centre for Women, E/ECA/ACW/RC.V/EXP/WP.4B.

Part V: *Women, Environment and Sustainable Development*, United Nations Economic Commission for Africa, African Centre for Women, E/ECA/ACW/RC.V/EXP/WP.5.

African Platform for Action adopted by the Fifth Regional Conference on Women, Dakar, 16–23 November 1994, Commission on the Status of Women, United Nations Economic and Social Council, E/CN.6/1995/5/Add.2, 29 December 1994.

The Platform for Action Critical Areas of Concern, the Fourth World Conference on Women, 4–15 September 1995, Beijing, China, United Nations.

Declaration on the Elimination of Violence Against Women, Resolution adopted by the General Assembly on the report of third Committee (A/48/629) Resolution 48/104.

1. African women: present realities and future directions

This chapter looks at areas in which African women are the key to the progress of their societies and ultimately to Africa's development and future. I attempt to establish factually the discriminations and injustices against women in various African countries. I also question how the conditions, needs and rights of African women are being tackled in governments' policies and in the programmes of international donor agencies and NGOs.

From a general overview and specific cases, areas of concern that are examined here include: African women's progress since Nairobi, 1985; education and training; women and the economy, dealing with the problems of SAPs, the question of economic empowerment for women, and favourable government policies enabling women to secure better jobs and easier access to credit; women and health, highlighting women's need for access to health services; environment, education and health; women and the state, dealing with war, repression and state violence; women and politics, dealing with leadership and political participation; women and rights and social justice, dealing with policy, legal reform and concrete actions to benefit women.

African women's progress

To present African women simply as destitute and in need of charity from the West is to do an injustice to women with a rich history of authentic leadership skills, economic enterprise and strategies of resistance to oppression. It is this rich legacy which has enabled African women to make historic contributions to anti-colonial resistance movements. They have had to resist European expansionist settler colonialism and pass laws as in countries such as South Africa, Zimbabwe and Kenya where racism and land appropriation were central to the colonialist policy and ideology of exploitation. Colonialist policies when applied elsewhere in Africa, for example in Ghana, Cameroon, Nigeria, Mozambique, Angola, Guinea and Cape Verde, also met with resistance from African women. It was precisely African women's grounding in economic production, particularly in agriculture, trade, marketing and management, and women's organizations which made it possible for them both to resist and to overcome the corrosive onslaughts of imperialism.

It is against this background that we must assess contemporary gender transformations and women's progress in Africa. The colonial introduction of a new capitalist economy, the imposition of new government systems, Islamic, church and state laws, changes in marriage practices and gender relations, property inheritance – all led to a new rigid gender ideology of power, demarcating public space and power as male to the exclusion of women. Male dominance was in effect written into law, resulting in new experiences of subordination for women. Unfortunately, backward and oppressive gender attitudes and cultures generated by the new institutions were carried over into many of the nationalist and liberation movements, so that, at the end of struggle, progressive gender equality promises were broken and African women found themselves more backward in terms of legal rights than they were in many pre-colonial socio-political systems which had clearly demarcated, instituted women's spaces and rights both in the private and public spheres, even if they were hotly contested.

Gender asymmetry in contemporary African nations has been made worse by both the earlier structuralist economists and later neo-classical economic notions of development which have guided post-independence African nations. These externally derived development plans of African states have generally been seen as a continuation of the colonial policy of foreign intervention in state economic plans and budget allocation, as for example the role of the World Bank and the international development agencies. Even the researches and reports of these institutions have revealed the negative effects of high capital-intensive projects on local communities and on gender relations. More particularly in the area of agriculture and current agricultural policies, there has been a failure of development planners to recognize areas of women's work and economic contribution and the high percentage of women-headed households. Economic development strategies, public policies and development projects have taken men as the central focus of development, enlisting female labour and production under male headship and upsetting traditional systems of gender complementarity and co-operation.

Development, rather than generating and supporting self-help initiatives, became aid-dependent projects, thereby dealing a serious blow to African women's independent efforts towards gender equality and a better life for all. It is not surprising, therefore, that current ILO and UN comparative data show a sharp decline in women's economic activity rates since 1970 in every African country (except South Africa and a few northern African countries with very low female economic input).

The fact is that African women have not benefited from the promises of development. For this reason, the UN End of the Decade for Women Conference in Nairobi in 1985, whose theme was Forward-Looking Strategies for the Advancement of Women, saw representatives of African women insisting on the specificity of the needs of majority African women. These were identified as basic needs. How have African women progressed since Nairobi's objectives of equality, development and peace?

A 1991 report by the Economic and Social Council of the UN in Addis Ababa argued that the restrictive economic climate of the 1980s, following World Bank-imposed neo-classical economics, limited the ability of government to mobilize the public sector for social and economic change. African women suffered most under the conditions of economic stagnation, cyclical debt crisis, and the crisis management mentality of Structural Adjustment Programmes, which put constraints on the normal economic and social activities of women as food providers and carers for their households, and as active participants in the development of their countries. In the areas of health, nutrition, education and training, economic opportunities and participation in decision-making, inequality between men and women has worsened due to these corrective policy measures. The report recommended improvements in women's technical skills, in education and training in science and technology, and in supportive policy and legal measures.

An even more comprehensive UN report on women's progress since Mexico 1975 was released in 1995 as an official document for the Fourth World Conference on Women. *The World's Women 1995: Trends and Statistics* provides statistical data aimed at forcing governments into action to implement the UN principle of gender equality. The report presents women in relation to men, thus highlighting areas of inequalities between the sexes. It shows that, in comparison to other regions, African women are still behind. In education, sub-Saharan Africa is among the regions where women and men aged fifteen and over have the highest illiteracy rate, with 70 per cent average for women in 1980 and just over 50 per cent for 1995. For men it was 48 per cent down to 33 per cent. In sub-Saharan Africa, only between 30 and 38 women per 100 men enter higher education.

While life expectancy has increased for women in northern Africa in the past two decades, one cannot say the same for the rest of the continent. Due to AIDS, the estimated life expectancy of both women and men dropped significantly in Uganda and Zambia, and it is expected to stagnate or decrease in eight other sub-Saharan countries during the next five years. However, in spite of high mortality, on reproductive issues, the

UN report shows that African women still have an average of six children. Adolescent fertility in sub-Saharan Africa is five to seven times higher than in developed regions. There is a worsening of maternal mortality in most of sub-Saharan African countries.

On the issue of work, the percentage of women reported as economically active was as low as 21 per cent in northern Africa. The economic activity rates for women did not show increases in sub-Saharan Africa.[1] A major source of injustice for women is the fact that women's work in subsistence agriculture in the rural areas and in the informal sector and in family enterprises is undercounted and underreported in official statistics, hence they are denied budget allocations commensurable with their economic contributions.

In the area of leadership, women are not learning politics and how to govern from having positions in government. Most African countries scored zero for women in upper government chambers. In 1994, Congo had 2 per cent, South Africa 18 per cent, with Swaziland scoring highest with 20 per cent.[2] In reality, African women learn leadership skills in their communities, in their traditional women's organizations and, some would argue, in their increasingly strong presence in non-governmental organizations. Individual professional women, to the detriment of grassroots women, have learned and developed leadership skills at the local, national and international level from involvement in the United Nations Decade for Women and international women's conferences.

In spite of their huge labour force, women do not exceed 1 or 2 per cent of top executive business positions if indeed one finds them at the top.[3] Women are still mostly in the traditionally female professions, such as the lower ranks in health and education. In the media, too, women are increasingly visible as presenters and reporters, but not as producers and editors where they remain poorly represented, for these are the more influential occupations.

When we compare the place of Danish women with that of their African sisters in the new gender equality index of the UN Development Programme's *Human Development Report 1995*, Denmark stands fourth in worldwide measure of women's income, education and health. Women hold 33 per cent of the seats in the Danish parliament and seven out of twenty cabinet posts. Nearly half the labour force is female, with women eligible for seven months of paid maternity leave. Many Danish women nevertheless say that equality is far from complete, citing an absence of women at the highest levels of government and the private sector. Danish women still have the main responsibility for home and family and they believe real equality would be achieved when men assume their share of those tasks.

Recognizing the link between economic power and political power,

Danish women are seeking management positions in the private sector, and striving for a higher proportion of women employers and self-employed in big companies, since the vast majority own small businesses rather than large companies. Like African women in government, the ministerial posts held by Danish women are most often in the 'soft' political areas such as social welfare and the arts. Denmark has never had a woman prime minister, foreign minister or UN ambassador. Again, comparing with the situation in Africa, women are largely absent at the top levels of Danish media where male opinion is dominant. The few Danish women reporters cover the traditional fields like social issues, health and education.

Education and training

UNESCO World Education Report 1995 contains up-to-date and projected analyses and statistics to the year 2000 on global educational trends and policy issues. The education of women and girls form the focus of this particular report. The facts are not encouraging; they show women's unequal educational opportunity to be global. Two-thirds of the world's illiterate adults are women, while it is girls who make up two-thirds of the world's out-of-school young people. In sub-Saharan Africa in 1995, out of the total adult population, only 56.8 per cent were literate, of which females made up only 47.3 per cent. Statistics for many countries show low school life expectancy for boys and girls and a gap between boys and girls as the girls are left behind before the age of sixteen.[4]

The education of girls remains an area of concern, as can be seen from the Ouagadougou Declaration 1993 under UNESCO'S Priority Africa Programme which called for action on girls' education in Africa, outlining strategies for educators and policy-makers to correct this fundamental social inequality.[5]

Illiteracy has been shown to breed poverty in the sense of the denial of equal opportunities. More importantly, it limits the crucial role that education plays in the development both of society and of human potential. While illiteracy and poverty are fellow-travellers, leading to abuse and exploitation, relevant education goes hand in hand with tolerance, respect for human rights, peace, justice and democracy. Education for African women is therefore a question of rights.[6]

Structural Adjustment Programmes (SAPs) and African women

Independent evidence shows that SAPs instituted by the World Bank and the International Monetary Fund (IMF) are breeding poverty and forcing maldevelopment on African women. There has been a rise in poverty with women in particular worse off today than they were a decade ago, before SAPs.

SAPs' measures have failed to deliver the promise to increase investment and savings rates, improve export performance, diminish debt, create jobs, bring about sustained growth, or improve the productive capacity of the poor, the majority of whom are women. Yet, what is still thought of by the World Bank and the IMF as an instrument of liberalization, 'macroeconomic stability' and economic growth and development, has turned into a nightmare in its ability to weaken African states to the extent that they are not able to pay salaries to their workers. So also has it broken women's autonomous economic sectors by exposing them to the cold profit calculations of market forces.

SAPs have forced changes in patterns of production, export and consumption on thirty-six countries in sub-Saharan Africa where more than half of the population lives in abject poverty. It is as if the ethics and morals of redistribution have been reversed so that poor nations pay the rich ones; for between 1990 and 1993, the region paid US$13.4 billion annually to its external creditors. This was more than its combined spending on health and education. As a debt that does not decrease but increases, in 1994 alone, it increased 3.2 per cent to US$313 billion. No wonder African nations predominate in the low human development category, while the creditor countries are in the top twenty of the high human development category in *The 1996 Human Development Report* published by the international Independent Commission on Population and the Quality of Life (ICPQL).[7] Nigeria, whose crude oil export is around 2 million bpd at over $15 per barrel, accounts for over 7 per cent of OPEC output and 40 per cent of US oil import, ranks low at number 137 in human development while the USA is second after Canada out of a total of 174 nations. Such glaring contradictions and the social destabilizing effects of SAPs *must* be exposed.

As debt has increased, so have the responsibilities and stresses in the health of African women. SAPs have meant more economic, family and community responsibilities for women in Africa, even as their traditional access to goods and services diminish with scarcity of cash or useless money as a result of currency devaluations and the rocketing of prices of basic commodities and essential household items. At the same time, there have been cuts in government subsidies on social welfare and health-care provisions in the few countries where these exist.

The economic stagnation of the 1980s saw a general decrease in formal sector employment, forcing more women into informal sector activity in order to supplement their earnings. Retrenchment from the formal sector is also forcing men into women's market sectors as pressure of more cash need in the household forces more children into the informal sector to supplement their mothers' earnings. Sub-Saharan Africa is the region with the highest rate of labour force participation of boys and girls aged ten to fourteen in 1990, recording 32 per cent compared to less than 8 per cent for northern Africa. Most of this child labour is in agriculture.[8]

African women produce more than 70 per cent of Africa's food. They do practically all the processing, accounting for more than 90 per cent of all time spent processing and preparing food, and provide the bulk of agricultural labour. African women are therefore clear about their needs in the agricultural sector and know the constraints on their output. They have complained about lack of credit, unequal access to land and labour, inadequate technical support for food processing and storage, low government interest in and valuation of women's more perishable food crops such as vegetables and fruits, hence lack of research to improve production and processing, and lack of protective tariffs on local food crops.

African women's commitment to family and community is such that, when possible, they are resistant to policies designed to move them away from food production and household provisioning into export-crop production, as for example in Tanzania, Senegal, Zambia. Other examples include peasant women's refusal of the Ugandan government's subsidies for bean production for export, and intensive use of women's labour for tobacco production as in Kenya. Female farmers and other small producers who cannot afford the higher prices of imported items are also unable to be part of the whole drive towards government-supported export production which is a male-dominated sector. Such a policy championed by the World Bank seeks to break women's autonomous markets and food-production systems.

As with subsistence agriculture and food processing, in most African countries, marketing is dominated by women. All are now experiencing low buying power as a result of higher prices. In Senegal and Ghana, for example, this has hit the once lucrative second-hand clothing sellers and market women traders.

Trade liberalization since 1984 has resulted in the closure of over 90 per cent of Tanzania's textile mills, and the loss of jobs for most workers who were women. Taiwanese imports are also putting pressure on the jobs of over 8,000 workers in Zimbabwe. All over Africa, import of cheap second-hand clothes threatens the livelihoods of small-scale seamstresses as well as larger textile concerns.

Ghana introduced SAPs in 1983. If SAPs are the saviour they are portrayed as, why would the government of Ghana introduce a Programme of Action to Mitigate the Social Costs of Adjustment (PAMSCAD) in 1985?

It did not stop high unemployment as a result of privatization. Nor did it bring down the high cost of medical care which has forced many women back to home delivery and higher incidence of maternal mortality. UNICEF's 1993 figures place maternal mortality rates in Ghana as high as 1,000 deaths to 100,000 births, one of the highest in sub-Saharan Africa. In Zimbabwe, the maternal mortality rate rose from 90 per 100,000 live births in 1990 to 168 per 100,000 in 1993 following the introduction of user fees. More girls are also dropping out of school for lack of school fees, thus further increasing the educational gap between boys and girls.

In most of these countries, decline in education budgets has led to a general collapse in support services: school inspection and supervision, in-service teacher education, curriculum development, school health services, and maintenance of school furniture. Equipment and physical facilities have deteriorated in most countries. Total public spending on education in sub-Saharan Africa fell in real terms between 1980 and 1988 from US$11 billion to US$7 billion. The withdrawal of state support resulted in a drop in gross enrolment rates at the primary-school level, which fell from 77.1 per cent in 1980 to an estimated 66.7 per cent in 1990. In Africa in the 1980s, female school enrolment rates dropped and drop-out rates increased. On average, only 37 per cent of school-age girls were enrolled in first or second levels of education in 1990.

There is a general increase in female-headed households as men leave or are unable to cope with the economic crisis. It is widely estimated that 30 per cent of African households are now headed by women.[9] Dependency ratios, which reflect the number of young children and older people per adult workers, are very high in these households. They are often also the households most marked by poverty and stress.

Opponents to SAPs have demanded increased participation at the grassroots level, and the inclusion of poor women in meaningful policy dialogue about money and economic matters. They have recommended gender-inclusive strategies that would involve these women in project designing, taking into account an accurate understanding of women and the poor, including gender and intra-household differences in production, consumption, access to resources and responsibilities. They have argued that women should be recognized as agents of development, and the kinds of work that they provide, visible or hidden, should be taken into account in economic research, national accounts and planning. This consequently means better access to education for women, property rights and financial credit.

Unlike the World Bank and the IMF, I hope to show later in my specific Nigerian case study that women see the answer to corruption, mismanagement and non-representative government in increased accountability, transparency and openness to citizens, not in the narrowing of the role of government to the function of financial budgeting and market facilitator. The vast majority of women have not benefited from the programmes and investments that were financed by the supposed African debt for whose repayment women and children are being punished. It is not surprising, therefore, that African women are in favour of debt cancellation and an end to SAPs.

AIDS and African women's health

Serious as death from AIDS-related infection might be, *The World's Women 1995* shows that between the late 1970s or early 1980s and 1994, 330,805 cases of AIDS were recorded for the whole of sub-Saharan Africa. A WHO 1993 report shows 45,000 cases of AIDS recorded for forty-two African countries compared to 80 million of malaria which kills the most, and 1.2 million cases of tuberculosis every year.

From 1994 WHO figures, approximately 52–55 per cent of sub-Saharan Africa's estimated 10 million cases of HIV-infected persons are women. In Africa, HIV is mostly transmitted heterosexually, with highest infection rates found in women sex-workers and young women between fifteen and twenty-five, mostly because of sexually transmitted diseases (STDs) and the underdeveloped thin lining in young vaginas. HIV manifestation in women is still hardly taken seriously either in research or in preventive measures which give the power of infection or prevention to men by the heavy stress placed on condom use. Yet, evidence shows a rise in newborn infection through mother-to-child transmission. In the AIDS tragedy, women are victims as well as the carers of the sick, the dying and the destitute in their families and communities.

Many have suggested that most lives would be saved with strong campaigns focusing on the prevention and cure of STDs, and, more importantly, with adequate, accessible and affordable health care for the poor. Women's reproductive role makes them the main users of blood transfusion. Some have therefore suggested health policies that would recognize AIDS as a blood-borne disease, just like malaria, tuberculosis and STDs, hence the need for massive investment in modernizing laboratories and blood banks in Africa, with specific emphasis on retraining of hospital technicians. There is also a demand for a holistic approach in keeping with African practice of healing the whole person in the context of community as opposed to curing a disease with no interest in the mind and welfare of the social person. This entails concerns about adequate food, home and right to land and employment; in other words, the rights of a full citizen.

Environment, education and health

The 1994 Cairo Population Conference, which urged rich nations to spend $17 billion a year by 2000 and $22 billion for its twenty-year plan on family planning, reproductive health and AIDS prevention, shows that donor agencies such as the United Nations and government-designed reproductive health services are begining to see a link between women's and girls' education, better education, better health and lower birth rate,[10] as opposed to a direct link between contraceptive provision and low birth rate. The World Health Organization (WHO) and the United Nations Population Fund (UNFPA) concern with women and health security at the UN Cairo Population and Development Conference was what set the stage for Beijing.

People resent public interference with their lives, in particular their sexuality, whereas with education and knowledge, people retain their privacy in such matters. But on all these issues, the illiterate and the poor have less access to legal rights and health provision. They are also more likely to live in unhealthy environments in refugee camps, urban shanty towns or villages with few or no basic amenities. In 1990, only five African countries had less than 40 per cent of their rural population without access to safe drinking water. Over 80 per cent of the rural population in Angola, Congo, Ethiopia, Madagascar, Sierra Leone and Sudan have no access to safe drinking water. Except for six countries, most urban African populations are without safe drinking water. Sanitation services are equally low.[11]

The huge financial calculations made at the Cairo conference remain pledges which are difficult to realize in the current climate of economic gloom. Who in any case has utilized most of these finances? The bureaucrats or the poor? We ought to remember that, long before the Cairo plan, several modestly designed development projects and literacy classes had been operating locally for years to instruct the poor, peasants and illiterate grassroots women on basic hygiene, literacy, sexual education, family planning, skills training and so on.

In opening the dialogue on women's reproductive role and rights, powerful agencies like the WHO have gone further than any other body in reaching into African villages with immunization programmes. However, when the WHO's Global Commission on Women's Health claims to have established goals for reproductive health services, basic education for children and adults and universal access to basic health care, with specific targets and provisions for monitoring and evaluation of women's health programmes, one wonders how the WHO can do this since it is not an African government. UNICEF is well placed to implement the plan of action and goals set up at the children summit in 1990. Like the

WHO, UNICEF is also able to reach the rural areas. UNICEF as a children's fund can focus on the needs of the girl child. Support for women and children is also consistent with UNDP's concerns and its pledge to assist countries with the improvement of the status of women through the eradication of poverty, job creation, sustainable development and environmental justice as contained in the UNDP-commissioned *Human Development Report 1995*.

In recommending strategies for empowerment, it is important that we adopt a structural, multi-issue approach and recognize the right to sovereignty, and the economic and social dimensions to women's health problems: for example, the stress and health hazards experienced by women juggling time, money, work, family and service to their communities. African women have said that they essentially need business capital, education and skills training, equal pay and benefits, child care, health care, community care provision for dependants, and flexi-time for those in the public sector. Put this way in a formalized language, these would seem to be the same issues that have been demanded the world over by women's groups, yet there are marked differences in their relationship to power and the global economy.

Violence against African women and the role of human rights groups

In their submissions to the Beijing conference in 1995, human rights groups such as Amnesty International insisted on the universality and indivisibility of human rights, demanding that words must result in action in a real, practical sense. Words and commitments are not new if we recall the Vienna Declaration and Programme of Action adopted by 171 governments at the 1993 UN World Conference on Human Rights which for one thing linked women's rights with those of the girl-child, and both to human rights. More importantly, the Vienna Declaration insisted that these rights should be integrated into all United Nations human rights activities. Governments, inter-governmental and non-governmental institutions should also integrate them into their activities. Similar commitments were made at other global conferences on the environment, population and social development.

Recognizing the question of sovereignty and contextualization, unlike most of the women's organizations, Amnesty International pointed out the fact that the most common form of violence experienced by women is perpetuated by the state. State violence against women, as was pointed out, includes torture, 'disappearances', and extra-judicial executions. With this kind of consciousness, it is such human rights groups which can put effective pressure on governments to ratify the Convention Against Torture and other relevant human rights instruments, since the evidence indicates that these conventions and instruments have not protected African women from mass rapes, massacres and humiliations and abuses in refugee camps.

In spite of all these global conferences and declarations, today, African women are the main victims of gross human rights violations and abuses. Of fifty-eight wars around the world, twenty are in Africa. Over the last decade, 1.5 million children have died in various wars; 4 million were permanently disabled; 85 million landmines remained scattered in sixty-two countries around the world, Africa being the most afflicted with 30 million landmines in eighteen countries. Recent years have seen devastating armed conflicts in African countries such as Rwanda, Burundi, Mozambique, Sudan, Eritrea and Ethiopia, Somalia, Sierra Leone, Liberia and Congo. With hundreds of villages destroyed, countless numbers of Africans are internally displaced or made refugees in neighbouring countries. Eighty per cent of the world's 18 million refugee population, that is 14.4 million, are from Africa; 75 per cent of all refugees (13.5 million) are women and children; and 75 per cent of all African refugees are women, a total of 10.8 million. Genocide, rape and other torture, murder and atrocities are shockingly men's weapons of war of which women and their children, particularly girl-children, bear the brunt. Armed conflicts have intensified poverty, trauma and malnourishment and have led to a breakdown of the basic infrastructure.

In addition to the human rights groups, development agencies such as the UNIFEM claim to deal with these concerns through the African Women in Crisis umbrella programme, and to promote women's participation in peace-building and conflict-resolution initiatives in Africa. But are these so-called initiatives not usually informed by macro-economic interests externally packaged and forced on local peoples? UNIFEM controls funds for setting up women's groups and networks, and can devise more effective ways of ensuring better conditions for refugee women to return back to full citizenship as well as the increased participation of women through its funding of development and relief programmes. UNIFEM in fact claims to act as a women's needs catalyst within the United Nations system, and also claims an autonomous association with the United Nations Development Programme (UNDP). An organization that is so powerful and able to do all these things can well be seen as a global women's government. If so, is there not a conflict between its stated mission of mainstreaming women through macro-economics and the observed adverse effects of SAPs on African women?

This is why I think that it is more likely that the independent human rights groups, with their literacy in the international humanitarian laws, known as the laws of war, which prohibit rape and other forms of torture, hostage-taking and extra-judicial execution, can use these avenues to defend and support African women. Like the right to education, civil rights are thought to be guarantors of peace, development and social justice. However, we cannot sit back and wait for externally formulated strategies to bring peace to our regions. We need also to look inwards and utilize traditionally tested methods of peace-making under the leadership of locally recognized authorities who will accept the involvement of women in mediation processes. Broad-based consultation and participation are good indications of a commitment to get to the root cause of conflicts to ensure lasting peace. The proof of good government is in the ability to facilitate such consultations, and to enforce reforms and change national laws, judicial systems, systems of criminal justice and policing. The ultimate test is in seeing changes through self-help and self-reliance in the situation of women and fewer and fewer human rights violations against women and other vulnerable and disadvantaged social groups.

African women and leadership

In spite of money spent on women's development by global donor agencies, and much rhetoric by women's groups, women are still absent from the top seats of African governments, a trend which, as I pointed out at the beginning of this chapter, is more contemporary than traditional. Whatever happened to the traditional concept of constitutional women chiefs and queen mothers?

During the nationalist movements and the liberation movements, African women were moving more into government seats encouraged by the pre-1988 Eastern European communist model. The western liberal democratic model being forced on Africans through SAPs, for all we can tell, is strongly against the presence of women in government. Yet, women's rights are said to be human rights. To fulfil this aspiration requires joint decisions on all policy matters, and equality in power-sharing.

If we take statistics from elsewhere, we see that Sweden has 40 per cent of women in parliament, the USA has less than 11 per cent, Japan has less than 3 per cent, the United Arab Emirates and Kuwait ban women from parliament. Bhutan, Mauritania, Papua New Guinea, the Comoros, Saint Kitts-Nevis, Palau, Micronesia, Kiribati and Djibouti do not have a single woman in parliament,[12] while in South Africa in 1995, 25 per cent of national assembly members were women.

Suggested strategies for increasing women's presence in government include instituting equal education, nominating women candidates and encouraging women's registration to vote. Since Nairobi, however, we have learned lessons of what power can do to women who have climbed through women's struggles, hence the growing demand for accountability to the women below, and collective or rotating leadership at the top. Expertise business management of these high-spending conferences must have a co-optive and corrupting effect on traditionally poor and independent NGOs, turning many away from community activism in the role of observers and advocates to that of participants and collaborators with governments. This issue is examined in the next chapter.

Notes

These are currently the dominant reports. There are a few more recent reports that show the same trends:

World Bank, *World Development Report 1997*, Oxford and New York: Oxford University Press 1997.

UNDP, *Human Development Report 1997*, Oxford and New York: Oxford University Press 1997.

UNICEF, *State of the World's Children 1998*, Oxford and New York: Oxford University Press 1998.

1. See Table 11, 'Indicators on economic activity', and Table 12, 'Indicators on the economy and women's work', in *The World's Women 1995*, pp. 142, 143, 148.

2. See Table 14, 'Women in public life', in *The World's Women 1995*, pp. 172 and 173.

3. See Chart 6.7, 'Women's overall representation among managerial and administrative workers', in *The World's Women 1995*, p. 155.

4. See Figure 2.8, 'Male and female survival rates to Grade 5 in selected countries, 1992', and Table 2.2, 'Male and female school life expectancy and school survival expectancy in selected countries, 1992', in *UNESCO World Education Report 1995*, pp. 37 and 38.

5. See Box 2.6, 'Call for action on girls' education in Africa', in *UNESCO World Education Report 1995*, p. 46.

6. UNICEF's *State of the World's Children 1998* shows some improvement in school enrolment of girls. However, more than 40 million children in Africa are growing up without access to basic education. Worldwide, the number is 130 million. It also shows a correlation between high school enrolment of up to 90 per cent and free education, for instance in Botswana, Cape Verde, Malawi, Mauritius, South Africa and Zimbabwe. In industrialized countries of the West, primary school enrolment is 100 per cent. More importantly, there is little difference between boys and girls in both primary and secondary schools. The UNICEF report insists on education as the right of every child and states that it is the responsibility of governments. Education is an essential human right and a force for social change.

7. See 'The triumph of avarice', *West Africa*, 11 August 1996.

8. See Chart 5.10A, 'Labour force participation rates of boys and girls 10–14 years old, 1990', in *The World's Women 1995*, p. 118.

9. See Table 2, 'Households, families and childbearing', and Chart 5.21, 'Poverty rates in households headed by women and men', in *The World's Women 1995*, pp. 29–30 and 130.

10. See Chart 4.8, 'Women's literacy and total fertility rate', and Chart 4.9, 'Total fertility rate according to years of completed education', in *The World's Women 1995*, p. 95.

11. See Table 4, 'Access to safe drinking water and sanitation services, 1990', in *The World's Women, 1995*, p. 58.

12. See Table 14, 'Women in public life', in *The World's Women 1995*, pp. 172–3; see also Chart 6.4, 'Percentage of women in decision-making positions in government by field, 1994', and Chart 6.5, , 'Average percentage of women in parliamentary assemblies', in *The World's Women 1995*, p. 154.

Sources

Network sources

I read thousands of pages of news, speeches and discussions, including documents and reports from the following organizations on the Beijing conference received on electronic mail from multiple recipients of NET list <hrnet.women@Germany. EU.net>

This information is provided by the United Nations Information Centre in Sydney for Australia, New Zealand and the South Pacific:

Amnesty International; ANC Dept Information & Publicity; Earth Times News Service; Report of the Inter-Parliamentary Union (IPU); The Development GAP Third World Network: Africa; Voice of America

Publications

Adepoju, Aderanti and Christine Oppong, 1994, *Gender, Work and Population in Sub-Saharan Africa*. Geneva: ILO.

Anderson, Mary, 1993, *Focusing on Women: UNIFEM'S Experience in Mainstreaming*. UNIFEM.

Decosas, Josef and Violette Pedneault, 1992, 'Women and AIDS in Africa: Demographic Implications for Health Promotion', *Health Policy and Planning*, vol. 7, no. 3.

Hay, Margaret Jean and Sharon Stichter (eds), 1995, *African Women South of the Saharah*, 2nd edn., Harlow: Longman.

Jacobson, Jodi, 1992, *Gender Bias: Roadblock to Sustainable Development*, Worldwatch Paper no. 110, Washington: Worldwatch Institute.

Kerr, Johanna, 1993, *Ours by Right: Women's Rights as Human Rights*. London: Zed Books.

King, Elizabeth and Anne Hill, 1993, *Women's Education in Developing Countries: Barriers, Benefits, and Policies*. Washington, DC: World Bank.

Parpart, Jane L. and Kathleen A. Staudt (eds) 1989, *Women and the State in Africa*. Boulder, CO: Lynne Rienner.

Seidel, Gill, 1993a, 'Women at Risk: Gender and AIDS in Africa', *Disasters*, vol. 17, no. 2.

— 1993b, 'The Competing Discourses of HIV/AIDS in Sub-Saharan Africa: Discourses of Rights and Employment vs Discourses of Control and Exclusion', *Social Science and Medicine*, vol. 36, no. 3.

Sparr, Pamela, 1994, *Mortgaging Women's Lives: Feminist Critiques of Structural Adjustment*. London: Zed Books.

Subbarao, K. and Laura Raney, 1993, *Social Gains from Female Education: A Crossnational Study*. Washington, DC: World Bank.

Reports

Advancing Women's Status: Women and Men Together? Royal Tropical Institute, Netherlands, 1995.

Changing Socio-economic Conditions of Women in Africa in the Context of the Nairobi Forward-looking Strategies for the Advancement of Women: Sectoral Analysis of Political Participation, Education, Employment and Law. UN Economic and Social Council, ECA, Addis Ababa, 1991.

Detailed Report on Situation of Raped, Widowed, Landless and Otherwise Traumatized Women in Rwanda Presented to Anti-discrimination Committee. Committee on Elimination of Discrimination Against Women, WOM/896, 15th Session, 306th Meeting (PM). 1 February 1996.

The World's Women 1995: Trends & Statistics. United Nations Publications, 1995.

Women, Health and Development: Progress Report by the Director-General, WHO, 1992.

World Education Report 1995. UNESCO, 1995.

Women and Economic Policies in Africa by the Organization of African Trade Unions Unity (OATUU), Economic Commission for Africa, Fifth Regional Conference on Women, 16–23 November, Dakar, Senegal, United Nations Economic and Social Council.

The Fourth World Conference on Women documents

Kampala Action Plan, Regional conference on Women and Peace, 22–25 November 1993, Kampala, Uganda. (Endorsed by UN Economic Commission for Africa [UN-ECA] and the Organization of African Unity [OAU].)

African Platform for Action Adopted by the Fifth Regional Conference on Women, held at Dakar from 16 to 23 November 1994. Commission on the Status of Women, United Nations Economic and Social Council, E/CN.6/1995/5/Add.2, 29 December 1994.

The Platform for Action Critical Areas of Concern. Fourth World Conference on Women, 4–15 September 1995, Beijing, China, United Nations.

Declaration on the Elimination of Violence Against Women, Resolution adopted by the General Assembly on the Report of Third Committee (A/48/629) Resolution 48/104.

2. A history of class transformations: contemporary women's organizations in Nigeria

Chapter 1 showed how increasing globalization resulted in greater inequality between African women in general, with women professionals and NGO leaders climbing to power through women's struggles, even as the conditions of most African women demand urgent improvement. The result is tensions between women's groups at the local level where class formation is not homogeneous. In this chapter focusing on Nigeria, Part I looks at the making of elite classes of women, and Part II examines the nature of their organizations, their relationships with traditional women in the project of class reproduction, tensions between and within various groups and how they are all differently related to the Nigerian state.

Class reproduction and the external factor

From the late nineteenth century to the early twentieth century, not many Nigerians had a European education. The British in fact created the entity known as Nigeria in 1914 when they amalgamated their three designated colonial entities, the Northern and Southern protectorates and the colony of Lagos, into one nation-state. During this early period, in the march to 'modern' nationhood, English-speaking Africans called Creoles were the carriers of European culture and education before native Africans. Those referred to as Creole were returned ex-African slaves with European surnames who came mostly from Freetown, Sierra Leone and Monrovia, Liberia. They formed a diaspora network all along the West African coast and were the first Africans after the Europeans to control the state bureaucracy and professions such as law, education and medicine. Many were also Christian missionaries. They feature as teachers and missionaries in Chinua Achebe's fictional narratives of changing traditional Igbo societies under colonial rule.

In his study of the Creole in the 1960s and 1970s Sierra Leone, Abner Cohen (in *The Politics of Elite Culture: Explorations in the Dramaturgy of Power in a Modern African Society,* University of California Press, 1981) points out that the Creole had their own cultural distinctiveness as part of the state elite, being located mostly in the civil service and the professions. The Creole who were in fact a mixed group during the colonial period and flexible enough to absorb or creolize the rising elite from other ethnic groups, following the exit of the British and the handover of power, continuously redefined their identity, either to belong with the provincial native African Temnes or Mendes or as city-based Freetown strangers, for economic and political advantage.

Cohen therefore considered the Creole a power group, and saw Creole women as the main agents in cultivating what he calls 'cults of eliteness', which constitute patterns of symbolic behaviour that can be observed and verified. These cults of eliteness are perpetuated in an ideology of eliteness through 'an elaborate body of symbols and dramatic perform-ances: manners, etiquette, styles of dress, accent, patterns of recreational activities, marriage rules, and a host of other traits that make up the group's life style' (Cohen 1981: 2–3).

Creole women are thus central to both biological reproduction and cultural reproduction in their role as socializers for eliteness. They carry out these roles in massive church attendance in European-style dress and hair, and in their dutiful services to the church, which they practically run. In this way, Creole women are major enhancers of the universalistic image which in this case is embedded in Christian virtue. Their associations, clubs and activities for the wider public, particularly their philanthropic associations, enlarge this image of universal concern. Some of their bourgeois activities include teaching, patronizing the arts, drama, acting as entertainers, hostesses and masters of ceremony on state occasions and at receptions for foreign diplomats and other foreign visitors.

In Nigeria, similar to the processes which took place in Sierra Leone, the production of cults of eliteness was achieved through the churches, schools and various church-linked women's associations. As such, Creole women and Creole culture played an important part in the development of contemporary women's organizations and the roles that these organ-izations played in southern Nigeria. The ideas generated from this culture spread to the southeast through individual women who had been trained in the Christian church and the various associations linked to the church and its ideologies, especially the Young Women's Christian Association (YWCA).

PART I

The Young Women's Christian Association (YWCA) of Nigeria

The YWCA as an instrument of socialization for eliteness preceded the Nigerian state in the project of class reproduction and the production of civil virtue. The YWCA is a branch of the British YWCA and was started in what was not even quite 'Nigeria' by upper-class women who were wives and daughters of the ruling elite. It was founded in Nigeria in 1906 by Bishop Tugwell. The inaugural service was conducted on 19 April at Abeokuta, and it spread from there to various Anglican churches. Lagos had its inaugural service in September 1906. The Onitsha branch was formed in 1911 by the Christian Missionary Society (CMS) as a centre to teach domestic science, especially to young brides.

The YWCA's Nigerian headquarters were founded in 1933 at 16 Broad Street, Lagos. In 1958, the government acquired that building, and the YWCA moved to 8 Moloney Street. The new quarters were erected with financial assistance from the Nigerian government, the Central Agency of German Churches, donations from a number of business firms, YWCA branches and 'good-spirited individuals'. It was opened in 1967 by Lady Oyinkan Abayomi, president of the national YWCA.

The YWCA had its roots in the class background of its founding members, who were basically 'ladies of leisure'. Some of these women found idleness frustrating and took up philanthropic work. They were soon joined by other professional women. The Benin branch, for example, was founded by Irene Elizabeth Ighodaro, the wife of Samuel Osarogie Ighodaro, a Benin lawyer. She had been born a Sierra Leonean and was the first black female doctor the people of that area had ever seen. Ighodaro was also secretary of the Nigerian YWCA. Later she became its president and vice-president of the international YWCA.

A press interview in 1986 suggests that Ighodaro's personal views were liberal rather than radical. She noted, for example, that 'one woman is equal to one man'. She argued for less interference by relatives in marriage and supported the nuclear, monogamous sense of family. Some of her views can be seen as contradictory. She felt, for example, that not enough women were having children, yet she also encouraged women to partici-pate in public life and to try to influence their social conditions: 'This cannot be done by sitting at home; women now get into Legislative Houses and Local Councils. They are participating as much as possible in public life.'[1] Some of the aims of the YWCA, according to Dr Ighodaro, were to seek unity among its members through activities that would promote their spiritual, mental, social and physical welfare; to instil in members a sense of social responsibility for the improvement of their communities; and to foster a spirit of understanding and appreciation of the beliefs and customs of member nationalities and races.

The YWCA provided accommodation and homes over the years to hundreds of girls and young women as residents or visitors. These hostels were quiet, neat and economical, but some found the atmosphere prison-like: visitors were not allowed in the rooms, and no visitors were allowed on the premises after 10 p.m. Some very strict parents, in fact, instructed that their daughters not be allowed any visitors at all. Discipline was supposed to be highly enforced, and the mode of dress controlled; for example, no trousers were allowed during lectures. Board members visited the hostels once a month to teach make-up. Claiming that their objective was to develop the youth morally, mentally and spiritually, the hostels encouraged needlework and crafts training. They provided leadership training for the home and the nation. As Dr Ighodaro said in the same interview: 'We have been in the vanguard and have always advocated that since we live in the world, we have to change with the dictates of the time.'

We can see how the orientation of the YWCA has changed since the early 1960s, when its 'practical design for modern living' was aimed at young girls moving to the cities from the rural villages. These village girls were taught how to use water cisterns, cookers, electric irons and other electrical appliances. They were taught how to dress like ladies, how to straighten their hair, and how to use the make-up then in vogue. Upper-class Yoruba and Creole women had brought the culture of a new western femininity – skin-lightening and hair-straightening and a different kind of romantic love and fantasy – to urban elite women. In the 1960s, they in turn carried the new culture into the 'hinterland'.

To a great extent, Lady Oyinkan Abayomi exemplifies the elite woman of this period. She was an upper-class woman whose father, Sir Kitoye Ajasa, and two uncles, Sir Eric Moore and Olaseni Moore, were colonial supporters and prominent in Lagos politics.[2] She was a founding member of Queen's College, Lagos, the most prestigious girls' secondary boarding-school in Nigeria. She herself was schooled in England, and it was there that she thought of reproducing Cheltenham College, Gloucestershire, in Nigeria. She teamed up with friends to do it.[3] At the hostel she ran, Abayomi groomed future 'ladies', teaching them housekeeping, home economics and home training in preparation for lives as married women. A few upper-class boys were also trained at the hostel. She is reputed to have been a strict disciplinarian. One woman recalled, at the celebration of her ninetieth birthday in 1987, 'I learned not to raise my voice while

talking, not to struggle with men, how to comport myself and what company not to keep. She absolutely was fussy about the business of being a
lady.'

Nina Mba considers Abayomi one of Nigeria's pioneer feminists and an
inspiring model for Nigerian women because of her commitment to public
service and her concern with raising the status and aspirations of Nigerian
women. This, I think, is debatable, since one must pose the question of
whether prudish ladies with white upper-class aspirations are feminists. If
they are, what is their brand of feminism? Abayomi's background of
inherited wealth and privilege and her cultural aspirations make her seem,
in today's parlance, more like an agent of colonial cultural imperialism (see,
for example, Fanon 1970). She is a daughter of imperialism.

In contrast to the acculturalization programmes of the 1960s, the
current programme of the YWCA is backward integration, by which they
mean teaching rural women to live comfortably in their rural environment
in order to combat what the YWCA sees as 'too much urbanization'.
Some of the current projects of the YWCA provide adult literacy classes,
which can lead to primary six examinations and give women a broader
outlook on life. During the Nigeria–Biafra war (1967–70), the YWCA was
involved in the rehabilitation and reconstruction of areas affected by the
war. After the war, it set up rehabilitation centres in Bende, Imo, Anambra
and River states to assist women and children who had been victims of
the war. During that period, it received aid from the international YWCA
and the US Agency for International Development (USAID), which sent
equipment, cars and other items to the Nigerian branch. The YWCA
claims that it was able to help send students back to school, locate relatives
and pay school fees.[4]

The Girl Guides Association

In its moral principles the Girl Guides Association is similar to the YWCA,
except that its allegiance is to the British monarchy rather than the church
(the British monarch is, of course, head of the Anglican Church). This
association, which was introduced into Nigeria in 1919, was founded in
England in 1910 by Agnes Baden-Powell, a sister of Lord Baden-Powell,
founder of the Boy Scout movement. Lady Olave Baden-Powell took over
from her sister-in-law.

In its rules and guiding principles, the leader of any group of Guides
is expected to help young people grow up in a guided manner. Guides are
required to acknowledge the existence of God; to try to know, love and
serve God and God's children; to be loyal to their country (before independence, to be loyal to the British monarch); and to accept a code of

self-discipline and behaviour spelled out in the Guide Law. June Paterson-Brown, Chief Commissioner for the United Kingdom and Common-wealth Girl Guides, has said that she wanted her Guides to turn out 'practical but still feminine; able to have children and pursue their own careers without feeling guilty about it; and to be possessed of the *joie de vivre* that is the hallmark of the movement'. She saw Princess Anne as the perfect role model for girls.[5]

This process of western cultural imperialism is designed to cover the full period of childhood development. Children aged four to ten join the Brownies; those from eleven to fifteen move on to the Guides; and those fifteen years and older become Cadets and Rangers who advise, support and guide the younger ones. Programmes and activities are designed to enhance physical, moral and spiritual development and to complement the work of parents, schools and church in giving positive training to future leaders. The association's activities include camping, from which the Guides learn endurance and togetherness. Its funds come from government subvention, fund-raising and dues from members.

From its inception, the influence of upper-class English women guided the aspirations of the Girl Guide movement through its founding members, who were essentially the same women who had started the YWCA. An insight into the life of these women of the 1920s is vividly given in an interview with Ayo Ogun entitled 'A Touch of Class.' The 'ready-made dresses' and shoes worn by the elite were ordered from England. Young men taught themselves ballroom dancing in the street. 'England ladies' (i.e. Nigerian women returning from abroad) were envied and emulated. '[They] wore a new dress every Sunday … and beautiful shoes to match. And then of course was the nice stepping they had picked up to let the rest of us know that they had been abroad.'[6] Most elite girls at that time went to the Girls' Seminary, after which they went abroad. It was through Girl Guide activities that most of these women were able to carry out their charitable and development work with less-privileged women.[7]

Girls sports' competitions were started by the Girl Guide movement, but they did not last. In 1950, Ogun and sixteen other women started the Ladies Sports Club.[8] Violet Odogwu, who did a lot of running for the club, went on to become the first Commonwealth Games woman medallist.

The Girls' Brigade

If the cultural imperialism of the Girl Guides was directed from London, that of a similar organization, the Girls' Brigade, came from Ireland. This international, inter-denominational and uniformed organization was founded in Dublin in 1902 by the National Sunday School Union. It was

known as the Girls' Life Brigade before 1968, when it changed its name
to the Girl's Brigade. Girls were encouraged to become followers of Christ
and, through reverence, self-control and a sense of responsibility, to find
true enrichment in life. Its motto was 'To seek, serve, and follow Christ'.
Girls could join at the age of five. The Brigade's principles upheld chastity
of womanhood; abstention from alcoholic drinks, gambling and smoking;
and service to home, church and nation. As with the Girl Guides, camping
was seen as a time for spiritual fellowship and adventure.

Organizations such as the YWCA of Nigeria, the Girl Guides Association, and the Girls' Brigade have been shown not only to be linked to the
colonizing culture, but to have originated from that culture. The values of
this culture were fundamental in forming the morality of the elite women
who carried these European values into the contemporary women's organizations. These socializing values did not act in a vacuum, but against
already existing cultures and their moral systems which constituted the
guiding principles of traditional women's organizations. How did the now
multicultural and multiethnic elite women in partnership with the state
bring these colonizing values into traditional women's organizations and
what was the nature of the new organizations?

PART 11

The National Council of Women's Societies
(NCWS)

Eastern Nigeria Njideka Nwokolo started the Women's Cultural and
Philanthropic Organization in eastern Nigeria as a result of what she saw
women doing west of the Niger. According to a history by Chief Mrs
Janet Mokelu, a founder-member,[9] she attended a YWCA welfare course
in London in 1958 on how to organize women. On her return, she founded
an 'umbrella embracing all women's organizations' to enable women to
exchange ideas and articulate their common interests. Oyibo Odinamadu
was elected the first president of the Women's Cultural and Philanthropic
Organization, and Eme Nwakanma Okoro (the former Miss Ikpe-Eme)
became its first secretary. Mrs Mokelu was their patron. Later that year,
the organization merged with the National Council of Women's Societies,
and Enugu became regional headquarters for the Eastern Region.

According to Mrs Mokelu, 'This fusion marked the beginning of group
articulation of interests by women and also a recognition by the Federal
government at that time of women's groups as part and parcel of the
political process.' Mokelu's claim is contentious if we consider issues of
class, representation, participation and the effect that this trend has had

on traditional systems of women's organization and women's political participation in public or civic politics. In fact, these new organizations provided elite women with extensive networks, which enabled them to participate in politics, the new economy and a new elite culture. As individuals, they could also pursue political ambitions and careers in the name of the female masses.

This is not to say that individual women did not sometimes participate in protests and demonstrations during this period. Indeed, the nature of women's movements changed as a result of the activities of these women. Nevertheless, the demonstrations did not lead to immediate gains for the generality of women, for it was the leadership roles played by individual elite women that were publicized. Under these individualistic and ambitious leaders, the female masses were often co-opted by having self-appointed or establishment-appointed women placed in leadership positions. With both economic and political interests now in the establishment, these 'leaders' began to see themselves as accountable to the establishment and not the generality of women, least of all masses of women in the rural villages.

Mrs Mokelu and Margaret Ekpo were already well-publicized political activists. They had led the 1949 protest that followed the bloody massacre of twenty-one protesting mine workers by the British colonial Captain Phillip and his troops at Iva Valley, Enugu. The women took their protest to the Executive Council of the National Convention of Nigerian Citizens (NCNC), and it was Mrs Mokelu who wrote, read and presented the address at the house of M. U. Adams along Ogui Road, Enugu.[10] Thus it is not surprising that Mrs Mokelu and Mrs Ekpo were appointed to the Eastern Nigeria House of Chiefs on 30 December 1959 by Robert de Stepledon-Stepledon, the colonial governor of eastern Nigeria. Both women were recommended by the premier, Nnamdi Azikiwe. According to Mrs Mokelu, their appointment was intended to ensure the full representation and participation of women in government and legislative debate. Both women also won election into the Eastern House of Assembly on the platform of the NCNC.

These appointments marked the beginning of a new era of female tokenism in an establishment which was not only masculine in composition but also masculine in character. Instead of insisting on collective participation by women in large numbers, however, these women seemed to enjoy their solo performances and ended their speeches with 'thanks to our men, who stood behind us'. This is not to say that they should not be supported by their men, but they had masses of women supporters whom they were supposed to be representing.

In addition to performing in the corridors of power, even in those of foreign governments, for that matter, there also began a trend of soliciting approval and good-will from the establishment. This can be seen from the list Mokelu provides of those who sent messages[11] to the Second Convention of the National Council of Women's Societies held at the United States Information Service building on Catholic Mission Street in Lagos in May 1963.[12] The convention was addressed by Lady Ademola, NCWS president. One of the issues she raised was the need for more employment opportunities for women in government departments and on statutory boards. In Mokelu's own words:

> Most women who played prominent roles in politics in eastern Nigeria[13] did so through the political party in power at the time. ... These women formed the foundation on which women were mobilized to gather support for the party in power. These women were mobilized and organized by the secretariat of the women's wing of the NCNC, headed by my humble self as the Secretary General.

Mobilizing women to give support to the political parties was seen as woman's role in the First Republic. The women who have been mentioned so far were all staunch Christians and urban-based wives of the elite class, whose activities were centred in the urban towns and regional capitals. Many of the same names resurface in the Second Republic, again servicing men's political parties.

In mid-western Nigeria, Mrs Bernice Uwanugo Kerry was a staunch Christian whose political career resembles that of Igbo women in eastern Nigeria. In 1986, an extensive interview charted her fascinating history. She was described as the first female senator[14] from Owerre-Olubor in Ika Local Government Area. Bernice Kerry represented the mid-western state, (which was changed to Bendel state and is now Delta state) in the House of Assembly of the First Republic from 1963 to 1966. She achieved that position out of the personal promise by the premier of the Mid-West, Chief Dennis Osadebay, to send women to both houses of parliament. Mrs Wuruda Esan was the other female appointed from the Mid-West by the Action Group Party.

In the House of Assembly, Kerry gained popular acceptance. She reveals that the men regarded women politicians as mothers and the women in turn offered men very useful advice. This is how she understood the meaning of women's liberation: 'We fought for women's liberation ... We tried to persuade them to leave the women to come out and participate in nation building. That is liberation, not saying they are liberated so they won't know their husbands again.'[15]

In the House, Mrs Kerry moved the motion that a man should be responsible for the upkeep of any child he fathers outside his marriage. In her belief, the family is the foundation of a solid and good educational background. The problem with Nigeria, in her opinion, is greed, and this can lead to armed robbery. Kerry, who was sixty-nine at the time of the interview had three children: a medical director of a hospital, a female university lecturer and an education officer at a state ministry of education.

Kerry went to the House on a NCNC platform and performed a number of government duties as a parliamentarian. In 1965, she was a government delegate to the Far East, and was a member of the Ika customary court, 1970–74.

Kerry is a household name in the Anglican Diocese of Benin as a distinguished religious and social worker. Her husband was the late Archbishop G. I. Kerry, and Bernice Kerry's pride is basically in her achievements as wife and mother, even though society might prefer to highlight other achievements. She is patron of the Society for the Promotion of Igbo Language and Culture; was involved in a long list of philanthropic projects, founded the Owerre-Olubor Grammar School in 1979, and was chair of the schools parent/teacher association; built the Owerre-Olubor dispensary; runs the Faith Maternity Hospital; does business and farming; has been a councillor, and local president of NCWS; and is an executive member of the Old Girls' Association of the famed St Monica's College, Ogbunike, in what is now Anambra state. St Monica's was a Christian missionary domestic science school and produced the first educated Igbo women. My mother also attended St Monica's.

Western Nigeria The 1949 massacre of trade unionists in Enugu saw the surfacing of female activists in the regional capital of the east. In the west, it was fighting for the abolition of women's flat-rate tax in Abeokuta which led to the mass meeting of the Abeokuta Women's Union (AWU) in May 1949. It was then that Funmilayo Ransome-Kuti proposed the formation of the Nigerian Women's Union (NWU) to unite all Nigerian women. She also suggested its affiliation with the International Federation of Women. The executive committee of the AWU became the same as that of the NWU, and the AWU soon became the Abeokuta branch of the NWU.

The women's first concerns were continuation of the fight against the flat-rate tax which was introduced by the colonial administration to replace the forced labour tribute practised in the southwestern provinces between 1917 and 1918 and the oppressive Sole Native Authority.[16] They were also fighting for enfranchisement for Nigerian women and equal participation in politics. Although the first branches of the NWU were located in the nearby provinces of Abeokuta and Ijebu, its first show of strength and support took place in Ijebuode over the water rate.

Since the movement focused on local issues, it is not clear why it was given a national title, the Nigerian Women's Union. Kuti and her colleagues, all elite women, were already in touch with international movements at this period, but their conditions and aspirations were very different from those of their sisters in the northern provinces, for they were more in tune with women in the urban towns of the eastern provinces. Rural development was not on the political agenda of the colonial administration during this period, and the elites who took over the administration continued the policy of marginalizing and isolating the rural areas. Most rural women had no tap water for which to pay rates, and they had no police to clash with, much less post offices or newspapers to which to send publicity or letters and rejoinders, all characteristics of the Abeokuta campaign.

Like those who led the Enugu 1949 protest, Kuti was well known nationwide, and her organization spread, but her constituency remained with urban-based women's organizations. The general strike of 1945 led to the formation of an Enugu Women's Association (EWA), whose primary aim was to assist the men who were jobless as a result of the strike. Its founders included Janet Okala, Mrs G. I. Okoye and Madam Peter Okoye.

In Aba, Mrs Kuti linked up with Mrs Ekpo, another woman with foreign contacts and influence. Ekpo had accompanied her husband to Ireland and had become politicized by her experiences with racism in Britain: 'These perceptions radicalized Mrs Ekpo's thinking about colonialism and feminism. She became a fierce opponent of colonialism and an advocate of the necessity for Nigerian women to demand the same civil rights that European women had' (Mba 1982: 169). This link between the two self-appointed leaders led the Nigerian Women's Association to change its name to the Nigerian Women's Union, Enugu Branch, in 1949. Enugu women related that Mrs Kuti, on her arrival, educated them on national unity and patriotism. Ekpo also credited her inspiration to Mrs Kuti. The two women envisioned an all-embracing National Women's Movement.

Mba indicates that the NWU spread to most towns in the Federation in both northern and southern Nigeria, but she does not tell us who made up the membership in the northern towns – i.e. whether they were northern women or diaspora southern women. However, we do learn that

the NWU was in effect a federation of autonomous branches: each branch was concerned primarily with the interests of the women in its area, with only a national executive committee which was more concerned with national issues affecting women. Mrs Kuti was the president of the NWU while remaining president of the Abeokuta branch, with Mrs Ekpo serving as national secretary while remaining president of the Aba branch. (Mba 1982: 173)

NWU's political objectives, contained in their 'Demands for Political Democracy', included enfranchisement for women, abolition of electoral colleges, proportional political representation for women, nomination of women representatives to local councils (which should no longer be headed by traditional rulers), and affiliation with no political party. Mba does not state whether the Enugu Women's Association gave up its membership in the NCNC when it joined NWU.

We do not know why in 1953 Kuti found it necessary to call a 'national' women's conference in Abeokuta, which she apparently described as a parliament of the women of Nigeria. What was born from this assembly was yet another organization called the Federation of Nigerian Women's Societies (FNWS). Offices were distributed among representatives throughout southern Nigeria. Kuti was named president-general. The resolutions of that conference echoed the objectives of the NWU, along with an added demand for universal adult suffrage and special care to ensure the participation of illiterate voters and consultation with FNWS prior to the introduction of laws. Mba lists FNWS' objectives as: (1) to encourage the womenfolk of Nigeria to take part in the political, social, cultural and economic life of Nigeria; (2) to create facilities for female education; and (3) to raise the status of women generally and to win for them equal opportunities with the men.

The arena of women's social existence and political participation was thus shifted by these elite women from the concrete situation of the greatest number of women in rural villages to an abstract one in the urban socio-political context. It was a new drama being acted out by elites. In Benin, the women talked of setting up a newspaper and co-operatives. In the Western Region, the women were concerned with primary and secondary education for girls. In Benin, in 1954, the women congratulated the Eastern Region for introducing universal suffrage on a non-taxation basis. Kuti moved her campaign to the north to demand women's enfranchisement.

Individually, members of the FNWS belonged to the NCNC, but the organization remained autonomous. However, the new leadership and political careers of these elite women meant that they could be easily enticed by political parties. The NCNC, for example, saw to it that its women members dropped out of the Federation of Nigerian Women's Societies. The organization seems to have worked through Ekpo, in spite of resistance from other women leaders from the east. The incident demonstrates a new issue of accountability and the loss of traditional built-in control mechanisms of the rural women's organizations. The Ngwa Women's Association condemned Ekpo for acting without the approval of her townswomen, and the national NCNC ordered its women members to withdraw from the FNWS. Enugu women, for their part, sought advice from Kuti, apparently because they liked her organization (FNWS), and Onitsha and Enugu remained members. What is interesting is that they saw FNWS as Kuti's organization. Kuti herself saw no conflict in remaining president of NWU and FNWS and the women's wing of the Western Region NCNC (1956–59).

In 1958, an alliance was formed between FNWS and the women's wing of the Northern Elements Progressive Union (NEPU). They took up the campaign for the enfranchisement of women in the north. Their argument was that if the Muslim north was not ready to give women the vote, it should halve its proportional representation in the Federal House of Representatives, but they failed to break the rigid patriarchal political monopoly that Islam held in the north. The leader of NEPU's women's wing was Mallama Gambo Sawaba, who became the sole mouthpiece and representative of northern women. The northern women who were being represented were, of course, in seclusion and not involved in this type of politics. It was only the 'Karuwas', free wives (often translated as prostitutes), who made up the women's wings of NCNC, AG and NUPU. The women were constantly harassed by local authorities and the NPC government in the Northern Region. They were also subjected to physical violence and moved in and out of gaol (Cohen 1969: 62–3; Mba 1982: 254–5).

Two international issues that concerned the NWU and FNWS were the French atomic-bomb tests in the Sahara and the South African treason trial. Kuti had been in contact with the Women's International Democratic Federation (WIDF) from 1947. She was instrumental in the NWU's decision to follow the WIDF in making the 8th of March a women's day. Through WIDF, Kuti made several international visits: to China in 1949, Vienna in 1952, Budapest in 1955, Peking in 1956, Budapest in 1961 and Moscow in 1962. She and Ekpo also went to Moscow in 1963 for the World Congress of Women. In 1953 Kuti became vice-president of the WIDF.

WIDF was regarded as a communist front organization by both the colonial and Nigerian governments, and Kuti's association with the organization resulted in an interrogation concerning her passport application for the 1956 Peking visit. In December 1957, the Balewa government decided not to renew her passport at all. The authorities feared that Kuti would infect women with communist ideas and policies. '[Kuti] asked if Balewa's visit to Egypt and Saudi Arabia made him an Arab out to Islamize Nigeria' (Mba 1982: 181). Kuti was, in fact, politically well-informed and well-connected to the Left, as can be seen from those who took up her cause: the Nigerian Trade Union Federation, for example; abroad, it was the Nigerian Students Union of Great Britain, a British

Member of Parliament, and secretary of the Movement for Colonial Freedom. Nigeria has yet to produce a female activist to equal Kuti.

Kuti was not a daughter of the establishment. If anything, she was a thorn in its flesh, and she applied African women's traditional methods of protest – insults and crying wolf – as can be seen from the letter she and the FNWS sent to the British Secretary of State for the Colonies: 'The rights of Nigerian women are now being assassinated by virtue of the Federal P.M.'s high office. A woman shall succeed him one day as P.M. Because we demand franchise for Balewa's North, women are called Communist. Because Nigerian women are used as tools in this country by various political parties, Balewa's speech was greeted by cheers' (Mba 1982: 181).

Power struggle in the new women's movement Kuti was ahead of her time and in the wrong socio-political setting for her level of political awareness and ideological commitment. At the World Congress of Women in 1963, Ekpo criticized Kuti's paper for presenting a negative picture of the position of women in Nigeria. More than twenty-two years later, this was echoed in the differences enunciated by the delegates from Women in Nigeria (WIN) and those from NCWS at the 1985 End of the Decade for Women Conference in Nairobi.

By 1952, other women leaders had surfaced in the Western Region. Elizabeth Adeyemi Adekogbe, who had become a member of the NCNC in 1950, had been trained as a schoolteacher and worked as a civil servant. She inaugurated the women's movement in 1952 in Ibadan. Its objectives were universal suffrage, admission of women to the Native Authority Councils, nomination of women from the movement to the Western House of Assembly, more secondary schools for girls, lowering of the bride-price, and controls over Syrian and Lebanese trading monopolies. Adekogbe and her colleagues hoped to persuade Nigerian women to accept the leadership of this movement on all political, economic and educational matters. They also aimed to remain independent but were prepared to form an alliance with any party having identical aims and objectives.

It was Adekogbe who, in 1953, suggested the formation of a National Women's Movement, but Kuti manipulated events so that the meeting was held in her territory, Abeokuta, under the auspices of her own NWU. This was how the Federation of Nigerian Women's Societies was formed, with Kuti as president and Adekogbe as vice-president. Adekogbe removed the Women's Movement, which was primarily Yoruba-based, from the FNWS, and the organization concentrated its efforts on forming women's co-operatives.

As a daughter of the establishment, she worked with the traditional rulers, most of whom became patrons of the Women's Movement and later the Action Group. She was Iyalaje of Ikija in 1953, while her husband became Oba of Ikija in 1954. Mba affirms that the Women's Movement can be said to have developed as an establishment organization and as a counter to Kuti's NWU. Like Kuti, Adekogbe had international links, especially with other establishment-supported women's organizations such as the International Council of Women which, unlike the WIDF, limited itself to non-communist countries.

Describing these women's organizations as being 'of the establishment' is not to say that they did not fight the pressures of political parties that wanted to control their organizations. Every one of them appears to have had this problem. But the aspirations and ideological orientations of their leaders were such that it was not difficult for men eventually to achieve control. Adekogbe (perhaps inspired by her other identity as a daughter of the Goddess in her capacity as Iyalaje) tried initially to fight off attempts by the Action Group, led by Awolowo, to incorporate the Women's Movement.

But if one woman proved stubborn, other women were available – which explains the 1953 decision to appoint Mrs Aiyedun as special member of the Western House of Assembly. She was not a member of the AWU or the NWU or the Women's Movement. She was, in fact, a member of the Egba Central Council. Adekogbe criticized the appointment openly, pointing out the dangers of men deciding who should represent women and of women who are seen and not heard. She believed that turning the Women's Movement into a women's wing of AG would result in the failure of women to organize themselves: 'Whilst the NCNC, NPC, or AG women's wings are political, ours is not. We are demanding the rights of women through a united effort of women. The problems of women are above party politics. That is why we do not propagandize for any special political party, although we may have our private leanings' (Mba 1982: 185).

Members of the AG responded with harassment and intimidation, ordering their wives to resign from the Women's Movement. Adekogbe's husband was forced to resign from the civil service, and she herself faced several problems as a contractor and headmistress. The Co-operative Bank of Western Nigeria refused the Women's Movement financial assistance. By 1954, Adekogbe had left the NCNC and joined AG, and active AG women, including Hannah Awolowo, wife of the party's leader, had taken over the executive council of the Women's Movement, which was renamed the Nigerian Council of Women (NCW). Adekogbe became organizing secretary of the AG women's wing. Mba describes the NCW as 'a one-woman show'. From 1954 to 1958, 'the Movement ceased its political propagandizing on behalf of women; it did not criticize any action of government; and it did not hold a general assembly' (Mba 1982: 187). By 1958, leading AG women, including Awolowo's wife, had become vice-presidents of the NCW.

In 1959, Adekogbe wrote to the Women's Improvement Society, which had been founded in Ibadan in 1948. The society was initially a social welfare scheme that worked with the YWCA and the women's section of the Ibadan Progressive Union, which was led by Wuraola Esan. Leaders of both these societies, like Adekogbe, were teachers. They inaugurated the National Council of Women's Societies in Ibadan in 1959, with the wife of the Chief Justice of Western Nigeria, Lady Ademola, as president; Mrs Ogunsheye, a lecturer at the University of Ibadan, was secretary; and the treasurer was Mrs Akran, wife of the Western Region Minister of Social Welfare. That same year, the National Council of Women's Societies replaced the Nigerian Council of Women as an affiliate member of the International Council of Women. Adekogbe noted, 'Before now, no women's organization in this country could claim to be national in any true sense. If, therefore, on the eve of independence, the National Council of Women's Societies has emerged, it should give one great pleasure' (Mba 1982: 188).

Tokenism and the loss of women's political autonomy The NCWS claimed to be the only true national women's organization and, from the outset, it also claimed to be non-political, concerned instead with welfare and educational matters. It received an annual government subvention and became the organization representing Nigerian women, with branches in all the capital towns of the three regions that existed at that time, including Lagos. Membership was on an individual basis or as a member of an organization. Lady Oyinkan Abayomi was head of the Lagos branch, which was composed of elite women, market women and female activist members of the two southern political parties. Other branches were made up primarily of elite, educated and wealthy women. Most had already been co-opted by the new political parties, which had used coercion and red tape to subvert the women's wings of various parties. The women's organizations thus came under the control of the party, and of men.

Ademola and Titola Sodeinde were named president and secretary at the first national conference which was held in Ibadan in 1961. At the conference, the NCWS called on the government to get women into boards and corporations and to set up an employment bureau for women and girls. The western branch was concerned with lobbying government to appoint women as ministers and to top positions in public services. They also demanded more schools for girls. The eastern branch, on the other hand, seems to have been concerned with the morality of youth, asking the government to ban them from public houses and hotels. That group also demanded that people of low moral character not be given positions of trust by the government. Eastern women were therefore already concerned with the issue of corruption, probity and accountability in the new political jungle. One cannot say that northern women were really involved in NCWS at this period because colonial and post-colonial state policies encouraged self-identification on the basis of ethnicity, irrespective of place of birth or residence. Even though delegates attended from Kaduna, the capital of the Northern Region, many were part of the diaspora of the south who merely resided in the north, and they were Christian women.

From the outset, because of the background of the women and the organizations from which they emerged and which they carried with them into NCWS, we see a tug-of-war between those of the Ladies Progressive Club in its concern with welfare, charity and philanthropy and political activists from the Women's Party and militant market women. NCNC, for example, recognized the pro-AG tendency of the National Council of Women's Societies, even though NCNC female activists like Madam Young, Miss Ededem and Mrs Mokelu were members of the NCWS in the Eastern Region. According to Mba, however, the council did not openly show support for any political party.

With the formation of the National Council of Women's Societies, we can see how women's protest strategies changed dramatically. Women could now write letters of appeal or summon representatives of women's organizations to the town hall. During the general strike in 1964, for example, their strategy was to send a letter of appeal to both the workers and the government to end the strike. In the 1964 political clash between factions of AG, NCWS prayed for a return to peace. It was the Benin branch that seems to have remained consistently political. It was successful in getting women appointed as court assessors and to an advisory committee that allocated market stalls. It also got the Benin city council to reserve six seats for women. It never stopped calling on government to appoint more women to government posts.

Mba concedes that the NCWS lacked the broad-based support that Abeokuta and Ibadan gave the Nigerian Women's Union, the Federation of Nigerian Women's Societies and the Women's Movement. Unlike these organizations, however, the National Council of Women's Societies was not focused on the charismatic leadership of a single leader like Kuti or Adekogbe. But the NCWS, in spite of ineffective leadership and lack of a broad-based constituency, continued to enjoy the support of each regime and to work for every government that Nigeria has had. As Mba (1982: 192) puts it: 'They bought recognition from government with their claim that they represented the women of Nigeria and that therefore they should be consulted by government on all decision-making which concerned women.' This monopolistic claim to women's leadership and representation by NCWS, in spite of its lack of broad-based legitimacy and its co-optation by the state, are issues on which the council has rarely been challenged.

Criticism of National Council of Women's Societies (NCWS)

Although various governments continued to use the NCWS as their out-reach to women, critics have relentlessly pointed out that the organization is non-representative and elitist. In recent years, this criticism has been voiced most frequently by the women the NCWS claims to represent. On 29 March 1987, the *Sunday Times* reported: 'The National Council of Women's Societies (NCWS) has been severely criticised for the narrowness of its operation. It has been accused of being elitist, parochial in its attitudes towards the improvement of the lot of women, ineffective, and irrelevant to the majority of Nigerian women, particularly those in the rural areas. It should be scrapped.'

Many women in Ibadan thought the NCWS was a church society; others thought it was another women's society. Those who knew more about it felt it had little relevance beyond urban areas, since the organization's leaders seemed ignorant of the plight of rural women, who were still exploited sexually and economically. As examples, they cited tax laws, *purdah* (Islamic seclusion of women), and neglect. Others saw the problems of Nigerian women as rooted in religion, customs and male chauvinism, yet the NCWS, they charged, concerned itself solely with the interests of a few professional women.

The NCWS' tactic of 'waiting for the government to act' also came under attack. Some believed that the NCWS should mount massive campaigns to hasten the eradication of practices such as child marriage. Critics also pointed to the monopolization of the council by a group of women who had not 'achieved anything ... yet refused to give way to women who represent a different generation with different experience as mothers and wives'. The ' old brigade', they felt, should remain in the background as advisers. Lastly, critics pointed out the need for the NCWS to become more community-service-oriented, designing programmes to organize and enlighten women.

Hilda Adefarasin, president of the NCWS until 1987, argued that it was inevitable that educated women should lead the council because of the national and international services it rendered and the sort of people it dealt with. The council, she asserted, was a forum for women of diverse interests and professional backgrounds. Past president Ifeyinwa Nzeako enumerated some of the NCWS' achievements: award of scholarships, promotion of the status of women, establishment of nursery institutions and crèches through various affiliates, liaison with government officials regarding the welfare of women, pilot schemes for family planning and adult education, acting as 'mothers' during various national crises, care of abandoned babies, speaking out for market women in times of escalating prices, and fighting discriminatory tax laws through its members in the legal profession.

Mrs Adefarasin felt the organization's most important achievement was creating awareness 'in our governments and men that women are a force to be recognised; also that women want to play their parts in nation-building and in all spheres of life', and she cited other achievements: organizing lectures and workshops to keep women informed, assisting the government in the Expanded Programme on Immunization (EPI) campaigns, and building hospital theatres for operations on young girls suffering from vestino vaginal fistula (VVF), which was rampant in northern Nigeria, presumably as a result of young girls' early marriage. The NCWS built the theatre and then handed it over to the government.

Despite the general criticisms of NCWS, officials of the organization were reluctant to give up their posts. The collaborative role of the NCWS with the state had been assured through the practice of having wives of heads of government assume patronage of the council. The NCWS had also been a stepping-stone for government appointments for women. Most state and federal presidents of the council have at one time or another served as ministers of state or state commissioners.

In the struggle over control of the NCWS hierarchy, especially the 1988 struggle for leadership at the Abuja convention, we can see how elite women have come to adopt some of the unsavoury political strategies of masculine party politics; how they are now truly daughters of imperialism. In place of women's solidarity, there is a vicious rivalry for control, power and supremacy within the context of a political economy based on capitalism and state patriarchy. In order for women to succeed in this system, they have to ignore their sisters, the daughters of the Goddess, and act as solo performers – iron ladies of the establishment – imitating men of power or servicing them. There is no true partnership of men and women in such a system.

Recent NCWS conventions The NCWS' eleventh biennial convention, held in Port Harcourt in 1986, seems to illustrate most of the contradictions embodied in the idea, character and aims of the council.[17]

The theme of the convention was 'Unity, Action and Progress', and it was attended by more than a thousand women. The plan was to discuss common problems, review past achievements, plan strategies and elect new officers. Sub-themes included youth in action for progress, women in action for national development, and community in action for national stability.

As has become habitual in these performances, the convention was opened by the state military governor (who is always a man). The nation's 'first lady' and some states' 'first ladies', patrons of the organization, read speeches which generally called on women to endorse and carry out government policies. The presence of establishment wives at these conferences means that the opening sessions receive all the publicity. They make their speeches and depart, and the press follows them, which means that the sessions themselves receive little publicity.

More important is the fact that the conventions are opened under the symbolic blessing and supervision of the establishment, which makes it unclear how the NCWS can claim to be non-governmental. Moreover, the voices of grassroots women are heard only in their capacity to entertain with songs and dances during a roll-call of the states.

At this particular convention, the speech by the then military president's wife, Maryam Babangida, exemplifies the contradictions that the NCWS itself encompasses. She began by offering several suggestions for improving the organization:

1. The council should be more consultative and act as liaison for its affiliates.
2. It should be more informed about the activities of its affiliates in order to foster and sustain a two-way communication.
3. It should reach out to other women's organizations and convince them of the merit of affiliation.
4. There should be an effort made to unite the council, since it can play a vital role in making women aware of their responsibilities by supporting government measures aimed at promoting the national interest.
5. The council should see itself as a vehicle for achieving national aims and aspirations.
6. Members of the council, as wives and mothers, should inculcate the right attitudes in the youth, in their communities, and in the nation.
7. They should set up a mechanism so the council can better co-operate with the public and private sectors to solve the problem of unemployment.
8. The NCWS should work with youth to achieve the aims of the National Orientation Movement.

These suggestions for structural change in the NCWS involved the formation of a co-ordinating committee involving the council and its affiliates, a publicity committee to enlighten the general public about the council's activities and provide up-to-date information to affiliates in rural areas, and an 'honour roll' for women who have made significant contributions to advancing the cause of women or who have rendered exemplary service to the council and its affiliate organizations – past patrons, presidents and the like.

Past struggles, said Maryam Babangida, where Nigerian women have united and fought for their rights, should serve as examples to the NCWS, and she reminded the participants of the achievements of Mrs Ransome-Kuti, Margaret Ekpo, Lady Ademola, Lady Abayomi, Hajiya Gambo Sawaba and Lady Gwari. She said: 'I therefore urge you, in like manner, to mobilise the women's societies to contribute and support all government and private programmes.'

On the other hand, she also advocated that 'as women, we should always identify ourselves with peace. There are many challenging divisive elements in our various communities, in each state and in the country as a whole. We should therefore use our feminine attributes of sympathy, intuition, and tact to influence our menfolk and the entire nation to surmount these divisive elements and thus maintain peace, unity, and stability.' Her sentiments seem to be echoed by the executive members of the council who paid a visit to the state governor, the 'host' of the convention. During the visit, the NCWS president stated it was their duty as mothers to co-operate with any government in power to ensure that the government's aims and aspirations were well publicized, especially to women in rural areas.[18] Earlier in the convention, a university professor had spoken on 'the role of women in national development' as part of the performance syndrome at the convention, where male 'experts' are invited to present papers. He lectured solemnly that 'women should feel gratified that it is a self-evident and inimitable fact that woman's proverbial place in the home cannot be deputed to the man'.[19]

What came out of the convention's deliberations included a call for more action for national development and more unity among women. It was also resolved that women must fight for their rights. The following resolutions were passed to parents, mothers and government:

1. Parents should be much more attuned to their responsibilities of inculcating in their children virtues like the fear of God, honesty, patriotism, capacity for hard work and discipline.
2. Adults should be aware of and understand the special needs of youth.
3. There is a need for women to evolve strategies to enable them to work together as a cohesive body to ensure unity and solidarity.

4. Women should work to maintain stable homes, to be self-reliant, and be encouraged to participate in politics in 1990.
5. Women should realize their responsibility for promoting and cementing unity in the country, bearing in mind their numerical strength and centrality in the home.

The reporter for the 1986 convention, Unoaku Ekwegbalu, wrote that 'politicking, negotiations, and alignments were continuous activities from the day of arrival until the elections were held … Final nominations showed that Nigerian political manoeuvre was at work once again … Complacency still seems to be the watchword. As it was yesterday, so it will be tomorrow. Posts are seen as personal properties which only enemies would seek to snatch from their owners.'[20] As a result, the 1986 convention failed to elect a new leadership, which meant another term in office for those already in power.

This struggle for control of the NCWS took a more violent turn during the next convention, which was held in August 1988 in the new federal capital, Abuja, a showpiece of the establishment. The convention ended abruptly as a result of a violent struggle for power:

> The convention's unceremonious conclusion was brought about when politics with the aroma of the Second Republic crept to the forefront during one of the heights of the meetings – the national elections. Observers say some of the contestants had been sponsored by some politicians and readily point to one of the aspirants, who was said to have paid for the accommodation and head-tax for several delegates.[21]

By NCWS rules, each state is entitled to twenty voting delegates. For the Abuja convention, some states seem to have had about seventy delegates, who, it was claimed, were needed as 'moral support' for their candidates. The women, like the men, were apparently getting ready for the Third Republic.

There were both regional and ethnic dimensions to the power struggle, as the 'northern' women seemed determined to seize the presidency of NCWS from the 'south'. Two of the aspiring presidents were active politicians in the Second Republic. The reigning president was quoted as saying, however: 'We don't have a North–South dichotomy, and rotational presidency is not democratic.' (The alternative of rotation had been rejected at the 1986 convention.) Babangida summoned a delegation from the NCWS to Dodan Barracks where she scolded them: 'I find it not too easy talking to you because as mature women, I expect you to advise me instead. But I would be frank with you all. I must begin by registering my disappointment at the unsuccessful convention held in Abuja. As women, mothers, and wives, you should know that unity and peace of the nation should rest in your hands.' The president of the NCWS claimed that 'there was no chaos, quarrelling, or physical combat. Do you think women of our calibre will throw [our weight] around?' Other women, however, reported that what took place was 'a bit of rowdiness'. The elections were postponed.

An extensive report of a summit with the new president of NCWS, Emily Aig-Imoukhuede, described the Abuja incident:

> Another frontal challenge to the established orthodoxy of the NCWS was last year's conference of the council in Abuja. The conference was to deliberate on amendments to the constitution and elect new national officers. One of the aspirants for the presidency was Laila Dongoyaro, whose radical credential is common knowledge. The government apparently was interested in the outcome of the election and had filled the hall with operatives of the State Security Service (SSS). When arguments got to an unladylike pitch, the SSS moved in, invited Adefarasin, Aig-Imoukhuede, who was in the race for the presidency, and others 'for a chat'. Immediately their leaders went to answer the call of the government's secret service, the delegates dispersed. The conference ended.[22]

Aig-Imoukhuede admitted being taken to the Abuja headquarters of the SSS but insisted that there was no need for SSS intervention and that she was only asked to identify herself.

The conference reconvened in Lagos in November 1988. Laila Dongoyaro did not attend, and Aig-Imoukhuede won the presidency. Both Mrs Aig-Imoukhuede and her predecessor were firmly grounded in the Christian mission tradition.

The reluctance of the NCWS leaders to give up their posts carries over to their appointments to public offices. The collaborative role of the organization *vis-à-vis* the state has resulted in the NCWS becoming a stepping-stone to government appointments. Most state and federal presidents of NCWS have at one time or another served as ministers of state or state commissioners. In a rejoinder to my criticism of the government's collaboration with the NCWS, as opposed to other national women's organizations,[23] a supporter of the NCWS had this to say:

> In the past, members of the NCWS have been encouraged and allowed to participate in politics and to join any political party of their choice. A case in point is that of Chief Mrs. J. Akinrinade who was a minister of state during the political days. She was a long-standing member of NCWS before joining politics. Today Chief Mrs. Akinrinade is the president of Oyo State branch of NCWS. The same applies to Dr. Simi Johnson. Dr.

Johnson is the president of the Lagos State branch of NCWS. We also know she too was a minister in the political days. We can also recall that these two women were not of the same political party, yet they were both members of NCWS.[24]

What we find is a situation where such a woman retains leadership of her state branch of the NCWS. For example, in June 1986, the Anambra state branch of NCWS honoured their president, Grace Obayi, who had been appointed State Commissioner for Education.[25] The women commended the state military governor on the appointment and hoped that more women would be called upon 'to serve'. The women also called on Obayi to look into the question of more appointments for women and the creation of employment opportunities. In her address, Obayi urged the women to be her watchdog. She retained the state presidency of the NCWS, yet women praised her for her selfless service and humanity. These women prove to be loyal daughters of the establishment.

This relationship with the establishment also applies to representatives of the NCWS and international women's organizations and their promotion of the policies and campaigns of their organizations, which basically serve western capitalist interests. In one interview, Victoria Nwigwe, a College of Education principal lecturer, national research co-ordinator, and president of the Imo state branch of the NCWS, reproduced western rhetoric about world peace on her return from an ICW conference[26] in London and condemned so-called terrorism in the words of American President Ronald Reagan and British Prime Minister Margaret Thatcher. She went on to say that the NCWS had plans to 'make inputs in the textbooks for use by schoolchildren to make sure that positive images towards peace are portrayed'. The NCWS planned to extend this campaign to the media.

On the relationship between her organization and rural women, Nwigwe said, 'Our annual conferences give every woman something to look forward to – for example, to the rural housewife, coming to Owerri is like going to London.' On the achievements of the NCWS in Imo state, she said: 'We are not engaged in women's liberation, whatever that means; we are out to mobilise and galvanise women to contribute meaningfully to society.' She also listed some of NCWS' achievements: about a hundred women employed in Aba in environmental sanitation, women cultivating yams on a large piece of land in Orlu LGA, women building a one-million-naira library in Aboh Mbaise, women building technical workshops for schools in over sixty communities in Imo state, and an NCWS representative at UNO who campaigned for and got the Expanded Programme on Immunization (EPI) and Oral Rehydration Therapy (ORT) executed through UNICEF.[27]

What Nwigwe does not say is that the NCWS did not finance any of these projects. Indeed, it does not have the budget to do so. What is happening is that in the Local Government Areas (LGAs) and communities of the eastern states, where women's organizations form part of the descent structures or lineage systems and are involved very effectively in self-help projects, the NCWS 'hijacks' success stories and glory, since it is assumed that the organizations are affiliated with the NCWS and some of the representatives of the rural organizations attend NCWS conferences and conventions.

When asked about the funding of the NCWS at the *Newswatch* summit in April 1989, the NCWS president, Aig-Imoukhuede, said:

> We go begging. Also we have a very small subvention from the federal government, which is not even enough to pay the bills for maintaining our secretariat. There was a time they were giving us about 8,000–10,000 *naira*, but this year, I think we may have about 30,000 *naira*. But what we do is that whatever project we have, we look for funding for the specific project. Even for workshops, we have to look for external funding from individuals, from corporations and bodies like yours.[28]

This chapter has looked at how the culture of the colonizers created a local elite, influencing individual women of specific ethnicities, and how these women were central to the reproduction of class through their leadership roles in girls' and women's associations which have their origins abroad in the colonial home country, Britain. With the nationalist movement towards independence, these elite women consolidated their power positions in alliance with political parties and the Nigerian state as leaders of regional and national contemporary women's organizations over and above already existing localized traditional women's organizations. This I believe resulted in tensions betweeen women's groups, raising the leadership questions of legitimacy, representation, accountability and corruption which I will examine in the next chapter.

Notes

1. *Guardian*, 21 May 1986.
2. *Guardian*, 4 March 1987.
3. In a tribute to the 'mother of Lagos', Nina Mba lists Abayomi's contributions to the history and development of Lagos as the founding of Queen's College, Lagos, in 1927; the founding of the New Era school in 1948; improvements in the conditions of Lagos markets; better health facilities for women and children in Lagos; setting up, in 1960, the Lagos branch of NCWS, the YWCA, and the Girl Guides Association in Lagos. *Guardian*, 4 March 1987.
4. *Guardian*, 28 May 1986.

5. *Observer* (London), 14 May 1989.

6. *Sunday Vanguard*, 26 April 1987. In Ogun's mother's time, such girls were completely schooled in England, and she named some of them: 'Lady Ajasa; the Robbins; my mother, who was Miss Pratt; Lady Abayomi, who was then Miss Ajasa, and my auntie Bola, her friend; then there was Joko Jibowu – Mrs Kuye; Aurora Kayode ... Then there was Mrs Obasa and Mrs Gibson; they were the people we admired in those days ... Mrs Obasa ... was unique and committed to helping all women. She was the first person to start a bus service. She also fought to get women employed in the government service, the railways, post and tele-graphs or in printing at a time when the colonial government only trained women as nurses and teachers.

'Lady Ajasa, the mother of Lady Abayomi, was one of the leading ladies, along with Mrs Henry Carr and Mrs Herbert Macaulay (Ogun's mother's eldest sister). Mrs Herbert Macaulay, like her husband, had been a musician. She died at a young age from a miscarriage, and her husband, the doyen of Nigerian politics at the time, was so affected that he wore black bow-tie for the rest of his life. Although he never remarried, "he had many well known children – from people of very good families too".'

7. Among the lieutenants who worked with Lady Abayomi in starting the Girl Guides company in Nigeria were Bisi Oluwole, wife of the Chief Scout; Mrs Sowunmi (formerly Miss Sowande); Mrs Olonode-Peters (formerly Miss Jibowu). Winifred MacEwen (formerly Winifred Ayo Onipede) became the first Nigerian Girl Guide to win the 'All-Round Cord'. She is described as a very staunch Catholic.

8. The women included Mrs Winifred MacEwen, Miss Grace Pepple (who later became Mrs Grace Guobadia), and Miss Juliet Odogwu, elder sister of Violet Odogwu (who became Mrs Nwajei).

9. Janet Mokelu. *Daily Star*, 11 June 1986. (I had the honour of chatting with Madam Mokelu in her house in Enugu in 1986 and working with her during the National Political Debate in the same year.)

10. This was recorded in *The Nation* (the official organ of the NCNC), vol. I, no. 8, April 1965.

11. They included Mrs Flora Azikiwe, wife of the governor-general; Chief J. M. Johnson, Federal Minister of Labour; the American Ambassador to Nigeria, Joseph Palmer II; and Allan Swin, director of the United States Information Service, Lagos.

12. Delegates who attended from eastern Nigeria included Mrs V. M. Amadi, Mrs M. W. Okezie, Mrs E. A. Obumselu, Mrs A. Duke, Mrs S. O. Onwuegbuna, Mrs Anazodo, Mrs C. Okolo, Mrs O. S. Long John, Mrs B. N. Chukueke, Mrs M. C. W. Njemanze, Mrs J. Halliday, Mrs M. Ekpo, Mrs J. M. Anyansi, Mrs C. R. N. Okagbue, Mrs Janet Peter Okoye, Mrs D. A. Ihezue, Mrs N. O. Ahamba, Mrs V. Onyiuke, Mrs Mary H. Umoh, and Mrs M. Udoji. They were the wives of important and powerful men in the establishment, as can be seen from street names in Enugu.

13. Because women never get mentioned in history books, I list these women who played a prominent role in politics in eastern Nigeria, irrespective of the fact that some would consider their role somewhat marginal. They are: Mrs Umana,

Mrs Banigo, Madam Mary Ironba, Mrs Mary Ededem, Mrs Ekpo Young for Calabar. Port Harcourt had Mrs Mary Nzimiro, Mrs A. Wogu, Mrs Long John, Mrs Comfort Okoye, Mrs Doris Amobi. Those at Aba included Mrs M. Ekpo, Mrs Ikwuemesi, Mrs J. Egbutchay. At Umuahia, there were Mrs Nwachukwu, Mrs Adamma Okpara, Mrs Phinah Onwudiwe, Mrs E. Iheukwumere. Enugu had Mrs Janet Mokelu, Madam Janet Peter Okoye, Mrs Christiana Okafor, Mrs M. Oraedu, Mrs E. Enweani, Mrs Matilda Okoye, Mrs Grace Okoye, Mrs Phoebe Okoye, Mrs Mabel Mbonye, Mrs Elizabeth Mgbemena, Mrs Malinda Onyekwe, Mrs Jemimah Nwadirim, Mrs Lucy Nwakobi, Mrs Marcellina Chiwetalu, Mrs Gbanite, Mrs Alice Afamefuna, Mrs Ugbut, Mrs Priscilla Onyia.

14. Ms Franka Afebua of the Second Republic, who was later claimed to be the first female senator, was nine years old when Mrs Kerry was already in the senate – one was nominated, the other was voted in. Afebua was elected. Also during Afebua's period, the House of Assembly became the House of Senate.

15. *Guardian Sunday*, 26 October 1986.

16. In 1949, the SNA system was abolished in Abeokuta and Ijebu Provinces.

17. *Daily Star*, 23 July 1986; *Guardian*, 18 July 1986.

18. *Daily Times*, 21 July 1986.

19. *Guardian*, 23 July 1986.

20. *Daily Star*, 23 July 1986.

21. *African Guardian*, 22 August 1988.

22. *Newswatch*, 2 October 1989.

23. Ifi Amadiume, 'Women and the Political Debate', *Guardian*, 19 May 1986.

24. Theresa Ogbuibe, 'Women and Political Future of Nigeria', *Daily Times*, 27 May 1986.

25. *Daily Star*, 11 June 1986.

26. The International Council of Women (ICW) has seventy-five national affiliates. It has five permanent representatives at UNO and a member in international agencies such as UNESCO, UNICEF and WHO.

27. 'Women at War', *IBC Journal*, August–September 1986.

28. *Newswatch*, 2 October 1989.

Sources

Cohen, Abner, 1969, *Custom and Politics in Urban Africa: A Study of Hausa Migrants in Yoruba Towns*. London: Routledge and Kegan Paul.

— 1981, *The Politics of Elite Culture: Explorations in the Dramaturgy of Power in a Modern African Society*. Berkeley: University of California Press.

Fanon, Frantz, 1982, *Black Skin, White Masks*. London: Paladin.

Mba, Nina, 1982, *Nigerian Women Mobilized: Women's Political Activities in Southern Nigeria, 1900–1965*. Berkeley: Institute of International Studies, University of California Press.

3. Speaking for women: class contestation in NCWS and other organizations

In the Introduction to this book, I used two Nigerian women, Chief Bankole and Mrs Establishment, to illustrate the contrasting concepts of daughters of the Goddess and daughters of imperialism. I am concerned with the question of legitimate authority and the structural position of these women in relation to grassroots women's organizations and local and state systems. On the basis of this, I raised questions of authority and accountability in Mrs Establishment's right to manage local women's finances through her community bank which would solicit external funding in the name of women's development. In contrast, as a trader and a traditionally titled woman, Chief Bankole, I felt, was in a structural position of legitimate authority and accountability *vis-à-vis* her local women's groups. My key interest, therefore, is in organically legitimate, organized structures of local women; the basis on which women can reap the fruits of their labour and glory in their own success. It is for this reason that I also raised doubts about Nwigwe's claims of local successes by NCWS in Imo state in the previous chapter.

Certainly, it is laudable that NCWS gives rural women an opportunity to witness and enjoy city life during its annual conferences. However, when Nwigwe talks about NCWS employing a hundred women in Aba in environmental sanitation, women cultivating yams on a large piece of land in Orlu LGA, women building a one million-naira-library in Aboh Mbaise, women building technical workshops for schools in over sixty communities in Imo state, you begin to wonder what the state policy is for women and rural development and what its implementation mechanisms are.

This chapter examines the competition between national women's organizations over who is best qualified to organize, represent and speak for women. I examine more contemporary factors in the development of other non-formal and formal women's organizations such as Women in Nigeria (WIN) and Nigeria Labour Congress Working Women's Wing (NLC/WWW) whose civil values are not based on Christian ethics, unlike earlier organizations and associations. First, I look at developments in the official organization for the implementation of the government's women and development policies, and how NCWS related to this organization.

The National Committee on Women and Development

A few events suggest that NCWS will not tolerate competition or rivalry in its 'monopoly' in representing all Nigerian women to the government. NCWS, for example, felt threatened by the government-appointed National Committee on Women and Development, which was placed under the Federal Ministry of Social Development, Youth, and Sports in 1984. The committee was set up in anticipated response to a resolution of the 1985 UN End of the Decade for Women Conference in Nairobi, which demanded the founding of a ministry of women's affairs. Consequently, the organization became effective in the states between 1985 and 1986. Inaugurated in Anambra state in June 1985, the committee, which included a chairperson, a vice-chairperson, a secretary and an assistant secretary, functioned as a fifteen-member body. All its members came from the civil service.

The Committee on Women and Development differs from other women's organizations in that it is a governmental body and not a voluntary organization. At the launching of the Anambra state committee in June 1985, its aims and objectives were:

- to examine concrete actions and measures to be taken to improve the status of women in the state, with special attention given to rural women
- to examine and evaluate the contributions made by women in various sectors of development (especially the priority needs of the states)
- to study areas where women's articulation should be initiated or strengthened
- to promote the full utilization of women, bringing about their acceptance in every state of development
- to improve the civic, political, social and economic participation of women in the development of the state
- to support the work of non-governmental organizations
- to play a co-ordinating role between government and state women's organizations

The committee's role was further elaborated by the Anambra state chairperson, Mrs M. N. David-Osuagwu, at a seminar on Women and Development – Strategies held at Enugu in 1986: 'We are not set up to be a rival group or to interfere with the role of the NCWS ... Having said that, however, it might be necessary to add that we are to interact with all women groups, while the NCWS caters to those groups which are affiliated with it.'[1]

Mrs David-Osuagwu went on to request of the Anambra state NCWS president, who attended the seminar, a list of all women's organizations in the Local Government Areas and a list of projects handled by these organizations. NCWS in Anambra state saw itself in competition with the committee, which prompted NCWS' national president, Mrs Adefarasin, to visit Enugu. There she gave an exclusive interview to the state newspaper, the *Daily Star*, in which she emphasized the status of the NCWS as an umbrella under which all women stood in order to speak with one voice.[2] She stressed unity and condemned those who portrayed Nigerian women as 'disunited'. She also called for an increase in the government's annual grant to the council to about 50,000 naira.

Suspecting that there was some confusion about the roles of the two organizations *vis-à-vis* women, especially in Anambra state, Mrs Adefarasin and Victoria Okobi, social welfare officer for women's affairs in the Ministry of Social Development, asked the Anambra state Commissioner for Information, Youths, Sports, and Culture to enlighten Anambra state on the functions of the Committee on Women and Development, which they saw as intended to advise the government on issues affecting women. To those in the NCWS, this meant that the committee would work with the NCWS, which was 'the government's recognized non-governmental voice for Nigerian women'. The commissioner tactfully promised maximum co-operation.

It is obvious that there are fundamental differences between NCWS and the Committee on Women and Development, both in their aims and objectives and in the political orientation of the women leading the organizations. This can be seen from some of the statements made during public occasions in Anambra state. On the role of women in rural development, Mrs Obayi, president of NCWS Anambra state and State Commissioner for Education, once said:

Igbo women are noted for forming cultural associations of one type or another as a means of fostering leadership potential and qualities in women, with special regard to development of their towns ... Attention should be drawn to the important role women play in the socialisation of children in the home. The hue and cry in our nation today on indiscipline and juvenile delinquency will be reduced to the barest minimum if women play their primary role as mothers and wives effectively.[3]

Statements by the Committee on Women and Development focused more on the needs of rural women. In July 1986, the committee called on the government to appoint women to leadership positions in the state and federal government and as chairpersons of LGAs.[4] The committee also demanded:

- that government train women for leadership roles, including project development and management roles
- equal benefits with men for equal work
- the creation and execution of a policy on family planning education for both men and women
- recognition of the 'natural' intelligence of rural women and an opportunity for them to contribute to the socio-economic development of the state
- provision of agricultural extension services and access to credit for rural women
- adult education for women, as well as education on food preservation, nutrition and health
- encouragement for women to embark on farming co-operatives, since over 60 per cent of Nigeria's farmers are women

This suggests that the Committee on Women and Development was highlighting the conditions of rural women as a result of direct contact and consultation. NCWS, on the other hand, was canvassing for money and power.

Women in Nigeria (WIN)

One reason behind the formation of Women in Nigeria (WIN) was the absence of any women's group or organization to study 'scientifically' the conditions and roles of women in society. Those who founded WIN were first involved in a study group which considered the life of women in Nigeria. This grew into the wider, inter-departmental Women's Social Sciences Group at the Ahmadu Bello University (ABU) in Zaria. At a small seminar organized on the ABU campus, it was agreed that a national organization should be formed. According to Ayesha Imam, first national secretary of WIN, they began to call their group Women in Nigeria.

WIN grew out of university campus politics to an independent national organization. In *The Win Document* it is stated that the organization originated from the interest and enthusiasm evoked by the first annual Women in Nigeria conference at ABU in 1982. Men and women who attended the conference had by 1983 established an organization committed to working for an improvement in the condition of Nigerian women.

The founding group believed that the liberation of women could not be achieved outside the context of the liberation of the oppressed and poor majority of the people of Nigeria, but they felt that there were aspects of women's oppression that they could work to alleviate. They felt it imperative that women organize and fight for full social and economic equality in the family, in the work-place, and in society in general, as part of the continuing struggle to create and develop a just society for all. First, they argued, they must know clearly how women's and men's lives are structured by the socio-economic and political conditions in which they live. Thus, research, policy-making, dissemination of information and action were all part of the organization's objectives.

The organization states that: (a) the majority of women, like the majority of men, suffer from the exploitative and oppressive character of the Nigerian society; (b) women suffer additional forms of exploitation and oppression; (c) women, therefore, suffer double oppression and exploitation – as members of subordinate classes and as women.

The organization's aims and objectives, as stated in its constitution, are:

- to promote the study of conditions of women in Nigeria, with the aim of combating discriminatory and sexist practices in the family, in the work-place, and in the wider society
- to defend the rights of women under the Nigerian Constitution and the United Nations Human Rights Convention
- to fight for non-sexist alternatives in government and institutional policies
- to fight against the harassment and sexual abuse of females in the family and elsewhere
- to promote an equitable distribution of domestic work in the family
- to provide a forum for women to express themselves
- to ensure for women equal access to equal education
- to combat sexist stereotypes in literature, the media and educational materials
- to provide the means of educating women on relevant issues
- to form links and work with other organizations and groups fighting sex and class oppression
- to fight for social justice

In terms of rhetoric, WIN is radically different from other contemporary national women's organizations in Nigeria, in that it is officially committed to change and it is ideologically orientated, even though the Marxist–Leninist or socialist ideology of some of its members is not explicitly stated. Some members claim that this omission is for strategic reasons, while others deny any association with socialism. This loophole,

I shall argue, poses a problem for WIN, as it means that the organization is really not self-defined.

WIN is urban-based. It publishes a quarterly newsletter and holds annual conferences to highlight different aspects of women's situations: Women in Nigeria (1982), Women and Education (1983), Women and the Family (1984), Women in Rural Areas (1985), Women's Awareness and Mobilization (1986). Proceedings from these conferences are published, providing a sizeable literature for women's workshops, study groups and researchers. Although membership is open to all, WIN members tend to be from the elite class. Unlike NCWS, however, WIN is essentially anti-establishment.

There are sixteen state branches of WIN in Nigeria, each headed by a co-ordinator. The state branches are relatively autonomous and concerned with local conditions. Activities include lectures, seminars, symposia, radio and television discussions, working with trade unions or other women's organizations, adult literacy, local cases of discrimination against women, public health lectures and so on. WIN is also reported to have fought individual women's cases such as rape cases and women's rights to benefits. In 1983, it blocked government efforts to close the road that connects the women's hostel and the mosque at Ahmadu Bello University on Fridays. There have been a few instances when WIN has fought parents and husbands who wished to withdraw girls from school.

WIN has often been critical of the government's anti-women policies such as the scapegoating of prostitutes under the Shagari government, when the police swooped on prostitutes or single women living on their own. It has also decried the knocking down of women's kiosks, the raising of store fees for traders and market women, the Babangida regime's reception of the British prime minister in spite of opposition to her visit to Nigeria because of her stand on sanctions against South Africa. WIN builds its programmes around the realities of women's situations. Its current research programme focuses on violence against women and children, child labour, female circumcision, domestic violence and vesico vaginal fistulae (VVF). In this area, the case of the murder of the child bride Hauwa (see Chapter 6) has become a mobilizing force. The theme for WIN's 1987 annual conference was violence against women and children.

In response to criticism of its elitism, WIN began in 1985 to shift its focus from academic and urban concerns to project work at the grassroots level. Since then it has undertaken development work such as adult education, setting up income-generating projects for women, housing and shelter groups. Women's awareness and mobilization formed the theme for its 1986 annual conference.

At a conference in London in March 1988, Ayesha Imam, one of the founding members and national co-ordinating secretary for the first four years, gave a critical assessment of WIN. One of the problems she saw was the fact that most of its members were in full-time employment, which limited the time they could spend working towards WIN's objectives. Another concerned the organization's financing, which was dependent on membership dues (unlike NCWS, WIN is not state-funded). WIN's radicalism created a problem with registration at the national level and in some states where it encountered threats and opposition. Another issue concerned male membership, which some WIN members opposed. When the organization was founded, men constituted a third of the membership, but their participation has gradually declined. A more serious issue currently dividing the organization is the question of affiliation to the NCWS, which some members favour. The most problematic issue, however, is the non-involvement of working-class, peasant and grassroots women because of WIN's university origins and its concern with research and conferences.

In the face of all these problems, WIN has found itself in a dilemma in terms of defining the scope of its ambitions. Should WIN act as a voice for women, or should it enable women to organize and speak for themselves? I believe – and suggested to WIN during my brief period of membership and work with the organization – that this dilemma stems from the fact that WIN's membership is undefined.[5] Side-stepping an explicit self-defining ideology has resulted in irreconcilable differences and contradictions in views, orientations and ambitions. Many WIN members I met would have been more comfortable with the aims of NCWS than with the more radical objectives of WIN, which were constantly called into question by populist members. These young women, however, found it easier to achieve a position in the hierarchy or gain public recognition through WIN than through NCWS, which is dominated by older women who are well-connected daughters of the establishment. Thus, the lack of ideological definition has left room for elite opportunism within WIN.

Confrontation at Nairobi, 1985

Newswatch recalled the workshop that gave birth to WIN at Ahmadu Bello University in May 1982 as 'a stormy one': 'Women from all over the country came to speak one by one about their common fate and fears. They could no longer trust exclusively the NCWS, which was dominated by allegedly conformist women, always ready to follow their husbands to dinners. They decided to do something about it, so WIN was born.'[6] This is a simplistic and provocative assessment which derives from media sensationalism. What the facts show is that there are generational, educational and ideological differences between members of both organizations. They came to the fore in Nairobi in 1985 at the UN's End of the Decade for Women Conference.

NCWS, which sees itself as the umbrella organization for all Nigerian women, went to Nairobi as a governmental body, led by the Minister of Information, a senior air force officer. This contradiction gave food for thought to Nigerian cartoonists, who added a headtie to his uniform. When asked in 1986 why a man led NCWS to Nairobi, Mrs Victoria Nwigwe, Imo state president of NCWS, responded: 'Such international conferences are usually led by a top woman in government or the wife or daughter of the country's Head of State. The Kenyan delegation, for example, was led by the daughter of late Jomo Kenyatta ... It was the time of Buhari, [but] his wife had not been seen around. I don't know why the Headquarters chose the then Minister of Information.'[7] The WIN co-ordinator from Imo state described the incident as 'a national embarrassment, if not disgrace'. She wondered if the minister felt comfortable in the midst of so many women and whether he remained to the end of the conference.

NCWS delegates at Nairobi objected to the presence of WIN members at the conference, even though WIN is independent. NCWS' antagonism exposed WIN members to harassment by Nigerian security agents and caused them a great deal of hardship, suggesting that NCWS tries to maintain its monopoly at any cost.

WIN's ten delegates to Nairobi included Ayesha Imam, lecturer in sociology at Ahmadu Bello University; Arlene Enebulele, research fellow at the Centre for Social and Environmental Research at the University of Benin; Ifeyinwa Iweirebor; Hannatu Omole; and New Ngur-Ade. Unlike NCWS, which went to Nairobi to represent the Nigerian government, WIN went to Nairobi to report to the UN and the world the Nigerian government's anti-female policies. WIN claims to have carried out intensive research into all aspects of the condition of women in Nigeria. Its findings were compiled into a 195-page document which included policy recommendations to the year 2000. The recommendations included:

- acknowledgement and remuneration of women's work
- abolition of all flat-rate taxes
- removal of obstacles to women's access to land use and ownership
- improvement of health care
- agricultural and technical training for rural women
- easy access to and qualification for credit
- autonomous organization of women in all sectors to fight for their rights
- input from women in the formulation of policies relating to women

- involvement and employment of women in all aspects of national development plans and programmes
- compulsory and free education for women
- discontinuation of rigid gender divisions in roles and jobs
- restructuring of curricula and reorientation of teachers to eliminate gender bias
- adult education programmes to enable rural women to acquire the skills necessary for them to earn higher incomes
- Minimum age for marriage
- Abolition of bride-price/dowry.

Since the constitution overrides all other laws in Nigeria, WIN quoted the sections which guarantee sexual equality. According to Section 39 (II) of the 1979 Constitution, there should be no discrimination or favour on the basis of ethnic origin, sex, political or religious opinion. The *WIN Document*, however, points to a few discriminatory laws. The law against loitering, for example, is used against women but not against the male clients and pimps who perpetuate female prostitution. (The twenty-six recommendations made by women workers during the 1986 political debate are very similar to WIN's recommendations.)[8]

Differences between WIN and NCWS

WIN has often been compared with the British women's movement in its emphasis on local issues and community problems. NCWS, on the other hand, has been compared to the American organization Rights of Women (ROW), which operates within the system, seeking legislative improvement. It denies that it is a liberation movement. At Nairobi, the confrontation between these women's movements culminated in a conflict which resulted in two platforms. One was a government platform, supported by the pro-establishment women's groups led by the daughters and wives of the establishment or by a government official. The other platform was that of the non-governmental women's groups, which some women found more exciting and 'sisterly'. It produced the conference resolutions and was supported by WIN, by radical feminist groups, and by women from the liberation struggle.

One assessor wrote:

> The difference of approach is firmly rooted in class. Liberalism, loose affiliation under a maternal wing, philanthropic projects, all characteristic of NCWS, are not threatening to the ruling-class men and are repaid by male approval and the inclusion of Mrs Adefarasin in the Political Bureau ... WIN's radicalism, uncompromising objectives, fearlessness in the face

of the dreaded 'feminist' tag, identification with rural and illiterate women, and a socialist perspective mean that it comes in for the same sort of public opprobrium as an organization like ASUU, with its taint of Marxism.[9]

These differences in orientation, commitment and goals are reflected in the responses of the two organizations to economic, social and political problems facing women. In the case of drug-trafficking, for example, the crime carried a death sentence under the Buhari regime. NCWS tended to condemn female heroin carriers in moral terms, as they did men. A member of a state branch of NCWS, who was also the wife of the state's military governor, condemned the 'indulgence of women in smuggling and drug-trafficking' as 'very disgraceful and capable of undermining the dignity of womanhood'.[10] The National Commission on Women's Development endorsed the proposed public execution of women found guilty of drug-trafficking, while WIN called for eradication of the causes of women's involvement in crime, pointing out that women bear the burden of economic responsibility for the family and that conditions of poverty and insecurity breed crime.

After the May 1986 riots and police massacre of students at Ahmadu Bello University, WIN demonstrated support and solidarity in practical terms with the rape victims. Together with the National Association of University Women (NAUW), it presented a memorandum to the Abisoye Commission of Enquiry:

> NAUW and WIN wish to express our sympathy to the parents of those who have lost their lives and the victims that were brutalised by the police as a result of the events of Thursday 22nd and Friday 23rd May 1986.
>
> It is very disheartening to see yet again peaceful students' demonstrations met with live ammunition and brutality. When the police were called to the campus, the students were peaceful, and we had seen no evidence of uncontrollable violence at all.
>
> Although many of our members were in and around the vicinity of the Senate Block all day Thursday, they went about their business without molestation by the students. Therefore we must deplore the rigid manner with which the university authorities responded to this peaceful demonstration.
>
> WIN and NAUW strongly condemn the brutality used by the police against unarmed and defenceless youth. NAUW and WIN are making this joint submission in view of the fact that the thrust of those assaults appears to have been directed at our female colleagues and younger sisters, many of whom are members of WIN or NAUW.
>
> NAUW and WIN are here going to cite some examples of the type of brutality that females were subjected to. All the cases mentioned were reported to us either by the victim or by an eye-witness.

A. A girl was stripped naked and taken away by six policemen. She returned later crying and bruised (eye-witness account).

B. A girl was raped by a policeman (eye-witness account).

C. Several girls complained of having their breasts squeezed or of being forced to strip and show their private parts or of being kicked in the private parts (victims' accounts and eye-witness accounts).

D. Several girls were forced to strip naked and lie on the floor. While the policemen were in the process of undressing, an elder policeman came by and persuaded them to leave the girls alone (victim's account).

E. Girls attempting to leave the hostels were chased, beaten, kicked, and dragged on the ground by police. This happened in the hostels, outside the hostels, and even outside the university gates when waiting for taxis in order to leave. It is particularly shocking that even pregnant women were not spared (victims' accounts and eye-witness accounts).

F. The policemen invaded the boys' quarters of members of staff and beat up students there also, including one girl whose external ear was damaged; she was hit on the back with the butt of a gun, and her breasts were squeezed (victims' accounts and eye-witness accounts).

G. Several girls were dragged out of the hostels (including out of their baths) in various states of undress and taken to police cells. When released from the cells, they still had no adequate clothing and appeared to have problems walking (eye-witness accounts).

H. One girl (who resides with a relation who is an ABU staff) has been unable to talk since the incident but screams when she is moved, which suggests that she has been brutalised either physically or psychologically.

I. Many people were beaten up, including both female staff and students and women not connected with ABU at all.

- a female staff member was assaulted in her car and had her blouse torn
- several women were beaten in the market and on the highway (i.e., *outside* ABU campus)
- police entered the premises of a business opposite the North Gate and beat up the business manager on the grounds that she looked like a student (victim's and eye-witness accounts).

There are also numerous unconfirmed reports of people still being missing and of other rapes, sexual assaults, and batteries.

In view of all these reports, many of which have been substantiated to us, WIN and NAUW make the following recommendations:

1. The Commission of Enquiry should extend its sitting for hearing evidence in order to investigate all sides. Most of the students (who have been the main victims of police assault) are not here to give evidence of what they experienced. In order to ensure that justice is done and

seen to be done, students must be enabled to come and give evidence. Provision should be made for their transportation, feeding, and accommodation. On our part, WIN and NAUW are willing to provide accommodation for female students coming to testify.

2. Bearing in mind the sensitive nature of any issues relating to sex and noting that worldwide a high proportion of women do not report rapes or sexual assaults for fear of the social stigma frequently attached to innocent victims, NAUW and WIN urgently recommend that the Commission make special arrangements to deal with testimonies related to these issues:

   a) The identity of women involved should be kept secret, and they should give their testimony *in camera*.

   b) Evidence could be given directly to Mrs Mohammed, who would represent the Commission, or a sub-commission composed of women should hear testimony, or a joint NAUW/WIN committee could take and investigate evidence.

3. NAUW and WIN call for stiff penalties for anyone guilty of killing, rape, sexual assault, or battery, in order to uphold respect for womanhood and as a check against any future occurrence.

WIN and NAUW find it extremely ironic to note that the suspension and expulsion of students which initiated this crisis was allegedly in order to defend the privacy of female students, even though they had not complained. As a result of the police coming to the campus, female students experienced not simply violation of privacy but of life, body, and property.

On the alleged miscarriage of justice at ABU, a state branch of WIN wondered about the non-suspension of ABU's vice-chancellor, noting that within twenty-four hours, the government had charged labour leaders with sedition and subversion. The statement reads: 'The organization is further distressed when we consider the irony that the National Labour Council leaders who were only protesting the ABU killings are now behind bars, while Ango Abdullahi and the Kaduna Police Commissioner, known architects of the killings, are safely treading the streets of our country.' After calling for the release of detained labour leaders and students, the statement continues: 'Rather than repress and intimidate, government should restructure the present socio-economic arrangement which heightens unemployment, illiteracy, armed robbery, inflation, and injustice.'[11]

With such fundamental differences, it is not surprising that one leader of NCWS, when asked if WIN was an affiliate member of the council, responded:

We don't know what WIN is all about, and that organization, from the little we know, cannot be an affiliate of our council. The composition does not make it eligible – for example, they are made up of men and women. It makes the organization suspicious and more of a political party under a cover. There is no parallel between WIN and NCWS. When WIN is properly constituted and structured and with clearly defined and acceptable objectives, we may consider any application for affiliation.[12]

At the *Newswatch* summit in 1989, the new national president of NCWS was still using male membership in WIN as an excuse for not admitting WIN into the council.

Given the ideological differences in the two organizations, WIN is not likely to seek affiliation with NCWS as long as its core founding members remain in control. Ayesha Imam said in 1986:

In general terms, WIN's position is that we don't want to affiliate with any women's organization, but we are happy to welcome any organization that has similar objectives and functions. We keep our doors open to any organization that can work with us. However, if there is any point for us and NCWS to have a common interest on any national issue, we will co-operate. In terms of the relationship between WIN and the NCWS, it can be said to be normal. The NCWS is always romancing the government of the day, maybe because they get recognition and support from the government, while WIN will only support any government action or policy that favours the generality of poor Nigerian women, especially those at the grass-root level. WIN is not looking for support from any government. The NCWS usually makes donations to various disabled houses, while WIN does not believe in that type of donation.[13]

Abdul Azeez concurs:

Women In Nigeria [WIN] is an association of women and men who are working for the improvement of life of Nigerian women. We are not an umbrella organization, and I am sure that our modes of mobilization of women are quite different from those of NCWS. This is because WIN concentrates its researches on the history of women's activities all over the country and uses it to make policy recommendations to the government. But the NCWS' activities, as I understand them, do not take to such projects at all. WIN, for instance, does not believe in the charity activities which NWCS undertakes.

Asked if she is a socialist, Imam answered, 'I am a Marxist'. This unequivocal ideological position is not stated by the organization itself, however.[14] The socialist background and ideological commitment of some of WIN's founding members is confirmed by Altine Mohammed, lecturer in architecture at Ahmadu Bello University and WIN's national secretary-general for the first four years (and therefore of the Imam leadership group). When asked by *New Horizon* what inclined her to a socialist ideology, she said:

> When I was in Zaria, I joined a progressive group at the ABU called MOJA [Movement of Justice for Africa], and it had impact on me. Later, when I went to Bayero University in Kano, I joined another socialist group called Organisation for the Salvation of Mother Africa [OSMA]. Here I became more conscious of the role of women in the struggle against oppression and discrimination in the developing countries of the world, especially Africa.

Another WIN member of the Imam group is Ladi Abdul Azeez, co-ordinator of WIN for Kwara state. Abdul Azeez is not a founding member of WIN. She joined WIN in Kwara state in 1983. When asked her opinion of *New Horizon*, she replied, 'Your magazine … is a kind of Marxist journal. As you know, Marxism to an ordinary Nigerian, especially the poor man in the street, has no meaning. Therefore, I will advise that your magazine should focus more attention on daily realities of the ordinary man.' Of the same magazine, Altine Mohammed said: 'Your magazine is the only mouth-piece for the Nigerian Marxists and the less privileged group in the society. The existence of your paper is very important to our struggle because until very recently, when the *Analyst* appeared, it had been the only magazine that gave the other side of our society.' Imam, for her part, is quoted as saying: 'I think the *New Horizon* magazine has been doing a good job in raising the consciousness of progressive Nigerians.'

When questioned about the type of political system that would bring Nigerian women to the 'promised land', Abdul Azeez does not commit herself:

> Any political system that can guarantee our human right, free and compulsory education, shelter and free health will be an ideal one. That government can exist under any name. You may call it socialist or welfarism – I am not really interested in the name. I am only interested in the substance of the government. After all, we have seen many countries in the Third World that claim to be socialist, and their women still suffer. And we have seen a country like Tunisia in Africa which does not call itself socialist but provides all the basic necessities of life for their women.

The secretary of WIN for Bendel state, Grace Osakwe, was asked if WIN agreed with the call for 'oppressed women to fight side by side with oppressed men for a socialist revolution'. Like Abdul Azeez, she was non-committal, although she agreed that 'socialism is the nearest ideology to the struggles and aspirations of the Nigerian oppressed women'. She went on to say: 'We shall therefore endorse and fight for any ideology that preaches equality of men, seeks to eliminate exploitation of man by man and which seeks to create a society that does not discriminate on sexist grounds.' (Grace Osakwe, incidentally, belongs to the post-Imam leadership group.)

What WIN has succeeded in doing is bringing into focus women and women's activities which have hitherto gone unmentioned in Nigerian political history at the national level. It has also provided an alternative model for political activities for younger women. In Kwara state, for example, as in all the other states, WIN has drawn its membership primarily from students and working women, which means it is a literate membership. Like other WIN chapters, it faces the problem of how to reach peasant and grassroots women. According to Abdul Azeez:

> In terms of membership, literate women are the dominant members now. But we realise that illiterate women should constitute the large membership of our organisation, and we are doing all we can to educate and bring them into our fold. Our major problems in these areas are the language barrier and organisation. Though WIN is not interested in making money, lack of it makes our activities slow here and there. We have therefore learnt to use our human resources to overcome part of these problems.

Bene Madunagu, a founding member of WIN and first co-ordinator of WIN's Cross River state chapter, has expressed WIN's aims and objectives in clear, uncompromising Marxist–Leninist terms based on formulations resulting from the material social history of patriarchy, political economy and capitalism in the West and the developments in the former Soviet Union. Some of her positions are open to question, as she subordinates gender to class and analyses the material conditions of African situations with a different political economy from the former USSR.

I agree that there is a need for a platform for women's expression, although the vanguard for liberation is contentious. According to Madunagu: 'By striving to provide a platform for women's expression, we should be able to reduce the specific expressions of exploitation of women. Thus it is hoped through all these activities and actions there will emerge a vanguard for the struggle of the oppressed peoples of our society and the world.'

No doubt WIN saw itself as a vanguard for liberation, even though by self-admission WIN's membership was literate and elitist. In spite of all its enthusiasm and determination, the organization had difficulty attracting grassroots women. It did not have the mobilizing capacity of NCWS. Is the Nigeria Labour Congress, Working Women's Wing (NLC/WWW), with an ideological orientation similar to that of WIN, more able to involve a broad section of working and labouring women?

Nigeria Labour Congress, Working Women's Wing (NLC/WWW)

Women workers in Nigeria demanded the creation of an NLC women's wing because of various discrimination against women: lack of equal opportunities within the NLC, payment of maternity leave entitlement only to some women, and the halving of vacation leave allowances by some employers. In spite of these demands, the creation of the women's wing resulted from a directive by the third ordinary congress of the Organization of African Trade Union Unity (OATUU) in Somalia in 1980. At that congress, the following resolution was passed:

> Aware of the immense contributions women in general and African working women in particular could make in the development of their countries; Conscious of the seriousness of the conditions of working women in Africa; Considering Resolutions Nos. 9 and GC/79/14/19 adopted by the Third and Fourth General Council meetings of the Organization of African Trade Union Unity in fulfilment of the Charter on the Economic, Social, Political, and Trade Union Rights adopted by the First Conference of the African Women held under its auspices in Accra in October 1976,
>
> 1. REITERATES its appeal to all national trade union centres to:
> a. Seriously study the best ways and means of encouraging the effective implementation of the Charter within the framework of socio-economic realities and to keep the OATUU Secretariat informed of the steps taken on the implementation of the Charter;
> b. Encourage women Trade Union activists to leadership positions within the Trade Union structure;
> c. Establish women's sections within their national Trade Union centres for those who have not yet done so.
>
> 2. FURTHER APPEALS to indicate their willingness to the OATUU Secretariat to host OATUU activities in the field of working women to make it carry out its programme according to plan.
> 3. INVITES the OATUU Secretariat to organize as a follow-up to the First Conference, on the Second Conference on African working women and development as a matter of priority.
> 4. FURTHER INVITES the OATUU Secretariat to comply with Resolution No. GC/79/14/19 of the Fourth General Council meeting and to establish a section responsible for the question of African women workers as soon as the necessary funds are available for that purpose.[15]

The NLC decided in 1983 to permit the formation of women's wings. Even then, permission was slow in coming and limited to a few states because of 'the differing levels of political and trade union consciousness'.

The role of the NLC has been in providing women with venues and inviting them to participate in activities such as ILO/NLC joint seminars. The NLC women's wing remains handicapped by financial and organizational problems – not to mention continuing chauvinism on the part of the NLC, which insists on controlling, supervising and directing its activities and relations with other women's organizations. Women's wing activities and programmes are subject to ratification by NLC national headquarters, and no woman holds a position in the hierarchy of the NLC. The women's wing is not even co-opted into the central working committee of the congress.

As of May 1986, the NLC women's wing had branches in five states of the nineteen states that existed in the federation at that time (Anambra, Lagos, Oyo, Imo and Bendel states). Women workers demanded more branches to provide a national outlook for the organization. When they met at a five-day seminar in July 1986, their demands were detailed and specific.[16] They included sound education for women and the provision of social security. The women called on government to promote equal access for women for all types of education and training for employment, especially vocational training for rural workers. They demanded that people leaving school be advised about areas of public employment in accordance with state and federal 'manpower' requirements.

Other demands made by the women included the creation and expansion of child health-care centres, with locations and timetables convenient for both the home and work-place. The NLC, the women felt, should work with the government to provide maternity leave coverage that would meet existing regulations. They argued too that the financing of special protection for working mothers should not involve costs directly related to their employment. They demanded equality of employment opportunities and that treatment of women be based on the fundamental principle that all human beings are equal, as recommended by the World Employment Conference of 1976. Government should take the measures necessary to ratify the equal remuneration provisions of Convention No. 100 of 1951, the Employment and Occupation Convention No. 111 of 1958, and other relevant conventions of the International Labour Organization (ILO) concerned with sex discrimination. They demanded that the NLC's national secretariat have a women's wing to represent and foster the interests of women within the hierarchy of the NLC. In conclusion, the women demanded the building of a women's wing into the infrastructure of the NLC.

Collectively, women might understand a women's wing as an integral part of the NLC but, as with all other women's organizations, individual members or state branches might understand its role differently, depending on their level of political awareness and commitment. Amoke Palmer, for example, assistant secretary of the Lagos state women's wing of the NLC, was quoted as saying, 'The movement is basically aimed at complementing the efforts of the men.'[17] Her branch chairperson, Rebecca Oliseh, was of a different opinion: 'We believe strongly that "what a man can do, a woman can also do", but our male counterparts are not usually happy about the challenge that women pose. Men would rather see women in the background of all activities concerning workers, and women are against being relegated to the background. Men's chauvinism is one of our main problems.'[18]

Male chauvinism, sexism and contradictions in the labour movement

Apete Azuike, chair of the NLC women's wing for Imo state, confirmed in interview[19] that women's wing activities and programmes were subject to ratification by NLC's national headquarters. She believed in 'a system where both men and women will participate in the decision-making process' and that 'women must rise and fight for their rights because it will not fall on their laps'. On relations with NWCS and WIN, she said, 'We have no relationship with the the NCWS. We see the NCWS as nothing more than a conglomeration of social clubs and not a fighting organisation of Nigerian women. As for WIN, we participate in some of their activities. The Nigerian Labour Congress will decide the pattern and nature of our future interaction with them.' In Imo state, she saw the basic problem as lack of financing and the members' low level of education.

The Lagos state branch saw its problem too as lack of financing, but another problem involved the low numbers of women in the organization. Several industrial unions simply did not permit their members to participate in the women's wing. This was the case with other employers as well. Amoke Palmer also spoke about the relationship of women's wings and WIN: 'The objectives of the NLC Women's Wing and that of WIN are the same. Any time any of these organisations has some activities like symposia or seminars, the other is invited. There is not much difference between their aims and objectives.' She was optimistic that the NLC Working Women's Wing would progress and become 'a virile [sic] organisation in the near future'.

There is, however, a difference in constituency between WIN and the NLC women's wings, for NLC women are mobilizing and fighting for women workers specifically; WIN fights on behalf of women in general. But even in their concern with women workers, the women's wings experience problems of elitism and tokenism, as grassroots women remain uninvolved. One Lagos state member, Patricia Bissong, said:

> Organisation of women at the grassroots is our problem. It is when we organise women from the grassroots like the men that our impact will be well felt. But since women are hand-picked to fill the various positions, this is problematic. Reports have it that in the industrial unions, women are hand-picked to be in the Women's Wing ... I remember last year when there was a women's seminar in the USSR, Nigeria had to send men instead of women. When they got there, the Soviet women asked them, 'Why are men representing women? Don't you have women in Nigeria?' This was the straw that broke the camel's back, and the men started to organise us. One could see that the men were doing this half-heartedly. They felt, if they carry the women along, one day the women will see above them – hence their lackadaisical attitude. Now there is no going back, and since we have already been inaugurated, our liberation struggle is a task that must be done. Whether they like it or not, the NLC Women's Wing has come to stay.

In March 1987, in a presentation at a symposium in Enugu to mark International Women's Day, Ethel Ngozi Nebo-Eze, state secretary of the Nigeria Union of Teachers (NUT), Anambra state wing, and its first and only (at that time) female secretary, gave an enlightening account of women's participation in trade unions. She described trade unionism as having been associated with 'violence, aggressiveness, insubordination, and rascality'. This background and public opinion, she felt, meant that 'trade union work was exclusively meant for men, as women could not involve themselves in everyday trouble'. However, with 'modern scientific trade unionism, based on mutual collective bargaining as opposed to table banging and fist clenching', Nebo-Eze believed that the situation has changed, and women can now participate respectably in trade union activities.

Nebo-Eze lists barriers affecting women's participation in union work as:

- domestic work combined with office/school work (union work will be an addition which could be avoided)
- frequent and irregular meetings and frequent travelling
- meetings lasting into the night
- husbands discouraging wives from active participation
- ignorance among women and lack of interest
- women discouraging other women who might be interested
- lack of encouragement by men, who have an advantage on all elective posts

- the attitude of some men towards their wives, as reflected in their regard and treatment of other women; most men feel that all women are the same
- lack of adequate training facilities and exposure
- child-bearing and frequent maternity leaves
- the fact that some women are mundane and materialistic, tending to pay more attention to externalities than to union work

She proposes the following solutions:

- unions should provide women with the means to enable them to determine their own role in the organization of the union
- women should attend branch meetings and stay throughout the meetings; adequate notices should be given
- women should cultivate an interest in various trade union publications
- they should participate in union activities
- women should ignore rumours and gossip and avoid running down women who aspire to lead; they should support forward-looking women
- provision of crèche and daycare facilities to allow women to combine domestic chores and child-rearing with active participation in union activities
- male workers should encourage wives who are working to participate actively in trade union activities
- women should be encouraged to hold elective posts
- regular seminars, workshops and training programmes should be organized for women
- there should be equitable representation of women and men in all trade union organizations
- women should not demand their rightful positions on the basis of feminine charms
- there is a need to check regularly on the progress of involving women in the organizational structure of the union
- unions should identify the barriers which militate against women's participation in union activities and find solutions to them
- a reasonable proportion of women should be allowed to participate in conferences, seminars and workshops on leadership skills and trade union activities to encourage greater membership participation, particularly by women
- husbands should be invited to social gatherings organized by the various trade unions
- the union should prepare and distribute resources, newsletters and material for women at the local level to inform members about the changing role of women

- women who possess the necessary qualifications, ability and determination should be elected to posts in the union

Nebo-Eze offers the following advice to women:

- They themselves should endeavour to be more serious and dedicated to union work. They should do their best when offered opportunities to participate in the organizational work of the union.
- Confidence begets confidence. It therefore behooves women to ensure that they earn the respect and confidence of their husbands and colleagues.
- Women must strive to be a shining example in their leadership roles, in which they chart a course of prudence and fair play in every aspect of their public life.
- They must see themselves as a factor in the machinery of the union's set-up, working assiduously alongside men toward the achievement of the much-desired unity, peace, and progress of the union. They must be prepared at all times to give or render honourable and effective service.
- Women, as members of a trade union, must possess humility to serve, courtesy and sociability to win the support of their homes, their states, their union and their nation.
- Women should ensure, above all, that their life-time of toil in the union yields dignity for themselves, their male colleagues, and a happier prospect for their children.[20]

At the same symposium, Cecilia Onyeka, state chair of the NLC women's wing for Anambra state, reminded everyone of the traditional unionism of Nigerian women. She said:

> It is important to note that the Aba Riot of 1929 and the Abeokuta Resistance of 1948 are good examples of what women can do once they identify their problems. Looking at those contributions makes the work of modern trade unions look light. Abolition of payment of tax by housewives and excesses of traditional rulers could have been one of the problems that trade unions are battling today ... Modern women should draw inspiration from the activities of the Aba and Abeokuta women and start now to work for a social contract.

She made the following recommendations to Nigerian labour leaders:

- efforts should be made towards conscious enlargement of women's groups, with special emphasis on rural areas, where members could be organized into co-operatives
- labour leaders should pull their resources together to see that daycare

centres are established at rates subsidized by the various institutions women work for

- they should see to it that trade union organizations include family planning in their education syllabus, as this could enable women to have a family of more manageable size so they can cope with their jobs as mothers and bread-winners
- they should struggle for a review of the statutory laws that heavily tax the incomes of married women, whose rebates are given to their husbands
- demand that fringe benefits be on the basis of rank and responsibilities and not on the basis of marital status
- demand equal opportunities for men and women
- encourage women workers to be effective in their jobs
- encourage female workers to acquire higher education and do more in-service courses to prepare them for managerial positions; this is the most important thing to give women an opportunity to tilt situations in their favour
- demand that women appointed to public offices represent the interest of women; they should be nominated by women and not hand-picked by men
- demand that equal numbers of men and women be appointed to public offices
- demand that child-bearing and child-rearing be regarded as a national service and see that adequate compensation is paid to nursing mothers
- demand the establishment of committees/bureaux to handle cases of sexual harassment, child abuse, and discrimination on grounds of religion or/and tribe of origin.[21]

It is clear that the opinions of women in the trade unions differ, as do their levels of political consciousness and ideological consistency. Even within the NLC Working Women's Wing, however, we can see the degree to which the 'performance syndrome' rules, as we witness the contradiction of male chauvinism and the opportunism of elite women (and their lack of ideological clarity), even on trade union platforms.

At the NLC WWW's symposium to commemorate the 1987 International Women's Day, as with other public events in Nigeria, wives and daughters of the establishment occupied the high chairs, and the press focused on them. More controversial, however, was the presence of senior men of the NLC at the high chairs during these women's events. What these male trade unionists had to say about women was bewildering. The Commissioner for Education, Anambra state, Grace Obayi, reminded women in her good-will message that 'our primary responsibility is our home, and the most positive contribution we can make to the development of our country is to give her well brought-up and disciplined children'.

The chair of the Anambra state council of the NLC, John Kamalu, said in his good-will message:

> I plead that you restrict your discussions to the well-being of your women-folk, international peace, and the general welfare of Nigerians, bearing in mind that you are mothers of the world. Please don't centre your discussion on equality with men. I know your capabilities. You can, with the materials at your disposal, turn the nation's table upside-down. Labour relies very much on the strength and capabilities of women and asks you to use them for the betterment of humanity. Women are extremists. Good ones are normally the best, while the bad ones the worst – there are examples of women heads of state and stories from the Christian Bible.

He went on to say: 'I know people are equally created, but because of women's extremity, people are careful in reminding you of your right.' He did acknowledge that Nigerian working women are denied daycare for their children and allowances for going on leave, even though they too pay the 'pay-as-you-earn' tax. He added:

> Nobody intends to provoke the women, bearing in mind the nature of your reactions, and consequences from the Aba women's riot are still fresh in our memories, but if we close our eyes to the non-proper recognition of womenfolk, we shall not be doing justice to our conscience … In conclusion, I passionately appeal to those of you whose husbands, boyfriends, and well-wishers are in authority to please use your bedroom voices to convince and possibly use your natural weapons to suppress the angers of your beloved ones in authority, because every man has a reflection of one or two attitudes of his beloved woman in him. Every successful man has a good woman behind him.

There were general mutterings of disapproval from some women, but most women clapped, and Kamalu took his chair again at the high table.

In my own presentation, I accused the labour union of sexism and squabbling over hierarchy. To the elite women, I said:

> It is not the Nigerian working-class or grassroots woman who opposes feminism, the fight for women's rights. The opposition comes from wives of the elite class – that is, the opportunists who are suffering an easily understood apologia in their sell-out of the women's struggle. Their denial that there is need for a women's liberation movement, their position that feminism is alien to African culture, and their utterances that men and women are not created equal is a cop-out and an insult to working-class women and the human rights movement as a whole.

There is a radical difference between the working-class socialist women's movement and the bourgeois women's movement in the way they are structured in the relations of production. It is similar to the difference between a servant and her mistress. This explains the difference in their commitment to the feminist struggle and their different priorities. One is seeking power within the establishment, and they succeed in gaining token appointments. They recognize and accept the privileges of the exploitative classes, derived from wealth or birth, and want to share in them. They are wives of different elite groups, mere appendages to titled men – the professional groups, the military men, the businessmen – that is, the *akajiakus*, *masuabus*, the *olowos*, who include the thieves and squanderers of the people's wealth – the real undisciplined class against whom the government should be waging its War Against Indiscipline, inequality, and 'squandermania'. They are the greatest supporters of their husbands, brothers, and fathers, content to be behind their success. They are the women who take pleasure in repeating the sexist and exploitative slogan, 'Behind every successful man is a woman'.

The other class of woman seeks radical transformation, for she is in the forefront in the labour market, expending time and energy for very little wages and few privileges. These women are part of the working class, doing menial jobs side by side with men. They are in the rural villages producing the food we eat. They clean up the urban towns, the blazing sun burning their bent backs, in the name of urban sanitation. It is this class of woman who needs shelter – adequate housing, designed with women and children's needs in mind; a decent wage and equal taxation system; better health care; a right to education and knowledge; freedom of choice in relation to her body; a guaranteed place in political decision-making processes; a better standard of living; better rights as a wife, a mother, or a single woman; a better quality of life.[22]

I feel that it is important that I present in as much detail as I can the direct voices of women active in these organizations in order to show the extent of women's involvement in civil political discourse in Nigeria. All these women and the organizations to which they belong sincerely feel the need to speak for women. Yet, every single one of these organizations admits its elitist leadership. Out of these four organizations, only the NCWS, with its Christian-derived ethics and a moral language dotted with notions of civil rights, has succeeded in mobilizing grassroots women at the local village level. It has well laid down structures to do this work, but is a very conservative organization that is tied to the state.

Even on the eve of the twenty-first century, NCWS has not shed its conservatism. It is even now more versed in the formalized internationalist rhetoric of development. The current president, Zainab Maina, has impressive credentials, both in education and organizational skills. She has also attended recent international conferences on women, including the Nairobi Forward-Looking Strategies for Advancement of Women, 1985 and the Fourth World Conference on Women in Beijing, 1995. Zainab Maina as a northern woman, whom one might argue was marginalized by her southern sisters' domination of NCWS and its presidency, given this opportunity, isn't doing much that is different from previous presidents of NCWS and their subservience to the establishment, as can be seen from a recent interview titled, 'We Reject Marginalisation', in *Newswatch*, 16 August 1999. NCWS still sees itself as a mobilization agent of the government and therefore entitled to greater government financial support. In this interview, Maina says, 'We undertake the mobilisation, enlightenment, and education of women to realise their rights and responsibilities as citizens of this country and what is expected of them in contributing toward national development' (ibid. p. 50).

If women in Nigeria, as indeed women in America, Britain, etc., are aiming for the presidency in the next millennium, it is quite likely that it is establishment's conservative women who will achieve this goal. In the United States, the world witnessed Hillary Clinton, even though betrayed in love and marriage vows, increasingly slide into conservatism, coupled with ambitions for political office, as she silently stood by her man, the US president Bill Clinton, during the Monica Lewinsky sex scandal in 1998–99. In the *Newswatch* interview, Zainab Maina seems to 'speak from two sides of her mouth'. She would not hesitate to call out women to lynch culprits of domestic violence, especially men who pour acid on their wives with the intention to deform, or those who turn their wives into a punch bag. Yet, in her own case, she gives the impression of subservience to her husband. Maina says:

> We are not fighting war with our men, our husbands, as there will be no respectable family that would exist without the man being the head of the family. Some of us are mothers that are happily married to our husbands and we respect them dearly. I have been a married woman for about 34 years now and no decision will I take without having the final nod and approval of my husband and so also any respectable woman. And no child would be happy to be called with his mother's name but always the father's name. So, we are all proud of our men, our fathers and husbands, and as such we want to appeal to them and to our governments to implement the 30% affirmative action to give the Nigerian woman her sense of belonging (ibid. p. 53).

What seems most important to these conservative women is high political appointments and filling women's quota that was stipulated by the affirmative action of the UN convention that eliminates all forms of discrimination against women. By this convention 30 per cent of all positions should be reserved for women.

Fighting for social and economic equality in the family and in society also involves a responsibility to challenge a husband and if necessary sacrifice a marriage. Daughters of the Goddess went as far as to organize sex strikes when these heterosexual women collectively would refuse men sex and food.

Unlike NCWS, WIN and NLC Women's Wing – with their politically correct language of rights based on civil notions of social justice – remain more effective as elite vanguards, quite removed from the general masses of women. The National Committee on Women and Development differs from these other organizations as a fact-finding and policy-implementing mechanism. As such, the committee is part of government structure with a different potentiality for empowering women. I shall return to this issue later. Meanwhile, in the next chapter, I wish to focus on the professional women to examine the extent to which their rhetoric of concern about women is put into practice.

Notes

1. Mrs M. N. David-Osuagwu, chairperson, Anambra State Committee on Women and Development. Address read at the seminar on Women and Development – Strategies, Enugu, 24 July 1986.

2. *Daily Star*, 16 July 1986.

3. *Daily Star*, 8 November 1986.

4. *Daily Star*, 31 July 1986.

5. Ifi Amadiume, 'Women and Political Development: Mobilisation and Awareness in Anambra State'. Paper presented at WIN training seminar on 'Awareness and Mobilisation', Fifth Annual Women in Nigeria Conference, University of Benin, 22–26 July 1986.

6. *Newswatch*, 22 July 1985.

7. 'Women at War: A New Radicalism Simmers', *IBC Journal*, August–September 1986.

8. *Guardian*, 30 July 1986.

9. Jane Bryce, 'Liberation, Feminism, and Nigeria', *Guardian Sunday*, 1 February 1987.

10. *Daily Times*, 16 July 1986.

11. *Sunday Concord*, 8 June 1986.

12. *IBC Journal*, August–September 1986.

13. This and the following quotations in this section are taken from 'Focus on Our New-Breed Women Militants', *New Horizon*, vol. 6, no. 8, September 1986.

14. It would be interesting to compare WIN's first four years, which were under the Imam group, and the post-Imam-group leadership from 1986.

15. 'Focus on Our New-Breed Women Militants'.

16. *Guardian*, 30 July 1986.

17. *Daily Star*, 21 May 1986.

18. 'Focus on Our New-Breed Women Militants'.

19. Ibid.

20. Ethel Ngozi Nebo-Eze, 'Women's Participation in Trade Unions'. Paper presented at a conference organized by Women in Nigeria, Anambra state, and the Awareness One Club in commemoration of 1987's International Women's Day, University of Nigeria, 7 March 1987.

21. Cecilia Onyeka, 'Contributions of Women in the Development of the Nigerian Labour Movement'. Paper presented at a symposium organized by Women in Nigeria, Anambra state, and the Awareness One Club in commemoration of 1987's International Women's Day, University of Nigeria, 7 March 1987.

22. Ifi Amadiume, 'The Role of Women Workers and Trade Unionism in the Development of National Economy'. Paper presented to the Anambra state National Labour Council Working Women's Wing Symposium, 5 March 1987; also published as 'Women Workers and Trade Unionism', *Guardian Sunday*, 15 March 1987.

4. Class and gender dynamics in professional women's organizations

Chapter 3 examined the tensions between national women's organizations over their dispute about who speaks for all women. The data presented showed a high level of women's political activities and civil debate. It was, however, evident that in spite of such competition these various organizations can all be criticized for their elitist leadership and agenda that excludes the majority of Nigerian women who are rural, poor and illiterate. Consequently, this chapter focuses on professional women and their organizations to show how they are generally viewed, the problems they face, and to assess their positions on rights and social justice.

There is no other group of women in whom ambivalence and contradictions about identity are more pronounced and more profound than in professional women. While grassroots churchwomen have often been accused of ignorance or 'backwardness' on feminist issues concerning women's place or power in contemporary society, highly 'educated' professional women cannot plead ignorance of the issues involved. Yet much of the distortion about African women's contribution to society and history comes not from the daughters of the Goddess, but from some of these professional women and the men they try to please. The result is a great disparity between theory and practice and between rhetoric and practice. This is evident in the contradiction between what professional women say as individuals and what their organizations claim as aims and objectives.

A typical distortion of history is a statement such as this that can be read daily in any Nigerian paper: 'Time was when women in positions of authority were an uncommon sight. Then women had no business with decision-making. Man was the head of the family and the community at large.' The usual argument goes that, with increasing educational opportunities for women, professional women have emerged who can perform as well as men in what used to be male preserves.

The 'arrival' of women in top professional positions has not been without strife, however. Female bosses are often criticized for being

Some Women's Organizations

1. National Council of Women's Societies   (NCWS)
2. National Commission for Women (NCW)
3. National Association of Women Journalists (NAWOJ)
4. Women in Nigeria (WIN)
5. Association of Professional Women Engineers (APWEN)
6. International Federation of Women Lawyers (FIDA)
7. Medical Women Association of Nigeria (MWAN)
8. Professional Insurance Ladies Association (PILA)
9. Society of Women Accountants of Nigeria (SWAN)
10. Association of Lady Pharmacists (ALPS)
11. Nigerian Army Officers' Wives' Association (NAOWA)
12. Naval Officers' Wives' Association (NOWA)
13. Nigerian Market Women Association (NMWA)
14. Police Officers' Wives' Association (POWA)
15. Nigerian Air Force Officers' Wives' Association (NAFOWA)
16. National Association of Women in Business (NAWB)
17. Women Health Research Network in Nigeria (WHERNIN)
18. National Association of Media Women (NAMW)

Source: Newswatch special edition, 'Women in Nigeria', 10 December 1990.

demanding and difficult to deal with. Many men claim they would not like to work for a woman. Such resentment has sometimes been attributed to men's social orientation, which makes them believe that only men are fit for positions of authority. But resentment of female superiors appears even more pronounced among women, for many women seem to be saying they would rather have no job at all (if they could afford to) than work under a woman. The dilemma these presumed contradictions poses is how to reconcile women's 'natural endowments' – motherly instincts and tendencies that make them 'gentle and kind' – with the tough 'masculine' bosses people have, rightly or wrongly, conjured up in their minds.

Female bosses argue that they have the added task of convincing people, especially men, that they can perform, and thus they have to work twice as hard as men. They claim they need to be tougher than men to be taken seriously. They have had to be high-handed, especially at the beginning. Top professional women include chiefs, finance directors, heads of units, bank directors, company presidents, managing directors, lecturers, professors, vice chancellors, and so on. These women say they find that men can be more petty than women are supposed to be.[1] Women in top management positions acknowledge that it is a tough journey to the top; that women are present only in token numbers in professions that used to be exclusively male; and that women are still discriminated against in staffing, remuneration, promotion and training opportunities.

Faced with this competition for power in contemporary society, stereo-typing in sex-role differentiation has intensified to such an extent that prejudices are being legitimized in language: for example, women are 'not as ambitious as men', are 'less rational', 'more dependent', 'conforming', 'passive', 'much more emotional than men'. In this contest, beliefs deriving from a western-colonized mind are employed, while those deriving from indigenous beliefs about motherhood – especially its selflessness and self-sacrifice and 'children should come first' aspects – are twisted and mani-pulated. Women must not show men disrespect or boss them about.

Some successful professional women resort to self-denial on the question of women's liberation and feminism, claiming they are not 'your average bra-burning, banner-waving, men-hating women's liberation type', writes Jane Bryce.[2] Bryce observed this contradiction in the recurring disclaimers of the 'liberated' label by women who outwardly appear on the path of liberation, and recognized that Nigerian women were trying to avoid the stereotyped image of the 'woman libber' as portrayed by Nigerian men. This apparent antagonism towards educated women was the subject of Molara Ogundipe-Leslie's New Year message in January 1987.[3] Ogundipe-Leslie who, as an outspoken feminist and columnist has been heavily criticized, wrote, 'A certain condition unites all educated women in Nigeria. This is the condition of hostility and fear from the menfolk. If you listen carefully, you will always hear statements of antagonism and negative criticism of the educated woman. She is the new demon that haunts the psyche of the Nigerian male of all classes. All social problems are un-critically attributed to her.' In Ogundipe-Leslie's opinion, Nigerian men want to move into the future, while keeping women in the past.

Top professional women acknowledge that 'only exceptional women, amidst the difficulties and barriers often thrown in their way, can reach the apex of an organization or the upper rungs of the ladder'. Chief Mrs Kuforiji-Olubi, chairperson of the United Bank of Africa Ltd, speaking on 'the journey to top management positions – how easy for women?', said: 'A man must confirm expectations for his success, whereas a woman must often disconfirm expectations for her failure.'[4]

A brief review of the progress of women in the professions shows that by the time of independence in 1960, the sexism inherent in the imposed British system had become well established. Women could do only certain jobs and those only in the areas of caring and nurturing. In 1962, the Lagos General Hospital had only one female doctor, Dr Olufunmilayo Odiakosa. Married women were employed only on contract and were not therefore given pensionable jobs, car loans or maternity leave. Periods of absence for maternity were in fact deducted from periods served.

In those days, professional women were classed as reverend sisters who should not marry. While on duty, however, they were not seen as sufficiently different to warrant a separate room. Odiakosa did not receive a promotion for six years on the grounds that she was happily married. At work, female professionals were worried incessantly about their competence, as it was continually being undermined. At home, they had to deal with suspicions of infidelity with male colleagues. According to Dr Odiakosa: 'This is responsible for the trouble in the homes of many female doctors. Few of us have intact homes; many are either divorced or separated because the level of development of some men cannot cope with such commitment to work.'[5]

Not all women are forthcoming about discrimination. Any who joined the professions in the late 1970s, especially those who have 'made it', deny experiencing sexism. One doctor, after denying that women are discriminated against, said, 'It is only in a few cases when you have a male patient with symptoms of a venereal disease and you have to examine his genitals, they insist on seeing a male doctor.'

Women seem to be concentrated in careers in urban health and ophthalmology, which are supposedly less discriminatory areas of medicine, where working hours are more regular. Likewise teaching – a field that has always employed many women – because, again, the working hours are more compatible with family life. Under centralized administration those women who, as heads of schools, were able to employ and dismiss staff, lost power to school management boards. However, the introduction of these boards was welcomed by younger female teachers who had often been subjected to harassment from male heads.

The International Federation of Women Lawyers (FIDA)

FIDA is one of the most articulate of the professional women's organizations. It believes in the study of comparative law and the promotion of the principles and aims of the United Nations. It is concerned with the legal and social aspects of the welfare of women and children. FIDA therefore has UN consultative status, and women lawyers are represented in the meetings of the United Nations Organization and its agencies. FIDA is also a member of the International Federation of Women. Mrs

Aduke Alakija, Nigerian ambassador to Sweden, is president of FIDA and was its representative at the UN until 1977. The present secretary-general, Mrs Adefunke Akinkugbe, is Nigerian.

Like their counterparts in the medical profession, female lawyers acknowledge the problems irregular working hours pose for married women with children. Married lawyers depend on having broad-minded and accommodating husbands. The lawyers and their association feel strongly about discriminatory tax laws, whereby a woman cannot automatically claim tax relief for children, though her male counterpart can. In the Ministry of Justice, even though there are now more female lawyers than males, females are still present only in token numbers as high court judges and commissioners.

The National Association of Media Women (NAMW)

One of the areas of greatest discrimination against women has been in the media, since they usually constitute the mouthpiece of the establishment. The entry of women journalists has been seen as an 'infiltration'. It is their growing presence, however, that gave birth to the NAMW.

In 1966, Toyin Johnson was the only female sub-editor at the *Morning Post*. 'In journalism', she said, 'you have a hectic social life, but there is a misconception bandied around that female journalists are loose women, as is said of nurses.'[6] The entry point for women journalists has usually been through the women's page, irrespective of an individual's qualifications. It was not until 1980 that Dr Hamidat Doyinsola Abiola became the first female editor of a national newspaper, the *National Concord*, but it is an independent publication owned by her millionaire husband. Today, as editor-in-chief and managing director of Concord Press of Nigeria, she heads a newspaper house which employs women in top editorial posts. Unfortunately, Abiola has come under fire from Women in Nigeria (WIN) for complacency on women's issues. The presence of a woman editor, WIN points out, has not made any impact on the sexist orientation of the paper or in the employment of women journalists.[7] It was apparently in response to this criticism that Abiola 'spoke out' in a 1986 lecture on 'Women and the Media in Nigeria',[8] which demonstrates the effectiveness of critical analysis and constructive criticism.

Abiola has the clout to use her paper as a platform. She can take as much space as she likes and can mobilize as many reporters as she pleases for research. Her tone on the issue of women and the media is that the media are male-controlled and -dominated. After citing International Labour Organization (ILO) statistics of women's contributions to the economy, she notes that 'while women still bear the age-old tag of the so-called "weaker sex", our national reality today is that it is this weaker sex that in fact constitutes the backbone of the nation'. Yet women are still regarded as second-class citizens in all aspects of the country's national development – as, for example, in the uneven development of education for boys and girls and in the provision of schools and access to professional and technical courses.

Rural women, in fact, constitute the most disadvantaged, under-privileged and belaboured segment of Nigerian society. They work under the most arduous conditions, with inadequate roads, no water and no electricity. In practice, they are the agricultural workers, but agricultural assistance and training are mostly given to men. Both WIN and NAMW have pointed out that the Nigerian media do not cover these issues affect-ing women's welfare. Some papers, in fact, devote less than a page to women's concerns, concentrating on family and home affairs or fads and fashions of the urban elite.

Both the print and electronic media have portrayed women as sex objects. There is even a nude girl pictured on page 3 of a certain national newspaper. One Lagos weekly is known for using women as bait to interest men in advertisements. All the papers are patronizing in their portrayal of women in service roles. According to Abiola: 'Only occasionally are the real issues of women's status and roles in a changing society discussed. And even on those few occasions when they are, such discussions are more often too brief, too superficial, intellectually impoverished, and totally devoid of any well-argued policy proposals worthy of serious governmental consideration.'

With the relatively recent infiltration of young, radical male and female journalists into the media, there has been a growing voice of opposition to the establishment and to the abuse of women and children. Some of the cases and issues referred to in the section on social abuses and campaigns indicate that these radical elements have been more concerned than the National Council of Women's Societies (NCWS). The younger journalists feel that they have improved the press and are leading the nation to a new realization that women are as talented and as intellectually endowed as men and, with encouragement, could excel.

According to Abiola, since 'the media represent the intention and influence of the power elite and social institutions of any given society', women should be represented at the decision-making level. There is, of course, a question here of meeting rhetoric with practice, when Abiola, herself the wife of the late Chief Abiola, one of the wealthiest men in Nigeria, writes that what the media should be doing is 'look[ing] at the realities of the society, inequality, discrimination, immoralities of the capitalist system where the rich get richer and the poor wallow in squalor' and that change should be sought in society's attitudes towards its female population.

The disparity between rhetoric and practice seems to be a characteristic of all the professional and elite women's organizations, primarily because they lack a broad base and because their individual members and leadership lack both a local and a rural base. In April 1986, for example, the Anambra state chapter of NAMW held a symposium on 'Towards Qualitative Family Life in Enugu'. It occurred during the National Political Debate (see Chapter 8) when there was general insistence that elites use local languages to ensure the participation of the rural grassroots population. It was therefore decided that media women should use the Igbo language at the symposium. What transpired was a piece of theatre during which the public realized that elite Igbo women found it difficult to express themselves in Igbo.

Usually at such meetings, the ordinary folk sit through the proceedings politely, not understanding a word, since the sessions are conducted in English. The 'performance' is more impressive than what is said. The wife of the military governor usually stresses wifehood and motherhood and the domestic duties of women, the nurturing and caring aspects of women's role; she talks about family planning and tells women to have fewer children. There is an obvious contradiction in the views of individual women who insist, on the one hand, that a successful mother should cook and care for her family, while on the other insisting that women be gainfully employed outside their homes.

In this particular symposium, the wife of the state governor said that women should not be haggard or untidy, thus showing the stress of their burden in 'bearing the family's cross'. They should keep their heads high at all times. Women were told to be devoted to their family, to be content with what they have, and to show selfless love in working for their children's happiness. The governor's wife appealed to husbands not to take their wives' pay packets and to ensure that marriage is built on trust and love.[9]

Other women's clubs

As well as organizations of women in specific professions, there are others such as the Zonta International Club of Lagos, made up of professional women, which see themselves as service organizations.

Zonta International's vice-president is Professor Jadesola Akande. Much of the work of the club is focused on welfare and charity. During the scandal surrounding the murder of Hauwa (see Chapter 6), the club, while presenting money and gifts to the Spinal Cord Injuries Association of Nigeria (SCIAN), called on the government to prosecute those involved in her death. The club subsequently planned a symposium on child marriage and called on the government to stipulate a minimum marriageable age for girls. Concerning the spread of AIDS, the vice-president of the club urged women to be sexually disciplined to reduce their chances of infection.

There are other women's clubs and associations which have retained more of the characteristics of indigenous women's organizations such as collectivistic ideologies of female solidarity; as such they are dominated by matrons and women who, although bourgeois daughters of imperialism, can also be described as 'daughters of the Goddess'. In the federal capital and in cities, these women who traditionally would have belonged to and functioned under their village women's organizations also do well in the contemporary urban-based organizations which, like the professional women's organizations, have acquired expertise in raising money. Women who belong to professional organizations also tend to belong to urban-based elite women's organizations, which place a great dela of emphasis on the women's state of origin. The Nka Ikemesit Iban Ibibio Society, described as a socio-cultural union of Ibibio women from Cross River state, for example, embarked on a project to erect a 2.5 million-naira civic centre in Lagos. This centre will contain a library, shopping centre, conference halls and, most unusually, a daycare centre. Their fundraising ceremony is to be hosted by the state governor.[10]

A similar organization is the Okwesili-Eze Club, which is made up of wealthy Igbo women. The club stresses self-help, sisterly love, charitable work, the promotion of Nigerian culture and instilling discipline in youth. They donate money, clothing and food to handicapped and motherless children's homes, the cancer society and state funds. Like the Nka Ikemesit Iban Ibibio Society, the Okwesili-Eze Club plans a daycare centre. Their emphasis on sisterly love and female solidarity has meant that the club has a well-developed welfare and bereavement scheme for its members. They pay entitlements to bereaved members and generally try to share each other's burdens. The principle that those who have should help others is embedded in their motto.

Wives of —— Associations

No other form of women's organization has evoked such outrage and condemnation as the associations of wives of the various male-dominated professions – wives of doctors, engineers, lawyers and so on. These associations have sometimes been dubbed 'mere appendages'. Some would prefer to see women join professional women's organizations rather than wives' associations. These associations tend to exercise power and control money or resources according to the importance of the husbands' profession at any given period in the political system. In 1986, for example, we find the Police Officers' Wives' Association (POWA), Imo state branch, planning to establish an 800,000-naira nursery school. According to the state president of the association, as their husbands work to maintain law and order, POWA members would ensure that their children are given adequate training. Since the military has ruled longer and has exercised more absolute power, I shall concentrate on the associations of military wives.

Nigerian Army Officers Wives' Association (NAOWA)   Over the years this association has emerged as the most powerful women's organization in the country. It has chapters in all brigades and units in the federation. Its aim is to provide a forum for women to unite and organize and be able to live on their own when their husbands are away.

The publication in 1988 of *The Home Front* by Maryam Babangida, wife of the military ruler at that time, gave an insight into the activities of the association, even as it raised questions and sparked debates. In the book, which appears to be based on the minutes and constitution of the NAOWA, Maryam Babangida writes, 'Since the officer is always on 24-hours duty, seven days a week, to defend his country, there is the need to have a wife who is responsible, efficient, and effective at the home front to oversee the activities there.' The need for 'a good rear management' is based on the assertion that 'soldiers work so hard that they need the comfort and warmth of a real home, not just a house, to which they retire when they have the rare opportunity of being idle, even if for an hour only'. It is not surprising that Dele Omotunde said: 'Sometimes the book appears to be a commissioned public relations job for the army.'[11] Another reviewer, Godwin Agbroko, stated: 'Maryam's immediate concern is not so much with the marriage institution per se as with the more specific role of the wife as a kind of institutional requirement for the successful career of an army officer.'[12]

Irrespective of the content or quality of the book, 700,000 naira was collected at its launch, and the royalties were pledged to Nigerian children; this was said to be a token of Maryam Babangida's commitment 'to the worthy cause of women and children in our society'.[13] She declared that the presidency of NAOWA had given her a 'fuller understanding and appreciation of the problems faced by not only the officers' wives, but by all women as mothers and wives'. She told all officers' wives to continue to care for their homes with calm and fortitude.

During the 'launching', as on other occasions, the might of the establishment was at Babangida's command, and it was full of praise for her 'achievement'. The chief 'launcher' was Lieutenant General Sani Abacha, then chief of army staff. The chairperson was Hannah Idowu Awolowo, widow of the late chief Obafemi Awolowo. Guest of honour was General Yakubu Gowon, one-time head of state of Nigeria. Others present included state governors, Armed Forces Ruling Council (AFRC) members, and many other eminent Nigerians.

In Chapter VII of Maryam Babangida's book, NAOWA is described as a forum where the wives of army officers can achieve a sense of social communion. It is therefore a social, philanthropic and charitable association with voluntary membership. Its main aim is to promote the welfare of the troops and their families and to foster friendship, unity and understanding among officers' wives (Babangida 1988: 63). Other stated aims are:

- promoting and undertaking social welfare schemes – such as sewing, cookery and handicrafts – and conducting health-care classes for soldier's wives
- undertaking philanthropic and social activities – such as visits to motherless children's homes, old people's homes, SOS village and handicapped people's homes
- assisting baby welfare clinics and baby shows as well as family planning clinics for soldiers' families
- organizing seminars, symposia, local and international tours to enable the association to participate fully in national and international welfare activities
- promoting self-help projects – such as daycare centres and playgrounds – and establishing libraries in barracks
- organizing visits to military hospitals with gifts

It is interesting how the history and role of this association have changed with the transformations in the Nigerian Army. When the association was formed in 1960, it was called the Army Wives' Association (AWA). Its activities were confined to the barracks, and most of the senior officers' wives were expatriates (i.e. wives of British colonialists). The wife of Major-General Welby Everald, commanding general officer, was the first national president of the organization. Subsequent presidents have included Victoria Aguiyi-Ironsi, Ayisha Usman Katsina, Mrs David Ejoor, Grace T. Y. Danjuma, Mrs G. S. Jalo, Maryam Babangida and Maryam Abacha. Usually, the wife of the chief of army staff has been the national president, and the wife of the commander in each military location has been branch president.[14]

Consistent with the transformation in the role of women during a crisis, the Nigeria–Biafra War (1967–70) saw the AWA emerging from the confines of the barracks into the national limelight, organizing donations and looking after the sick and wounded and the families left behind. It was through this role that the AWA is said to have achieved 'its vision of a "partner-in-progress" to the Nigerian Army'. After the war, the AWA reverted to welfare activities.

In the earlier days of the AWA, many men did not allow their wives to join the association, which was seen as an outlet for gossip where officers' wives met to 'put on airs according to the ranks of their husbands and show off their latest acquisitions in clothes, cosmetics, and jewelry' (Babangida 1988: 65). As the Nigerian Army moved from the traditional military role of defence and combat into politics and economic and political power, so too did the wives grow in importance, to such an extent that men who had banned their wives from joining AWA now changed their minds. These same men would go to the secretariat to try to get identity cards for their wives. Membership in the NAOWA became rewarding in 'raising funds', developing the 'spirit of helping the needy', giving women a 'sense of belonging in the society', interacting with women from different cultures and religions, gaining organizational experience, and so forth.

With a growing sense of their class, the women changed the all-embracing name Army Wives' Association, which they described as 'bland and nondescript', to the Nigerian Army Officers' Wives' Association (NAOWA). They established a secretariat in an officers' mess in Lagos, reviewed their constitution, and made it mandatory that the wife of the chief of army staff assume the presidency of NAOWA. They created a logo, drew up a code of conduct, and issued identity cards for members. NAOWA's code of conduct contains the following injunctions to wives:

An officer's wife must:

1. Maintain proper public manners to reflect the high standards of the military.
2. Respect other people's feelings and be tolerant.
3. Be courteous, polite, loving, and kind.
4. Maintain high self-esteem in the home for good up-bringing of children.
5. Be a complement to her husband's success.
6. Be eager to listen and reluctant to talk.
7. Love and respect her neighbors.
8. Pay particular attention to the children's behavior and up-bringing.
9. Be punctual for all engagements.
10. Create a conducive atmosphere for peace in the home and her environment at all times.
11. Be neatly dressed and maintain a good turn-out at all times.

12. Keep her home and surroundings clean.
13. Teach her children to respect the laws of the land and their elders.
14. Intensify cultural and moral values in the home.
15. Bring up their children with the fear of God in them.

Don'ts:

1. Do not take undue advantage of your husband's position in the Army.
2. Do not fight in public.
3. Do not quarrel before children.
4. Do not disagree with your husband publicly.
5. Do not disgrace your husband in public.
6. Do not gossip. Avoid idleness.
7. Do not disregard your husband's comments, especially on food or cleanliness of the home. Take them in good faith.
8. Do not carry rifts between you and your husband over to the next day.
9. Do not indulge in destructive criticisms.
10. Do not engage in any dubious activities that can cause embarrassment to your husband.
11. Do not indulge your children in luxury items or high spending. (Babangida 1988: 73–4)

Maryam Babangida wrote of these changes:

People became so interested in the way things were moving that the mess was often jammed to capacity at our meetings, and husbands encouraged their wives to join. The officers even helped their wives with their assignments on behalf of the Association. I was told that there was growing a new kind of rapport between officers and their wives. At one of the meetings, I saw many pregnant officers' wives and wondered why. One of them got up to say, quite unexpectedly, that I was responsible! 'You have brought peace to our homes. Our husbands now respect us more', she said. I thought she was joking until others lent her support with vigorous nods and a hail of 'Yes! Yes! Yes!' (pp. 67–8)

Other achievements of Maryam Babangida's presidency include the building of a nursery school in Ojo cantonment and raising funds for hospitals and homes for the disabled.[15] The association also founded a NAOWA farm on the Ojo–Badagry road on land acquired from the Lagos state government. General achievements of NAOWA over the years have included the building of several schools in the barracks, provision of school buses, donation of medical items to hospitals and medical reception stations in the barracks, promotion of the government's Expanded Programme on Immunization (EPI), teaching women about the benefits of family planning, and building a vocational centre at the Ojo cantonment to teach various trades to wives and children of soldiers – hair-dressing, cooking, dress-making, handicrafts and so on. In accordance with its welfare policy, the association looks after sick members, whether at home or in hospital. Bereaved members are also given support, and husbands who are widowed receive financial support. New wives are socialized in NAOWA for the reproduction of the cult of military eliteness.

Northern Women: the Federation of Muslim Women's Association of Nigeria (FOMWAN)

How do northern Nigerian women fit into these structures of women's organizations in the contemporary Nigerian nation-state? As the masses of women in the northern states are relatively invisible in academic scholarship, so too are they invisible in the patterns and structures of contemporary women's organizations. Those who do have a presence in this structure are Christian girls and women, and this presence is the result of shared western elite cultures generated through churches and formal education. Northern Christian females associate with their southern counterparts primarily through international organizations – the Red Cross, the YWCA, and the Girl Guides – and through social clubs such as Club 29, which organizes children's games and bazaars. They are able, through these means, to interact with women from the south, but this is not true for Muslim women.

Muslim women's organizations have generally been seen as the female wing of Islamic fundamentalism, since they seem to promote sharia law (laws based on Islamic constitution), and the total obedience of women to Islamic concepts of propriety. The Federation of Muslim Women's Association of Nigeria (FOMWAN), for example, works within accepted and safe grounds. For this reason, Bryce reached the conclusion that northern feminists feel more akin to Women in Nigeria (WIN). She posed the question of whether Islam intends for women only the roles of mother and wife, and she correctly stated that *purdah* (the seclusion of women) is misinterpreted by Muslim men for selfish purposes. Bryce, who has never been apologetic about feminism, addressed conservative Muslim women when she wrote: 'We are attempting by our practice to re-educate men and our more timid sisters not to accept "natural" categories, not to be afraid of breaking with convention.'[16]

With FOMWAN, we find the same trend as in other women's organizations whereby officials of the organizations make statements according to their level of political awareness. Thus, while some members of FOMWAN are reactionary, others are radical or progressive.[17] During the May Day celebrations in 1986, FOMWAN highlighted the problems of rural women workers, especially farmers. They called for the provision of good drinking water, basic health facilities, and simple mechanical gadgets that would make women's work less tedious and assist in the processing of food. They also called for an enhanced earning capacity, literacy programmes, and education in co-operative ventures. Child-bearing, they argued, should be regarded as an important contribution to labour and production, and women workers should not be victimized for absence from work for maternity reasons. In the same message, they called on the government to uphold 'the dignity of women by giving women their fundamental human rights of having access to education, health facilities and freedom to practice their religion without hindrance'.[18]

In this chapter, as in the previous one, I have presented data which demonstrate the diversity of opinion among women in the professions and their organizations. The data show that although elite women spend a lot of time talking about enlightening and civilizing their rural sisters, they themselves as professional women face negative and stereotypical representations at home and in the work-place. The data also indicate that they are more credible when articulating their own experiences in the civil ethics language of rights and social justice, than when they speak for grassroots women in the class-loaded and patronizing language of imperialism. This I believe accounts for the contradictions between rhetoric and practice in professional and elite women's discourses on women's empowerment.

Do these professional women's associations have the choice of not involving themselves in issues of rural development? What accounts for the fact that, in Africa, civic associations find themselves so overstretched that they assume the responsibilities of the state? This is the question I intend to examine in the next chapter by looking at some campaign programmes and areas of responsibilities shared between state agencies and women's organizations.

Notes

1. 'Female Executives: How Human Are They?' *Guardian*, 22 April 1987.

2. Jane Bryce, 'Liberation, Feminism and Nigeria', *Guardian Sunday*, 25 January 1987.

3. Molara Ogundipe-Leslie, 'A New Year Message to Women', *Guardian*, 5 January 1987.

4. *National Concord*, 6 October 1986.

5. 'Women and the Professions Since 1960', *Guardian*, 1 October 1986.

6. Ibid.

7. *The WIN Document*, 1985, p. 120.

8. *National Concord*, 21 July 1986.

9. *Daily Star*, 16 April 1986.

10. *Guardian*, 26 April 1986.

11. Dele Omotunde, 'Still, a hidden treasure: Maryam Babangida's book reveals little of her own life', *Newswatch*, 3 October 1988.

12. Godwin Agbroko, 'Managing the rear: Maryam provides guidelines on military matrimony', *African Guardian*, 26 September 1988.

13. 'Maryam's day of glory', *Newswatch*, 3 October 1988.

14. This was revealed in Esther Bali's interview in *Quality* (vol. 4, no. 15, 19 October 1989). At the launching of her own book for children, Esther Bali, wife of General Damkat Bali, Minister of Defence and Chairman of the Joint Chiefs of Staff, received over 100,000 naira.

15. The opening of this nursery school was Babangida's first official assignment when her husband became president.

16. Jane Bryce, 'Liberation, Feminism, and Nigeria', *Guardian Sunday*, 1 February 1987.

17. The financial secretary of FOMWAM, for example, sociologist Zainab Kabir, has said: 'I think men use religion and all other complaints to project their macho image and justify their actions against women … Every man feels threatened by an accomplished woman. And it is more so in the North' (*Guardian Sunday*, 27 July 1986).

18. *New Nigeria*, 3 May 1986.

Source

Babangida, Maryam, 1988, *The Home Front*. Fountain Publications.

5. Gender and class in campaigns and civil discourse

This chapter looks at a wide range of issues involving women's oppression in contemporary Nigeria, the intensity of debate on issues of everyday life, and the struggle for survival by ordinary folks. It shows how the responses to campaign issues further reveal the differences in political awareness and political interests of the various women's groups mentioned in Chapter 4, thus calling into question the degree to which there is a coherent women's movement in contemporary Nigeria.

First, I look at several campaigns recognized and financed by the Nigerian government. These show that since the government are not clear about how to carry out or co-ordinate such campaigns, it has relied on voluntary women's organizations or civic groups to do this for them. When they involve rural women, we find that, unfortunately, the villages have little control over the programmes, and village and poor women suffer abuse.

Women in Health Development Programme

The Women in Health Development Programme of the Federal Ministry of Health hopes to improve the standards of rural communities by involving women's organizations in the preliminary health-care delivery system. Specific objectives include involving more villages in primary health care (PHC) through community participation, increasing immunization coverage, eliminating locally prevalent health problems, improving the nutritional status of children, bringing potable water closer to rural households, raising the functional literacy of village women by at least 30 per cent, making essential drugs available in the villages and raising living standards through family planning. The programme was initiated in 1982 based on guidelines laid down by the World Health Organization (WHO) which continues to assist by providing consultants to help participating villages prepare project documents.

Other health-care programmes left to informal organizations are the

Oral Rehydration Therapy (ORT) and the Expanded Programmes on Immunization (EPI). State branches of the Medical Women's Association of Nigeria are usually asked to organize lectures and rallies in the villages to educate the rural populace about the programmes.

Women's Education Campaign

A Women's Education Campaign was first discussed in June 1986 when the minister of education urged women to study science and technical subjects instead of regarding them as subjects suitable only for men. He reported that the ministry had designed a supplementary education programme for women and had allocated 500,000 naira for it. However, it was not until September 1986 that there was a serious national effort to do something about women's education, beginning with a four-day seminar/workshop at Abuja. At the opening ceremony, attended by representatives of the departments of education from all nineteen states, voluntary women's organizations, professional groups and secondary school pupils, Minister of Education Jibril Aminu identified women's education as a priority. The women's education unit in the schools and educational services division of the Ministry of Education was to co-ordinate the programme.

The objectives of the Women's Education Campaign were listed as provision of equal educational opportunities for boys and girls, and the education of parents, traditional rulers and society in general on the need to modify attitudes towards women's education. According to the minister:

> The blueprint will be a master plan for women's education in the country over a long period. With clear objectives set from this master plan, we shall then make action plans for shorter periods, co-terminal with the National Development Plans, setting forth achievable targets, until the master plan is eventually implemented in the country by succeeding generations of educational policy-makers, planners, developers, and managers at both state and federal levels.[1]

The apparent lack of gender-sensitive language in this statement of a 'master plan' indicates that the policy and plans for women's education were to be left to the male establishment, for the policy-makers, planners, developers and managers are all men. Vanguard and civic women's groups would be right to intervene at this level to demand the rephrasing of policy statements and to follow up implementation plans.

Basic education under the UNESCO–UNICEF Co-operative Programme is defined as:

The minimum provision of knowledge, attitudes, values, and experiences, which should be made available to every individual and would be common to all. It should be aimed at enabling each individual to develop his or her own potential, creativity, and critical mind, both for his or her own fulfill- ment and happiness and for serving as a useful citizen and producer for the development of the community to which he or she belongs.

Given this definition, as we have seen, most Nigerian girls and women lack basic education. Education for girls usually stops at the primary level. Figures from the statistics division of the Ministry of Education show that females constituted 44 per cent of the total primary school population (14,383,487) in the 1983–84 school year. Lagos state schools, with 329,947 females, had the highest rate (51.7 per cent).[2]

Despite the government's stated commitment to the 'emancipation' or 'liberation' of women through education, there is a disparity in the views of those in authority in the various states. In Jos, for example, the military governor told girls to consider the study of science a challenge they must face. In Anambra, the governor declared that the preference for male education was outdated. He believed that the Women's Education Cam- paign would ensure the success of other, related programmes, such as the War Against Indiscipline (WAI), the Women's Development Campaign, and the Environmental Sanitation and Health for All Programme. But the commissioner of education in the same state (a woman, incidentally) told women that the campaign should not be seen as part of the 'so-called' women's liberation movement, which she described as 'alien to our cul- ture'.[3] In Sokoto, on the other hand, the Grand Khadi stated that Islam commanded men and women to seek knowledge. He added that the prophet Muhammad allowed his wife Aisha not only to learn, but also to teach. In Niger, a unit designed to focus attention on the mass education of women at all levels was set up in the Ministry of Education.

The Sokoto state Committee on Women's Education went further and established an endowment fund for the education of women who had been unable to attend primary school and to provide centres for literary and practically-oriented classes in the nineteen Local Government Areas (LGAs). All the LGAs were mandated to open monitoring units for the proper identification of women's problems. (An edict prohibiting the withdrawal of female children from school already existed.) Free education for girls at all levels was also intended to help women improve their educational skills. The head of the women's education unit of the Federal Ministry of Education, on her part, appealed to older women to take advantage of this second chance for education, to participate in vocational training, and to send their daughters to school.

In March 1987, Bauchi, Borno, Gongola, Kano and Plateau states organized a zonal workshop for a Population and Family/Awareness Campaign for local women councillors. At this workshop, twenty was suggested as the minimum age for girls to marry. The participants also stressed the government's encouragement of women's education at all levels and the participation of religious and community leaders in family planning programmes.

At its launching of the Women's Education Campaign in Cross River state, the governor gave as reasons for the campaign the imbalance in the education of women in Nigeria, the need for enhancement of women's status and the need to eradicate the erroneous impression that a woman's place is in the kitchen: 'The time has arrived', he said, 'when Nigerian women should be made an integral part of the development process in Nigeria. They should no more be left to play second fiddle'.[4]

Other campaign issues

The responses to other campaign issues further reveal not only the differences in political awareness and political interests of the various women's groups, but again the highly developed level of civic engagement with public issues and the keen interest in civil debate.

The women and inheritance debate has involved discussions on a review of the Marriage Act. It has been one of the strongest campaigns waged by the NCWS, which seeks an amendment to entitle wives of ten years' standing to half the family property should the marriage break up under whatever circumstances. Sections 72 and 73 of the Matrimonial Causes Act of 1970 allow a deserted wife and her children to remain undisturbed in the matrimonial home. Divorced women, however, have no right to the property of their former husbands. NCWS argues that a divorced woman has a legitimate claim to half her husband's property, since she has contributed to his wealth over the ten years of the marriage.

The Ordinance Law stipulates that the requirements of a husband's will should be followed on his death. When there is no will, and the marriage was contracted under the terms of the Marriage Act, the widow and other dependants are entitled to the husband's property, although the executors of the husband's estate may use their discretion.

Under customary laws, the rules vary, and women are often discriminated against. With the Igbo, a wife has nothing, since the property reverts to her husband's family. Among the Yoruba, a surviving spouse is not entitled to succeed to the other's property. The Yoruba also appear to have something equivalent to the Igbo options of division of property according to the number of wives or according to the number of children.

Their *Idi-igi* rule involves the division of property according to the number of wives, while *orio joris* involves the division of property according to the number of children.

In the case of Muslim women, those contributing to the dialogue do not draw comparisons from what might have been customary Hausa practice; instead, they refer to the laws of Islam. Mrs Bilikisu, for example, writes on behalf of Muslim women's groups: 'We are trying to make women realise their rights and how they can get them without being aggressive.'[5] As editor of the *Sunday Triumph*, Bilikisu is a typical professional Nigerian woman. She has domestic help. She studied political science and international relations before joining the media. Although she is speaking as public relations officer of the Federation of Muslim Women's Associations of Nigeria (FOMWAN), she may not be especially representative of Nigerian Muslim women.

Bilikisu points out that *kule* (seclusion of women) was introduced by men, not the Qu'ran. She cites examples of Muslim women who have gone to war – such as Aisha, one of the wives of the Prophet Muhammad, and Queen Amina of Zaria, a formidable sixteenth-century Hausa warrior queen and empire-builder. There are, she says, positive aspects of Sharia which have meant that moral discipline in Muslim societies is superior to that of the West. The Qu'ran prescribes one wife. If a man takes more, he is compelled to treat them equally. Bilikisu herself is not committed to the veil, but dresses well.

Property law is well spelt out in the Qu'ran. After payment of funeral expenses, debts, legacies and other charges, the widow receives one-quarter of the estate (Sura 4: 12), and the children each get one-eighth. In practice, however, 'anything goes', from total neglect of widows by relatives to total dispossession by the husband's relatives, irrespective of the Qu'ran. The few who are not dispossessed are fortunate.

The dialogue concerning the condition of Nigerian widows centres on both inheritance and the customary 'punishment' of widows following the death of their husbands. At a seminar on 'Traditional Practices of Widowhood in Calabar', organized by the Catholic Women's Organization of the Calabar Diocese in August 1986, there were extensive discussions of how widows are accused of the death of their husbands and victimized, tortured and generally regarded as unacceptable in society. They are made to sit on ashes, dress in sacks, go without food or a bath, and forced to eat from broken plates.

A Nigerian Widows' Association (NISA) was formed in Lagos in 1943. Its president Agnes Ibekwe describes it as a non-religious voluntary organization to provide a forum for Nigerian widows.

Discriminatory tax laws

Discriminatory tax laws is an issue one might expect the Nigerian Labour Congress (NLC) or the NLC Working Women's Wing to take up, but this has not been the case. The issue has, in fact, become a priority for the Federation of Women Lawyers (FIDA). It is a rare example of how professional clout, irrespective of class differences, can be applied for the general advantage of women. American women lawyers, for example, have used this kind of professional clout to the advantage of less privileged women. There we find middle-class women lawyers banding together to defend, with some success, women accused of murdering husbands who have abused, battered and 'damaged' them.

The facts and figures published by FIDA in 1987 show that the annual tax for a typical man is 305 naira, while that for a typical woman is 660 naira. In other words, a woman pays twice as much as a man who earns the same salary.[6] Under the old taxation system, both personal and dependent relatives' allowances were claimed by both men and women, but spouse's and children's allowances could be claimed only by men. Mothers who are widowed, separated, divorced or single must show proof of their status by a letter from their children's father and, where applicable, provide a death certificate or Decree Absolute. The 1987 Tax Relief Law provides an increase in the spouse's allowance (from 300 to 500 naira) and an increase (from 250 to 400 naira per child) for the children's allowance for up to four children.

Women's protests against the discriminatory tax laws intensified, with FIDA pointing out that the relief is not really a 'spouse' allowance but a 'wife' allowance, since females are ineligible for the allowance. The requirement for proof of status puts women under the control of ex-husbands and subjects them to the caprices of tax officials, who decide whether or not they should be granted relief. FIDA's strategy for fighting this campaign includes collecting signatures and presenting them to the Minister of Finance.

Hawking and street trading

Women, harassed and discriminated against in paid employment, are treated no more respectfully in other ventures in which they find themselves struggling to make ends meet. As hawkers and petty traders, whether in a stall or on the streets, they are harassed by council workers around garbage-filled gutters and roadsides. War Against Indiscipline (WAI) preachers and urban sanitation preachers pick on street traders as scapegoats.

In most cases, women street traders are widows with small children. Their trays contain small items that fetch about 50 naira. Since only a fraction of the contents are sold each day, a woman's earnings are about 10–20 naira per day. It is a trade that results from a dire need of cash to supplement what the women produce at home from their own creative economic efforts. In reality, it is struggle, and women 'make do', as child care and poor health allow. If there is a husband in the picture, he is usually unemployed, sick or infirm. In such families, older children often combine street trading with schooling.

In the metropolis and its suburbs, street trading provides a complete mobile market. The trade, which was peaceful and lively in the past, is dominated by women selling processed food and petty commodities: soap, ballpoint pens, matches, cigarettes, talcum powder. Everyone patronizes the street sellers, even task force officials and the police. Some commentators have pointed out the irony that street traders are harassed on Martins, Marina and Broad Streets, the financial backbone of the country, where 'a lot of financial transactions, legal and illegal, take place all around. In fact the whole area is a money market zone – millions cross hands here, so why should street traders who want quick disposal of their wares for quick and meagre returns not be allowed to transact a straightforward business of selling and buying?'[7]

The Illegal Market Edict is ineffective, given the socio-economic context. It has resulted in victimization of the disadvantaged and powerless, the abuse of young girls and women, and further corruption of government officials. A similar edict, enacted in 1953 in Ibadan, the largest indigenous African city south of the Sahara, also proved a failure. The colonial Lieutenant-Governor of the Western Region, T. M. Shankland, signed into law the Ibadan District Native Authority (Control of Street Trading) Rules in 1953. According to the edict, 'No person shall erect stalls or sell, hawk, or expose for sale any wares within five feet of the edge of any road or street.' Conviction carried a fine of 12 shillings or fourteen days' imprisonment.

This prompts us to question a thesis held by some southern African scholars that, during West African integration into the capitalist system, the colonialists were not interested in the movement of Africans but in the cash crops they brought to the trading posts.[8] These scholars have contrasted the vibrancy of West African cities with those of southern Africa, where the colonialists were more interested in the management of labour than of commodities – as can be seen from the pass laws and labour reserves. Thus, in southern Africa, all cultural life was managed by the authorities. This control bred alcoholism, violence and various forms of urban anomie. The labour reserves, coupled with apartheid, resulted in political management of geographical space, which has meant that Africans have no social claims to the city centres. Thandika Mkandawire concludes:

> The remarkable and paradoxical thing about all this is how much of it has persisted after independence. And even more paradoxical is that post-independence governments have not sought to come to grips with this historical heritage. Instead, a number of them have sought to 'maintain standards' – a euphemism for maintaining the urban status quo, which is, in our case, the 'apartheid model of urbanisation'.[9]

Basic facts about street trading, apart from its being an institutionalized cultural heritage, include its economic rationality. Most street traders are poor and illiterate. Their earnings are not enough to hire shops, which rent for 30 to 100 naira a month. For those who can pay rent, the waiting list for stalls stretches to years since not enough market stalls are provided by the municipal or local governments. This has worked in favour of government officials who take bribes and force some women to pay for stalls with their 'bottom' (bodies). In Ibadan, as in Lagos, it is the economic nerve centre of the city that suffers the 'menace' of street traders.

In spite of the enormous amount of energy devoted to their trade, by the end of 1986, only a month after the International Monetary Fund (IMF) imposed the second-tier foreign exchange market, the families of street traders and other poor families were just about surviving by sticking strictly to basic dietary needs and not wants. As their spending power diminished, even basic necessities were eliminated. Frozen fish or beans replaced meat. Gari or millet replaced semolina and rice. In some families, children ate beans three times a day. Chewing sticks replaced toothpaste and brushes; local soda replaced detergent powder. For some, boiled eggs replaced meat. Local black soap replaced soap tablets. Some now used shea butter instead of vaseline on their skin.

When these poorly fed women are not eking out a living street selling, they are employed by the state governments in the name of environmental sanitation to sweep public places, including those special zones where they may not trade. Armed with baskets and brooms, they clear paper and empty cans and boxes of drinks and whatever else litters the streets. In many towns, the women do not live in the cities but come from the suburbs or nearby villages. Those who do live in the cities live in shanty areas. Many are elderly. They are paid 70 naira a month. In River and Anambra states, their equipment consists of rakes, brushes, wheelbarrows and an orange reflective rubber jacket. (So much for the traditional dignity of the African mother or female elder, the daughters of the Goddess!)

Drug-trafficking

It is within the socio-economic context of poor Nigerian women that the issue of women's involvement in crime and drug-trafficking must be examined. The growing economic hardship has worsened gender relations and intensified the abuse of women. When men are not verbally abusing women, they are physically beating them up for not meeting economic expectations. Any redress open through the law court depends on the personal disposition of the judges, who often put aside legal judgments and pass moral ones, especially in the case of drug-trafficking.

There are some exceptions. For example, in one case, a judge acquitted a housewife who killed her husband in self-defence. According to the judge, 'She has not used more force than was necessary in the circumstances to preserve her life.'[10] The twenty-seven-year-old woman claimed that her husband had returned from a drinking spree and asked her for food. When she said that there was no food to be cooked, a fight had ensued. Her husband held her by the throat, and in self-defence, she took a piece of wood and hit him on the forehead. He died the same day.

Another woman faced with the same problem might have felt forced to procure something to cook, only to earn another kind of judgement by Nigerian men:

> I had always held women in great esteem, but now no longer, particularly some of the so-called modern women. For example, today, what is the difference between a prostitute and a housewife? There is practically no difference, and that is not what it used to be. Take a woman who goes to bed with any man who gives her a certain amount of cash. You agree that she is a prostitute. Then take another woman who does not actually accept cash but lets boy friends pay her rent or buy things for her. Now is there any real difference between that girl and the first girl? That's what happens between a husband and wife in modern setting.[11]

In another letter, the attack on women is even more vicious:

> For the past three years, we have been witnessing the fact that some women have made crime a full-time occupation or part and parcel of their character through robbery, drug trafficking, prostitution, smuggling, forgery, fraud, and murder. We also have reports of women abandoning innocent babies; in most cases, the abandoned babies are usually dumped in the most unhealthy places – dust-bins, bush, river banks, and toilets. Such behaviour really negates the pride and importance of womanhood.[12]

The figures concerning people involved in drug-trafficking, categorized by sex or by the amount of drugs trafficked, indicate that women are not the culprits we have been made to believe. The media and the magistrates punish women more for the use they have made of their vaginas than for the actual crime of trafficking.

Under the Buhari/Idiagbon regime (1983–85), drug-trafficking carried the death penalty. This has since been altered to court sentences involving different terms of imprisonment, a change which is generally believed to have increased the incidence of trafficking.[13] Those arrested increased from twenty-five in 1985 to 119 in 1986. Profits have also increased. For example, the value of twenty-five drug seizures in 1985 was 4.545 million naira. The value of 116 seizures in 1986 was 36.965 million naira. Twenty-two males and four females were arrested in 1985, seventy-five males and forty-six females in 1986.

By 1988, the picture was beginning to change as the national culture was also changing. Drug-trafficking was seen as a part of international criminal cartels necessitating co-operative action. On 2 November 1987, Nigeria and the United States signed the Mutual Law Enforcement Agreement, making for more efficient tackling of narcotics. Between January and June 1988, 146 traffickers were arrested, bringing the number of arrests between 1984 and June 1988 to a toal of 516; and ninety-nine were women, while 417 were men.[14]

According to figures from the Murtala Muhammed airport security agents, in 1985, six of those arrested concealed the drug on their persons, eleven in their anuses, four in their hand luggage, one in his/her shoe sole and two in stockings. In 1986, twenty-seven of those arrested concealed the drug on their persons, sixty in anuses, twenty-one in hand luggage, five in their shoe soles, five in kettle flasks, and one in the luggage. If 'persons' mean women's vaginas, then it seems that the anus supersedes the vagina as a vehicle for carrying drugs.

The problem of drug-trafficking has been linked to financial gain, which in fact applies only to male traffickers and drug barons; male traffickers were caught with 2.4 kg of cocaine valued at 2.4 million naira, much more than the few grammes for which women were being sent to prison. Many of the women were couriers for men, 'mules', and have found themselves serving long terms in foreign prisons. By July 1990, Holloway, a women's prison in north London, held forty-two West African women, said to be mostly from Nigeria. Out of the 317 women sentenced in England and Wales in 30 June 1989, more than half are claimed to be from Nigeria, Ghana and Jamaica.[15] Many of the women involved are illiterate and believed that they were carrying harmless white powder, or were duped into taking a bag for someone. Some swallow condoms full of drugs which sometimes rupture and kill the courier.[16] Other reasons stated for trafficking include economic hardship and unemployment. The burden of family responsibilities has also been cited as well as ignorance of the long jail sentences for the crime – anything from four to fourteen years.

While customs officers detain their stereotypical African woman drug mule, it is reported that 'suited businessmen with attache cases slip through with much larger quantities of drugs'. Harry Fletcher, assistant general secretary of the National Association of Probation Officers, said in 1990 that these women are 'the exploited pawns of the drug barons and are being pushed as if they were master criminals'.[17] Heightened awareness and co-operation have led to a shift in favour of community involvement in drug prevention programmes, thus encouraging voluntary groups and women's organizations such as Nigeria's International Women Lawyers to join the fight against drugs.

Land appropriation

Land is to the rural grassroots farmer as cow and oxen are to the pastoralist. Most rural Nigerian women are involved in the farm on which their subsistence economy is based. Just as we see petty traders being squeezed out of the city centres by big business and bureaucratic elites, we also find women in the villages losing access to farmland and vegetable gardens as a result of a new culture of big-time farming by urban elites. This has resulted in a situation where rural communities find themselves seeking redress from the people who are dispossessing them of their lands. The case of the Uzo-Uwani LGA, one of the least 'developed' LGAs in Anambra state, is a good example of this trend.[18]

In 1986, thousands of villagers who had lost their farmlands to land speculators sent urgent appeals to the state governor to stop the land-grabbers. They stressed that acquisition of the land violated the 1978 Land-Use Decree. Unfortunately, those involved were so powerful that they could falsify certificates of occupancy to indicate that the land was acquired before the Land-Use Decree became effective. They were exposed, however, by the fact that some of the companies that bought the lands were not viable legal entities before the decree. Their survey plans also showed the Onitsha–Adani expressway, which did not come into existence until 1982–83. Some of the land speculators acquired more than 100 hectares in a single customary right of occupancy from the local government authority, without reference to or approval by the state military governor. Some of the lawyers who managed the deals were not qualified in the year that the buyers claimed to have bought the lands.

One of the affected villages expressed its fear that people were being turned into 'beggars and wanderers' in their own land. Another community warned that the sale of its land would sentence future generations to 'slavery', as land is the principal source of survival and subsistence. The villagers reminded the military governor that the Anambra River Basin and Rural Development Authority took about 10,000 hectares of their land for rice projects, yet what the villagers cultivate are yams, maize, cassava and other tubers. In 1973, this particular community had in fact decided to invest the power to sell land in their community as a whole and not in sections of that community or in any particular individuals.

The questions these communities put to the government were: Who were the vendors, and what were their ages in 1978? When were these farmlands actually leased or sold? Who was the lawyer that executed the deeds of conveyance? What were the companies that bought or leased the farmlands? Were the companies in existence in 1978? Seventy companies had taken over at least one square mile. The protest against this land appropriation involved the members of the town union, their sons in other parts of the country, the local ruler, and some age grades, which threatened to use force to stop 'greedy and disgruntled elements who lease/sell land to speculators'.

This and other cases reported from all over the country indicate the growing force of rural capitalism, through which poor men and women are losing their means of livelihood. It also exposes the multicultural and multiethnic networks of the powerful, which link various elite groups – titled men, local chiefs, those in business, government and the bureaucracy – in economic, social and political self-interest.

Ordination of women

In 1984, the Synod of the Anglican Church voted in favour of ordaining women priests. The Episcopal Church in the USA and the Anglican Church in Canada have ordained 1,250 women priests since the early 1970s; New Zealand and Hong Kong have also ordained women into the priesthood. In 1986, however, the Church of England's General Synod ruled that women ordained as priests within the Anglican Church abroad could not conduct services in Britain. Catholic Rome has said that the ordination of women poses an obstacle to an eventual reunion between Rome and the Anglican Church, which was set up in 1534 with the repudiation of the authority of Rome.

In 1986, the United Church of Canada decided to include female images in the Bible in response to demands by feminists in Canada, USA and Britain, who protested the male domination of Christianity. One example they cited was that, in the English translation of the Bible, God equals male, although in Hebrew and Greek the word is genderless. The

Hebrew word Elohim for God is plural in form, and Yaweh, which means Jehovah, has no male connotation.

What is the position of Nigerian men in this debate on the representation of women in religion? The Archbishop of Ibadan and Primate of the Anglican Church of Nigeria, Reverend Timothy Olufosoye, has pursued an argument based on prejudice.[19] He fears that if women are made priests, they will also demand to be made bishops, and there has never been a female bishop in the history of the episcopate. According to Olufosoye, Jesus chose twelve disciples, and they were all male. He points out that women themselves believe they are unclean during menstruation and cannot enter a place of worship, let alone be priests at the altar consecrating bread and wine for holy communion and offering benediction. 'Will married women be accepted?' he asked. 'What about pregnancy?' Since theological colleges are male institutions, 'Where will women be trained?' In the Anglican Church in Nigeria, a deaconess can perform quasi-priestly functions. As such, she can baptize children, conduct church services, preach sermons and lead prayer sessions, but she cannot administer communion.

At a seminar organized by Women in Church and the Society of the World Council of Churches, held in August and September of 1986 in Zimbabwe, rural and peripheral urban women leaders in Africa called on church leaders to ordain women priests who have the calling and the necessary qualifications.[20] The debate which followed the recommendations of the seminar was so heated that it drew a rejoinder from a newspaper columnist who set out the history of the Christian priesthood, its patriarchal Jewish origin, and the concept of priesthood from the New Testament.[21]

> The point I wish to drive home is that women should stop splitting hair over the question of priesthood in the 'churches'. Women Christians are priests, as the word 'priest' is a generic term which refers to all Christians. Some people give the present-day priesthood in the church a different interpretation as if we are still under the Levi era of the Old Testament.[22]

More recently, following the Anglicans' Lambeth Conference of 1988, there was a wide survey of the opinions of religious leaders in Nigeria concerning the ordination of women.[23] Reverend Jeremiah Iroakazi Egekwu of God Church, Owerri, made the point that Jewish cultural prejudice against women is reproduced in the Old Testament. 'The Bible seems to be against women being priests, but this is not so. On the day of the Pentecost, believers went to Jerusalem and there 120 men and women were baptised. Women were there when Jesus died. When he was resurrected, it was women who took the message to the disciples.'

Pastor Simon Job Okochi, president of the Seventh-Day Adventist Church in Rivers state, said:

> From all indications, there is a strong opposition to women in the priesthood and the reason is that throughout the ministry of Christ, Jesus had a lot of women but none of them was ordained. So ordaining them would amount to going beyond what Jesus himself did ... I have yet to come across any portion of the Bible that authorizes it.

The most contradictory statement came from Dr Godfrey Otubu, Baba Aladura, Chief Priest of the Eternal Sacred Order of Cherubin and Seraphim and member of the national executive committee of the Christian Association of Nigeria (CAN). He is quoted as saying: 'There are restrictions that they must learn in silence. Women who have issue of blood [who are menstruating] cannot enter the prayer house, not to talk of the chancery. The same thing applies eight days after she delivers a baby.' Yet Otobu's church is one where women have made the greatest inroads in spiritual leadership and mass participation, although the church's finances and general administration are controlled by men.

The survey also sounded the opinion of Nigerian Muslims. Prominent Nigerian Muslim novelist Zaynab Alkali pointed out that men have interpreted the Qu'ran and Hadith as it suits them and in a way demeaning to Muslim women. For Muslim men and those of the Sufi sects, theological differences centre on doctrine and not gender. Muslims do not contemplate a debate on possible demands by women to become Imams.

Men's commitment to self-interest and privilege can be seen in their determination to retain control of their exclusive networks and clubs. It is revealing that of the two controversial issues debated at Lambeth, implementation of which was left to individual dioceses, it was polygyny that the African churches were quick to adopt and implement, while they collectively opposed the issue of women's ordination. Only weeks after the Lambeth Conference, the Nigerian Anglican Church endorsed polygamy and adopted Resolution LC 88/26 on the 'Church and Polygamy', which Bishop Ajayi Crowther, the first African bishop, first talked about in 1888. In August 1988, African bishops claimed that it was adopted with the calculated purpose of holding its converts against the attractions of Islam. The church was in fact regularizing what has been happening, since African men never gave up polygyny.

The argument from the African bishops against the acceptance of women into the priesthood was that there were more pressing priorities for the church in the Third World: hunger and poverty, development, debt crisis, liberation struggles. Clearly, these men, whose forefathers were sons of the Goddess, did not see the representation and participation of women in the power structures of the church as part of the struggle for liberation and democracy.

Data presented in this chapter show that while government officials and international agencies send out policy statements and reports which are full of grandiose plans and promises of women's development, it is women's organizations and civic groups which are taking on the implementation of many of these development programmes. We also find that formalized developmentalist rhetoric does not capture the complexity of issues and areas of women's oppression in contemporary Nigeria. The picture changes when focus is shifted from the top to the ground and we experience a high level of civil discourse and debate on issues of women's rights in education, property and inheritance, tax laws, trading, the justice system and the priesthood.

This focus on civil discourse continues in the next chapter which examines the issue of class and gender in child abuse in Nigeria.

Notes

1. *Guardian*, 23 September 1986.

2. *Guardian*, 20 September 1986.

3. *Guardian*, 18 February 1987. This is a good example of how daughters of the establishment 'sell out' other women in their single-minded determination to perform efficiently.

4. *Guardian*, 4 March 1987. While in the 1980s in Anambra state the concern was to encourage female education, today it seems that the present governor is more interested in how to increase male enrolment. Chinwoke Mbadinuju, in an interview in *The News*, 6 September 1999, revealed his plan to introduce a compulsory free education programme from primary to secondary school by the next school year, with the stated hope of bringing male children to school, rather than an intention to increase general enrolment.

5. *Guardian*, 30 July 1986.

6. *Guardian*, 18 February 1987.

7. 'The Survival World of Street Traders', *Guardian*, Sunday Supplement, 13 July 1986.

8. See, for example, Thandika Mkandawire, 'Letter from West Africa', *Southern Africa Political and Economic Monthly* 7, April 1988.

9. Ibid.

10. *Sunday Tribune*, 10 August 1986.

11. *Daily Star*, 25 August 1986.

12. Ibid.

13. *Guardian*, 16 January 1987.

14. 'Narcotics Arrests hit all time high', *Newbreed*, 2 October 1988.

15. 'Foreign drug "mules" swell female jails', and 'Pawns in drug traffickers' game of chance', *Guardian* (London), 30 July 1990.

16. 'Third drug "mule" dies as packets burst', *Guardian* (London), 10 November 1992.

17. 'Foreign drug "mules" swell female jails', *Guardian* (London), 30 July 1990.

18. *National Concord*, 24 September 1986.

19. *Guardian*, 12 April 1987.

20. *Weekly Star*, 21 September 1986.

21. In support he cited Exodus 28: 1; 40: 12–25; Hebrews 7: 14–28; Timothy 2: 9–15. The reference in Exodus claims that the everlasting priesthood was given to Aaron and his sons. In the Hebrews reference, it is the Son who is consecrated for ever. In the First Epistle of Paul to Timothy (2: 9–15), women are to learn in silence. They should not teach. They should be silent and not usurp authority over men. For the transgression of Eve, women can seek salvation through child-bearing, 'if they continue in faith and charity and holiness with sobriety'.

22. *Daily Star*, 15 October 1986.

23. This and subsequent quotations in this section appeared in *African Guardian*, 5 September 1988.

6. Class and gender in child abuse

This chapter picks up the topic of child abuse, particularly child marriage, and makes connections between this issue and the abuse of women in general. Few will deny the irony that in this age of globalized campaigns for human rights, individual and societal abuses against children have been on the increase. In the past few years, publicized cases of sexual abuse of children in both Britain and the USA have shown that abusers in these western countries come from all classes and ethnic groups. They are nearly always men.

Child abuse in Nigeria has its own complexity and reflects new structures of patriarchal and class privilege, thus pointing to an economic factor: victims tend to come from poor families. Research into child labour reveals that underage hawkers, street sellers, housemaids and apprentice mechanics have often been pushed into the marketplace by parents who need the extra earnings to supplement family income.[1] The children suffer physical, mental and psychological damage including stunted growth (from head-loading), malnutrition and fatigue from long working hours. Mental damage also results from the child's knowledge of injustice and abuse. Such powerless and unprotected children also suffer overt abuse: sexual abuse, flogging, early marriage. Some children work in unsuitable surroundings – brothels, for example. Others serve as domestics for families of the privileged classes.

In indigenous customary law on child abuse and neglect, some commentators have stated that there are no clearly formulated and enforceable legal rules, except moral condemnation.[2] A child abuser would be regarded as unfit to look after children. His or her 'wickedness' would be seen as a family trait, and the family would be perceived as unfit to be married into. Under general law, which consists primarily of received English law and local statutes, common law stipulates that the employment of extra help is the responsibility of the wife. A father is under no legal obligation to pay third parties for necessities supplied to his child. Three concepts are introduced here: the patriarchal, authoritarian western concept of the husband and father as an unaccountable and distant head of the family; the privileges of the legitimate or legal child as the only one worthy of protection; and the wife as the first domestic servant of the family (who may employ additional servants). Here we have clear evidence of the legalized disempowerment of women and children.

Under statutory rule, the Children and Young Persons Act of 1943 has its roots in the Victorian concept of the monogamous family. The Act deals with children 'in need of care and protection' – protection from begging; protection from association with prostitutes, criminals or thieves – and children who are ill-treated, neglected or in the care of drunken or wicked parents. This can be compared to the problems that have arisen out of the child sex-abuse cases in Britain with a provision intended only for the removal of innocent children from guilty parents, not for disputes between parents. There has been no revision of legislation since Nigerian independence.

The rhetoric of women's organizations against marriage and inheritance laws does not include demands for changes in the Children and Young Persons Act. Instead of effective legislation, the Ministry of Social Development, Youth and Sports was contemplating a child welfare policy. This was announced at the third biennial conference of the African Network for the Prevention and Protection of the Nigerian Child Against Abuse and Neglect in October 1988.[3] The policy is intended to fulfil the United Nations mandate on the rights of the child. As we know, policy is not legislation.

Trade in children

One of the consequences of the absence of enforceable legal rules against child abuse has been the growing commercialization of child labour. Child labour is a big business. There is, for example, the notorious case of 'slave trade' in Ukelle in the Ogoja LGA of Cross River state.[4] The seriousness of the case forced the government to set up an investigative committee. Wanokom, Wanikade and Wanishem were the villages hardest hit. Influential men there used the poor as buying agents. About 2,000 children under the age of fifteen disappeared, reportedly sold to people in the Shagamu area in Ogun state. Children who were not sold were used for slave labour at a fee of 20–50 naira a month. Recruiters usually received six months' payment in advance.

According to the clan head of North Ukelle: 'Dealers visit the village very late at night and lure away children who have been brainwashed about an unseen "utopian" paradise somewhere.' Some children seem to have left without the knowledge or consent of their parents. Others were sold by their parents, whose compensation ranged from a head of tobacco to 50–80 naira a year per child. The monthly payment of 20–50 naira means that recruiters make 150 per cent profit on each child procured. In 1981–82, one villager claimed that they had more than twenty-six teachers. In 1987, the exodus of children had reduced this number to six. In this theft of children, many are lost, and parents are sometimes seen making fruitless journeys in search of their children.

It was not the government but the local communities and their diaspora community at Lagos who devised strategies to arrest the outflow of village children. Their strategies included fines for those who were caught, alerting police posts to search lorries for children, and recruiters were ordered to return children. But recruiters began to move at night and early morning to avoid the 'eagle-eyed villagers'. Some willing children have also been known to trek 25 kilometres of bush paths or have escaped on bikes and motorbikes. Ogun state is reported to be the base of three traders in child labour. The strongest children are usually sent to cocoa plantations in the three western states; the rest are employed in households in Ibadan and Lagos as domestics.

Child marriage

Closely associated with child abuse and the trade in children is child marriage which, in the present 'modern' setting, has lost most of the traditional and customary rules that governed this practice in pre-colonial African societies. By this I mean strong sex taboos and initiation rituals under the control of uncorrupted matriarchs (daughters of the Goddess), functioning in autonomous women's systems. This is hardly the case in so-called traditional practices today. A few incidents in 1986 and 1987 which involved the deaths of very young girls shocked many in the nation into articulating a collective opposition to child marriage.

It was during this heightened consciousness that a chief medical officer pointed out that the custom of early child marriage cuts across ethnic groups, religion and traditions. He had witnessed 'the mounting deaths resulting from the delinquency and recklessness of our privileged men, who impregnate unripe and biologically underdeveloped girls'.[5] He cited the case of a child named Fatima, who was engaged at the age of nine and married at the age of twelve. It was this early marriage which caused Fatima's vesico vaginal fistulae (VVF), perforation of the bladder into the vagina, which results in the uncontrollable drainage of urine into the open space. He knew of more than 5,000 such cases in the northern Nigerian town of Kano alone.

VVF is one of the ailments to which young wives are susceptible due to early childbirth, because the pelvis is not sufficiently developed to allow the passage of a child's head through the vaginal canal. This results in prolonged labour and a trapped foetus. Long-term consequences include incontinence and infertility. At a seminar where some of these facts were reported by medical specialists, the UNICEF representative in Nigeria confirmed that Nigeria's maternal mortality rate is one of the highest in the 'developing countries', despite a large investment in medical care and dedicated staff.

In 1982, a draft presented to the House of Representatives on the marital age of Nigerian youths was suppressed by powerful elements from the northern Nigerian states.[6] However, in 1987, the death of twelve-year-old Hauwa Abubakar of Sokoto state due to punishment meted out to her for daring to run away from the old man her father had married her to, resurrected the debate. This time the Nigerian media and some national women's organizations were determined to politicize the case.

The story of Hauwa, child heroine Hauwa Abubakar of Sokoto state was nine years old when she was betrothed to Mallam Shehu Kiriwa, a cattle farmer from Bena village in the Zuru LGA of Sokoto state. At the age of twelve, Hauwa was forced to live with Shehu. When Hauwa ran away from her marital home, Shehu asserted his authority by meting out punishment. He began to cut off her fingers. In November 1986, after Hauwa ran away for the second time and had been taken back to Shehu by her parents, Shehu decided to chop off her legs. Hauwa was not deterred and continued to resist her marriage by refusing to eat.

Hauwa's wounds became infected. She was rushed to the local hospital which referred her case to the Sokoto University Teaching Hospital (SUTH). Her father, Malam Abubakar, continued to move the girl between herbal healers and local clinics within the local vicinity, however, and it was not until 8 January 1987 that Hauwa was rushed to SUTH. By then it was far too late, and she died on 4 March 1987. Shehu was charged with culpable homicide by the Sokoto state police. Hauwa's father (whose family had been sustained by Shehu for three years) had found it difficult to condemn Shehu and explained his daughter's death as the will of Allah. Indeed, he asked that the case be tried in a Sharia court according to Islamic law.

In an interview, the doctor who treated Hauwa in the paediatric department at SUTH corrected some of the media's misrepresentations of the case. According to the doctor, Hauwa's legs had not been completely chopped off by Shehu, but the doctor had recommended amputation because of the massive infection. He also reported that Hauwa's rejection of food was a normal consequence of the shock of amputation and not a hunger strike.[7]

Public response to Hauwa's murder   In addition to the haphazard casting of blame, there was a general anger at the failure of women's organizations to take legal action and a counter-response by feminists to that criticism. More important was the debate on women's health and reproductive rights which this incident opened up. There was an open attack on the power elites such as judges, lawyers, heads of state and policemen who in order to drive the attack home, were referred to as the elder brethren. It was not expected that those who perpetrate barbarism in the name of privilege would willingly give up that privilege. In this case, young men were also angry at the old men and seemed more open to change.

In one letter, which was widely quoted, a woman invited the NCWS to sell her jewellery to provide funds for a prosecution:

> I am highly disgusted by the barbaric and Satanic murder of twelve-year-old Hauwa because she refused to marry an old man forced on her by her parents. The incident is a dirty slap on our National Council of Women Societies. If the NCWS or its President, Mrs. Hilda Adefarasin, cannot afford the legal fees to hire a lawyer to effect the prosecution of Shehu, the alleged 'husband-murderer', I hereby offer my jewelry to be sold and its proceeds used to fight this out through a civilised process. The expected victory will redeem our name and serve as a deterrent to the Shehus of this country.[8]

Another, open letter to Hilda Adefarasin, President of NCWS, read:

> I am writing you this letter in your double role as the president of the National Council of Women Societies and secondly as a mother. This letter is prompted by your tacit consent over the Hauwa issue. One would have expected the NCWS to have issued a statement condemning the murder of this innocent girl. And at least on a rhetorical level, ask the authorities to bring to book all those that have a hand in the killing of Hauwa. Though she is dead, one fights the cause of the dead to make the living live. But as of this writing there has been no press statement, no petition – not even a passing mention ... of indignation against the murder of someone you claimed it is your duty to look after. All we have is silence, silence, and more deafening silence.[9]

Hauwa's death also drew the attention of Amma Ogan, editor of the highly acclaimed *Sunday Guardian*. She remarked on the surprising fact that it was young men who responded to Hauwa's case in 'libber'-like language, and she attributed this to the fact that they, better than older men who have 'savoured the pleasures of a multi-cultural marriage system', are more inclined to welcome change. Recalling her experience as a correspondent in the National Assembly during the Second Republic, Ogan noted that the legislature, which functioned as a male cartel, threw out a motion which sought to institutionalize the law of bigamy and codify a recognized form of marriage which would allow either partner to challenge the other on bigamy. This was done with the active support of token females who feared losing out to co-wives. As Ogan said: 'In those days of the Second Republic, where money bubbled like champagne, the air, for many confident law-makers and hard-nosed women, was conducive to marriages of all kinds.'[10]

In response to these letters of criticism, NCWS president Hilda Adefarasin declared that the council had no *locus standi* to prosecute. She did not understand the fuss over this particular case, since there were many such cases. As one newspaper report stated: 'The NCWS president preferred to be circumspect on comments regarding Hauwa because of the sensitivity of the case and the possibility that she might be stepping on toes.'[11]

Men who spoke out gave some feminists a chance to charge collective guilt in the crime. Newspaper columnist and university lecturer, Professor Molara Ogundipe-Leslie, called Nigerian men 'women-hecklers'. She pointed out the negative coverage of women's activities, the constant attacks on women activists, and listed several instances of denial of existing social facts:

> We are told daily that women in Nigeria are totally liberated, having no problems whatsoever except those created by alienated and Oyinbo-nised Nigerian women of the butter-eating class who want to bring poisonous foreign values into our African paradise. It is a mystery how the case of Hauwa can occur in such a free country as ours, where women are not generally given in child marriages, forced marriages, or marriage sales known as bride price in which women are tagged for education, youth, and fecundity, and never in the south of the country, either. How could Hauwa's case have occurred in a country where women are no longer genitally mutilated in the name of culture in rites of female circumcision, whether they are educated or not, rural or urban; where no Sharia court exists which will make Abubakar [Shehu Kiriwa], the "father-husband" suffer only slight punishment, if at all, while his kind of mentality is not produced in large numbers by a social system which spawns his type; in a country where, as FOMWAN [the Federation of Muslim Women's Association of Nigeria] declared, women have been liberated under the Sharia law for thousands of years; a country where widows are not subjected to various forms of social, psychological, and economic terrorism by their husband's families even in modern settings. It really beggars the mind how the case of Hauwa could be.

The truth is that there are many and similar Hauwa cases which happen unseen and unheard. Instead of rallying with women to improve the realities of the condition of women in Nigeria, instead of struggling together with women as fellow citizens to stamp out injustice and tyranny wherever they appear in our society, and not to men only, most of our menfolk spend their time attacking and demoralizing women, within and outside organizations.[12]

Response of women's organizations The position of the International Federation of Women Lawyers (FIDA) was clear. They would press charges. The Federation of Muslim Women's Associations of Nigeria (FOMWAN), very much in line with its conservative counterpart NCWS, stated that Hauwa's was one of many such cases and pointed out that there is no stipulated marital age in the Qu'ran, although it emphasizes maturity in and consent by both partners. Significantly, those who spoke from FOMWAN did so anonymously. They believed that poverty and ignorance were primarily to blame for early marriages. These women – they would not call themselves socialists or Marxists – claimed that rich people in the north would never give their daughters in marriage as early as twelve. They believed that child marriage would continue as long as social conditions existed compelling people to submit to others, and that no law would change the system until something drastic was done to improve social conditions.

All these comments have touched on gender and class analysis, which shows the consequences of class differences among women in the various organizations. In contemporary society, you have a submissive class of domestics serving elite women. Like the 'father-husbands', elite women are also guilty of using young children in domestic and extra-domestic employment.

An important fact which came to light in the debate over Hauwa's murder is that virgin marriage means early marriage. Some of the consequences of early child-bearing include the figure of 20,000 cases of VVF in Kano state alone. The NCWS' response was to build a 3-million-naira treatment and rehabilitation centre for VVF patients in northern Nigeria.

Nationwide response to the crime against Hauwa led to a series of seminars and conferences all over the country. At a conference in April 1987 at Minna in Niger state, the Committee on Women and Development condemned forced marriages and suggested eighteen as the minimum age for brides. The women also condemned what they termed the inhuman treatment of widows – for example, shaving their hair with pieces of broken bottle. They questioned the practice of giving custody of children to men. They called for access to loans and modern agricultural technology for women, since they produce about 80 per cent of the country's food supply. They called for a decree to facilitate the acquisition of land by women. They called on the government to implement the UN convention on the elimination of discrimination against women.

The response of the relatively more radical women's organization, Women in Nigeria (WIN), was different. WIN had its northern branches press murder charges against both Hauwa's so-called husband and her father. At its annual conference in March 1987 at Calabar, Cross River state, WIN called on the government to ban traditional and customary practices which sustained the oppression of women – for example, forced marriage. They too called for a minimum age for marriage of eighteen, and for free and compulsory education for children as outlined in the UN's Declaration of Universal Human Rights. The national organization demanded that Mallam Shehu Kiriwa be prosecuted for the murder of Hauwa Abubakar. To immortalize her, WIN launched a nationwide Hauwa Abubakar Memorial Campaign against child abuse and forced marriage.

Having made an analysis of the socio-economic causes of the problem, WIN called on the government to review its Structural Adjustment Programme to ameliorate the burden on women. They pointed out that inflation had weakened the purchasing power of poor farmers and workers and made life more difficult for women who are responsible for feeding the household. They asked that the government repeal the minimum wage amendment decree and refrain from raising fuel prices. They also pointed out the tax disparity between men and women and demanded a uniform tax policy.

The conference did not omit criticism of WIN as an elite organization and called on members to create an alternative vision for dealing with the oppression and liberation of rural women. WIN was to create conditions for both rural and urban women to work together. As a result, WIN resolved to work on community projects which centred round the immediate needs of women. Members made plans to help improve the skills of rural women through informal adult education schemes and to sensitize the public and the government about illnesses peculiar to women, especially the victims of VVF in Kaduna state.

Also as a result of Hauwa's case, young male journalists probed more into such abusive practices and related issues. *African Concord* carried a feature on child-wives, pointing out that it was common practice in many parts of the country, especially in the Nigerian northern states of Niger, Katsina, Sokoto, Kaduna, Kano and Bauchi.[13] In Kano, for example, 68 per cent of women were married when they were under fourteen years of age. This, of course, meant that girls were withdrawn from school – if they were sent to school at all. At a school in Daura, local government officials revealed that of the 132 pioneer pupils in 1980, only forty completed secondary school. Most of those who left were girls about to be married. Among many ethnic groups in Nigeria, particularly the Igbo, Urhobo and Ibibio, the demands of western education finally overrode the customary practice of child marriage.

An interview with officials of WIN revealed that its northern branches have been offering legal aid and advice to girls who wish to divorce husbands forced on them. Sometimes they have had to fight village heads as well as parents and husbands. Asebe Musa, a young girl whose father had died, had been cared for by her village head who felt that he could retrieve money spent on her through a forced marriage. The Kaduna state WIN branch helped Asebe secure a court ruling against the marriage, and she was able to return to school.

The Kano state branch of NCWS and the Ministry of Social Welfare worked together in a campaign against early and forced marriages. Although there were some successes in urban centres, the practice proved difficult to tackle in the villages.

The problems caused by the practices are both medical and social. The incontinence associated with VVF as a result of a perforated anus and torn vagina results in a constant dripping of urine through the birth canal, which causes offensive odour. A young girl suffering from VVF is shunned by her husband and by society. Only a few lucky ones get to a hospital; most are hidden away in the villages or end up begging on the streets. There is usually a long wait for a bed and treatment, which may involve a series of operations over long periods of time. Much of the damage is never corrected.

Young girls are also victims of recto-vaginal fistula (RVF), where the rectum is perforated into the vaginal tract. This means the leakage of both faeces and urine. When this occurs, doctors sometimes have to make an opening in the abdomen for the passage of faeces.

A new operating theatre at the Murtala Mohammed Hospital (MMH) in Kano eased the wait of more than 1,000 VVF patients living on hospital floors. MMH had been operating on only one VVF victim a day; with the addition of the new theatre, VVF operations increased to between two to four a day. The NCWS also planned a rehabilitation centre for VVF patients, where they would be educated and taught skills so they could take care of themselves. This appears to be the equivalent of a village quarantine house to which incurable VVF victims are banished.

Medical treatment for VVF and RVF does not necessarily mean a happy ending, since in many cases incisions reopen. Some girls can have up to two or three VVF operations and end up with a colostomy. These young women usually have complicated deliveries and often lose their babies. Financial responsibility for them falls to their parents or to themselves, since many are rejected by both their husband and their family.

Early and forced marriages also contribute to the high rate of divorce and prostitution. As with certain forms of circumcision (see Chapter 7), what is at issue is the control of female sexuality. Some people believe, for example, that delaying marriage for girls encourages sexual promiscuity. Islam, which prescribes marriage after a girl's ninth menstrual cycle, also insists that the couple consent to marriage and that a girl, even if married, must be sexually mature prior to intercourse. Islamic Malik law authorizes a father to give a daughter in marriage.

At the Nigerian Law Review seminar in 1986, the NCWS proposed eighteen as the minimum marriage age for girls. That would keep girls in secondary school until they are well into their teens. The general consensus was that education is the best answer to the problem of early or forced marriage. Scholarly research in some northern Muslim towns, although acknowledging the special emphasis Islam places on the status of women and the protections it provides for them, also points to education and urban migration as modernizing and emancipating forces opening opportunities and expanding life choices (Coles 1983, 1984; Callaway 1986, 1987; Callaway and Creevy 1994).

Teenage pregnancy and abortion

Physical damage because of early pregnancy is not confined to child wives but applies equally to the general problem of teenage pregnancy. Young girls with unwanted pregnancies run the same risks of physical damage during childbirth or as a result of crude and ineffective abortion practices. According to the director of the Planned Parenthood Federation of Nigeria (PPFN), about 50,000 teenage girls find themselves with unwanted pregnancies every year,[14] but the very large number of illegal abortions make such statistics only an estimation. Even so, there is a high incidence of abandoned babies. Commissioners and ministers of health and departments of social studies at various universities are informed about these facts and make public statements about the problem without proposing government policy.

The increased number of school drop-outs because of poverty has a strong correlation with teenage pregnancy. According to a social scientist at the University of Lagos, thousands of young girls are forced to fend for themselves early in life. They take jobs as waitresses or in petrol stations; occupations that expose them to men. The parents of such children often encourage their association with men. The president of the NCWS blames old men who pick up teenagers from the street for small sums of money. They corrupt the girls, who are mostly naive and ignorant, and they disappear when the girl becomes pregnant. Others blame the general corruption of a post-war, oil-boom consumer economy and a materialistic culture. Women are also used as symbols to reflect a man's wealth.

Without legal and free abortion, many frightened and desperate girls attempt to abort their unwanted foetus with sharp instruments or what an Enugu doctor described as 'superficial contraceptives' – sugar, purgatives, potassium, salt or codeine. Such methods frequently result in serious damage to the girls.

Abandoned babies

Closely related to the problem of sexual abuse of immature girls is the issue of abandoned babies, which, in patriarchal language, is referred to as 'the brutal killing of innocent babies'. It is not unusual to find this sort of entry in the daily paper: 'This inhuman action is the height of inhumanity to human and an ungrateful act to God by some of our wicked female folk.' In some cases, search parties ravage the area where a baby is abandoned to track down 'the heartless mother'.[15]

Given the multi-dimensional sources of the problem, the incidence of abandoned babies is of course very high. Indeed, there is evidence to suggest it is a growing problem. Statistics from Anambra, Imo and Rivers states indicate that more than 190 babies were abandoned between 1978 and 1985. Figures from the social welfare division of the plateau state Ministry of Information showed that in Jos at least four children a month were abandoned by their mothers,[16] and these are only the reported cases. Most of the abandoned babies were a day old when found – usually in motor parks, railway stations, makeshift bridges and hospitals. Some are found strangled or dead from dehydration.

As with other social issues, there is no state policy dealing with abandoned babies, other than a general call for intensification of family planning and the usual public appeals to assist poor parents, especially those with triplets and quadruplets. A state commissioner for information and social development observed: 'If the public and charitable organizations do not help in alleviating the problems faced by these parents, others in similar circumstances might be compelled to abandon their children.'[17]

The lack of government policy and law on these issues and the absence of a state welfare system means that voluntary organizations pick up the pieces. Suggested solutions to teenage pregnancy usually include sex education, counselling and provision of contraceptives. The YWCA, for example, provides education, counselling and accommodation for teen-agers who have dropped out of school. The NCWS provides similar services, as well as instruction in domestic sciences, dyeing, dress-making and cooking.

This chapter has looked at the complex issue of child abuse in Nigeria: child labour, trade in children, child marriage, teenage pregnancy, abortion and abandoned babies. The data presented show that all these problems have a socio-economic explanation and relate very much to class inequality between women. While the evidence shows public awareness and pas-sionate civil debate about issues of women's oppression, the state remains ineffective and almost invisible as an instrument for effecting citizens' rights and the social contract. Although we see how the responses to campaign issues reveal the differences in political awareness and political interests of the various women's groups, it is these voluntary women's organizations that are responding to campaign issues rather than the Nigerian govern-ment.

The same pattern can be seen in the next chapter which discusses other controversial issues of women's reproductive health and repro-ductive rights, from both a local and an international point of view, including African, European, Christian and African Islamic perspectives.

Notes

1. Emeka Okara, 'Child Abuse', *Daily Star*, 30 July 1986.

2. E. I. Nwogwugwu, 'Legal Dimensions of Child Abuse and Neglect', *Daily Star*, 12 November 1986.

3. *New Outlook*, 30 October 1988.

4. *Guardian*, 8 February 1987; *Guardian*, 15 April 1987.

5. *Guardian*, 7 December 1986.

6. *Guardian*, 19 April 1987.

7. *This Week*, vol. 3, no. 12, 23 March 1987.

8. *Guardian*, 13 April 1987.

9. *Guardian*, 13 March 1987.

10. *Guardian*, 29 March 1987.

11. Ibid.

12. M. Ogundipe-Leslie, 'Hauwa Is Everybody's Problem', *Guardian*, 23 March, 1987.

13. *African Concord*, 7 April 1987.

14. *Newswatch*, 26 January 1987.

15. *Weekly Star*, 26 October 1986.

16. *Guardian*, 13 September 1986.

17. Ibid.

Sources

Callaway, Barbara, 1986, *Education and the Emancipation of Hausa Muslim Women in Nigeria*, Working Paper no. 129, Michigan: Michigan State University, Office of Women in International Development.

— 1987, *Muslim Hausa Women in Nigeria: Tradition and Change.* Syracuse, NY : Syracuse University Press.

Callaway, Barbara and Lucy Creevey, 1994, *The Heritage of Islam: Women, Religion, and Politics in West Africa.* Boulder, CO: Lynne Rienner.

Coles, Catherine M., 1984, 'Muslim Women in Town: Social Change among The Hausa of Northern Nigeria', PhD thesis. University of Wisconsin-Madison, University Microfilms International.

— 1983, 'Urban Muslim Women and Social Change in Northern Nigeria', Working Paper no. 19, Michigan: Michigan State University, Office of Women in International Development.

Coles, Catherine and Beverly Mack (eds), 1991, *Hausa Women in the Twentieth Century.* Madison: University of Wisconsin Press.

7. Women's health care and discourses on reproductive health

It cannot be stressed too often that it is important to keep in mind the specific viewpoints of native and local Africans in understanding and utilizing available information about reproductive health. It is essential that African women's reproductive health needs are addressed in culturally appropriate plans of action so that they can take charge of matters concerning their health and the health and welfare of their children.

Local African discourse on these matters contrasts with western concern about single issues. These now dominate discourses on what used to be a general interest in women's well-being, referred to as women's health care, the popular term used before the current concern about women's reproductive rights. The interest has shifted from general health care surrounding pregnancy and birth to more controversial single issues relating to the genitalia and reproductive sex, such as circumcision and genital mutilations, abortion, contraception, rape and prostitution.

This chapter deals with some of these controversial issues, giving the facts as argued by various local interests in Nigeria, as well as the supposed traditional African explanations for practices related to women's reproductive health and reproductive rights. It includes the involvement of women's groups in articulating how Nigerian women perceive their reproductive needs, and strategies of power for women for reproductive health. The approach is discursive and comparative, including African, European, Christian and African Islamic perspectives. By employing a structuralist and class analysis, that is, by identifying the logic of the system, I hope to demonstrate the socio-economic basis of the abuse of both women and children, the ideological falsifications used to deny the material reality, and how all these issues are linked and can therefore be understood within a broad framework which subjects all related factors and interested parties to critical evaluation.

Bride-price

In the discourse regarding the abuse of women, it becomes even more clear how the language of culture and ritual is falsified with shifts in historical contexts in order to maintain absolute control over women and female sexuality. With the loss of traditional women's rituals of collective solidarity, new and false validating claims are constructed in the context of change. In the case of child marriage, fear of women turning to prostitution was one of the reasons given for the early marriage of girls. We see this excuse used again in the debate on bride-price.

Within our living memory, we have witnessed changes in old institutions. We have, for example, seen how bride-price (and its variants such as dowry and bride service), a traditional custom of kinship exchange, redistribution and filiation through marriage payments, has been reduced to the 'pricing and selling' of women in the name of marriage, which is how feminists have attacked the practice. Most of what is done today as a 'traditional practice' is a distorted mixture of old customs, practised out of context. Old institutions and old economies have changed as they have been affected by the post-Nigeria–Biafra war (1967–70) economy and its changing cultures. Social ceremonies have been affected by the general inflation, yet traditional custom still requires parents to give their daughters marriage gifts. These gifts directly influence what Nigerians call bride-price, but it is in fact only part of a marriage payment.

The high and growing cost of bride-price has been the subject of intense and heated public debate in male-dominated modern institutions such as churches, town unions and the government. It is only recently that women's organizations have joined the debate. During my field work in 1986, the bride-price of a wife was something like 5,000–7,000 naira for teachers and nurses, 8,000 naira and more for graduates. The government of eastern Nigeria, under Michael Okpara, reduced bride-price to almost nothing in 1960 when a flat rate of 60 naira was decreed. Unfortunately, the attempt failed because only Jehovah's Witnesses abided by the reduction.

Where bride-price is low, the added expenses are usually high. For this reason, the Methodist Church in Imo state decided to fix bride-price at 500 naira and to remove the non-monetary gifts (gas stoves, refrigerators, television sets). Abriba state required that bride-price be 7 naira for all girls and that there be no additional expenses. Abriba communities cannot afford high bride-price since they practise mass weddings involving up to 500 couples. In other Igbo societies, individual communities also appear to be limiting the costs of weddings: one community in the Ideato LGA in Imo state, for example, has forbidden beer and hot drinks and allows only palm wine. It has also set up a bride-price review committee.

Female analysts who have joined in the bride-price debate have had a different view of the problem, maintaining that it is a selfish concern of men.[1] They contend that there is no reputable study that shows that high bride-price causes prostitution (men had claimed that high bride-price prevented them from marrying, suggesting that women were being left 'on the shelf' and thus turning to prostitution).

During this debate in 1986, the wife of the military governor of Anambra state spoke on the role of women in the 'war against indiscipline' and called on women's organizations to help reduce bride-price and expenses associated with marriage ceremonies. She cited the case of Umuoji, where women had helped to influence the local ruler, the Igwe, and the community to reduce bride-price. She ended her speech with an attack on women: 'A situation where we abandon our children every Saturday to attend extravagant ceremonies, cannot make for healthy development of the society.'[2] From the controversy that hit Enugwu-Ukwu in 1986 over its new marriage law, it is doubtful that women of Umuoji truly influenced the decision of the local ruler. Indeed, the Enugwu-Ukwu case revealed the divisions in the male establishment in the rural communities. The interest group that these laws affected – that is, women – is not part of the decision-making process.

After the Igwe of Enugwu-Ukwu declared his own 'free marriage' laws, the Town Development Union issued a statement:

> The Enugwu-Ukwu Community Development Union [ECDU] wishes to dissociate itself from the recent announcement by Igwe Osita Agwuna over bride-price in Enugwu-Ukwu. The announcement was an arbitrary decision made by the Igwe, without consultation with the town union, the village unions, and women's organizations in Enugwu-Ukwu, so that the announcement, when it came, took Enugwu-Ukwu people unaware. The ECDU wishes to remind the Igwe that he cannot make any Marriage Law for the town without due consultation with – and, indeed, the consent of – the majority of the relevant bodies, particularly the women who give birth to and nurture daughters to marriageable age.
>
> 'Free marriage' in Enugwu-Ukwu, as the Igwe pretends to advocate, is quite untenable, as it can encourage a situation where Enugwu-Ukwu daughters can be picked like mangos, without parental consent or knowledge. The ECDU therefore advocates a bride-price within the reach of bachelors and will set up a committee to approach relevant groups and organizations in Enugwu-Ukwu to collect their views. The recommendations of this committee will be forwarded to the Igwe in due course.
>
> Furthermore, the ECDU believes the Igwe's over-orchestrated announcement is part of his scheme to raise money for his private use in the launching of a book entitled *Marriage without Tears*, scheduled at his

Obuofonri on Saturday 30th August 1986. The invitation card and the supporting campaign clearly state that the proceeds of this launching will be used to support the Obuofonri Museum, which is solely owned by Igwe Osita Agwuna. It is therefore clear that Igwe Osita Agwuna has no sympathy for bachelors, but only wants to capitalise on the bride-price issue to launch a book and make money …

All citizens, relations, and friends of Enugwu-Ukwu are strongly advised to ignore the launching of any book at the Obuofonri on Saturday 30th August 1986 or any other date.[3]

Prostitution

The increase in prostitution is in reality directly linked to the general deterioration of the economy and the hardship and moral deterioration that the government's Structural Adjustment Programmes have unleashed on the poor. In prostitution, we have another example of the cost to women of class privileges. It is from the accounts of conflicts between prostitutes and their clients that one begins to gain an insight into the decadence and meanness of many wealthy Nigerian men. In most cases, young girls and women are abandoned with children unprovided for. In many cases, prostitutes are not paid, but humiliated and abused after they have provided sexual service.

Because of the direct economic relationship between women and prostitution, we find that prostitutes are mostly mothers – widows, divorcees and unemployed teenagers. Most Nigerian female prostitutes go into the business to raise the capital to begin a trade or to educate their children. Many 'retire' after they have achieved their goals, and many become 'somebody'. The post-colonial culture in Nigeria is such that 'money talks' – i.e. wealth is respected, regardless of the means by which it has been acquired.

A feature article on prostitution had this to say about the booming business of the trade in sex:

The frontier of commercial sex seems steadily on the increase. It is to be supposed that the Acquired Immune Deficiency Syndrome [AIDS] plus harsh economic times would mean less casual and promiscuous sex. Right? Well, quite wrong. Despite AIDS and the bite of the economy, prostitution is an industry on the upward swing in a country where easy sex has become a staple necessity.[4]

Among the new classes of prostitutes mentioned are students in institutions of higher education, graduates, workers and businesswomen. They are described as part-time prostitutes who bring a new sophistication and professional touch to the business. There is obviously competition between the old-fashioned prostitutes and the new sleek strategists who operate in the clubs, hotels and houses of the upper classes, while the traditional types eke out a living in the shanty areas and back streets of the cities.

The same article describes Lagos as 'the country's capital of dingy sex'. In most cities, prostitutes are concentrated in the 'desolate and highly populated slummy areas'. Such areas in Lagos include Ajegunle, Amukoko, Okokomaiko, OrileIganmu, Maroko, Ketu and Agege:

> So common has prostitution become, and so widespread, that some are unable to see a distinction between prostitutes and those who are not. In Akure, the capital of the cocoa-producing Ondo State, residential prostitutes are scarcely to be found. Yet girls, especially students of secondary schools, colleges of education, as well as workers, can be seen laundering their boredom at drinking and eating places, waiting for customers.

In many of the hotels, male waiters and porters operate as pimps, pairing off male lodgers with girls. Prostitutes are forbidden to enter the hotel lobbies, except when they are with men. Lodgers who desire the services of call-girls find the security men eager to make arrangements. As a male waiter at the Owena Motel in Akure said: 'The very young, pretty, and educated girls are having a field day here. This is because the hotel is always fully booked. The cocoa trade attracts many rich businessmen.'

It is not only pimps who profit from the sexual abuse of women. Landlords too make handsome profits; more than the prostitutes make, in fact. In 1987, in the high concentration areas, prostitutes charged 5–10 naira; in popular hotels, the rate was 30–100 naira. Out of this, prostitutes must pay 10–15 naira a day for a room in the slums and 20–30 naira a day in the big hotels. A landlord's return for renting rooms to prostitutes was 300–1,000 naira a month. With this kind of profit, landlords are able to convert their houses to hotels and brothels, thereby causing a shortage of rental accommodation for the general public in the cities.

There are also reports of the conditions of teenage drop-outs, and those from homes where domestic discipline has collapsed, walking the streets aimlessly without money and being forced into prostitution by sex-hungry men. Some of them are described as so desperate that they quite innocently ask for no more than food, a drink, or money for a taxi, and 'a place to lay their heads for a night or two before commencing a directionless journey through the streets'.

Among those prostitutes who are 'more polished' and referred to as 'club girls' are undergraduates paying their way through college and unemployed university graduates. They earn about 200 naira a month and shift base according to the shift of power in government:

The luring of students into prostitution became quite fashionable during the flamboyant days of the Second Republic. 1004 [1004 Estate, Victoria Island, Lagos], the official abode of federal legislators, became 'Mecca' to many female students. The legislators went for teenage undergraduates, whom they took on tours abroad or kept in expensive hotels at government expense. When the politicians fell from grace, most of their courtesans decamped to military officers.

Some of the girls were earning up to 5,000 naira a month. They spent weekends in Paris, London or New York. In these liaisons, material and immaterial wealth – for example, business contracts and classified information – are exchanged for sex. Some of the women set up their own businesses, factories or manufacturing industries. Some gained political office. It was this culture which gave rise to the term 'bottom power'. I have heard bitter male intellectuals quote women as saying, 'I have this country in my vagina!'[5]

Sections 223, 224 and 225 of the Criminal Code prohibit brothels and prostitution and carry a penalty of six months' to two years' imprisonment if convicted. From media reports, only poor women are harassed under this law.

For prostitutes who do not end up as wives of elite men, there is no pension. The fates awaiting 'old broken whores' include 'selling odd items, merchandise or giving their body to old customers who drop in for old times' sake. For these hags, the price of a life of prostitution is already a painful reality' according to the *African Guardian*'s article on prostitution.

It is not only women who render sexual services to the privileged classes in an unequal relationship, however. There are also underprivileged men prostituting themselves, servicing powerful and wealthy men. In one report on homosexuality in Nigeria, we learn that it was the imperialist patriarchs of the different colonial rulers in Africa – first the Arabs and then British government officials, priests, teachers and traders – who 'introduced' Nigerian men to homosexuality. In both cases, the colonialists initially left their wives behind and used local men as domestic servants and sexual partners. It was a master–servant relationship typical of wifehood in a strong patriarchy, which is typical of the colonialists' cultures.

By 1940, many of these boys had completed their 'homosexual tutelage' and set up businesses in most northern urban centres as full-time professional homosexuals. This is the origin of the Hausa institution of *Dan Daudu*. *Yan Daudu* [plural] are men who dress in women's clothes, talk like women, cook and sell food and generally run brothels from whence both male and female prostitutes can be hired on payment of a commission.[6]

The *Yan Daudu* not only pimp, they also train young boys and girls in prostitution. The girls are primarily child-brides who have run away.

Female homosexuality (*Madiko* in Hausa), according to the same article, is supposed to be a feature of the upper middle class and the feudal oligarchy:

> It is particularly prevalent among the wives of traditional rulers, business-men, and high-ranking bureaucrats. But unlike male homosexuality [called *Ludu* in Hausa], the partners in the relationship are usually their peers, almost of the same age bracket and social and economic status. Sometimes, they are even wives of the same husband. Of course, the practice of teenage forced marriage to husbands of advanced age as well as polygamy encourage *Madiko* in various ways.

The incidence of lesbianism, when compared to male homosexuality, is seen as a temporary or transient occurrence, however, especially in the case of girls in all-female hostels and boarding schools. Girls claim they had such a relationship because they were afraid of getting pregnant while at school or because of fear based on cruel stories about men. With 'maturity', they are said to reject lesbianism.

The inequality between male homosexual partners can be seen in the fact that those providing the service are young, handsome, smartly dressed and perfumed. They are students, clerks, middle-level public servants, unemployed graduates and so on. Those paying for their services are much older, traditional title-holders, prominent politicians, high-ranking bureau-crats, university administrators, religious leaders, businessmen, college principals and top military officers. It is 'a club of exotic sex, swirling wealth, double-crossings, swaps, and spine-chilling intrigues'.

According to the *African Guardian*: young male homosexual prostitutes 'flaunt their flashy, sleek cars, their designer shoes and dresses, and carry themselves with a conspicuous presence. Because their wealthy clients never hold back monetary and other material gifts, these young gays spend money with reckless prodigality and live a life that is often brutish, nasty, and short.'

The same young men are said to 'go after girls with the same hunger with which their gay seniors come after them'. And of these 'seniors', it is said:

> After attaining a level of immersion in homosexuality, some of these men cease to have any meaningful use for women. Some homosexuals who occasionally socialise with women are known to prefer anal intercourse. In Kano, most prostitutes have had to undergo orientation into anal sex so as to cater to the new tastes and retain their increasingly homosexual clientele … Several unstable marriages have been linked to homosexuality.

Very much like the 'club girls', these young men may say that they have the country in their anus, as many of them, for the secrets they keep, claim a high price – limousines, houses, expensive trips abroad.

There are a few myths and beliefs used by men to justify their masculinism, patriarchal monopolies and homosexuality. Their analysis, I am sure, will intrigue feminist and social science theorists. It is said, for example, that homosexuals are more prosperous than heterosexuals. It is also said that sex with a mad woman or a domestic animal is a magical route to riches.

More than the reported cases of depression, anxiety and alcoholism among homosexuals are the reported consequences for women of anal intercourse. They include typhoid, hepatitis, syphilis, incontinence and AIDS. Even in the face of an AIDS epidemic, patriarchal authority reigns above reason. The position of the Catholic Church was made clear by the Archbishop of Lagos, Dr Olubunmi Okogie, who cited the Sixth Commandment (Thou shalt not commit adultery) as the only way to deal with the problem. He stated categorically that priests cannot say, 'Use a condom'.[7] As the archbishop was making these pronouncements, there were reports of two women becoming the 'first' AIDS victims. Both women were said to be of 'easy virtue'.[8] This was, ironically, some fifteen months after a report of the death of six patients from AIDS at University College Hospital, Ibadan.[9] (AIDS is, in fact, rendered in the vernacular as 'woman disease'. Indeed, any venereal disease is called 'woman disease'.)

Homosexuality, unlike female prostitution, to the traditional African remains a thing of revulsion: 'Homosexuals are like lepers. It is a taboo and a dirty subject to talk about.' The report also claims that it is practised more openly in the Islamicized areas of the north than in other parts of Nigeria.

Rape

It is in the act of rape that we see embodied the fundamental principle governing all these abuses. In Nigeria, it usually takes a horrendous experience to shock the nation into public statements and debates. The Ahamadu Bello University (ABU) rape cases of 1986 provide a good example. During the students' demonstration in April of that year, the police shot a number of students and also raped female students. Jane Bryce theorizes that men rape because:

> Men are almost universally socialized to treasure their virility, which by definition means their power, the strength to enforce their will by all the means available, including the physical. It is no accident that one of the highest terms of approbation in Nigeria is 'virile'. We seek a virile govern-

ment, a virile press, a virile education system, a virile language, a virile economy.[10]

Among the users and promoters of this masculine language of dominance and power are educated elite women. The problems resulting from this are fundamental and destructive. It goes along with what I have called the 'performance syndrome'.

What happened at ABU was not a simple case of rape but a symbolic enactment of anger, competition and inferiority complexes on the part of the men. The class inferiority complex of the police meant that the women were seen as prized objects of the rich and thus objects of hate, resentment and defilement.

On university campuses, this antagonism was sharpest during the oil boom period, especially during the First and Second Republics. Male students on the campuses had begun to lose girlfriends to wealthy men of the establishment and, in retaliation, they began to despise and abuse female students. A case in point was the Lady Ibiam Solidarity Front (LISOF) of 1985. Gender relations on the campus had become so bitter that a few female students decided to form a front which would look into the roots of the problem. They planned to invite men for discussions on how to bring about a more cordial relationship. The men's response was to band together and unleash violent verbal and physical attacks on the women. The women were so demoralized that they disbanded LISOF.[11]

Apart from specific cases of violence against women, the rape of women goes on daily in different contexts. DANSANDA, the police newsletter, recorded 2,796 cases of rape and indecent assault in 1985 even though such incidents are not usually reported to the police.[12] Other organized rape incidents involve 'Yandaba', ' terrorists' in Kano, who are described as members of a gang of criminals who carry out burglaries, rape and abduction of wives. They also function as paid assassins.[13]

On this subject of rape, we have a paradoxical situation in which African realism and tolerance, which works quite well when faced with difficult and unpleasant choices, is countered by hypocritical western bourgeois sensibility with its roots in conservative Judeo-Christian morality. Africa has seen many wars and disasters since colonization and after, and has had to face the tragedies of war-gang-rape of women. This is a good case to use when discussing traditional African attitudes and solutions to forced pregnancy and the question of abortion. In post-civil war Rwanda, when babies of rape victims were being born, how did the international agencies handle the situation and what specific choices were the African women themselves making?

Much as civil discourses on rights focus on legislation, rigid state regulation is not a characteristic of African traditional societies and cultures as it is of capitalist formations and imperialism. The reports at the time of the Rwandan crisis led us to understand that thousands of both Tutsi and Hutu women and girls were being raped by Hutu soldiers and militiamen and also by Tutsi-led rebels in their counter-offensive. Women were either massacred or raped. They reacted with shame and concealment. Only now are hospitals exposing the facts as women come in for treatment; hospital workers report that nearly all the women reject their pregnancy, preferring the babies to die, and making a direct association between the crime and their repulsion. They wanted abortion or, like many Nigerian teenagers, carried out self-abortions risking infection and death. Some simply ran away from the babies after birth. Suicidal feelings and guilt were reported as common characteristics of these our sisters.

Where such a powerful organization such as the UN Security Council was forced to recognized war rape as a crime against humanity, the Catholic Church, to which most of these women belong, insists on birth and love and care. Catholic nuns are taking the rejected babies who thus become tagged and categorized, whereas in the traditional cyclic or re-cycling system, the principle of tolerance meant that they would quickly melt into large family compounds under the identity of compound names, or their mothers would find security in marriages and kinship systems, or have an abortion that would not be mentioned. In any case, such tragedies did not happen on such a huge scale.

Here then is a good case to contrast with what is going on in the USA today where men tell women what to do with their bodies and their values and aspirations. Anti-abortion violence took the form of murder for the first time on 10 March 1993 at the Pensacola Women's Medical Services when Michael F. Griffin shot and killed Dr David Gunn. There have been more anti-abortion killings since then, including the deaths of two women workers at a women's health clinic in Boston in December 1994.

The question is, of course, what these murders are about; whether they are about the upholding of morality, which is contested anyway since there are many moralities, or whether the issue is about power over women's reproductive rights and sexuality. One thing is clear, though: it is not for the love of the babies, since conservative church morality is to force the women to go full term and then give away the baby. So the issue is really the right of the woman to choose what is best for her.

Family planning

The term 'family planning' is another manifestation of African realism and the principle of tolerance, for it has come to include abortion practice.

Even the fast-growing Christian fundamentalists in Nigeria pretend they do not know that abortion is carried out under the guise of the more acceptable term 'family planning'.

Unfortunately, promotion of family planning in Africa is associated with fears about rapid population growth, hence the attack on cultural beliefs and the causes and consequences of the high demand for children and the low demand for contraception (Acsadi et al 1990; David 1974). Even Islam, we are told, is not opposed to family planning since Islam has always been concerned with child spacing and family planning, even in the absence of compelling population pressures (Omran 1992).

Official anxiety about the population explosion in Africa has led to the scapegoating of women and the abuse of their bodies by exposing them to drugs and contraceptives already banned in the West. A draft copy of the National Population Policy gives a general picture of population trends in contemporary Nigeria. Infant mortality stood at 90 out of every 1,000 children born. In the 1960s, it was 187 out of every 1,000 children born. The death rate was 13–16 for every 1,000 persons. In the 1960s, it was 27. This means an increase in life expectancy from thirty-seven to fifty years. The 1960s population growth rate was 2.5 per cent; it is now 3.3 per cent. If this rate continues, Nigeria's population is projected to be 280 million by the year 2015, which would make it the most populous nation in Africa and the tenth most populous nation in the world. The draft did not recommend a population-control policy but left the choice of family planning to the individual.[14] This means that there are no government policies recommending health monitoring of contraceptive users.

Where does this leave women? Data from the UN International Children's Emergency Fund (UNICEF) show that 65,000 women die in pregnancy and childbirth yearly in Nigeria. Some 200,000 children under five years old lose their mothers each year.[15] Other figures indicate that the average Nigerian woman has seven pregnancies, and 10 per cent of Nigerian women die in childbirth. The dangers of childbirth result from mothers being too young or too old or their pregnancies being too close or too many.

Ben Gyepi-Garbrah, a demographic consultant to the World Bank, confirmed that all the countries in the sub-Saharan African region now have population or family planning policies and programmes, while in 1974, only four countries had such programmes. He praised Africans for their good progress in birth control, and called for additional family planning methods to be introduced.[16] Nevertheless, contraceptives should not be the means of checking the fertility of African women because of fear of population explosion. World Bank studies have shown that it is the education and political participation of women which reduce the birth rate. A World Bank 1993 publication on a cross-national study based on data on seventy-two developing countries shows that doubling the enrolment in female secondary education and improved health and family planning services reduce fertility and mortality considerably. To talk about the status of children and mothers is to be concerned about the health and welfare of women and children, and one cannot do so without acknowledging the fact that these issues are linked to illiteracy and discrimination in education and training – experiences which are needed to motivate meaningful and relevant change.

Speaking at a UNICEF workshop on the status of children and mothers in Nigeria, the Minister of Social Development, Youth and Sports, Air Commodore Bayo Lawal, indicated grave concern about the health and welfare of women and children: 'As long as women remain illiterate and are subjected to discrimination in education and training, the motivation for change so badly needed to improve the quality of life for all will fail.'[17] In the formalized rhetoric, there were the usual proclamations about programmes and projects to promote the welfare and development of women and children and the usual financial assistance from international agencies. UNICEF, for example, announced that it was giving $42 million dollars (US) for the five-year period from 1986 to 1990. The chief of general staff had earlier announced a comprehensive social development policy to ensure the welfare of women and children: 'We need to visualise women's position as they grapple with the running of our homes with appropriate technology and resources, bringing up our children and trying to improve their lot and achieve self-fulfilment.'[18]

It is interesting to note that reports about these policies on women never discuss the effectiveness of existing machinery or structures for implementation of the new policy. Further analysis shows some contradictions in the concern expressed about the health and welfare of women. On the one hand, there is a formal reinforcement of the patriarchal family, with its ideal wife and mother; on the other hand, the policies usually make women responsible for family planning, regardless of its cost to their autonomy and health.

In March 1987, the state hijacked what was universally regarded as a Women's Day and turned it into a Family Week, supervising and monopolizing the activities which took place. At the end of the event, the government pledged to pursue programmes which would improve the family. Air Commodore Lawal pledged that the Ministry of Social Development, Youth, and Sports would implement programmes – e.g. Women and development, training and daycare centres – to forge a stable family system. The then Minister of Education, Jibril Aminu, advised family heads to ensure the unity of their families, pointing out that the family was a fundamental organization of society. Family Week ended with a carnival involving family units, voluntary organizations, market women, school-children and students. Lawal and Aminu led the carnival procession in what was a very symbolic expression of state patriarchy.[19]

In the concern about women's health, the contradictory positions taken on the contraceptive drug Depo-Provera are instructive. Depo-Provera is widely used in Third World countries. Documented side-effects include amenorrhoea, heavy bleeding, irregular bleeding and waist pain, head-aches, weight gain, dizziness and abdominal discomfort. In spite of these serious side-effects, however, the head of the department of obstetrics and gynaecology at University College Hospital, Ibadan, O. A. Ladipo, claimed that the advantages of the injectable contraceptive far outweigh its side-effects, and use of the drug should be encouraged. A single injec-tion, it is pointed out, gives virtually complete protection from pregnancy for three months, whereas the pill must be taken daily.[20]

General market surveys indicate that Depo-Provera is also the cheapest available contraceptive.[21] In November 1986, condoms cost 10 kobo apiece at family planning clinics and 5 naira for three at chemists' shops. One month's supply of pills cost 1 naira at family planning clinics and 10–15 naira at chemists' shops. Loops and coils each cost 1 naira and are inserted at no charge at family planning clinics; they cost 30 naira, plus an addi-tional 100 naira for insertion, at chemists' shops. Diaphragms cost 5 naira each at the family planning clinic and 20 naira at chemists' shops. Depo-Provera injections, which last for up to six months, cost 3 naira at the family planning clinic and 5 naira at chemists' shops.

In December 1986, a new report revealed that the injectable contra-ceptive was known to cause cancer.[22] It was banned in Nigeria ten years after it had been outlawed in Europe and America. The drug was intro-duced into Nigeria in 1970 by Upjohn, an American company. About 286,941 units were distributed by the United Nations Fund for Population Activities (UNFPA) between 1970 and 1986, followed by a further 235,000 units. The United States Food and Drug Administration (USFDA) notified the Nigerian Ministry of Health in 1978 that the drug had been banned in the USA because it had been linked to benign and malignant breast tumours in dogs and endometrial cancer in monkeys. It also caused irregular menstruation, which necessitated the administration of oestrogen (itself an additional risk). In additon, there is a risk of malformation if the drug fails and pregnancy occurs. In other words, the risks outweighed the benefits.

The main lobby against use of the drug consisted of feminists, con-sumers and government scientists. The World Health Organization Toxicology Review Panel, the International Medical Advisory Panel of the International Planned Parenthood Federation (IPPF), and the American College of Obstetrics and Gynecology approved the drug on grounds that epidemiological research and twenty years of use by humans had not shown any severe side-effects. In March 1987, the Nigerian government set up a committee to review use of the drug.

In the debate that ensued concerning the safety of female contraceptives, women pointed out that campaigns on family planning were usually directed at them, although men are the greatest obstacle to the acceptance and practice of family planning in all African societies. Men fear female infidelity and believe that pregnancy will expose it. As we have seen in the cases of teenage pregnancy, however, women will take terrible risks to terminate an unwanted pregnancy. Furthermore, in actual practice, extra-marital affairs are more common among men than women.

A medical doctor pointed out that, as he put it, 'men possess the main powers of population explosion in terms of their unlimited fecundity. The Nigerian male is sexually very active and thus responsible for three to four pregnancies annually, thereby creating situations that many times end up in abortions.'[23] Experts have always pointed out that a woman, no matter how sexually active, can produce only one child annually. Thus, they argue, male contraception is the most effective, safest and simplest form of birth control. The most effective method available to men is vasectomy, a quick and simple surgical procedure carried out under local anaesthesia (and it is reversible). Other methods, which are not 100 per cent effective, include oral contraceptives to make sperm cells inactive, condoms and the hardly effective *coitus interruptus*.

In the concern about women's health, the answer is not to dump dangerous drugs such as Depo-Provera on Third World countries. Women need to be given a wide range of choices of contraceptive devices. Women need easy access to family planning clinics with adequate equipment, well co-ordinated hospital referral schemes and appropriate health education packages.

Abortion and preventive measures As I have shown over the sale or dumping of dangerous drugs in Africa, there is a wider international context involving multinational financial interests simply out for profit; as well as the other context of cultural imperialism involving western governments and development agencies. And there is yet another context of liberation movements, whether feminist and liberal or religious and fundamentalist. All have a vested interest in controlling and deciding the use of the female body according to the knowledge and power systems that they control.

Knowledge and information mean informed choices. All the available materials should be accessible to women so they can make informed decisions about their reproductive lives. However, African women usually take the position that men also need to have access to available information, since these issues result from relationships involving both men and women. It has been argued that choice should also entail the choice for preventive measures. The idea of the power to choose thus needs to be contextualized culturally, and both gender and class dimensions should be considered.

Women's health provision should include: pregnancy prevention counselling, pregnancy testing, pre-natal care, cancer screening, screening for sexually transmitted diseases, provision for health support systems for victims of rape and other forms of domestic violence, shelters for women for various problems, particularly battered women's refuges.

In vitro fertilization (IVF)

Another important issue is western advances in reproductive technologies. IVF was developed in the 1970s in Britain and the USA to treat specific cases of infertility. It is the technique whereby a woman's egg is taken out of her body and fertilized with sperm in a dish under laboratory conditions. The fertilized egg (pre-embryo) is then implanted in the womb. The world's first test-tube baby, 'Baby Louise', was born in Britain in 1978. Moral voices from churches, the general public and the state questioned and continue to question this supposed manipulation of nature.

Hot as the ethical debate surrounding IVF is (one of its two American inventors, Dr Howard Jones, said recently at a lecture at Dartmouth College that it should have been called a 'fallopian tube bypass' to make people feel more comfortable in relating it to other accepted bypass surgeries), the practice is likely to meet with less resistance from Africans than it did in the industrialized West. I suspect that this is a good example of traditional cultural beliefs and practices playing a crucial role in supporting needy and infertile women, although poor women are less likely to have the benefit of this option than the rich. A culture that gives barren women the gift of faith and hope in magical or mystery fables of 'rag-to-baby' is hardly likely to condemn the miracle of test-tube babies! Nor is a culture which believes that babies are not to be named or planned for until a specific period after they are born and have become human beings likely to be as uncompromising as modern scientific views on the personhood of a pre-embryo cell outside the womb, a developing embryo and a foetus.

However, I expect attitudes will change when faced with more contemporary issues of choice in sexual orientation. Rag-to-baby miraculous tales were most often related in connection with old or married barren women who had sought children all their lives and never had one; suddenly one day a rag placed by the river turns into a baby for them! Stigmatized or disadvantaged as such women were, they were still located within central societal norms. Such stories are not told about young women, let alone single women or lesbian women. From the reply given by Dr Jones to questions put to him at the Dartmouth College lecture, I suspect that the founders of in vitro fertilization techniques were probably quite traditional in their moral thinking, believing that they were treating infertility in conventional marriages.

A particular tendency in contemporary modern feminist discourse on women's health and empowerment would argue for a radical departure from traditional methods of system flexibility in marriage patterns which include polygamy. The fact still remains that kinship roles and adoption took care of the reallocation of men, women, children and babies, including orphans, children of rape victims and so-called illegitimate children, without fear of radical readjustment in the social institutions of society. At the moment, most African societies are not faced with such radical agendas, and, in fact, African women and couples constitute the largest number of patients in fertility clinics that they can afford. Some feminists would see as exploitation what these women see as a unique opportunity to fulfil a deep hunger for pregnancy and the experience of giving birth.

From a feminist perspective, Janice Raymond (1994) refers to the birth of Baby Louise Brown in 1978 as 'the technological made flesh'. For Raymond, interference involving the use of drugs and tools is simply medical violence against women, for it includes procedures that are dangerous, destructive, debilitating and demeaning. Surrogacy becomes 'a traffic in women's bodies'. Raymond's position would be misunderstood if it were not seen in the international context of unequal relations between North and South. As far as she is concerned, this relationship of inequality creates baby markets in the poorer countries for adoptable babies and foetuses. I think she scores a point particularly on the use of technological, contractual and degendered language to delegitimize biological motherhood by referring to mothers in technical terms as substitutes, reproductive vehicles, maternal environments and incubators, terms which imply nonparental status, while sperm that has been emitted and placed in a testtube is referred to as the biological father.

In talking about choice, one should also consider the injury done to women as experimental objects. I am in agreement with Raymond's characterization of such individualistic freedom as amoral neutrality in contractual industrialized breeding, as a particularly western ideology.

Women should be informed of the fact that the whole procedure is experimental, has a very low success rate, and involves risks such as over-stimulation of the ovaries and the development of cysts. Recent events in Britain such as the destruction of thousands of unclaimed foetuses,[24] the debate over who has the right to IVF treatment, and media involvement in and commercialization of multiple pregnancies resulting from such treatments, have focused public attention on the ethics of male techno-logical manipulation of life and birth.[25]

By separating the status of the foetus from that of the mother, western industrial society has dealt the final blow to mother-right, a notion that was tied to the knowledge systems of the daughters of the Goddess and women's power. On further discussion of these issues with my colleague Professor Ronald Green, who is director of the Dartmouth Ethics In-stitute, he argued for choice for women and the principles of tolerance and social responsibility. He felt that this choice should include female solidarity in surrogacy with effective legislation to control abuses and exploitation.

Female circumcision

I have left the issue of so-called female circumcision to the end since some feminists think this is one area in which the control and abuse of female sexuality is complete. More importantly, I wanted to demonstrate that it is not a single-issue campaign and that all areas of Nigeria face the problem of physical damage to females, either as a result of early child marriage, early teenage pregnancy, abortion, dangerous contraception, rape or female circumcision.

Scilla McLean's report (1980) claims that, in Nigeria, the major ethnic groups, the Yoruba, the Igbo and the Hausa, do practise female circum-cision, but not the Nupe or the Fulani. Also, according to Dr Nwankwo Ezeabasili, although a dying custom, female circumcision is still practised in many parts of Nigeria.[26] The Igbo *ibe ugwu*, according to Ezeabasili, involves excision of the clitoris or labia minora or both. In the Ezeagu and Idemili LGAs, circumcision involves removal of the labia minora. In the Orlu and Nkwerre LGAs it includes the excision of the clitoris. Usually this is done between seven and twenty-one days after birth and after separation of the umbilical stump. In Abakaliki, circumcision is done at puberty. In Ogbaru in Bendel state, it is done during the first month of the first pregnancy. The claim is that the cutting is done with a razor and without anaesthesia. During the operation, other parts of the body are sometimes damaged inadvertently – usually the vagina, the rectum or the urethra. Bleeding is controlled with medicinal herbs dissolved in palm oil.

Between 1973 and 1980, two Igbo doctors, V. E. Egwuatu, a consulting obstetrician and gynaecologist, and N. E. N. Agugua, a consulting paediatric surgeon, carried out a study at the University of Nigeria Teaching Hospital (UNTH) on forty-three female children and fifteen female adults treated at the hospital (Egwuatu and Agugua 1981). They found that most circumcised women require elective episiotomy at their first delivery and that an anterior episiotomy is sometimes necessary to prevent tearing of the circumcision scar. There was also a high rate of mortality among the babies, as well as a high rate of deformity – for example, implantation dermoid, a small bag-like structure caused by part of the skin being driven into the body tissue. Other problems include cryptomenorrhoea, where the symptoms of menstruation are experienced but no external bleeding occurs; chronic vaginitis or inflammation of the vagina; vulval stenosis or narrowing of the vulva; and infibulation, sealing up of the labia majora, which prevents sexual intercourse.

The UNTH researchers also reported a case involving a three-year-old patient. As a result of careless cutting, a large opening formed between her rectum and her vagina, so that faeces passed through the vagina. The damage could be corrected only by a colostomy. Here we have a three-year-old girl with a recto-vaginal fistula (RVF), the condition which often afflicts child-mothers or child-wives (see Chapter 6). The posterior wall of the vagina and the anterior wall of the rectum had been cut off during circumcision. There are also reports that a stunted penis, a genital deformity, is sometimes amputated in the mistaken belief that the child is female.

In another study, Odujinrin et al. (1989) report the random selection of 181 women from those attending the family planning clinic of the Department of Community Health, College of Medicine, University of Lagos. Of these, 84.7 per cent were aged between twenty-five and forty-four years, and most of them were Yorubas (70.7 per cent). The Edo had the highest percentage of circumcised women (76.7 per cent), followed by the Igbo (61 per cent), and the Efiks with the least (20 per cent). Studies also revealed that the Igbo and Yoruba had the highest rates of infant circumcision. Some of the respondents were reported to be aware of the consequences associated with female circumcision and it was found that the more educated the women were, the less likely they were to have their daughters circumcised. Almost all of the circumcised daughters had mothers who had also been circumcised.

A different study by B. C. Ozumba (1992) also reports a retrospective analysis of seventy-eight patients who had previously presented with acquired vaginal stenosis in a ten-year review of experience in the management of acquired gynetresia at the University of Nigeria Teaching Hospital at Enugu. It shows ritual circumcision to be its leading cause.

The medical consequences of malpractice by circumcisers are consistent, not so the reasons given for the custom. It is usually said that those who practise female circumcision in Nigeria do so to satisfy cultural/ethnic demands. However, the facts show that the custom is rationalized by false and contradictory claims. The Igbo claim that it makes females more effeminate and therefore more attractive to men. Some claim it promotes cleanliness by reducing vaginal discharge. It is also supposed to reduce women's sexual desire and thus promote their chastity and fidelity. But, as Ezeabasili notes, the fact that most of the prostitutes in Anambra state come from areas where female circumcision is obligatory makes rubbish of the claim that it stops promiscuity. The prostitution of these women is directly related to their poverty.

Medical ethics and female circumcision Those who embrace the idea of a culturally sensitive approach to eradicate the adverse effects of such traditions argue that circumcision is culturally defensible to the extent that African women have 'accepted this practice as the norm defining their culture'. They take the position, however, that physicians should be compelled by medical ethics to advise patients against the harmful consequences of infibulation in order to protect them. This culturally sensitive approach suggests double ignorance. It is saying that those who are doing it do not know what they are doing, and those who are supposed to treat the medical complications do understand what has been done, but don't know why it is done and should mind their own business. It all amounts to a clinical language devoid of meaning. In actual fact, Africans know full well what they intend to achieve as Tobe Levin (1986) pointed out years ago in her critique of Ngugi Wa Thiong'o's use of female circumcision to define Kikuyu national identity in his novel *The River Between*. Both the Kikuyu themselves and the colonizing Christian British had also seen the ritual practice as a useful instrument in a political contest to determine Kikuyu future. Women in all cases became objects in the hands of men.

When we move beyond the clinical language of diagnosis, we find that even the informed medical profession can mislead the public by the mixing up of information in pure medical jargon. We don't know exactly what is going on. For example, circumcision is usually divided into three categories of severity: (1) Sunna, the removal of the clitoral prepuce; (2) excision, the removal of the clitoris and all or part of the labia minora; and (3) infibulation, the removal of the clitoris, labia minora, and part of the medial aspect of the labia majora.

If these are varieties of the practice, in simple biological terms, it is only things outside the vaginal canal that are removed, whether prepuce, or the labia. Only in the case of infibulation, that is the least widespread, being practised in Somalia, Sudan and Mali, do we get the problem of stitching up. All three types involve medical risks of infection and complications. They also involve risk of malpractice whereby more than is intended can be removed or stitched up. Looking carefully at the data, mostly released by the medical professions (for how else would the public have access to the structure and content of the genitals of African women?), what is being reported are cases of malpractice in the procedure. What is not being reported is the percentage of malpractice. These figures are nowhere near the numbers of fistulae from child marriage. Are the fistulae circumcision-linked or do they result from an underdeveloped pelvis in young mothers?

For the eradicationists and campaign propagandists, female genital mutilation is simply a cruel and antiquated practice which has persisted uninfluenced by the 'rational and scientific ideas' of western countries; a perverted paradox in countries which value a woman's reproductive capacity and at the same time subject her to this 'hazardous' practice. Even western-dominated international agencies such as the World Health Organization have no worries in circulating statistical 'facts and figures' whose accuracy no one knows because no one will ask how they were collected. A huge money-guzzling bureaucracy has grown around this single issue, and facts and figures, brochures and campaign materials have been produced. They remain static on paper while the ground shifts in a dynamic way that no amount of bureaucracy could ever monitor. The propagandists continue to circulate the same 'facts and figures' without history.

Every year since the early 1980s when this campaign took the form of single-issue politics, we have read that the practice of female circumcision/genital mutilation is worldwide and that about 80 million young girls and women in over thirty countries of Africa, the Middle East and Southeast Asia have undergone it. We have heard claims that though the practice has strong traditional and cultural underpinnings, it has become a (world) health issue to the extent that it adversely affects the physical and mental well-being of many of the women subjected to it, resulting in the usual physical, mental and marital problems.

The misinformation is even more damaging when a clear distinction is not made between the implications of the various types of the practice for the women's sexual arousal. We are often told that clitoridectomy is the mildest form, and that even this supposed mild form should not be equated with male circumcision, since it generally involves far more extensive damage to the sexual organs, and more often has long-lasting side-effects. In its mildest form, it has been argued that a clitoridectomy is structurally analogous to the amputation of the penis.

As I understand it, the clitoris is an erotic red spot hidden at the base of the prepuce. The removal of the prepuce hood would give easier access to it. Therefore, the removal of the prepuce and even the minor labia (the two wings folded over the clitoris and the entrance to the vaginal canal) need not affect the clitoris since they are stretched and cut. Only in malpractice would more areas including the clitoris be removed.

The situation is different when the intention is to gouge out everything outside the vaginal canal in order to achieve a flatness as in the case of infibulation. This aesthetics of flatness, if this interpretation is correct, would seem to be the opposite of the appreciation of the mons veneris in European aesthetics. Those Europeans and Europeanized Africans who have worked in the Sudan and other areas where infibulation is practised tend to be more horrified and repulsed by the practice. They should constantly stress the fact that they are talking about genital mutilation and not prepuce circumcision.

I wish to be provocative and broaden this discussion by asking if more focused and concentrated erotic sensations inside the vagina and womb are achieved by the removal of the clitoris. There are obviously people for whom heterosexuality is at the centre of their identity, and lesbian women would be justified in attacking these practices from their own points of interest. Certainly statements by men from infibulating cultures point to the tightly stitched up enclosure or refusal of entry as the problem. Once the entrance is opened up, they say, they and their partners enjoy normal sex, or maybe even more sex. We may wish to compare this with revelations in Germaine Greer's *The Female Eunuch* about European women's (and, I must add, we the Europeanized African women's) ignorance of the full structure and potential of their genitalia and the tendency to fake orgasm when they even have the courage to show that they enjoy sex. I wonder how far bourgeois women have gone since *The Female Eunuch* was published in 1971? In Africa, I know we tell everyday bawdy stories and jokes about grassroots women and their loud enjoyment of sex.

It is also remarkable that writers on this subject of female circumcision are not clear about its origins and history but rely very much on the symbolic expressions of local peoples. However, reasons given by the Africans for the practice show a clear knowledge of the structure and erotic potential of the female genitalia, hence the constructed direct statements, or sometimes indirect excuses, for eliminating the prepuce 'maleness' in the female which they see as being in direct competition with the penis. These are statements about power and gendering.

O. Koso-Thomas (1987), a mature writer on the subject, stresses the point that circumcision has a strong religious and cultural base without which it would not be in existence today. It is because this base structure has for so long been shrouded with secrecy and protected by strong communal ties, that the eradication of female circumcision must, therefore, involve the social, religious and cultural transformation of certain communities, rather than overturning or uprooting this base by rapid legal decrees. Nevertheless, she believes that the medical consequences of maintaining such a tradition have become so great that the social and cultural conditions, the vectors giving rise to it, must be removed in order to ensure its eradication. Koso-Thomas knows what she is talking about because she has her country's Sande women's religion as a reference point. This women's religion, and many similar ones in traditional African cultures, makes a good case study for the comparison of women's health and rights under systems of knowledge controlled by traditional matriarchs (Amadiume 1997), daughters of the Goddess and those manipulated by men and corrupt women.

In suggesting strategies for empowerment, there is a significant association between poverty, illiteracy, the low status of women and the practice of circumcision today. By far the most common suggestion is the proposal for educational awareness of the entire community, with the active involvement of native health workers and trained medical practitioners, local leaders and women's groups, not just the sentimental concerns of 'outsiders'. Even more critical to this effort is the education of men towards improving the status of women in their respective communities.

However, in such a programme directed at those who practise female circumcision proper, that is prepuce removal, what will the women be told? Will they be given purely hygienic facts which can only address mistakes or the malpractice of local doctors? Or will the educators talk about the erotic zones of orgasm? Female genital mutilation involves many social roles; it relates to superstition, religion, local customs, health practices, childbearing, concepts of sexual fulfilment and a range of other important social issues. In this light, changing attitudes about the practices will inevitably involve change in the overall situation of women. Even though women must not allow the marginalization of this issue, it cannot be separated from other women's or social justice issues as I hope I have now demonstrated. Women should resist being categorized into simplistic but damaging genitalia-based dichotomies in the politics of otherness.

In many of these controversial and sensitive matters, such as female circumcision, child marriage, family planning, abortion and condom provision campaigns, there is a strong resentment of direct interference with people's private decisions and sensibilities about sexual habits. Whereas with relevant education and knowledge, people retain their privacy about such matters.

End note

I would like to call attention to an earlier and commendable effort to raise some of these controversial issues at a national conference initiated from within and fully documented (Kalu and Osinbajo 1989). The 1989 national conference on Better Protection for Women and Children was a recognition by the Nigerian government, the policy-makers, the Ministry of Justice and a broad section of the public that, in spite of culture, law is an effective instrument of change. There was a common agreement that the two groups least protected by law were women and children.

Its thirty-two-point communiqué and its proposals for reform constitute a comprehensive assessment of the state of the law and policy on women and children which I have summarized as: women are chattel; cultural traditions claim women are inferior to men; constitutions and charters have not changed discrimination against women; cultural mentalities persist in spite of legislation; legislation itself is sexist and needs changing; inflation of bride-price turns women into chattel and should be legislated against; there should be equitable and non-sexist distribution of matrimonial property, and protection for all wives, not just for the monogamous ones, in all types of marriages in the Evidence Act; mass enlightenment and education campaigns on rights of Muslim women under the Sharia are needed; specific laws against spouse-battering and male adultery should be generally recognized under the Penal Code.

Point 14 of the communiqué states: 'bodily mutilations such as female circumcision, inhuman widowhood rites and other customary practices which debase womanhood should be prohibited by law'. There is need for legislation against sexual intimidation in the work-place, for the equal right of women to stand as sureties, for equal tax relief to both spouses, and for the age of maturity and of marriage to be fixed at eighteen years.

On children's rights, point 19 reads:

> Government should use all efforts to ensure that children enjoy certain minimum rights namely, right to good food, shelter, clothing, medical care, education, maturity before marriage and parenthood, and freedom from physical, sociological or sexual abuse; special education and facilities at government expense should also be made available to disabled children. The Children and Young Persons legislation should be modernised to incorporate the principles enshrined in the United Nations Standard Minimum rules for the Administration of Juvenile Justice.

There is a need for wider mobilization in the war against child abuse, for better organized centres and units for the counselling and enlightenment of 'women with unwanted pregnancies and children on options open to them', for less discrimination against the rural child on basic needs and rights. In all legislation and definitions, a person under the age of fourteen should be considered a child.

There should be more representation for women in public offices and the legislative assemblies; legal justice for women must be ensured even if this requires preferential affirmative action; cultural and religious differences must count in the making of new laws; a woman should not be dependent on her husband's consent to obtain a passport. Point 32 states: 'provision should be made for girls who drop out of school on account of early marriages or pregnancies to continue their education'.

Notes

1. *Guardian*, 25 August 1986.

2. *Daily Star*, 25 October 1986; *Daily Star*, 29 October 1986.

3. *Daily Star*, 28 August 1986.

4. *African Guardian*, 19 November 1987.

5. In 1999 there is little change in this business. Sylvester Asoya's 'Bar beach at night', *The News*, 6 September 1999, portrays Lagos Bar Beach as a gateway to many desires and many heavens, where white-garment spirit possession religions pray and cast out demons. There too erotic desires command worship in makeshift tents for 'short-time' (quick sex) at night. At the peak of business, prostitutes are paid between 800 and 1,000 naira But in the small hours of the morning the pay falls to 100–200 naira. In the sleazy atmosphere of the beach, there does not seem to be much interest in condom use.

6. *African Guardian*, 14 May 1987.

7. *Guardian*, 31 March 1987.

8. *Guardian*, 9 March 1987.

9. *Guardian*, 15 December 1985.

10. Jane Bryce, 'Rape: An Act of Sexual Dominance', *Guardian*, 15 June 1986.

11. 'Feminism for Girls', a discussion at a forum on 'Sisterhood: Towards a Consolidated Women's Movement in Nigeria', 6–7 March 1987, Enugu.

12. Sunday *Vanguard*, 23 November 1986.

13. *Guardian*, 28 August 1986.

14. Ibid.

15. *Guardian*, 17 June 1986.

16. *West Africa*, 19–25 December 1988.

17. *Daily Star*, 6 December 1986.

18. *Daily Star*, 17 June 1986.

19. *Guardian*, 17 March 1987.

20. *Weekly Star*, 30 November 1986.

21. *Sunday Vanguard*, 30 November 1986.

22. *Guardian*, 3 December 1986.

23. *Guardian*, 27 August 1986.

24. 'Women sell their eggs through agent for £750', *Sunday Times* (London), 16 June 1996; on the Director of Public Prosecutions' order that thousands of frozen human embryos be destroyed, and how the women who produced 'these potential children feel', see *Guardian* (London), 24 July 1996; 'Couples in last-minute bid to save embryos', see *Guardian* (London), 1 August 1996; 'Clinic starts destruction of embryos', *Guardian* (London), 2 August 1996.

25. There was public outcry and a debate about the ethics of the fertility treatment given to Ms Allwood, a British mother pregnant with octuplets who sold her story to the media: 'Science that produces more death than life', *Guardian* (London), 1 August 1996; 'On the edges of ethics: One tragic case doesn't mean the law is wrong', *Guardian* (London), 6 August 1996; 'Medical morality: Advances in fertility treatment pose unheard-of dilemmas. Do we have the ethics to match?', *Observer* (London), 11 August 1996; 'Eight-foetus mother seeks million-pound sponsorship deal', *Observer* (London), 11 August 1996; 'Fury at 8-baby birth bonus: Parent may make £125,000 per child', and 'Woman could die bearing octuplets: Pregnancy creates controversy after period of personal trauma for "independent" minded mother', *Guardian* (London), 12 August 1996; 'Doctor attacks 8-birth deal', and 'Conception of a multiple nightmare: The hopes and joys of new life have exploded in the faces of Mandy Allwood and Paul Hudson', and 'Stop the freak show: Fertility issues deserve an informed debate', *Guardian* (London), 13 August 1996.

26. *Weekly Star*, 12 October 1986.

Sources

Books

Acsadi, G., et al. (eds), 1990, *Population Growth and Reproduction in Sub-Saharan Africa: Technical Analysis of Fertility and Its Consequences*. Washington, DC : World Bank.

Amadiume, Ifi, 1997, *Male Daughters, Female Husbands: Gender and Sex in an African Society*. London: Zed Books.

David, H. P. (ed.), 1974, *Abortion Research: International Experience*. Lexington, MA: Lexington Books.

Dorkenoo, Efua, 1992, *Female Genital Mutilation: Proposals for Change*. Manchester, UK: Manchester Free Press.

El Dareer, Asma, 1983, *Woman, Why Do You Weep? Circumcision and Its Consequences*. London: Zed Books.

Hosken, Fran P., 1993 (4th revised edn), *The Hosken Report: Genital and Sexual Mutilation of Females*. Lexington, MA: Women's International Network News.

Kalu, Awa U. and Yemi Osinbajo (eds), 1989, 'Women and Children under Nigerian Law', *Federal Ministry of Law Review Series*. Ibadan, Nigeria: Intec Printers.

Koso-Thomas, Olayinka, 1987, *Circumcision of Women: A Strategy for Eradication*. London: Zed Books.

Levin, Tobe, 1986, 'Women as Scapegoats of Culture and Cult: An Activist's View of Female Circumcision in Ngugi's *The River Between*', in Carole Boyce Davies and Anne Adams Graves (eds), *NGAMBIKA: Studies of Women in African Literature*, Lawrenceville, NJ: African World Press.

Lightfoot-Klein, Hanny, 1989, *Prisoners of Ritual: An Odyssey into Female Genital Circumcision in Africa*. New York: Haworth Press.

Matory, James Lorand, 1994, *Sex and the Empire That is No More: Gender and the Politics of Metaphor in Oyo Yoruba Religion*, Minneapolis: University of Minnesota Press.

McLean, Scilla (ed.), 1980, *Female Circumcision, Excision and Infibulation: The Facts and Proposals for Change*. London: Expedite Graphic Limited.

Mickelwait, Donald R., Mary Ann Riegelman and Charles Sweet, 1976, *Women in Rural Development*. Washington, DC: Westview Press.

Ogundipe-Leslie, Molara, 1994, *Recreating Ourselves: African Women and Critical Transformations*, Lawrenceville, NJ: Africa World Press.

Okonjo, Isabel Kamene, 1984, 'The Role of Women in Social Change among the Igbo of Southeastern Nigeria Living West of the River Niger', Boston University Graduate School, PhD, Sociology, Individual and Family Studies. Michigan: University Microfilms International.

Omran, Abdel R., 1992, *Family Planning in the Legacy of Islam*. New York: Routledge.

Raymond, Janice G., 1994, *Women as Wombs: Reproductive Technologies and the Battle over Women's Freedom*. San Francisco: Harper.

Sanderson, Lilian Passmore, 1981, *Against the Mutilation of Women: The Struggle to End Unnecessary Suffering*. London: Ithaca Press.

Toubia, Nahid, 1993, *Female Genital Mutilation: A Call for Global Action*. New York: Rasco.

Women in Nigeria Today, 1985, Editorial Committee, Women in Nigeria. London: Zed Books.

Journal articles

Bien-Aimé, T. and J. Neuwirth, 1994, 'A Challenge to the Ethics of Calder, Neutrality on the Medically Harmful Practice of Female Genital Mutilation', *American Journal of Obstetrics and Gynecology*, vol. 171, no. 4 (October 1994), 1160–1.

Calder, B. L., Y. M. Brown and D. I. Rae, 1993, 'Female Circumcision/Genital Mutilation: Culturally Sensitive Care', *Health Care for Women International*, vol. 14, no. 3 (May–June 1993), 227–38.

Davies, J. H., 1992, 'Female Genital Mutilation – A Practice That Should Have Vanished', *Midwives Chronicle*, vol. 105, no. 1249 (February 1992), 33.

Egwuatu, V. E. and N. E. N. Agugua, 1981, 'Complications of Female Circumcision in Nigerian Igbos,' *British Journal of Obstetrics and Gynaecology*, vol. 88, no. 11 (November 1981), 1090–93.

Eregie, C. O., 1994, 'Uvulectomy as an Epidemiological Factor in Neonatal Tetanus Mortality: Observations from a Cluster Survey', *West African Journal of Medicine*, vol. 13, no. 1 (January–March 1994), 56–8.

'Female Circumcision. Female Genital Mutilation. World Health Organization.

International Federation of Gynecology and Obstetrics', *European Journal of Obstetrics, Gynecology and Reproductive Biology*, vol. 45, no. 2 (3 July 1992), 153–4.

Johnson, K. E. and S. Rodgers, 1994, 'When Cultural Practices are Health Risks: The Dilemma of Female Circumcision', *Holistic Nursing Practice*, vol. 8, no. 2 (January 1994), 70–8.

Lightfoot-Klein, H. and E. Shaw, 1991, 'Special Needs of Ritually Circumcised Women Patients', *Journal of Obstetric, Gynecologic, and Neonatal Nursing*, vol. 20, no. 2 (March–April 1991), 102–7.

Murray, Jocelyn, 1976, 'The Church Missionary Society and the "Female Circumcision" Issue in Kenya, 1929–32', *Journal of Religion in Africa*, vol. VIII, facs. 2 (1976), 92–104.

Odujinrin, O. M., C. O. Akitoye, and M. A. Oyediran, 1989, 'A Study on Female Circumcision in Nigeria', *West African Journal of Medicine*, vol. 8, no. 3 (July–September 1989), 183–92.

Ozumba, B. C., 1992, 'Acquired Gynetresia in Eastern Nigeria', *International Journal of Gynecology and Obstetrics*, vol. 37, no. 2 (February 1992), 105–9.

Rehnstrom, J., 1994, 'Female Genital Mutilation', *American Journal of Obstetrics and Gynecology*, vol. 171, no. 4 (October 1994), 1160.

Toubia, N., 1994, 'Female Circumcision as a Public Health Issue', *New England Journal of Medicine*, vol. 331, no. 11 (15 September 1994), 712–16.

8. Women and the 1986 National Political Debate

This chapter presents a variety of women's voices to show how the gender- and class-informed local language of civil debate about social contracts and justice contrasts with the local language of rights presented in Chapters 6 and 7. It will be seen how this language differs again from the formalized international language of rights as a laundry list presented in Chapter 1. In this chapter, we hear directly the voices of different women, and assess their level of political awareness and their integrity. In the laundry list format of elite women's rhetoric, which says nothing about their own private morality and public ethics, African women are presented as ignorant objects to be civilized, helped and managed. The data presented here on the National Political Debate in 1986 contradicts this negative image of African women.

On 13 January 1986, the Nigerian military president, Major General Ibrahim Babangida, inaugurated the Political Bureau in the new federal capital, Abuja. In the president's speech, carried in all the newspapers, the Political Bureau was mandated to provide an objective and in-depth critique of Nigeria's past political experience, to identify the basic faults and what went wrong to serve as background information for the National Political Debate. Its second term of reference was to identify a philosophy of government which would determine goals and serve as a guide to the activities of government. The bureau was also to guide, monitor, analyse and document the debate. At the end of the debate, the bureau was to suggest a blueprint to promote meaningful socio-economic development in the country: 'You must see the search for the new political order as a launching pad for the new Nigeria: prosperous, humanist and stable at home; a nation that possesses real capacity in the African context, and one that commands and compels respect in international affairs.' Two things were sacrosanct and non-negotiable: the federal arrangement and the revenue allocation formula.

Rules of the debate In a full-paged newspaper article, the Political

Bureau gave its interpretation of the president's mandate as: (a) to review Nigeria's political history, identify the problems which led to failure and suggest ways of resolving and coping with those problems; (b) to identify a philosophy of government to determine goals and serve as a guide to government activities; (c) to collect information and data for the government and identify political problems that may arise from the debate; (d) to gather, collate and evaluate the contributions of Nigerians to the search for a viable political future and to provide guidelines for the attainment of the consensus objectives; (e) to deliberate on other political problems that may be referred to from time to time.

Women's voices Theme 14 on women in Nigerian politics gave women's groups an entry into the debate, while theme 17 on the rural population in Nigerian politics also meant that the voices of grassroots women were sought. Needless to say, this extensive programme for a national debate afforded researchers a golden opportunity to collect first-hand material and to assess the opinions of individuals and interest groups on several issues. My concerns were with women's interests. I took extensive notes, as can be seen from the wealth of data, presented several papers[1] and participated in several organizations, primarily in the eastern and mid-western states. I shall report, as much as possible in their own words, what women said in the meetings I attended during this debate.

WIN debates

Anambra state On 17 May 986, the Anambra state chairperson of the NLC/WW, Cecilia Onyeka, and I, organized a state-wide one-day symposium at the Enugu Municipal Hall on the WIN platform. Women's organizations in the state, especially those in the rural villages, were to have extensive discussions in their localities. Their views, delivered verbally or in writing, were taken to the Enugu meeting by their representatives. Discussions centred round the following themes:

1. An analysis of Nigeria's political past and women's participation in it.
2. A history of women's (and women's organizations') mobilization and political participation.
3. Nigeria's political future and women's place in it.
4. Conditions necessary to ensure women's awareness and participation in development.

The symposium, which was conducted entirely in the Igbo language, was led by veteran politician Chief Madam Janet Mokelu, who examined women's past roles and their history. She challenged the prejudices, dating back to the colonial period, that relegated women to the background and saw them as unconcerned with politics. With the struggle for independence, attitudes changed, and women became involved. At the same time, however, women had to contend with opposition. Their participation in rallies and other gatherings was disapproved of by society. The Women's War of 1929 sharpened women's awareness, and they began to seek an education, especially because men preferred to marry educated women. This was the background for Mokelu's own political consciousness. Women began to realize that Nigeria was their country as much as it was the men's and that they had to participate in its growth and development. The shooting of local miners at Iva Valley in 1949 gave birth to women's active participation in politics in eastern Nigeria. Women were determined to protect their sons. Mokelu wrote the letter of protest that followed the massacre of the miners, and women thus became involved in national politics.

On 30 December 1959, Dr Nnamdi Azikiwe, to show his gratitude for women's support and to encourage their political awareness, sent Mokelu and Margaret Ekpo on a National Convention of Nigerian Citizens (NCNC) platform to the House of Chiefs as representatives of women. He also proposed their admission to the House of Assembly. Both women stood for election on 16 November 1961 and won the right to represent both men and women. Mrs Mokelu, who remained in the House for quite some time, said that men supported them during that period, but she is not sure if men are as supportive of women today. In those days also, women's associations were autonomous.

Mrs Mokelu closed her presentation by telling men to stop monopolizing everything and to support women as they used to. Having set the scene, she relinquished the floor to women from various parts of the state.

UNOAKU, a journalist, listed the achievements of queens and queen-mothers in the old African empires, the functions and achievements of traditional descent- or lineage-based women's organizations, and the important role of women in the family as the keepers of food, peace and law. With the advent of colonial rule, the Christian Church and education, political participation for women carried a social stigma. The white man's religion taught that a woman was to be subservient to her husband, whether he was good or bad. Women who raised their voices were regarded as wild and wayward. This contributed to women's backwardness in politics and leadership. Women were used only for campaigns and to vote for men. Men operated a strategy of 'divide and rule'. Unoaku felt that women should therefore get together to devise a new political system, a 'feminocracy', in which leadership would be in the hands of women. Men have messed up, she said; women are more principled.

CECILIA, a labour activist, called on women to forge a strong unity towards 1990, one which would supersede ethnic, religious and social barriers. This was necessary if women were to take their rightful position. Women, she said, must come out and speak. She attacked the male habit of monopolization and of deceiving women with the idea of women's wings. Women are socialist by nature, and socialism should be the system for Nigeria. Since women are experienced in family management, they would manage Nigeria well; women are not as hard as men and therefore not as corrupt. Women constitute the majority of the population in the rural areas, so co-operative movements should be set up by the government to assist and monitor various development projects there. This would ensure women's active involvement and allow an equitable distribution of wealth to become a reality. She advocated a school-to-land project for the country, as well as women's access to loans and farm settlements. She called on women to muster the courage in 1990 to stand for any post for which they thought themselves fit, whether president or governor, and she proposed a mixed-sex government – that is, a male president and a female vice-president.

GRACE, a grassroots woman, thanked God that they have produced children who can speak like this, saying in Igbo, '*Nwanyi bu ife*' (A woman has worth). She said that a lot of work needed to be done, and they would support us to do the job. Regarding problems in the home, she said that women worry about their children, since children these days are not easy to control. Poor people are suffering, and there is no money to buy food.

CATHERINE, an elderly grassroots woman, said there was much to be done. They, the elders, know things but are not as articulate as younger people. However, from earliest times in Igbo society, women had a say. They even defied custom and began to keep twins when twins were taboo. Women have been fighting for a long time. She thanked us for our presentations and said that they now felt strong and would go anywhere we tell them to go. The men they had put in power in the past did not even greet them after they got there. 'When they come across you, they speed past!' she said. 'Don't just you eat – share. Let's support sister women. We will still support men, though, but not just men any more. People eat more than their share. Women come out and support knowledgeable women. We will teach them, and they will listen to what we will say.'

ADA, another elderly grassroots woman, told women that she came to support them: 'We are here to support you. Government said we should speak. Don't be afraid. The youth are saying maybe we should call back white people to rule us again, since men have done badly. But they said, before going for white people, the women are there. Let us try them. It probably would be the way out for Nigeria.'

ALICE, a village schoolteacher, spoke about her impressions of NCWS

and WIN, saying that she had seen a difference between the two organizations: 'While NCWS says they are not political and are with government, WIN gives you the chance to have your own opinion.' Government
denies women a say. Women have a great deal to say, but no forum or
mouth. WIN helps them say it. It is necessary for women to have a unified
voice to express their dissatisfaction with some government policies and
decisions – for example, market levies. She said that education was rapidly
becoming a female prerogative, as boys now leave school early in search
of money due to high school fees and levies. This will result in a terrible
imbalance in the future. Secondary school fees should be reduced so that
boys can also go to school. 'These days, we worship money,' she said. Our
children are only concerned with money. In the villages, grassroots people
feel that socialism is for Russia and that Russians don't acknowledge God.
The villagers need enlightenment on socialism as a form of government.
We should arrange and enter villages and speak to rural women. In the
villages, women have built dispensaries and handed them over to local
councils, yet there are no medicines for the women who built them.

AGNES, a market woman, heard we were having a meeting and decided
to attend. She enumerated the sufferings of Nigerian women today: 'No
jobs for the educated, theft, pain for mothers. For those in the civil service,
it is retrenchment and starvation. They used to get compensation, but not
now. Government must compensate if it must retire people. How are the
unemployed to pay the various levies demanded by the government?'

JANET called on women to stop playing the part of second-class
citizens. Looking towards 1990, women should not just be voters, but
should actively contest elections. The Second Republic used women to
entertain and to vote, 'but in eating, they forgot us'. In her family, when
things get difficult, her father and mother put their heads together. Women
are equal to men and should be supported.

EUGENIA was pleased with the politics of the discussion; it was not
just about the kitchen. She said that before coming to the meeting, she
had been talking to a woman about the closure of their market sheds,
and both women concluded that this meeting would not be about the
market sheds. Still she came to the meeting and was pleased that the
discussion was about her shed. Government was destroying women's
means of earning an income, without paying compensation. Facts about
these difficult positions that women are in should be taken to government.
Women's worry is about feeding their children. Government should send
women into the villages to get their opinion.

MADAM ILOABACHIE, a YWCA leader, chaired the meeting. In her
closing remarks, she affirmed that socialism would not prevent Nigerians
from practising their beliefs. As a member of the older generation, she

called upon her peers to prepare younger people to take over from where they stopped: 'Let us open our mouths and say what we want and support these children. The men support us and acknowledge that the men who ruled committed murder. These younger ones will support socialism and will stand by us. We want free health care, especially for childbirth and blood transfusions.'

At the end of the meeting, a resolution was passed calling for sisterhood and love among women; for no campaign politics but nominations; and for women councillors to affiliate with WIN. My contribution to the debate concentrated on a mechanism that would ensure women's full participation in government, that is, effective self-government, particularly in local government. I suggested the women's committee system and a Ministry for Women's Affairs, having had first-hand experience of how this system works (see Chapter 10).

Imo, Anambra, Rivers and Cross River states On the 23rd and 24th of May 1986, representatives of various women's organizations and individual women met on the WIN platform for a political symposium on 'Women and Nigeria's Political Development' at the multipurpose hall in Owerri, Imo state. This was the most exciting of all the National Political Debates in which I participated. We were on the home ground of the Women's War of 1929, and from the women's confidence, oratory and audacity, it was clear that these fearless matriarchs were true daughters of the Goddess. They were beautifully solid and supportive and, at the same time, full of careless laughter and gaiety. Their excitement and enthusiasm for action were such that even after the meeting had been declared closed the grassroots women leaders hung around. They were waiting for action. They participated in the tedious process of summarizing papers and writing the summary report and communiqué. They insisted on being informed of everything, seeking clarification on points, and they had suggestions to make on everything. The meetings were conducted in both Igbo and English. Here is what some of the women said.

ROSE demanded that rules in the civil service be purged of sex discrimination and that there be laws for adequate provision for widows, divorcees, working mothers, the handicapped, abandoned babies and neglected children and that government put as many women as possible in positions of responsibility and put an end to tokenism. She demanded the creation of a Ministry for Women's Affairs at both the federal and state levels, as recommended by the UN, to monitor the emancipation of women and to act as a watchdog in matters relating to sex discrimination and sexual harassment. The ministry would also have the power to take defaulters to court. She pointed out that Norway has a woman prime minister and seven women in her cabinet. The Philippines has Mrs Aquino, Britain has Margaret Thatcher; Golda Meir has made Israel a great power; Sri Lanka has had Mrs Bandranaike, and India Indira Gandhi. Nigeria has had female activists, such as Mrs Ransome-Kuti, Margaret Ekpo, and Mrs Nzimiro. 'The new political order', she said, 'should have for its watchword merit, selfless service, probity and accountability, integrity, honour, wisdom, and honesty of purpose – the very qualities that seem to have eluded most of our leaders ... We are here in search of a new political order. We are being asked to make known to our anxious people what part we can play. We shall not disappoint those who have called on us. The large crowd of women here is adequate testimony of our new-found strength in a united front.'

CONFORT said: 'The Igbo women of the past constituted what was accepted in various communities as formidable vigilantes. Vigilantism of the womenfolk maintained law and order far better than the well-thought-out and written edicts are doing today. Community development and environmental sanitation were added responsibilities undertaken by women in the past.' The Women's War of 1929 ushered in women's mobilization movements 'as the silent majority of the era turned momentarily into the vocal majority when the need arose'. During the First Republic, women made the least impact, due to lack of education, the fact that girls were groomed for early marriage, and the minimal exposure of women to national and world affairs. Nevertheless, a few women did make an impact, which has influenced women into playing active politics today.

The Nigerian civil war saw the sharpening of women's political aware-ness, and politicians made use of women's mobilizing abilities. During the Second Republic, 'women's political involvement reached its zenith, when they were led to believe they were indispensable for campaigning. At such times, men made use of "women leaders" who were able to mobil-ize various women's organizations to vote for men. The organizations voted in a bloc, not for the "right candidate", but for the person who offered more cups of rice, salt, chunks of stockfish, or even money. This practice was the result of poverty, hunger and women's desire for material goods. The blame for this anomaly lies in Nigeria's poor economic system, which has made it impossible for the average person to live a modest life. Women, as well as men, mortgage their conscience because they must find a means of providing for their families.'

She argued that the women's wings of various political parties have been 'used to impress and confuse the majority of the female population. It raises a false hope for many, who see the token of one female permanent secretary, one minister, one commissioner among several men.' With education, women have come to have an awareness of their identity and their mission in life. Yet few inroads have been made in the present military regime, despite the fact that the government has given women token appointments. 'Women have been mobilized into various women's organizations, associations, social clubs, and the like. The number of such associations and their varying objectives have in no way strengthened the cause of women. They have tended to detract from rather than strengthen women's participation in government. More painful still is the in-battle to gain supremacy over other women's organizations and the arrogance of some women's organizations, which look down on others. Men are also accusing women of being their own worst enemies. Some men, who capitalize on the division and apparent lack of strategy by the women, accuse women's organizations of not knowing what they want.'

She accused those in government of failure: 'They have failed to provide any degree of stability in the country. They have, with the aid of some women, left our treasury empty; they enter the government poor and come out millionaires. They ask women to farm but make no provisions for preserving what is produced in the annual budget; they have not even provided adequately for the education of the children. They are exposing our youth too soon to the luxuries of life. In concluding, she said that the Nigerian woman 'wants a place under the sun to maximize her endowments and potentialities. She is not asking anything more than that which reflects basic universal human rights. The challenge today is to deliberate on the past, to learn from our mistakes, and take a plunge into changing the country to what we want.'

CATHERINE from Nnobi said that women had ruled in the past and had power; today, men rule women, but should not subdue them. The older women look up to the younger women and support them. Younger women should take the lead.

Another woman said: 'Women did rule, and we support that women should rule. Margaret Ekpo and others, they ruled. Now we have women more educated than Margaret Ekpo.' A woman from Awka said that women have already taken the plunge and have come out. There is no looking back: 'We tried our best in the last two republics but must do more work.' She attacked the token appointment of women, pointing out that women outnumber men in the population. She too used the home metaphor as a reference point to argue that women's ability to manage and keep peace in the home proved their ability to manage the nation.

A Rivers state woman attacked the orthodox view that politics is for men, while the domestic work is for women. Politics affects women, and laws which are made also affect women. She said that the voting rights of women have been exploited by men. Rivers women want to be more active in politics and want more females in power. 'It is the woman who lifts the man to higher goals, for behind every successful man is a woman. So also behind any successful government development project, there has to be a woman.' She demanded 40 per cent involvement of women in government and services and called for a women's united front, a combination of socialism and democracy – that is, socialism in tune with African norms. She called for an end to work-place discrimination and a say for women in family planning. 'The government, in particular, should embark on compulsory and free education for women because once you educate a woman, you educate the nation; whereas if you educate a man, you educate an individual.' Women should be encouraged to go into 'masculine jobs' such as bus-driving, train-driving, carpentry, space-craft pilot, and so on.

CHIEF MRS ADA ANYANWU holds the title Ada-Emeabiam I of Owerri and was a member of the Imo state House of Assembly during the Second Republic. She asked how genuine the request for women's views was: 'Should we women believe that our opinions, whether as individuals or groups, are sincerely required by the menfolk who are asking us to participate in this debate? Or are we, for purposes of sexual balance, being asked to say something and then have our contributions thrown into a dustbin? ... Most Nigerians know that Nigerian men have been at the helm of affairs before and after independence. For twenty-six years since 1960, the political stage of Nigeria has been dominated by men. Alhaji Tafawa Balewa was our first post-independence prime minister. General Babangida is on the seat now. Between the former and the latter are twenty-six years. Of what? Of political turmoil presided over by menfolk. In Parliament, it was particularly men all over. At the state level, men have held sway. At the local government level too, it has been men ... There seems to be a cordial relationship between Nigerian men and bad government. We should, in any future political arrangement, break this cordiality by switching to a higher representation of women in government.'

She enumerated the failures of male rulership in Nigeria: unsuccessful and unreliable census counts in 1963 and 1973; four controversial and bloody elections in 1959, 1964, 1979 and 1983; a civil war from 1967 to 1970. 'All these troubles were caused by men ... Our women are particularly honest. No one has ever heard that a Nigerian female political leader was impeached or jailed for embezzlement. No one has ever heard that a Nigerian woman built financial empires for herself at the expense of ordinary Nigerians.' She suggested a mixed-sex leadership – that is, if there is a male president, there should be a female vice-president. At the state level, there should be a woman deputy governor and a woman deputy chairperson at local government. Internationally, women have shown a great sense of leadership, and she listed the familiar names of female heads of state. Her conclusion was that women have shown competence when given the chance. Their natural concerns with motherhood make them more committed to peace and stability which are necessary conditions for national economic growth. A female head of state would check both male and ethnic rivalry.

Nigeria needs more women in important government positions – in managing natural resources, in banks, in private and public companies, as accountants and bank managers – because 'women are more honest than men. They are also more afraid of committing crimes. Today, men mismanage and embezzle money and then set buildings on fire to cover their wrongdoings. Can you imagine a woman setting a twenty-storey building on fire to hide her crime? ... There should be more women magistrates and judges because they are more honest and more resistant to bribery than men.' She concluded by calling on Nigerian women to join hands in love and unity, with honesty of purpose, sincerity, and hard work in 'a crusade to salvage this nation'.

Both the president and the secretary of Imo state's NCWS were present and used the platform to enumerate the achievements of the NCWS and outline its programme for the Political Debate.

MRS EZE, a retired chief inspector of education, blamed the failure of both the parliamentary and presidential political systems in Nigeria on 'the avaricious, insatiable appetites of our politicians and the wrong values of our society'. Having cited Plato's definition of three classes of men – namely, the appetitives or the acquisitive, the ambitious or the honour seeking, and the philosophical or lovers of truth – she said: 'The type of democracy we experienced in the Second Republic was government by all the appetitives in unbridled competition. The political scene degenerated to Hobbes' "man in the state of nature". Politicians acquired and looted the country's wealth, not just for themselves, but for their children and their children's children. The question now is how Nigeria can correct the errors of the past and build a virile, stable and secure society.'

She called for an amendment to the 1979 Constitution to grant public servants leaves of absence to enable them to run for office. This would maximize the chance of recruiting the right type of people, men and women. Also, politics should be made financially less attractive in order to attract the right kind: 'Politics has been perceived by Nigerians as the quickest means of making money ... As soon as candidates are elected, they grow puffy and become unreasonable lords ... The time has come for Nigeria to make full use of her women of honour and integrity.' She too enumerated the names of female heads of state, and she quoted Nehru: 'In order to awaken a people, it is the women who have to be awakened. Once they are on the move, the household moves, the village moves, the country moves.'

Urging women on, she said: 'In order to make a useful contribution in society, the woman has to literally force her way out of her conforming role. If we look back at the number of participating women politicians, the number is insignificant compared with the population, but their contribution was significant. In the First Republic, we had the Janet Mokelus and the Margaret Ekpos. If our mothers could achieve so much with little or no education, the sky will be our limit if we try half as much. *You* have to say you are before anybody else says "thou art". So women, we are not asking for preferential treatment. You, women, must realize that you have to consistently prove your competence, efficiency, and effectiveness for your contribution to be accepted by the public.'

On concrete contributions by village grassroots women, Eze said: 'In the much-talked-about going-back-to-land as a means of revamping Nigeria's economy, the women are in the forefront. At the village level, one marvels at the activities of women in the building and equipping of schools, churches, hospitals, civic centres, seeing to the installation of pipe-borne water, electricity. In urban areas, the situation is the same. Women contribute their quota wherever they are. Women have abundant un-tapped resources and talents which government should harness to make the new political order flourish. If government discovers men to put them in positions of trust, let it discover women too. Whatever criteria are adopted to recruit men should be applied to women as well. If the government were to borrow a leaf from church and other social organizations, it would place women in its key sensitive areas. Women could be in charge of scholarship boards, public examinations boards, etcetera. For one thing, society finds it easier to tempt men in high places than it does women. How many people will have the guts to visit women at night to lobby them for one thing or another? Women show greater restraint than men when exposed to opportunities for amassing wealth.

'Positions of trust will help women to participate in control of the nation's purse. Because of women's high sense of justice, they will guard the nation's account so religiously that Nigeria's economy will flourish. Problems of unemployment will be greatly minimized. Our youth will cease to roam the streets and find life more meaningful. They will realize the dignity of labour. Their sense of value will change, and a new species of youth will emerge. Policies making it possible to bridge the gap be-tween the haves and the have-nots should be introduced. This govern-ment could be advised to make laws that, for example, limit the number of houses landlords may own. Funds for putting up more buildings could be utilized by such landlords, individuals or as corporations to establish small-scale industries. This would be another way of solving unemployment.

'I am not advocating a government of Plato's Philosophy Kings nor am I trying to build a utopian society. I am only advocating a government that will be responsive to the needs of the people. Permit me to add here that the Nigerian Army should be reorganized and made to realize its role in the modern, civilized society Nigeria is aspiring to be. In this respect, there ought not to be any more coups to allow Nigerians a chance to learn from her mistakes. Finally, I am optimistic that if the right type of people are recruited to politics, if women of honour and integrity are voted in and placed in key sensitive areas, if the measures proposed are given a chance to work, we will have gone a long way towards building a nation we can proudly and meaningfully say is "free from poverty, ignorance, and disease", and "we are bound in love, peace and unity".'

MRS UPKABI, who was the only woman on the fifty-member 1979 Constitution Committee, reminded us that it was the inclusion of a sexual equality guarantee in the 1979 Constitution that made it possible to accommodate what was being said. History has shown that, when given the opportunity, we have proved ourselves: 'Whether government is serious or not about wanting our opinion, we are serious.'

Another woman questioned the participation of men in WIN, while a YWCA woman expressed delight at the large representation of women at the meeting. According to this woman: 'Women are in the majority in Nigeria. We need women in the seats of government to fight for us. We should educate female children in order to ensure awareness. Women are like those carried by the river; where they land, they stay and work.'

CONFORT AGWU of the Ministry of Agriculture, Imo state, expressed concern about the gap between educated and illiterate women. She argued that if we are to have a female president, that woman must come from the villages: 'Educated women do not attend village women's meetings. These educated women should also help in the church. We should not wait until 1990 but start mobilizing now. Elite women should therefore get into village meetings and begin the job of enlightenment now, so that, by 1990, village women will know them if they wish to be supported.'

ROSE ACHALONU, co-ordinator of WIN, Imo state, intervened to say that we were not there to talk about individual women to be elected but the political system we wish to propose. She acknowledged that there were male members in WIN but explained that men were there for support – for example, her husband was in WIN and very supportive.

ROSELYN OKOYE, a grassroots woman who had attended WIN's Enugu debate, said: 'I heard this talk already at Enugu, and I was very happy. My opinion for 1990 is that we must get women in government, especially for the presidency. This will guarantee us maternity benefits, for example, and milk for mums. They are bearing Nigerian children. They should get things from government and not be taxed.' A woman whom I described in my notes as a Christian fundamentalist said: 'God blessed children. The bad world today is from the men.'

MRS OKAFOR pointed out the importance of educating youth to guarantee their progress. She complained bitterly about the levy on women, among whom are many widows: 'It is wicked to make education dependent on tax clearance. Where will we get it? Women will consider these things if in power.'

Most women from Imo state proposed a one-party system. According to one woman, this would mean that women would not run for election but would be appointed. She felt that educated women should be in the vanguard. Women would then vote for the women so nominated. Dynamic women in the villages should be involved in pulling in their communities. Like most Nigerian women, she stressed women's honesty: 'Women don't build three-storey buildings.'

Another Imo woman who proposed a one-party system said that an opposition should be picked to watch those in the party. We should support enlightened women. Women are being overtaxed; therefore, women need women to fight for them in government.

A grassroots Nnobi woman complained about the government's policy of passing all exams before allowing a job in the civil service, especially in teaching: 'To the women's government we are expecting in 1990, please look into this.'

Another woman expressed concern about the bad economy. She called for more trade exchange to encourage the flow of money.

Yet another woman called for a one-party system because 'it prevents greedy politics'. She wanted more women involved and a female president. She also wanted to see the government encourage production of raw material so we can get things to export. She called for a return to the old regions, since she felt that statism was a problem. She called for a rotational presidency.

Another woman who called for a one-party system said: 'The British Queen is a good example. Let women rule. I support it.'

A woman from Owerri called for communism, saying that oil from the south was being used to develop the north: 'Redistribute the wealth so that I too can shop like Mrs Babangida.'

A trade union woman said: 'Naturally, women are perfect finishers; they do their best to project the image of womanhood. They are incorruptible judges – for instance, during the civil war in Nigeria, many women fought the war without arms, many joined the militia; some were the architects of the food supply. They made ends meet by making do with what they had and worked very hard, because they are better managers at home.'

CHIEF MRS ANYANWU, contributing from the floor, said: 'Any party is useless if women do not rush into it. Set up enlightenment committees and get into the villages. Some educated women do not even know their rights. I won election because of the support of women. There were no men in the inner circle of my campaign, only women.'

A woman commented that we don't really have one Nigeria; if we must be one Nigeria, there must be equal employment opportunities in all the states. She called for women to get into the seats of power.

Another woman said that civil servants ought not to resign their jobs to engage in politics. They should take leave without pay, so that they don't embezzle and to protect against redundancy.

For another woman, 'government depends on what we make of it. Women who fear God and know planning should dominate in government.'

CHIEF MRS UZOMA said: 'God bless us all. What we are saying here affects even the unborn child. God gave women special intelligence from time, but men don't want to use it. We have educated women. If we don't come out as women, no one will recognize us. Mrs Nwankwo, as a commissioner, has done wonders in Imo state. It is women who know women's needs. Men are just the umbrella for taking shade when the need arises. We can move mountains if we are together. In Orlu local government, what we have is only an Enlightenment Committee, which I hear has to do with sanitation and not politics. We should not wait for 1990 but must start campaigning right now. Men have cheated us too much.'

A young student demanded that students be given a livable wage. She felt that women should rule, since they are honest and not corrupt. She also suggested the presence of church leaders in government for mutual support and expressed anguish over the tempting and corruption of young female students by wealthy men flaunting their money, and she described how the girls are being harassed and left pregnant. The girl's presentation drew loud applause, angry sighs, and even tears from some of the women.

A grassroots woman said: 'Let women rule us. We have to agree on what the woman should be paid. Those in government should not be paid a lot of money. It is love of country that motivates service. You don't use forceful rule on women. Rural government is hard. Since men have been ruling, we have been eating sand. They should be removed.' She proposed a mixed-sex leadership, with a woman from one party and a man from another. She also suggested moderate pay for workers as a way to check greed. 'Come 1990, women must rule Nigeria.' She called on

mothers to start educating both their male and female children. The last
woman who spoke from the floor called for a review of the Nigerian
constitution to find out how it favours or discriminates against women
and urged that the government make amendments where necessary. More
women should be included in this ratification of the constitution, she
concluded.

At the end of the debate, a communiqué was published.[2] It contains
the main points of the summary report of what was said and the decisions
taken.

Bendel state The Bendel state WIN political debate on 'Women in
Politics: Towards 1990 in Nigeria', held on 30–31 May 1986, at the YWCA,
Benin City, was attended by many organizations and representatives of
WIN from other states. It was also attended by leaders of the NCWS and
NLC in Bendel state. The audience was very mixed, characterized by the
'performance syndrome', and very much dominated by its male members.
It was, characteristically, opened by the state's commissioner of informa-
tion, a man.

In his address, the commissioner said the meeting was important because it was 'by' women: 'From the militancy exhibited, women will take
over in 1990. Let us try them.' Unfortunately, his speech was detached
from the realities of women's lives and concentrated on national and
international matters, attacking the plunder of the Nigerian economy,
looting and external debt. He said that women were needed to rejuvenate
the country towards noble ideals: 'Nigeria is rich in natural resources. If
WIN can mobilize the nation to check the siphoning of our wealth to
foreign countries, we would be real winners, and I can't see how we can't
win.' The pun drew laughter and applause.

In her speech, another state commissioner, a woman, made no mention
of grassroots women or any effort to include them in the debate.

The formal character of the debate continued with the reading of
papers until it was suggested that there should be a translation into Creole.
(Bendel state is multiethnic and often referred to as a mini-Nigeria, since
it exhibits all the national differences and contradictions at the state level,
unlike most other states, which are usually composed of a dominant ethnic
group.)

One woman said there was nothing wrong with the Nigerian system
but the operators. Indigenous structures were not taken into consideration
by the colonialists: 'This was the initial mistake.' She called for a confederation. Since women are now being heard and not just seen, there
should be no limit to our aspirations, and she cited the names of women
presidents and prime ministers elsewhere.

A male WIN member explained the role of the organization as a forum for awareness. WIN, as a conscious agitator and constructive motivator, is concerned about women in development in Nigeria and about gender contradictions. Gender education is necessary and should not be assumed. The level of development of a nation is measured by the level of the development of its women. He stressed the right of the oppressed to organize around their oppression, and he called for a women's committee to be instituted in 1990 to mobilize, educate and sensitize the womenfolk. He concluded by saying that God is neither man nor woman.

A woman said that men had failed in the past because they did not listen to women. Now we women must take over. If women take over in 1990, they should be supported by organizations like WIN. She called for a parliamentary system, as she felt it was less expensive and changing government in that system was easier. She too felt that the Nigerian system was not faulty and that the problem lay with the operators.

For another woman, it was important that women educate other women. Since each woman belongs to several organizations and associations, it is good to discuss things with women and look into these issues.

A man from the Club of Matured Mind Benin City did not say much in terms of women, but he criticized the past failures of government. A student from a girls' college cited Winnie Mandela as a good model. She said that if women can keep the money in the home, why can't they keep the country's. Her mum keeps her dad's money very well. In her words, 'Men are diets. Women are the balanced diet.'

The chair of the National Association of Nurses and Midwives, a man, saw women as the most potent collective force, one that could be mobilized through women's associations only to vote for men. (In my notes, I called him 'a patronizing idiot'.)

The representatives from Onitsha Ukpo said this was their second meeting with WIN. They supported the decision that women should rule in 1990. A very, very old man from the Urobo Social Club amused the audience with his historical account. He said that at one time in Benin history, a woman in Benin was made Oba, but on the crowning day, she started her menses and therefore was not crowned: 'That was the end of crowning women Oba. What a tragedy! Yet again, Victoria was Queen of England when the British attacked Benin. What a tragedy! However, since independence, there has been trouble in Nigeria because of men. Women are full of gas and should be given the government of Nigeria'.

A tough-looking young girl dressed in her uniform from the St John Ambulance Brigade made a fist and said that women should handle the battle and fight. They should subdue the men.

The Igbanke Progressive Union of Students said that their own involvement was in the villages. WIN should get branches into the villages and involve grassroots women. They demanded universal free education.

At the end of the debate, a report was issued as a press release.

NCWS Debates

Anambra state On 26 June 1986, NCWS, Anambra state, held a political debate at the Women's Training College in Enugu. It was the most formal of all the women's debates I attended. It began with an opening prayer, and an introduction to the chair and guest speakers. There followed the presentation of papers by guest speakers, short remarks by the guest of honour, contributions from the floor and the views of the council by the state secretary. After light refreshments, a vote of thanks was made, there were closing remarks from the chair, and closing prayers.

Unlike other women's meetings I attended, at the NCWS debate there were differences and antagonism between members of the audience and the women leaders, including women highly placed in the government and civil service, who occupied the front rows. This antagonism took the form of mutterings and murmured criticism as the important women and patrons of NCWS were introduced. The 'introduction' followed the political party practice of praise-singing. For example, well-established female politicians were called their praise names, such as *Onu n'ekwulu ora* (the mouth which speaks for all) or *Onye a malu amalu* (one that is well known, or a famous person). A politician led the opening prayers, and she prayed in the name of Jesus Christ. It was also significant that the four guest speakers were all university lecturers, two men and two women.

A lot of the contradictions at this gathering were encompassed in the chair's opening address: there is opposition to women becoming involved in politics, since custom is against women competing with men. Women should therefore wake up from sleep and come out. However, women and men will never be equal, since their bodies are different, but their roles can be complementary in working together. If things get better for women, the country will get better.

DR EWELUKWA, a male lecturer at the University of Nigeria, said that when God made the world, he made the family; he made man and woman. In development, however, it seems that women are trailing behind or going backwards. Yet, no family can stand without the firm support of father and mother. The importance of a woman in the home is the same importance due her in the government. It is because of the absence of women in politics that men have done so badly due to absence of control. Women should become involved in economic development and in politics. Women should be determined that what men can do, they can do as well.

Some women are so strong that they land a man on the ground in a fight. This male speaker, who appeared to be a better feminist than the women, especially the chair, acknowledged that God's gifts differ in our varied talents. Since women now predominate in the rural areas, any industry there would be in the hands of women. Times have changed; there is nothing that women cannot do now: 'Those hard things they never used to be able to do will now be done by machines. Stop running. Our country is not complete without women. Job gender stereotypes imposed from overseas have been broken. In government, they have also been broken. Men in this country have ruled one government after another without success. If women do not come out, things will not be corrected.'

DR FELICIA EKEJIUBA, also of the University of Nigeria, criticized the absence of rural women at the symposium. She provided facts and figures to show that women work very hard and have contributed a lot to development: 'Women are out. They should however not be frightened into receding. They have produced all of you educated women and the politicians. Eighty per cent of the rural population is female. Women do all the work there, including farming and trading. They have built houses, post offices, maternities, and churches, and they fill the churches on Sundays. Why is it important to them that they build these things? Because of their children. Rural women are more concerned than those in towns about maintaining moral standards of the villages. Women have proved that whatever they do, they do well, so let men give way to us to rule.'

DR AMUCHEAZI, a male lecturer at the University of Nigeria, like Ekejiuba, pointed out the importance of involving rural women and criticized the NCWS for the way it marginalized rural women in the debate. He had strong words for Nigeria's past governments: 'Things are getting worse. Now we live in fear. African politicians are like tin gods and very oppressive. The poor are made millionaires overnight and the rich made paupers. What is needed is equitable distribution of resources by government. It is the only solution.' He advocated a national government – that is, representation from all the states at the centre and a pluralistic system, with proportional representation of interest groups.

ANTHONIETTE NDULUE, of the Anambra State University of Technology, went through the history of Nigeria to enumerate powerful women who played an important role in government. She called up the old Oyo empire and the roles of queen mothers, widows of the king who were priestesses, and women who were the supporters of the king. Among the Ogboni, one member must be a female. Women were in charge in the palace of the Oba. In the old Benin empire, women were important and had several titles. It was the same in Onitsha, where there were Omu titled queens. She also referred to the 1929 Women's War and the role of Mrs

Ransome-Kuti and the Abeokuta Women's Union. In Muslim northern Nigerian history, there was Queen Amina. In the contemporary situation, however, she said that women are not keen to participate in politics: 'There is no federal woman minister. In the states, only one position is reserved for a woman commissioner. Women are not chairs of local government councils. Yet women have proven themselves when given a chance.' Women, she said, are begging for a fair chance.

MRS OBAYI, state commissioner for education and state president of the NCWS, said that her job did not give her time to attend NCWS meetings but that her mind and interest were still in NCWS meetings. She said that the NCWS was representative of all women, even grassroots women. The reason women are not seen in power is because our custom is still backward. She said that we women will still cook the food, but after cooking, we should wash ourselves and come out. Men contribute to making women go backwards: 'People do not relinquish power voluntarily. I have tasted power; power is sweet. God created Eve and gave her to Adam. Men and women are not equal. If women do the work involved in politics, they will get a position. Women are their own condemners by calling women who rule names. It is not politics which corrupts women.' She, like most of the women, cited women who have ruled in other countries. 'Women do not have the wickedness to commit crimes with impunity. Without women, the country is losing over half of its potential. The roles of the sexes should be complementary.'

Then the invitees spoke. A representative of women contractors: 'Women helped male politicians get into power during political election, but when it is time for the sharing of contracts, men take everything or give to their wives. A woman can be illiterate but still determined that her children will be educated. There are widows. There are also those with retrenched husbands. Wherever they put two men, let them put one woman to speak for women.'

A female student reminded everyone that usually, when men get stuck, they call on their mothers to help. She pleaded for help for students who cannot afford school fees.

A market woman said that women were not able to get import licences. A woman from the Women's Teaching College spoke of the problem of unemployment for people who leave school.

A woman from an LGA complained of the levies being extracted from villagers, although there was no money in the rural villages and no roads.

A civil servant complained of discrimination, that women in the civil service are given menial jobs. At the administrative and decision-making levels there are no women; there is no female permanent secretary. Men take women's allowances. There are no women on the ASET Fund Committee. She said that members have no confidence in the NCWS, since their executive officers are with government and defend the government: 'All they do is talk, and then everyone disperses.' This last criticism received very loud applause.

Unlike the other debates, where rapporteurs read out a summary of what was said and everyone agreed on the main points forming the communiqué or resolution, a statement was distributed prior to the meeting and later published[3] as the contribution of NCWS, Anambra state.

Northern states Some of the resolutions released following WIN's organized debates in the northern states are similar to those from the eastern and western states. An beautiful analogy which came out of the debate held jointly by Niger and Kwara states is the Yoruba saying, 'Women, the shell of the snail', a woman and house analogy made by other Nigerian women. A general complaint expressed by the northern states had to do with the difficulty of reaching women who are restricted by Islamic seclusion. Through committed female politicians, youth groups, youth associations and adult education classes for Islamic knowledge and literacy in Hausa, organizers ran workshops and, using representatives from these groups, were able to collate the women's opinions.

Generally, participants called for a government of the *talakawa* (the poor, grassroots proletariat, the masses); a comfortable life for all Nigerians; elimination of exploitation, oppression and subordination; the right of women to participate in policy- and decision-making; and a government which excludes the current owners of enormous amounts of jewellery and/or estates – a socialist political party. Analysis of these demands led WIN members to conclude that the women unanimously supported a socialist alternative, even though some could not call it by the English term. I should add that these northern, Islamic-ruled empires have for centuries had a class opposition or polarization of *talakawas*, the peasantry, and the *sarakunas* (the ruling aristocracy and a middle merchant class) under a political economy of both feudal and merchant capitalism. It is perhaps for this reason that class consciousness is sharpest in the northern states of Nigeria and on its university campuses.

Government's White Paper on the Political Bureau

Following the National Political Debate, on 27 March 1987 a report was submitted by the bureau to the federal government. On 1 July the government released a 169-page White Paper on the Report of the Political Bureau.[4] The White Paper was widely criticized for rejecting some of the most important popular demands and for being more concerned with the mechanics of government than with the basis of socio-political organization.[5]

I refer here only to those aspects of the White Paper that concern women and how the government responded to the bureau's recommended policies to meet women's needs. The bureau classified Nigerian society into the social strata: traditional rulers; landed gentry; industrial/commercial elites; intellectual and military elites; the quasi-proletariat; and workers, peasants and unemployed. In the thinking of the bureau: 'The failure to maximally and positively exploit the potential of each class for the well-being of the Nigerian people remains one of the clearest indications of the failure of our past political systems.' From what women said during the debate, we saw that they perceive themselves as a distinct class with distinct interests. More importantly, they perceive themselves as exploited, in the sense that there was only minimal remuneration for their labour and indirect appropriation and exploitation through compulsory levies, tolls and taxes.

On the philosophy of government, the bureau reported suggestions for meritocracy, Afrocracy, triarchy, capitalism, socialism, Islamic theocracy and African communalism. It did not report feminocracy or the mixed-sex government that women demanded. The bureau identified Nigerians' expectations of a new social order as:

a. Provision of social justice and welfare for the people.
b. Eradication of alienation and marginalization of the masses from the decision-making process.
c. Maximization of production and assurance of equitable distribution of resources.
d. Establishment and operation of a truly democratic political system and promotion of national unity by reducing areas of tension.

In recommending socialism, the bureau argued:

Capitalism, the dominant ideology in Nigeria, tends to foster poverty, ignorance, disease, and squalor among the masses. The Bureau recommends that Nigeria adopt a socialist socio-economic system in which the state shall be committed to the nationalisation and socialisation of the commanding heights of the national economy which fall under the following categories:

a. public utilities
b. enterprises which require heavy capital expenditure
c. enterprises and property which are tied up with the political integrity and security of the nation
d. other monopoly-type enterprises which generate imperfection in the

market and prevent resources from being put to their most efficient use, such as the distribution of essential commodities.

This should be without prejudice to the existence of a private sector of the economy. This private sector should be co-operative or non-monopolistic in character. The Bureau emphasises that non-monopolistic private enterprises should not be allowed to grow into conglomerates and also that the profits which accrue to such enterprises should be distributed annually among workers, managers, and the investors in proportion to the degree of contribution made by each category of these people to the pro-duction of the profit. The private sector should be limited to agriculture and small/medium-scale enterprises.

The military government was clear in its rejection of the popular demand for socialism:

Government rejects the imposition of a political ideology on the nation. Government believes that an ideology will eventually evolve with time and political maturity. Government is satisfied with the goals set out in the Second Development Plan (1970–1974). These goals are: a united, strong, and self-reliant nation; a great and dynamic economy; a just and egalitarian society; a land of bright and full opportunities for all citizens; a free and democratic society. These ideals of a greater and better Nigeria are also expanded by the Fundamental Objectives and Directive Principles of State Policy in Chapter II of the 1979 Constitution and buttressed by Chapter IV on Fundamental Human Rights.

Government wishes to emphasise that whenever the concept of a 'new social order' or 'new philosophy of government' is mentioned in this report, it should be construed as referring to the principle of democracy and social justice.

On the question of free access to land, the backbone of the rural African economy which is traditionally dominated by women and village farmers in general, the government again rejected the bureau's recom-mendations for a new political economy for Nigeria:

In light of the fundamental significance of land to the new social and economic order proposed in this report, the Bureau recommended that government should formulate a comprehensive land policy for the country. Such a policy should have the following features: making land available on freehold to any peasant farmer willing and able to cultivate it; making it possible for every adult, irrespective of sex, to acquire and cultivate lands in his or her own right; and making it possible that people whose lands have been compulsorily acquired for public purposes are adequately com-pensated, preferably with alternative land.

Industry, Parastatals, and Privatisation:

a. In view of the apparent contradiction of privatisation of parastatals and government policy of social justice, and in view of the recommended new philosophy of government in this Report, the present government policy and posture on privatisation should be re-examined with a view to identifying which of the existing parastatals at the federal and state levels deserves to be commercialised. Meanwhile, until the re-examination is done, government should stop privatisation.

b. Government should pursue with urgency the nationalisation of the entire oil industry.

c. All government companies and parastatals should be properly classified according to their roles and functions.

d. Government should step up its policy of establishing basic and capital goods industries such as iron and steel, machine tools, petro-chemicals, etc.

e. Government should invigorate its policy of taxing excess profits, and it should institute a profit-sharing system involving workers, management, and owners of capital, proportionate to their contributions to annual profits.

f. Industrial locations should be diversified deliberately so as to stem the rural–urban dichotomy and uneven geographical spread in the country. In doing this, however, industrial locations should be dictated by economic factors.

The government rejected (a) and (b), but pledged to take measures to increase effective Nigerian participation in the entire oil industry. The government accepted (c) and (d), noted (e), and accepted (f).

The bureau recommended the presidential system, in spite of noting that it is cautious of 'the danger of dictatorship in a single presidential executive'. It noted that the Nigerian military had political ambitions and that

traditional rulers compete against the nation for allegiance, represent a force against the principle of popular democracy and are dysfunctional reminders of sub-national differences. Besides, there is considerable rivalry and open politicking within the highest level of traditional leaders in almost every state of the federation. The Bureau therefore was not persuaded by the arguments for diarchy or triarchy because neither is capable of providing insurance for progress, stability, and a guarantee of peaceful continuity.

Under forms of representation, the bureau recommended the representation of women and labour in each of the legislative houses:

The case for women is obvious. Despite their numerical strength in the total population, it has been difficult to have any reasonable representation of this group of Nigerians in public policy-making at any level of government. Some may regard this recommendation as reverse discrimination against men. In the circumstances of our times, this cannot be avoided. Similarly, the working people of the country have been totally left out in the promotion of their interests. To reverse this situation, the Bureau recommends that in each legislative assembly at the federal, state, or local government levels, 5 percent of the seats be allocated to women and 5 percent be allocated to labour. Candidates to fill these seats should be nominated from the women's and labour groups by political parties in the ratio of their relative numerical strength in each legislature. Such nominations must be confirmed by the National Commission on Political Parties and Elections. The representation of these groups in the political system is, in the Bureau's view, central to our quest for stability and a new social order.

Government response was:

Government notes the reasons for the Bureau's recommendation on representation of women and labour groups. But government does not accept the implication of reverse discrimination embedded in that recommendation. Government believes in equality of sexes, individuals, and groups. Given equal opportunities in political parties and other institutions, government believes that these groups can effectively stand on their own without special constitutional provision.

On the constitutional system, the bureau said:

Although the Bureau appreciated the expression of a sense of structural alienation and the manifest need to correct the ills of certain aspects of the existing system, the Bureau did not find any compelling merit in the case for confederalism or in the case for a unitary system of government for Nigeria. In fact, the Bureau does not see any other accommodation and healthier arrangement for Nigeria than continuation of the system of federalism. The Bureau accordingly recommends as follows:

a. That Nigeria continue with a federal system of government
b. That the present three-tier arrangement of government –
   namely, federal, state, and local – should continue.

Government accepted these recommendations 'with more emphasis on local government'.
On the role of the military, the bureau stated:

The Armed Forces are largely a part of the vestiges of colonial bureaucracy in Africa. It was raised both for imperial defence and for internal security. Its post-colonial intervention in politics is part of the crisis of development, which is promoted by the corporate and bureaucratic orientation of the military and the socio-political and economic environment of Nigeria. In most cases, the intervention of the Armed Forces is goaded by organ- isational and collegial conflicts, internal rivalries, and struggle within the military, on the one hand, and that between the military and the post- independence civilian regime, on the other ... The reasons adduced for military interventions are systemic collapse; crisis of legitimacy indicated by corruption, ineptitude, gross indiscipline and bad leadership; influence of self-seeking or powerful civilians; personal and self-interest of the military coup makers ... The intervention of the military has had social, economic, political, and organisational consequences, which include, among others, the reduction in running of government expenses, coupled with more expenditures on military-related projects and welfare; attract- iveness of the military as a profession; regimented governance; emergence of an authoritarian culture; diminished professionalism; depletion of the officer corps; and politicisation of the military.

Echoing the moral language of the women's political debate, the bureau stated:

The popular view is for military disengagement and the emergence of a new social and political order that is stable, progressive, and responsive to the needs of Nigerians and insured against intervention of the military, whose function should be limited to its traditional role of defending the nation. The view that there is need for a civilian/military co-operation or supervisory role for the military in the new social order was not accepted. The politician is expected to have responsibility for setting the goals of state policy without interfering in internal and professional matters within the military.

Government noted the recommendations on the role of the military. On women, the government report stated:

The Bureau shared the widely voiced view that women constitute an oppressed, exploited, and underprivileged group in Nigeria, as in most Third World countries. Noting that the 1979 constitution granted them equality with men, it pointed out that the government has taken steps to integrate them into the mainstream of Nigeria development. It advocated full involvement for women in politics in order to assure the defence and promotion of women's interest in society. It, therefore, recommended that 5 percent of the legislative seats be allocated to women in all three tiers of government, to be filled by nomination through the political parties.

The government did not accept this recommendation.

The bureau's report continued: 'The Bureau notes that the Federal Government has not formulated a national policy on women and development. The Bureau recommends the formulation of this policy which should be consistent with the philosophy of government proposed in Chapter IV of the report.' The government's response was:

> Government notes this recommendation. Government is of the view that since women have been accepted as full citizens of this nation, government does not see the need for formulation of a national policy on women. However, in areas where women are considered to be at a disadvantage, special efforts are being made for their welfare. For example:
>
> a. A blueprint on women's education in Nigeria is being implemented throughout the country to remove the imbalance in the education of women.
> b. The Home Economics Department of the Ministry of Agriculture designs programmes to boost the efforts of women in agriculture.
> c. The Women in Development Committee of the Ministry of Social Development, Youth, and Sports is set up to highlight areas of hardship and discrimination against women for the attention of government.

On the highly contentious Revenue Allocation, the bureau stated:

> Revenue Allocation or statutory distribution of revenue from the Federation Account among different levels of government has been one of the most contentious and controversial issues in the nation's political life. None of the thirteen formulae under different regimes since 1964 has gained general acceptability among the component units of the country, and the issue has become the first problem every incoming government grapples with.
>
> There is a consensus by contributors that the present formulae for revenue allocation need to be reviewed and revised. It was argued that, among the tiers of government, the Local Governments are best placed for effective grassroots development and mobilisation of the people and also that the Federal Government seems to have taken on too much responsibility, which should constitutionally be assigned to the states and local governments. It argues for a reallocation of responsibilities, which would result in a reduction of revenue to the federal government.
>
> … The Bureau therefore advocates the sharing of revenue in such a way that the Federal Government will get 40 percent, State Governments 40 percent, and Local Governments 20 percent. It was also of the view that funds meant for local governments should be sent directly to them from the Federation Account. Local Governments would thus be encour-

aged to play their proper role as the third tier of government, one whose activities have direct impact on the welfare of the rural masses.

Government responded: 'Government will immediately rectify this by setting up a Technical Revenue Mobilisation Commission which will in future emphasise Revenue Sharing and not Revenue Allocation. Government also notes the importance of the federal presence in the states. This will be used as a factor in sharing revenue in future.'

On mobilization, the bureau stated:

The need for the inauguration of a new political culture is an indispensable condition for the success of the social, political, and economic order. That culture must emphasise public enlightenment, education, and mass mobilisation toward the goals and objectives of the Nigerian state. There is clear evidence that the behaviour of Nigerians in the political process has been largely negative. The low consciousness of the people makes them vulnerable to manipulation by the power elite of the society. The backlash from such actions has been the emergence of a culture of helplessness, apathy, and indifference to the political process.

There has been an argument that the malaise was not due to the system but to the people. The Bureau is convinced that both the system and the people are to blame. It shares a concern for urgent and concerted efforts toward the creation of the right political culture in Nigeria, which should be achieved through a coherent, thorough, and clearly guided and executed programme of social mobilisation and political education based on the recommended new philosophy of government. . . .

Social mobilisation must be seen as encouraging people to take part actively and freely in discussions and decisions affecting their general welfare. Its goal is the creation of a new culture that will transcend the multitude of negative factors in the Nigerian nation. It should make the citizen more efficient and active; impart new values and attitudes to their countrymen; make them more accommodating of the beliefs of one another; enable them to effectively participate in the decision-making process; eliminate ignorance and disease; and instill a sense of pride in, and loyalty to, the Nigerian State.

The Bureau is of the view that the present use of unrelated and uncoordinated government and social institutions on an ad hoc basis for social mobilisation programmes should stop. The new programme should use institutions like the co-operative unions, women's organisations, youth and student's organisations, age grades, village wards, and clan councils, which should be institutionalised and given specific functions to perform in the political system. Government agencies, traditional authorities, and the mass media should also play vital roles.

The government accepted most of the recommendations on mobilization of the masses. Indeed, that became the sole mission and project of the government and the elites. Instead of the bureau's recommended National Directorate of Social Mobilization and Political Education as the body to achieve the objectives, however, the government preferred to call it the National Directorate of Social Mobilization.

On corruption and indiscipline, the bureau stated:

> Corruption and indiscipline are two of the most serious problems in the Nigerian political process since independence, and any efforts to erect a new political order without tackling the twin problems will result in a failure. The Bureau is convinced that a lasting solution can only be achieved by the creation of structures that would diminish the two malaises. The leadership must display transparent honesty, be purposeful, and show commitment to the ideals of the society, to be able to command respect and followership from the larger society. In order to squarely deal with the problems of corruption, indiscipline, lawlessness, and disorder in our society, the Bureau recommends that:
>
> a.   Nigerian leaders should fully commit themselves to principles of social justice for all citizens, as enunciated in the philosophy of government in this report. To this end, they should be seen by members of the public to be a shining example of accountability and discipline in the society.
> b.   The strategy and programmes for fighting corruption, indiscipline, and other problems in our society, as spelt out in the other section of this chapter, should be faithfully implemented as the necessary minimum steps towards eradicating, or at least minimising, the hydra-headed monster of indiscipline, corruption, and lawlessness in our country.

Government accented the recommendations, which it said 'should apply to all Nigerian leaders, both in the public and the private sectors, in and out of office'.

In accordance with the White Paper, the following programme for the transition to civilian rule (which was postponed from 1990 to 1992) was issued by the government:

1987, third quarter

- establishment of Directorate of Social Mobilization
- establishment of National Electoral Commission
- establishment of Constitution Drafting Committee

1987, fourth quarter

- election to local governments on non-party basis

1988, first quarter
- establishment of National Population Commission
- establishment of Code of Conduct Bureau
- establishment of Code of Conduct Tribunal
- establishment of Constituent Assembly
- inauguration of National Revenue Mobilization Commission

1988, second quarter
- termination of Structural Adjustment Programme (SAP)

1988, third and fourth quarters
- consolidation of the gains of the SAP

1989, first quarter
- emergence of new constitution
- release of new fiscal arrangement

1989, second quarter
- ban on party politics to be lifted

1989, third quarter
- announcement of two recognized and registered political parties

1989, fourth quarter
- elections to local governments on political party basis

1990, first and second quarters
- election to state legislatures and state executives

1990, third quarter
- convening of state legislatures

1990, fourth quarter
- convening of state legislatures
- swearing in of state executives

1991, first, second and third quarters
- census

1991, fourth quarter
- local government elections

1992, first and second quarters
- election to federal legislatures and convening of National Assembly

1992, third and fourth quarters

• Final disengagement by the armed forces

In real history General Ibrahim Babangida's military regime hung on
to power even after the 1993 elections contested between Bashorun
M. K. O. Abiola and Alhaji Bashir Tofa. The result, which would have
delared M.K.O. Abiola the winner, was cancelled by Babangida. Babangida was finally forced out of office by a popular movement and had to
hand over power to an interim government consisting of civilians and the
military. In November 1993 General Sani Abacha grabbed power from
the interim government headed by Shonekan and declared himself head
of state, nominating a provisional ruling council. M. K. O. Abiola declared
himself the elected president and was thrown in jail by Abacha. (For further
developments see pp. xi–xix: 'Nigeria: statistics, chronology, human rights'.)

On 29 May 1999 the final disengagement by the armed forces took
place, launching Nigeria's Fourth Republic when retired General Olusegun
Obasanjo took office as a civilian president. Obasanjo's policies are only
just unfolding and dissent and debate have already gained momentum. It
seems Nigerians have been hungry for their democratic rights. There are
several issues of interest that have been raised by public analysis of Obasanjo's appointments. The most interesting of all is the appointment of
Dupe Adelaja from Ogun state as minister of state, a strong position in
the Ministry of Defence. Women had asked for a mixed-sex presidency
and did not get it. This appointment has been linked to allegations of
ethnicity in Obasanjo's policies, since Dupe Adelaja is the daughter of
Abraham Adesanya, the leader of Afenifere, a pan-Yoruba group, which
constitutes the Alliance for Democracy party (AD). Obasanjo has been
accused of building a South-West zone political base for elections in 2003.
Consequently, the question is whether President Obasanjo, who was not
voted into power by the Yoruba, is now implementing a Yoruba agenda,
that is, an Afenifere or AD agenda (*Newswatch*, 6 September 1999). In any
case, what are the implications of the appointment of a woman minister
of state for the empowerment of grassroots women in Nigeria? What will
be the drive in this woman's policies – gender, class or ethnicity?

Another question for Obasanjo's government concerns the distribution
of revenue allocation. Will the new civilian government change the revenue sharing formula, which is currently 48.5 per cent to the federal
government, 24 per cent to the states, 20 per cent to local governments,
and 7.5 per cent to special funds such as the Oil Minerals Producing
Development Commission (OMPADEC) and the Ecological Fund?

Conclusions

The 1986 National Political Debate involved civic groups from the urban and rural areas. It would have been impossible to attend the hundreds of meetings to sample the opinions of all Nigerian women. However, a representative selection of views appears in this chapter and elsewhere in this book.

We gain a comparable perspective on women's participation by looking at a national debate from Kenya. Tabitha Kanongo of the History Department, Kenyatta University, Kenya, saw women's participation in Kenya's political debate in 1992 as a chance to hear the many voices of women as peasant farmers, social workers, petty traders, university lecturers, professional and business women, civic leaders and political aspirants. Since women constitute over half the population of Kenya, Kanongo considers Kenyan women 'a critical mass that had it within its power to determine the destiny of the country: the vote was a weapon that women could utilize to their advantage and for the general good of society. The vote was to be used wisely to elect candidates (female and male) who would be sensitive to the totality of women's realities and aspirations.'[6]

With this view, we can see how the call would be couched in the now standardized rhetoric for 'adequate representation of women at all key decision-making and policy formulating bodies'; to ensure passage and implementation of 'gender-sensitive legislation'; to correct inadequate credit facilities; to correct insufficient representation at decision- and policy-making fora; to discredit the trivialization of women's labour in the domestic arena; to inform women of their legal rights; to redress their lack of control of resources, especially land; and to protest their relegation to inferior social status. We can see that these are complaints and not demands for a change of political system. Suggestions about ways to deal with these complaints have often led to tokenistic co-optation and corruption and not transformation of the masculinized state.

Stocktaking of the political performance of the neo-colonial state in Africa shows that representation is not a guaranteed solution to the gender question. If we look at the main concerns of delegates to Kenya's first National Women's Convention as reported by Kanongo, we see the varied interests that cannot constitute one mass at the grassroots participatory level, but representatives of these varied interests can easily present a face of unity in a controlled situation of performance, a characteristic of contemporary European state systems in Africa. People speak, the audience claps, and a communiqué is issued as if there was a general consensus. Even if the communiqué contains irreconcilable differences, words frozen on paper are not live voices that can continue to cause trouble.

I have taken a different perspective to show that gender and class are key factors in the Nigerian debates, and I have shown major differences between the demands of rural or grassroots women, and those of bourgeois women, whether progressive or conservative. The idea of women's rule or women ruling was seen as quite realizable by the daughters of the Goddess who proposed a women's government. On the other hand, elite women saw women in government in terms of percentage or proportional representation. Both tendencies believed in co-operation with men. I believe that these differences in the women's perceptions of government are directly linked to differences in their experiences of women's organizations; national women's organizations have lost the sense of women's organizational autonomy which in some situations is still a reality for rural women in their kinship, descent and village groups. The memory of organizational autonomy is more vivid in the minds of the daughters of the Goddess. The next chapter looks at their home domain, the local government, for comparative data on the contextual political setting in which rural women operate.

Notes

1. Ifi Amadiume, 'The Local Government System: The Institution of a Women's Committee'. Paper delivered at the National Political Debate organized by the Nigerian Union of Journalists, Anambra State Council, Enugu, 14 May 1986; 'Women and the Political Debate', *Guardian*, 19 May 1986; Ifi Amadiume, 'Conditions Needed to Ensure Women's Awareness and Participation in Development'. Paper presented at the National Political Debate Symposium on 'Women and Nigeria's Political Development' organized by Women in Nigeria (WIN), Anambra, Imo, Rivers, and Cross River states, Owerri, 23–24 May 1986; Ifi Amadiume, 'Women and Development: Another Development with Women in Nigeria'. Paper presented at the National Political Debate Seminar on 'The Nigerian Economic System and Political Order' organized by the Institute for Development Studies, University of Nigeria, Enugu, 9–11 September 1986; Ifi Amadiume, 'Unitary System of Government Versus Grassroots Democracy'. Paper presented at the National Political Debate Forum on 'Nigeria's Political Order: In Search of a Viable Popular Democracy' organized by the Department of Political Science, University of Nigeria, Nsukka, 23–24 September 1986.

2. *Daily Star*, 9 and 16 July 1986.

3. *Daily Star*, 2 July 1986.

4. Excerpts of the report are serialized in *West Africa*, 3, 10, 17, 24 and 31 August 1987.

5. For a Marxian critique of the report, see Edwin Madunagu's manifesto in the *African Guardian*, 6 and 13 August 1987. Madunagu's differences with the Political Bureau led to his expulsion from the bureau in December 1986.

6. Tabitha Kanongo, 'Perceiving Women in Kenya's History' in *Africa World Review*, May–October 1992.

9. Women in local government: a comparison

Advocates of rights and social justice often seek legitimacy by claiming that they speak for the generality of women, more especially working-class and rural women. This is particularly true of national women's organizations in Africa. We saw how all the competing women's organizations in Nigeria claimed to be concerned about empowering grassroots and rural women in the villages who make up the largest population of females in the nation. The Political Bureau and the government White Paper also acknowledged the importance of women's contribution in society, and local government as the tier of government best suited for mobilization of the population for national development, since over 80 per cent of the population is rural and females constitute more than 55 per cent of this population:

> The Bureau is of the view that the present use of unrelated and unco-ordinated government and social institutions on an ad hoc basis for social mobilization programmes should stop. The new programme should use institutions like the co-operative unions, women's organisations, youth and students' organisations, age grades, village wards, and clan councils, which should be institutionalised and given specific functions to perform in the political system. Government agencies, traditional authorities, and the mass media should also play vital roles.[1]

As such, the bureau called for more equitable revenue allocation to enable local governments to function more effectively. This chapter looks briefly at the history of local government in Nigeria and examines the effectiveness of government rural development strategies. Concluding with a specific case study, it examines the state of development in Nnobi and women's involvement in development programmes. What role are daughters of the Goddess playing in advancing their towns and villages, and women's cultures? What are the problems they encounter and what strategies do they employ?

Local administration in Nigeria

Until 1954, the British ruled Nigeria through a unitary system of government under one governor-general, directors of services and heads of departments based at the centre, Lagos; then a parliamentary system was introduced in a federation of the regions (see Awa 1976; Akinyemi et al. 1979).

A British Protectorate was established in 1885, following the meetings in Berlin (1884–85) during which the imperial states of Europe shared out the African continent between themselves (Gavin and Betley 1983). Britain claimed the area which later became known as Nigeria when the Northern and Southern Protectorates were amalgamated in 1914. Prior to this, there was no Nigeria, only politically and culturally diverse and relatively independent ethnic groups and nationalities. Experiments with unification in Nigeria began with British colonial unitary administration which was different from the traditional uniform administrative practice in Britain.

I know that Scotland and Wales now have their own assemblies, but until quite recently Great Britain was usually described as a kind of unitary government, comprising four ethnic regions under one political constitution and a monarchy. It has a centralized government in the parliamentary system and a democratic local government with a long history and tradition pre-dating parliament itself and even the Norman invasion of 1066 (Webb and Klebb 1963). A feature of the British unitary government system is the preservation and strengthening of the autonomy of the local authorities, even though general policies are laid down by ministries in London. Concepts were, however, interpreted differently when dealing with 'natives'. The British operated a Native Authority system in the Northern Protectorate, based on Lugard's 'indirect rule'. The traditional rulers ruled and collected revenue through the existing and efficient traditional bureaucracy of the northern emirates, while the British supervised and advised, sharing the collected revenue with the emirs (Heussler 1968). With amalgamation, Lugard's indirect rule was extended to the south and seen as a means of administrative unification. This resulted in ethnic and religious divisions, since different policies on education were applied in the different regions. The south-eastern communities also felt an infringement on their traditional political systems by the imposition of 'Warrant Chiefs' and a Native Authority.

The catastrophic consequences of Lugard's colonialist universal system of local administration in other parts of Africa, and the revolts against it, are well documented (see Perham 1962; Cohen 1959; Morris and Read 1964; Ogot 1972). Similarly, the enforcement of this system in Igboland and the militant actions led by Igbo women which toppled it have also been well analysed (Afigbo 1972; Nwabara 1977). In spite of courageous efforts to oppose this form of imperialism, local government reforms remained unpopular; they were undemocratic (and ineffective), and they marginalized women, peasants and youth. By 1946, change was in the air: a section of the educated elites had begun to mount a powerful criticism of the whole structure of native administration; a nationalist movement for independence had begun; and in Britain a Labour government had taken office and initiated the so-called post-war consensus on democracy and human rights.

Against this background, in 1947, directives for a grassroots democracy were given to the African colonies by Arthur Creech-Jones, Secretary of State for the Colonies, as a prerequisite for African independence. Progress, in his view, 'depend[ed] on developing in African communities a sense of community obligation and social responsibility and service. In this, local government plays a conspicuous part' (Kirk-Greene 1965). Thus, there was a call for a grassroots democratic system of local government with participation through elected councils, as in Britain, but instead, there emerged an alliance between educated African elites and the colonial government (sons and daughters of imperialism).

On 1 January 1947 a paternalistic constitution was invented by the colonial governor-general, Sir Arthur Richards. His constitution focused on unity, diversity and the participation of Africans, all without consultation. As soon as the Richards' constitution brought regional autonomy in local government, the Eastern Region became the first West African government formally to abolish the hated Native Authority System. The result was promulgation of the relatively radical Eastern Region Local Government Ordinance No. 16 of 1950. What was adopted was the English local government model. Since it favoured educated elites, the county councils and district councils that emerged became incompetent bureaucratic administrative entities which were far removed from the illiterate grassroots population.

As Bello-Imam (1983) points out, local government did not become the base for training future politicians for national leadership, as it did not attract educated people. They instead went to the urban centres where resources and power were concentrated. As local governments covered very large areas and lacked resources, development efforts were left to initiatives within specific communities. Responsibility for local social services remained with regional departments and were not allocated to local governments.

The final change was completed on 1 July 1960, when the Eastern Region Independence Local Government Law shifted control of legislative, judicial and executive power from colonial officers to indigenous

Nigerian men. Participatory local government remained an illusion in the rural communities because local government headquarters in distant towns were out of reach for most rural people. Improvement and Town Unions in rural Igbo communities and non-governmental organizations (NGOs) in all African communities emerged to fill the huge vacuum of effective local government and social services. Under these circumstances, NGOs grew in importance and became dictatorial.

Rural development

With the increasing imperialism of developmentalists and NGOs in Africa, local government has sadly become synonymous with rural development as conceived by international funding agencies. The 1976 Nationwide Local Government Reform, however, proved a major transformation in local administration in Nigeria. Colonial rule in Africa, although it rationalized its imperialism in its mission to educate and civilize 'savage Africans', never reinvested even minimal amounts of the national revenue in the rural villages where most Africans live. It was not until 1976 that the federal revenue allocation to local governments was increased from 5 to 10 per cent.

The reform also tried to ensure more grassroots participation by creating more local government areas (LGAs) and limiting LGA population to 150,000–800,000. Aimed at making people politically responsible, it prescribed 75 per cent elected council members and 25 per cent nominated to represent special-interest groups. This 25 per cent was actually a provision for the presence of the traditional ruler's council, but it was an improvement in some LGAs, where traditional rulers constituted the entire local government council. This was especially true in some northern states.

The local government council, as it operated in Anambra state, was headed by an elected chairman, who was the chief executive of the council. There were also two to five elected supervisory councillors who executed the policies of the council through their departments, which were directed by committees. There were a total of four committees and six administrative departments (see Figure 9.1).

The military regime under Buhari–Idiagbon (1983–85) brought an end to democracy, and Nigeria reverted to indirect rule through sole administrators, but a new focus on rural development also began with that regime. It is only under the development policies of the Babangida regime (1985–93) and a new local government system that rural development has been made a priority for the first time.

Implementing rural development   In its blueprint for rural develop-

Local Government Council
Chairman

Standing Committee	Secretary
Finance and General	Finance Department
Purposes Committee	
Education Committee	Education Department
Works and Planning	Works and Planning
Committee	Department
Agriculture and Health Committee	Health Department
Elected Members Side	Natural Resources
	Department
	Administration Department
	Information and Public
	Enlightenment Unit
	Social Welfare Unit
	Local Government Officers Side

Figure 9.1 Anambra state: administrative structure of local government
(*source*: Bello-Imam 1983: 43)

ment, Anambra state lists as its specific objectives:

- provision of all-season roads
- rural electrification
- self-sufficiency in food production
- siting of industries in rural areas
- establishment of village polytechnics or craft centres, basic care centres, cottage hospitals and general hospitals

It gives its implementation strategies as:

The various town/community development unions, age grades, and other similar organisations will be effectively mobilised for the purpose of rural development. In this regard, well-organised town unions will be registered and formally recognised by the State and Local Governments.

According to the World Bank Rural Development Sector Policy Paper of February 1975, rural development is 'a strategy designed to improve the economic and social conditions of a specific group of people – the rural poor. It involves extending the benefits of development to the poorest among those who seek a livelihood in the rural areas'. It follows, therefore, that in order to achieve this objective, there will be a structural linkage between the Local Governments and the respective town or community unions, age grades, and other similar organisations within each Local Government Area, since the major objectives of these unions are essentially geared toward the improvement of the standard of living of their towns and communities by providing them with modern amenities.

Efforts will be made to spell out how best the resources of the community welfare organisations can be harnessed towards the objectives of developing their rural communities. These local organisations will be given or made to have a psychological sense of importance because of their patriotic efforts in the development of their rural communities.

The idea is to involve the rural people fully through their town unions, age grades, and other similar organisations in planning and implementing policies that are designed to improve their economic, social, political, and cultural development. This will enable them to make positive contributions to both rural and national development. The effective involvement of the local people in this manner will in course of time lead to the attainment of self-reliance. The emphasis will, therefore, be on a concerted approach to mobilising of the people and their resources through the town/community unions, age grades, and other similar organisations in partnership with the local authorities.

This direct involvement of the local people will not only help to harness their potential resources for developmental purposes but will also, in the spirit of the War Against Indiscipline, result in leadership training and patriotism.

There is enough evidence to show that local voluntary organisations are interested in rural development at the grassroots level. They will thus be encouraged and motivated to be the primary vehicles for such development.

The well-to-do and most active members of these local organisations may not necessarily live in the rural areas but may, in fact, be resident in the urban areas. They are usually closely bound by their common allegiance to their home towns and communities. These men and women can be forthcoming in offering their financial and moral help in the development of their rural areas with proper encouragement and awareness that the State Government recognises their ability and that of their union members to mobilise resources within and outside their communities for rural development.

Operational structure

The Organogram hereunder represents an operational structure formulated for effective rural development. It is expected that this structural arrangement will encourage active popular participation and control.

Operational Chair

State Rural Development
  Implementation Authority

Ministry Responsible for
  Rural Development

Zonal Rural Development Committee		Zonal Rural Works Unit
Local Government Rural Development Committees	Local Government Council	Local Government Traditional Rulers' Advisory Council
Development Area Committee (where necessary)		Traditional Rulers' Advisory Council

Town/Village Development Committee
(age grades, women's organisations, work groups, etc.)

Chairman of Town/Village i/c[2]

Problems with this strategy Making local organizations the primary vehicle for rural development poses serious problems. There are fundamental contradictions in the structures of local organizations, especially those that are non-traditional or invented under colonialism. In Nnobi, we saw how ineffective the local government council has been as an instrument of rural development or even as a means of mobilizing the people (Amadiume 1987: ch. 9). It was in fact the town union, the Nnobi Welfare Organization (NWO), that actually administered the affairs of the local community, while other non-governmental organizations contributed by initiating and funding projects.

We also saw the political disadvantages for some sectors of the community that this state of affairs entailed. Town unions are dominated by males and elites; women and youth have little say (or confidence) in these organizations. The unions have also had acute problems with mismanagement, have proven incompetent in administering rural community development projects and they have often succumbed to partisan politics. Yet the state pledges formal recognition of 'well-organized town unions'.

The same charges can be levelled at social clubs, which are elitist in their display of wealth as a means to political appointment. Most poor villagers cannot afford the expense of the private hospitals built by these social clubs in the name of self-help and philanthropy.

What we see time and time again is that the ineffectiveness of the local government system, especially in the provision of funds for social and economic development in rural communities – in development jargon: 'de-linking' – has given amazing power to the private sector, thereby encouraging feudalism and rural capitalism, to the detriment of the rural masses. For this reason, the final paragraph of the implementation strategy, which calls on the 'well-to-do' urban-dwellers for financial and moral help for rural development, should give cause for alarm. It cannot be viewed in isolation from the ever-increasing patron–client relationship between the Nigerian government and wealthy individuals in the private sector.[3]

The new strategy for rural development has provided a Local Government Traditional Rulers' Advisory Council, whose responsibility is to advise the Local Government Development Committee and assist in public enlightenment. The composition of the typical council of traditional rulers is made up of the 'well-do-do' – i.e. business and educational elites who have acquired the capital necessary to buy traditional titles. The typical council also includes those who have gained titles through the patronage of the traditional rulers. Thus it is composed of the upper and bourgeois classes. How can such a group 'enlighten' the poor rural masses?

The contents of the blueprint suggest that there is a terrible misunderstanding of three crucial words used in relation to the rural populace: 'awareness', 'mobilization' and 'development'. In Nnobi – and, no doubt, everywhere else in Nigeria – rural people have always been aware of what is needed for social and economic development. They have mobilized themselves to meet these needs but have lacked adequate assistance from the government. Government, on the other hand, has concentrated funding for development projects in the capitals and urban centres and, in so doing, has helped the 'well-do-do' to do even better. Nigeria's uneven development has been well documented (Nwosu 1985).

As can be seen from Anambra state's implementation strategy, the World Bank's definition of rural development is accepted. If rural development is about improving the conditions of the poorest in the rural areas, how can the government shift responsibility to that class of exploiters whose very existence creates the poverty of the majority of the poor? Rural communities are not homogeneous entities, economically or socially. There are the poor and powerless, on the one hand, and, on the other, the rich and powerful.

Some researchers who have worked in rural communities in Asia have defined development as a process of liberation of initiatives, as opposed to the imposition of development programmes on people. Because of the basic contradictions entailed in class polarization, they argue, development projects should be aimed at balancing power between the rich and the poor.[4] It follows that a true initiator of such relevant development cannot come from the exploiters within the communities – that is, from the capitalists in the private sector. It can come about only through a strong grassroots democratic local government.

The primary concern of such an initiator, the authors argue, would be geared towards helping rural people organize themselves into co-operatives for employment and income-generating programmes. This would accelerate the de-linking process, which will lead to relative autonomy from the exploitative classes. It is only then that the grassroots will be a fertile base for social and political education – that is to say, true public enlightenment for awareness and consciousness-raising.

A strong grassroots democratic local government system

Launching the White Paper on the new local government administration which was implemented on 1 April 1986, chief of general staff, Commodore Ukiwe said: 'It is pertinent to remind ourselves that by the tail end of the defunct civilian administration – i.e., by December 1983 – local government structures and modes of administration throughout the federation had virtually been in total disarray as a result of the use to which the erstwhile politicians put them.' Ukiwe also quoted President Babangida's silver jubilee celebration speech of 1985: 'This government is committed to the principle of citizen participation at all levels of decision-making. An effort will be made to utilise the local government system for encouragement of grassroots mobilisation, community, governance, and self-fulfilment.'[5] These objectives are reflected in the White Paper on the new local government system.

Since the military government believed that the 1976 nationwide local government reform failed for operative reasons and not because of structural problems, the 1976 structure has been retained. The main area of change was the appointment by the military governors of a chairperson and councillors. Another change was the rule which mandated inclusion of one woman among the councillors.

I have pointed out elsewhere some problems in relation to women with this new scheme.[6] These include gender biases and prejudices carried into the management structure of the new Local Government Councils. There was, for example, from references to a 'he' or a 'chairman', a general assumption that men should chair the councils. With regard to the token females in the councils, questions that could be raised include the basis of their selection, their credentials, whom they represented, and to whom they were accountable. Most of all, how would the masculine town unions relate to them?

In the introduction to the blueprint for rural development, it is clearly stated that some 80 per cent of Anambra state's populations live in rural areas. It would thus seem reasonable to assume that social and infrastructural amenities would be distributed between the rural and urban areas at a ratio of 80 to 20 per cent. Such logic notwithstanding, 10 per cent of the federation account and 10 per cent of states' internally generated revenue is all that is given to local governments. The government's new emphasis on rural development has not been translated into a need to increase revenue allocation. If anything, more financial responsibility has been shifted on to local governments by the federal government. The federal government, for example, instituted free primary education, but it has left the responsibility for teachers' salaries to state and local governments. It was this that prompted Anambra state's military governor, Group Captain Emeka Omeruah, to say that local government should be the richest of the three tiers of government, since it holds the bulk of the population. Omeruah said: 'We do not kill the goose that will lay the golden egg ... The rural area is the best index of the development of any country.'[7] It was not long before the state and local governments began to levy parents and demand school fees. This led to rioting by women in Bendel state.[8]

Another major contradiction was that the body through which rural development was to be achieved was instituted as a separate community development committee (CDC), not as an integral part of the structure of the local government council. The CDC was expected to constitute representatives of all local organizations in each community in Anambra state: town unions, clubs and associations, age grades, women's and youth's organizations, religious organizations, elders and traditional rulers. Ironically, it is they who would constitute the most important committee of a true grassroots democratic local government council.

Recommendations

An alternative proposal for a strong grassroots democratic local government system to guarantee rural development entails:

• a reorganization of LGAs on the basis of spatial area and population
• a restructuring of the local government council
• an increase in local government grants

Lagos Metropolis found it necessary in 1980 to institute fundamental changes in the 1976 Local Government Reform. The large size of LGAs carved out by the 1976 reform made it impossible to fulfil the purpose of local government – to bring government closer to the people (Bello-Imam 1983). Lagos reduced its council population areas to 25,000–300,000. Lagos is a metropolis where there is a large population concentrated in a small geographical area. Thus, local people were not necessarily living far from their local councils, and they had ready access to transportation.

This is in sharp contrast to the situation in rural areas. Even in areas of heavy population density in Anambra state, LGAs are very large. They include several villages and towns, and both transportation and communication are difficult. In the Idemili LGA, for example, none of the nineteen towns has a population of less than 20,000. Someone from Nnobi had to travel to Ogidi, where the LGA headquarters was located, to see the council's chairperson or the councillors. This is too far a distance for rural folks who basically walk. It is too far for citizens to walk to reach their local government council. The 1986 local government White Paper specified five councillors, which meant that not all of the nineteen towns in the Idemili LGA were represented at the council's headquarters.

To speed up the government's policy of rural development and make it meaningful, every community/village/town/village-group of 10,000 or so should have a local government council and a town hall. Nnobi, which has a population of more than 20,000, is made up of three villages. The village of Ebenesi, the first in seniority, has a population of more than 10,000, and should have a local government council and a town hall. Nnobi should thus have two LGCs, one for Ebenesi and the other for Ngo and Awuda, the other two villages. Nnobi as a town would then have a two-tier system of local government, where the lowest level of the LGC, the village council, would operate as a village assembly. The second level, the town council, would operate on a committee basis, and final decisions would be taken at town council meetings. A third tier of the LGC would include closely related towns. A fourth tier would be at the level of the present LGA.

A restructuring of the councils would involve committees, which should be comprised of elected or nominated councillors from local government wards within each village LGC area, co-opted members of traditional and non-traditional local organizations, and villagers who wish to attend particular council committee meetings. Development committees should not be independent non-governmental bodies but one or more committees of the LGC – that is, part of the LGC structure. I have also argued elsewhere (and do so again in the next chapter) for the institution of a women's committee and a women's unit in the LGC structure, whose concern would be the specific interests and needs of local women.[9] I have also argued for a rotating system of chairing for the council committees.

These changes would entail a massive decentralization of the civil service, the transfer of personnel to rural communities, and a reorganization of the budget so that more money goes to the provision of services, agriculture and allied industries for the majority of the population who live in rural areas.

The shortage of revenue that the LGCs have experienced accounts, to a large extent, for their ineffectiveness. In the British system, more than 50 per cent of local government grants came from central government (Bello-Imam 1983). (It is now 75 per cent, and the compulsory levy in the form of a poll tax enacted by the Conservative government to raise the remaining 25 per cent led to demonstrations and riots all over Britain in April 1990.) Unlike rural Nigeria, however, Britain has a well-developed infrastructure which can be taxed to generate revenue.

The ability of local governments in Nigeria to generate adequate internal revenue is based on assumptions. Furthermore, the government's present policy of taxing and levying the rural populace is exploitative, since the government has done little or nothing for the rural communities. Since matching grants lead to uneven development, they should be abolished. An increase in the federation allocation to local governments is imperative. We saw in Chapter 8 that the Political Bureau recommended an increase to 20 per cent. Ideally, a stated, level amount in grants should be allocated to each LGC, and those communities would then decide how to spend their portion.

It is significant that only Lagos has managed to generate operational revenue. Bello-Imam writes:

> The Lagos City Council stands out among other councils in the country in that, since its inception, it has always derived the bulk of its internal revenue from the property rate instead of personal income tax. For instance, in 1962–63, this accounted for about 85 per cent of its internal revenue and 51 per cent of its total revenue. (Bello-Imam 1983: 34)

Since infrastructural amenities have been concentrated in the capital by both colonial and Nigerian governments, Lagos has the property to tax. This is not true in the rural areas.

'Who pays the piper', they say, 'calls the tune.' Town unions have become more experienced and knowledgeable about government finance, especially revenue. In the wake of the government's new-found interest in rural areas as a source of revenue, I believe there will be a lot of competition between town unions and LGCs for control and management of development projects. The government's search for revenue is part of the process of restructuring the Nigerian economy in response to directives from the World Bank and the International Monetary Fund.

How old institutions of power and the organized collective power of women have been undermined and how the needs of the rural masses have been affected by this competition will be examined in the rest of this chapter as I look specifically at the women in Nnobi.

State of development in Nnobi

Table 9.1 shows the full state of development in Nnobi in 1986 – namely, a list of projects completed and on-going. It also shows financing

Table 9.1 Projects of the Nnobi community up to 1986

Name of project	Responsible body	Estimated cost	Stage of completion	Remarks
1. Afor Market	Nnobi Welfare Organization for Nnobi Community	N 2,000,000	On-going	Design and planning completed, drainage started
2. Electricity	Nnobi Welfare Organization for Nnobi Community	N 1,000,000	On-going	N 500,000 spent to date
3. Pipe-borne water	Nnobi Welfare Organization for Nnobi Community	N 500,000	On-going	N 200,000 spent to date
4. Nnobi General Hospital	Abalukwu Social Club, Nnobi; Federation of Nnobi Age Grades; Nnobi Welfare Organization for Nnobi Community; People's Club of Nigeria, Nnobi Chapter	N1,000,000	On-going	N 600,000 spent to date
5. Village roads	Nnobi Welfare Organization for Nnobi Community	N 130,000	On-going	Ebenesi-50 km, Ngo-43 km, Awuda-30 km
6. Biscuit factory	Nnobi Multi-purpose Co-operative Society Ltd	N 500,000	Completed	Factory completed, machines installed; project awaiting commissioning
7. Petrol station	Nnobi Multi-purpose Co-operative Society Ltd	N 60,000	On-going	N 35,000 spent to date
8. Erosion control	Awuda Community, Nnobi	N500,000	On-going	N 114,000 spent to date
9. Erosion control	Umuagu and Ndam Ngo, Nnobi	N 400,000	On-going	N 40,000 spent to date
10. Travel goods industries	Dozini Industries Ltd, Nnobi	N 500,000	On-going	N 135,000 spent to date
11. Onumonu battery industry	Onumonu and Sons Nigeria, Nnobi	N 2,000,000	On-going	N 600,000 spent to date
12. Technology workshop	PTA, Girls Secondary School, Nnobi	N 80,000	On-going	N 50,000 spent to date

No.	Project	Organization	Amount	Status	Notes
13.	Madonna Catholic Hospital	Madonna Catholic Community, Nnobi	N 1,200,000	On-going	Two buildings completed and the third in progress; N 600,000 spent to date, nearing completion;
14.	Church building	St Simon's CMS Church Members, Nnobi	N 1,000,000	On-going	N 800,000 spent to date
15.	Church building	St Andrew's (CMS) Church Members, Nnobi	N 800,000	On-going	N 300,000 spent to date
16.	Church building	St Paul's (CMS) Church, Ebenesi-Nnobi Members	N 600,000	On-going	N 300,000 spent to date
17.	High Temple and Tabernacle	Christ the King Sabbath Mission	N 10,000,000	On-going	
18.	Nursery, primary and secondary schools	Christ the King Sabbath Mission	N 6,000,000	On-going	Nursery completed and commissioned
19.	Village hall	Umuru Brothers Association Ebenesi, Nnobi	N 300,000	On-going	N 140,000 spent to date
20.	Community hall	Awuda Community, Nnobi	N 80,000	On-going	N 50,000 spent to date
21.	Village hall	Umuaemelum village, Awuda, Nnobi	N 120,000	On-going	N 20,000 spent to date
22.	Village hall	Umunna Umugamuma, Awuda, Nnobi	N 25,000	On-going	N 15,000 spent to date
23.	Village hall	Umudinya village, Awuda, Nnobi	N 115,000	On-going	N 50,000 spent to date
24.	Village hall	Ifite village, Ebenesi, Nnobi	N 400,000	On-going	N 110,000 spent to date
25.	Village hall	Amadunu village, Ebenesi, Nnobi	N 50,000	On-going	N 35,000 spent to date
26.	Village hall	Workers Ndam, Ngo, Nnobi	N 150,000	On-going	N 70,000 spent to date
27.	Village hall	Umunebo, Ngo, Nnobi	N 120,000	On-going	N 50,000 spent to date
28.	Village hall	Umuegbu, Ngo, Nnobi	N 200,000	On-going	N 80,000 spent to date
29.	Village hall	Dununebo, Amadunu Ebenesi, Nnobi	N 40,000	On-going	N 30,000 spent to date
30.	Culverts	Ebenesi, Ngo, Awuda	N 195,000	On-going	N 170,000 spent to date
31.	Primary school extension	PTA, United Primary School, Umuagu Community	N 20,000	On-going	N 8,000 spent to date
32.	Primary school extension	PTA, Awuda Schools	N 40,000	On-going	N 15,000 spent to date
33.	Primary school extension	PTA, Central School, Nnobi	N 30,000	On-going	N 25,000 spent to date

responsibility for the projects, the estimated cost of each project, and the amount spent up to 1986. About 75 per cent of the projects were for infrastructural amenities such as roads, electricity, pipe-borne water, village halls, culverts and a marketplace. Only three projects were for industries – a biscuit factory, travel goods industries and a battery industry. Only one project was aimed at women, and it is, ironically, a technology work-shop (in reality, a craft workshop).

With 75 per cent of the projects in the area of physical infrastructure, one would expect a strong governmental presence. It is, however, non-governmental bodies – town unions, social clubs, churches, villages – which are financing these projects.

Women's involvement Discussions with the president of NWO and several Nnobi women, including members of the Women's Council, make it clear that women have been marginalized in the decision-making pro-cesses, and their interests are not taken into consideration in the planning and execution of development projects (but their financial contribution is heavily relied upon). Nnobi women do not have separate projects but contribute to infrastructural projects undertaken by the town. Con-sequently, most of the projects undertaken by the Nnobi Women's Council have been in the provision of social amenities for the common good of the people of Nnobi – taking care of and equipping maternity homes, for example. But its most important activity is looking after the marketplaces, and everyone in Nnobi acknowledges the fact that the market has been the responsibility of the Women's Council ever since Nnobi was born. The cost of modernization of the market has made it necessary, as a result of the government's ineffectiveness and lack of clear policies on women's rights, to bring men into the marketplace. The politics surrounding Nnobi's central market, Afor Nnobi, provides a good example of changing gender relations in Nnobi and the place of women in development.

The struggle for economic justice in Nnobi: control of the marketplace During the 1977 arrests, when Nnobi women failed to act collectively, there were some events based on a traditional strategy of female militancy, resistance and direct action. In the marketplace, an African woman's second home, they booed and insulted those they knew to have been responsible for their arrest. Instead of the traditional Nnobi women's strategy of *isi nta* (a kind of tug-of-war), they used satire and innuendo, the strategy of the less powerful (Amadiume 1987). The import-ant point is that it was at the marketplace that they felt strong enough to do so. The contemporary situation represents a general struggle by rural women all over Africa to maintain control of the marketplace, traditionally a woman's domain in the indigenous African economy. In many ways, this struggle symbolizes the onslaught by capitalism on the traditional agriculture and subsistence economy, the appropriation of rural women's rights and their exploitation by the new elites and their pseudo-state systems.

In 1986, the politics around the Nnobi central market came to the fore again, as a result of the new government's rural development policy. With the effect of the International Monetary Fund's (IMF) Structural Adjustment Programme, local and state governments have found it necessary to generate revenue, but they find it difficult to contribute money to rural projects. Thus government wants villages to build markets and hand them over to the government to control. This was the case with the Afor market project in Nnobi, where NWO decided to construct a modern market at an estimated cost of 2 million naira, as described in the following interview with the presidents of NWO and the president of Nnobi Women's Council (Inyom Nnobi) in August 1986.

NWO: Inyom Nnobi can be called a cultural organization for women, where all women, regardless of religious or any other affiliation, belong. It includes all Nnobi. Most of its projects provide social amenities for the good of all people in Nnobi, such as taking care of the maternity home. The women keep the market neat, sweeping it after each market day. That is their responsibility right from the time Nnobi started. They keep order in the market. In other words, the market is totally controlled by Inyom Nnobi.

AMADIUME: You've just said they are in complete control of the market. Who are the market masters?

NWO: We say control of the market in the sense that 90 per cent of the people in the market are women. Inyom Nnobi keeps the market clean. It controls women trading in that market. If you fight in the market, the women take up the case, charge you or fine you if you are found guilty. They recommend any further development in the market to the Town Union. The Town Union works in close co-operation with the women. The women advise what should be done in the market and how it is controlled. The NWO is the overall government of Nnobi. The market master is a staff person paid by the NWO.

AMADIUME: I happen to know the history behind the development of market masters. At that time, you were not the president of NWO. Was Inyom Nnobi party to the initial decision to install market masters? Was it consulted?

NWO: We've had market masters as far back as the 1950s.

AMADIUME: You mean during the colonial period?

NWO: Yes, In those days, it was something like local councils. The local council controlled the market in collaboration with the NWO. The market master was discontinued, reinstated, stopped and started again. The controversy with the market is not about the market master but about the introduction of toll collection. The toll collection started in 1983, when the chairs of the three villages in Nnobi met together and made that decision. They met with the Igwe, and the Igwe approved it. As you know, innovation is not immediately welcomed. Objections were raised by market women and other people who attended Nnobi market from other towns. They did not wish to pay the toll at first, but later they accepted it.

AMADIUME: What was Inyom Nnobi's role in that?

NWO: Its role is to convince women that the money collected goes to the central Nnobi purse. Since the women comprise about 90 per cent of the market's population, immediately they are won, the battle is over. Even when we set up the Market Committee of the NWO, we had about six women on the committee to represent Inyom Nnobi, two from each village. Women have controlled the market from the beginning. It is only now, because development needs money, that men have come into the market. Before that, even the construction of market stalls was done by women.

AMADIUME: You mean the stalls on the periphery which men occupy?

NWO: Yes. Women built them. They are grouped according to villages, then patrilineages. The women then construct the sheds.

AMADIUME: But this is a project. It can be listed as a women's project.

NWO: At Afor market, the structures are constructed by Nnobi women in groups. They collect money in groups and construct one line, two lines, and so on, and they use them as their permanent sheds. The cost of modernization has made it necessary for men to come in. The market has to be planned and designed, and larger buildings have to be constructed. Still, women contribute.

AMADIUME: Is there money collected and set aside for the market? What is the political situation of the market?

NWO: We have decided to construct a modern market at Afor. We have set up a committee of experts – designers, a surveyor, architects – which is working on it now. An engineer is chair of the committee, and a university lecturer is secretary. They are now drawing up a plan. We are marking 2 million naira. We hope to raise one million through contributions, donations and loans. We are negotiating with the Nnobi branch of the National Bank of Nigeria to contribute the remaining one million.

AMADIUME: What about the local government? It seems that the government wants revenue, but it does not want to contribute money to rural projects. Government, for example, wants villages to build markets and hand control over them to the government. This is a wrong policy.

NWO: The Market Committee of the Idemili local government in Ogidi approached us, and wanted the market for management only, but we are very reluctant to hand over the market to local government because Afor Igwe in Umudioka was handed over to the Onitsha Northern District Council in the 1930s, and it has never been developed. They simply say it is their market – no development, but they want money. We decided that Nnobi should build its market, and if the local government wants to manage it, we will have to negotiate terms. The revised development of local governments reform of 1976 gave local government the power to manage markets. That document stated that local government will take over existing markets only by negotiation and not by force. We feel we will be at an advantage in handing over a built-up market. If we spend two million, local government will refund that money before taking over the market. We also expect to retain a percentage of the total collected from the market, which will give us a source of funding for our other development projects. The market is the easiest way of getting that revenue.

AMADIUME: Remember you said that the market as it stands now was built by Nnobi women? Have you thought about recognizing the Nnobi market as a women's project? Now that government claims to recognize women's economic contribution and is interested in funding or assisting women's projects, I see a need to specify some projects as belonging to women to give them some economic autonomy. Obviously, not all NWO members are as progressive as you are in terms of women's issues; with some, I believe we won't even be discussing it.

NWO: You are right. Under the previous president, we wouldn't even be discussing this.

AMADIUME: I have it on record how the NWO 'killed' Inyom Nnobi and put it under NWO supervision. Isn't it ridiculous that NWO has to decide what should be called women's projects? Isn't it right that revenue collected from women's projects should be invested in projects which will yield income for women? Take the market, for example. When you negotiate revenue shares with the government, will you be bearing in mind that a certain percentage should go to Inyom Nnobi? I feel that Inyom Nnobi has a right to an independent purse – money which they can use for other women's projects, as, for example, a co-operative since this land is not fertile for agriculture.

NWO, INYOM NNOBI: We have no land.

NWO: There is no government, at the family level or any other level, that can succeed if women do not support it. When I was elected president, my first action was to go to the women – that is, Inyom Nnobi – to tell them, 'Now Nnobi says I am going to be president. I see what has happened in the past. I know that if we dwell on the politics of who should rule or who owns this etc., only Nnobi and our children will suffer.' Any Nnobi person knows that the problems we have concerning women's autonomy in Igboland have been old ones. In the past, in Nnobi, in 90 per cent of families, the man was either a farmer or a trader, and this was the same for women. After farming, men have their own share and women theirs. In most cases, when the farm produce is taken to market, it is women who sell it, and because of that, women own the shed in the market. Men never used to go and sit in the marketplace. Men used to have collection or gathering spots where they would sit and drink or take snuff, or where they would stay and call for drinks if in-laws were coming to take a new wife. They stay at these spots and drink in the morning and then disperse after a few hours, while women traded in the market. So you see that even though all along women controlled the market because they used it more, at the same time, women have always been aware that the market was owned collectively by all Nnobi, that they owned it with men. They also knew that the government system in Nnobi was such that if there was something to be done, men and women got together to do it. If things get difficult, you can go to the women. The women contribute ideas which the men take to their meeting; both views are combined, and the project is carried out. There has never been a time when a line of demarcation said, 'This is solely men's, and this is women's.' There is no project in Nnobi that men can claim they carried out completely.

INYOM NNOBI: Take the hospital, for example. It was equipped by women – the beds, I went to buy them.

NWO: Things change with time. In Nnobi, we are not known in Igboland as those who are quarrelling with their wives. If there is anything going on which involves supporting women, Nnobi will not be among the last. We will be among the first to do so. We are not quarrelling. Nothing will prevent us from co-operating. We know that if women benefit, they bring that benefit to Nnobi; if men benefit, they bring it to Nnobi. We co-operate. It will be difficult for women alone to raise the 2 million naira that we need for the market. There is better progression in co-operation. But if it becomes necessary to help women identify their role in any project, NWO will automatically encourage it to any length.

AMADIUME: You have made a diplomatic speech. Now, how are we going to send to the Women and Development Committee a list of all the

women's organizations in Nnobi and the projects they have undertaken? Other areas are getting assistance, equipment, and so forth. In
the absence of literate women who could have been nearby to write
out all these things for them, I see a role for NWO, since you co-
operate with the women. The women have given you a lot of support.
Your men also visit home frequently and are more in touch with what
is happening at home than the elite women are. How are you going to
set about doing something? Are you going to form a committee to do
a feasibility study of the economic situation? For example, lots of
machines are now being designed here in Nigeria in line with self-
reliance and indigenous technology – crop-driers, fish ponds, etc. The
departments of agriculture, rural development units, all have ideas.

NWO: One of the problems we face is ignorance, which breeds suspicion.
Once you mention co-operative, they immediately say that that person
is looking for a way to enrich himself. That kills businesses and organizations started in Nnobi. Each person approaches the other with
suspicion.

INYOM NNOBI: That is true.

NWO: There are also denominational differences which divide the women.

AMADIUME: *Odinani* [followers of indigenous religion] people are also
excluded from many things. With each group speaking only to women
from within their own group, they create rivalry.

NWO: This is true and these are some of the big problems which we are
facing in the rural areas.

AMADIUME: I suggest they take a section of the market as their project.
What about forming guilds along the line of the various commodities?

NWO: The elites have played a disuniting part.

INYOM NNOBI: Yes, especially the previous leader of NWO. This man
here respects women and consults us. With the hospital, for example,
there is a particularly bad bush, we cleared it because of his respect for
us. We sweep and clean the hospital, rotating in villages, and we do it
with a clean heart.

NWO: I'll go any length to back anything that will project the name of the
town, and I'll convince the members of the executive to do so too.
There is nothing personal to gain except the joy that when names are
called, let us also call the name of our town. You yourself also have a
role in informing us. If it is an economic venture, we will try our best
to see it started, and then the women can take it up. Perhaps this will
attract back the elite women, for they also stand to gain by being the
ones to go and represent Nnobi outside. Also, I suggest that any time
you be chance to visit Nnobi, you inform Mrs Chukwuka here to summon Inyom Nnobi so that you can address them.

AMADIUME: Yes, even she herself has invited me twice.

NWO: Your suggestion about the market project needs careful deliberation. This approach to women's economy is new. In terms of social amenities, women have done very well. If they are convinced, their laws are very firm. Keeping the hospital clean used to cost us 300 naira a month, but now the job has been taken over by Inyom Nnobi. They sweep Afor market monthly, and they sweep their village squares.

AMADIUME: I know, because some years ago, I went to sweep the Idemili square with *Odinani* women.

NWO: Women of different denominations have their own projects within the church. We have women members in the co-operative society, but that is a joint venture.

AMADIUME: Can't the women in this co-operative use their experience to get other women together and form a women's co-operative? Co-operatives grow out of other co-operatives. You can invite experts to advise the women.

NWO: At the moment, we have a wrong notion of what a co-operative society is supposed to be. They operate in secrecy and restrict membership. In a real co-operative, everybody is equal and contributes an equal amount. Co-operatives do not pay taxes. I believe the women can do it well.

AMADIUME: I have a great admiration for Nnobi women.

NWO: You should have. But things have changed with modern Nnobi men, who tend to believe that women should remain at home and be given food.

INYOM NNOBI: If women go out, people begin to talk about them. Someone like myself, they say, 'You'll never find her at home. She's off to meetings or to market.'

NWO: But this is changing. After the Biafran War [1967–70] when we returned to Onitsha, you'll find a woman who has been married for fifteen or twenty years and does not trade!

INYOM NNOBI: It is education that causes it.

NWO: No, an educated person has an opportunity to get white-collar jobs. For a woman without education, it is trading, but her husband won't allow her to do that.

INYOM NNOBI: The fact that women went off to market caused unrest in Nnobi recently. After the Biafran War, Inyom Nnobi made a law that any woman who did not leave home before 7.00 a.m. had to pay a 6-pence fine. We used to block the roads. One elder opposed us because he believed that women should stay at home and cook and serve meals.

NWO, AMADIUME: That is a colonial mentality, not a traditional one. Staying at home became prestigious.

INYOM NNOBI: That view won at the time and they made the market operate between 11.00 a.m. and 2.00 p.m. The struggle continued until we won the right to stay at the market all day.

AMADIUME: In the published constitution of Nnobi, why is Inyom Nnobi not a member of the central executive?

NWO: It is a mistake. When I became president, I wanted to start with the committees and I wanted women to be represented on all the committees because NWO operates through the committees – health, market, works, etcetera. When the constitution is amended, if the majority find it necessary, we shall include them. In the past, men used to say the sexes should hold separate meetings. After men's meetings, if there is something concerning women, then they will be invited.

AMADIUME: How can a central executive which functions on the basis of representation not include women? Some of your members actually assume that Inyom Nnobi is in the executive council. I had to show them the constitution.

INYOM NNOBI: We used to attend, but one man said he didn't want to see us.

NWO: It was missed in the constitution, and the man who operated the first government after the constitution felt that women should not contribute at all, but should be kept far away. He could still have invited them to meetings until the importance of their participation would be realized, but he didn't. This omission in the constitution could also have been a way to prevent bringing a non-Nnobi person to the central executive.

INYOM NNOBI: Non-Nnobi wives are not represented on the executive committee of Inyom Nnobi either.

NWO: Once, a child of a non-Nnobi woman became chair of NWO and wanted to use his position to enforce a rule that non-Nnobi wives could be representatives on the Inyom Nnobi executive, but we opposed it.

AMADIUME: I'd like to ask you now about the government's recommended community development committees. Have you constituted yours yet? Are women on it?

NWO: Yes, we have, and women are on it – that is, representatives of Inyom Nnobi.

AMADIUME: You suggested to them that women should be on all the committees. Have they done so?

NWO: Yes.

AMADIUME: Who makes up the central executive?

NWO: All officers of NWO, all *ichie* titled men, two representatives from each branch of NWO, special members from each village – that is, three each – plus chairs of the committees.

AMADIUME: Have there been any recommendations to revive women's titles?

NWO: Not yet.

AMADIUME: Have you given this any thought? – seeing that certain levels of representation consist of the titled. Mrs Chukwuka came to Imo state with us for the WIN political debate and saw the number of women chiefs who spoke there. When politics resume, they will be at an advantage. Look, I am not saying that I support the chieftaincy institution.

NWO: We believe that Nnobi is an ancient town. We are reluctant to introduce some of these artificial titles. We've thought of reviving the old traditional title for women, modifying it to suit religious positions – for example, the Onitsha maintain the Otu Odu society, one of the highest women's societies. We shall think about reviving these things.

AMADIUME: Even the Anglicans have finally accepted *ichi Ozo* [taking the Ozo title].

NWO: The various towns have to negotiate this with the church.

AMADIUME: I hear Nnobi has agreed with them.

INYOM NNOBI: It won't happen here. It is heathenism. They practise it at night, and in the day they go to church.

AMADIUME: That's not so. I have witnessed one title taken here in Nnobi. Ezudona and Ekechukwu, as priests of Aho, performed their own rituals. Then the Catholic priest arrived and performed his.

INYOM NNOBI [in disgust]: We are working on one idea. You know that when a man takes a title, he is given fowl and yams. But these titled men don't seem to give anyone anything. We want to make a rule that they give something when a new child is born.

AMADIUME: You women should get your ideas together and list things that you want in the constitution because a constitution is a binding law for a community or a town. I can see that this title thing is going to cause trouble: church women don't want it, but *Odinani* women support it. The idea is to expunge it of 'bad' practices. Some of the symbols people condemn are not bad; it is from white people's wrong interpretations that they get these ideas.

NWO: Yes, I agree. Look, for example, at when they ordain a bishop. He sits on a stone, yet it is this stone they say we used to worship!

AMADIUME: Wasn't Peter told that he would be the rock on which the church would be built? It is a question of how symbols are interpreted.

NWO: Father Ikeobi has explained the positive symbolism of a lot of these things that were thought bad.

AMADIUME: Mama, I can see that if NWO comes out now to support the taking of titles, it is you Christian women who will oppose it.

INYOM NNOBI: We will say which we will do and which we will not do.

AMADIUME: You will be the ones to lose.

NWO: They believe that once their husband is titled, they are too.

INYOM NNOBI: Do you know that we were not there when this constitution was written. Imagine! You bear a child, and an *ichie* will not give you anything. They've given *ichie* to greedy men! They things they ask for from the patrilineage are not in the constitution. They have not even given us copies of the constitution.

AMADIUME: You hear that!

NWO: I will buy about six copies and give them to Inyom Nnobi. They only cost 1 naira each.

AMADIUME: But they are more than six. I'll contribute 5 naira so they can have more. I recommend that they translate it into Igbo so the villagers can buy and read and refer to it.

INYOM NNOBI: [continues to talk about the right of a woman who has given birth to receive a gift from a man who has been named an *ichie*].

NWO: It is the protocol of not eating food in public that prompted the *ichie* to insist that if they go anywhere, they are to be given fowl and yams. In the past, you had to give them fowl before they would eat your food. It was understood. They did not have to say it. NWO has decided that the rule about giving fowl should not be compulsory. If an *ichie* visits and you have a fowl to give, you can give it. If you don't have a fowl, you don't give, and the *ichie* will not accept your food. It is not compulsory.

AMADIUME: You see, women are concerned because they are the ones the husbands ask for the fowls to give.

INYOM NNOBI: They don't even pay school fees.

NWO: The *ichie* are quite undisciplined, and I have declared total 'war' on them. We fined two *ichie* 250 naira each. If they don't pay within three months, we will take away their titles. We want to operate a government where everyone knows their rights. We need a 75 per cent consensus to amend the constitution. Things will be corrected. By December, we will set up a committee to review the constitution. Inyom Nnobi can register a protest then.

AMADIUME: One last thing. I understand there was a controversy between Inyom Nnobi and the neighbouring village of Awka-Etiti involving the market and the collection of toll.

INYOM NNOBI: There was a 20 kobo flat levy and 50 kobo for those who had shops. The responsibility for collecting the levy was handed over to a committee which sold the 50 kobo tickets. The booklet finished, and they did not print more. Instead, they decided to take 20 kobo from everyone.

NWO: This was under Okongwu's regime. When I came in, we decided that the flat rate was unfair and that we should charge 1 naira, 50 kobo, and 20 kobo according to the commodity being sold. Meat sellers and those who sell from vans pay 1 naira; those with sheds and articles and wholesalers – like women selling cassava in bags – pay 50 kobo. All others pay 20 kobo. The misunderstanding came as a result of shortcomings of toll-collectors. But there is a 'cold war' between us and Awka-Etiti. Ezenwa [the traditional ruler of Awka-Etiti] wrote, and we wrote a rejoinder, but we were tricked and our article was not published. Igwe got hold of what Ezenwa published and denied all he said, and we finally got the truth published.[10] Then Ezenwa looked for a way to retaliate, and when we ruled this levy, he cashed in on it by ruling that any Awka-Etiti person who attends Afor Nnobi would pay a 100-naira fine. He also approached Nnokwa and Nnewi, asking them to withdraw. We also got information that they lured some of our people to cause trouble in Nnobi. We quickly mobilized Inyom Nnobi. There was an internal split in Awka-Etiti. Awka-Etiti people wanted Eke to be a daily market, and if they took their produce elsewhere, the Eke market would not attract enough attendance. They wanted to eclipse Afor. But that decision was made by a wealthy person, not the poor, who need to sell. There is in fact an Awka-Etiti woman who sells fish worth 2,000 naira every Afor market day. They even offered to pay her that amount to stop going to Afor. But this is what you tell a fool. Some obeyed the order to stay away from Afor, but after a few months, they protested to their Igwe.

AMADIUME: Was Inyom Nnobi party to the decision to levy?

NWO: No.

INYOM NNOBI: After they talked about this thing, we called a meeting of Inyom Nnobi and it started a rumour. We talked about it and decided to kill it, but they came and begged us not to. We also knew that the present president of NWO is our ally. They called on us to explain and lead, and we ruled that the women should pay without protest.

NWO: The problem was caused by the weakness of the chair of the market committee. We gave the market committee three weeks to call a meeting to involve women in the discussion. Then they were supposed to make an announcement at the market for three consecutive market days to alert people to the change. Instead of doing this, the chair rushed to the market and made the announcement, without even consulting its committee, which includes six Inyom Nnobi members.

INYOM NNOBI: The chair objected to our membership and said we would be observers, despite the fact that more than 90 per cent of the people in the market are women.

NWO: These are some of the problems I am fighting. We hope women's issues will improve with time, especially as those in Inyom Nnobi are understanding and stand ready to help.

AMADIUME: Yes, you need a lot of support in that. There is a great deal of change coming in the situation of women. Even Babangida's government recognizes this.

The role of women in development described for Nnobi in 1986 raises several problematic questions for researchers and developmentalists. We saw that Nnobi women did not have a knowledge of development as something separate from their daily lives, activities and struggles, as an integral part of the progress of their town, culture and society. Women's projects were for the whole society and could not be itemized on a sheet of paper. This means that they were embedded in the local process and therefore locally accountable. This in my opinion generates social responsibility.

What were the consequences for this local system when the government, through its Committee for Women and Development, asked for a list of women's projects? What would be the consequences for this local system when an international donor agency steps in to fund individual projects? How do these externally generated processes reproduce class and corruption?

From the interview with the president of the Nnobi Town Union, it is obvious what women's roles are in Nnobi. We also learn that Nnobi women still employ traditional strategies of resistance, particularly their method of strike action. What is not so obvious is the women's strategy of tactfulness. The president of Inyom Nnobi appeared silent at the beginning of the interview. This is not because she was lost or had nothing to say. She listened quietly, studying our 'tone of voice', and deliberated on the degree of risk that whatever she said, disclosed or challenged would involve. Local conditions determined her decisions and actions. Being an Nnobi daughter gave me rights of belonging, but outside residence meant that I could take more risks. In this instance, I took more risks because I had been briefed and empowered by the women's council of Nnobi to speak for them on the issues that I raised in the interview. The president of NWO was right to say that they were not quarrelling with their women. Issues of rights raised contextually were matters for deliberation, negotiation and co-operation in the closely-knit communities. They are not intended to result in a total rupture of local systems and absolute gender polarization in the way that the western-imposed rhetoric of rights demands immediate change, even if the world of traditional villagers collapses in the process. (The western world, in any case, is now quite comfortable these days to see Africans live permanently in refugee camps behind barbed wires. In connection with the recent war in Zaire, it was admitted that there were more than forty refugee camps in Zaire, and Zaire had the largest refugee camp in the world – a camp of 400,000 to 700,000 Africans subsisting on handouts from Europe. More money is claimed to be spent on refugees than these communities ever saw in their entire history on their home ground.) I have used these examples to raise the question of external intervention in local processes when people come as 'civilizers' and developers and disrupt village structures in places where local government systems are non-existent or underdeveloped.

Village women's lives have been disrupted and their traditional power systems corroded in the name of modernization. In the case of Nnobi, women contribute money towards this modernization, which will result in the erosion of their traditional power around the marketplace economy. In this process of 'modernization', the forces against women's traditional rights seem to come from all directions. Government policies, for example, which have made local organizations the primary vehicle for rural development, have only strengthened the power of town unions, social clubs and the private sector. Given this reality, the next chapter looks at what women in other Igbo communities are doing and the role of external agencies before re-examining the question: What system can best ensure women's full participation in local government?

Notes

1. From excerpts of the report serialized in *West Africa*, 3, 10, 17, 24 and 31 August 1987.

2. See E. Ukiwe's keynote address to the national conference of the commissioners responsible for local government on the implementation of the military government's White Paper on local government review, Enugu, 11 March 1986. See also the speech delivered by Emeka Omeruah, military governor of Anambra state, to the same conference; H. N. Nwosu (Commissioner for Local Government, Rural Development, and Chieftaincy Matters, Anambra State), 'The Rule of Traditional Rulers in Rural Development of Anambra state', paper delivered at State House of Assembly, Enugu, 30 May 1986; communiqué on conference of commissioners responsible for local government matters in the federation, 11–12 March 1986; and *Blueprint for Rural Development in Anambra State*, Official Document no. 1, 1986.

3. In 1986, Anambra state embarked on massive fund-raising under the Anambra State Education and Technology (ASET) Fund. Big private donors were promised immortality in the 'Anambra State Tower of Light' (*Daily Star*, 25 June 1986). The project was another illustration of corruption in the relationship between the private sector and government. During field work in 1994, each time I rode past, disgusted taxi drivers would point at the redundant and delapidated monument as another example of government lies and deceit.

4. See a publication by Asian scholars working with the United Nations' Asian Development Institute in Bangkok (UNADI): 'Towards a Theory of Rural Development', *Development Dialogue* 1–2 (1977–78), Dag Hammarskjold Foundation, Uppsala.

5. E. Ukiwe, keynote address (see note 1).

6. Ifi Amadiume, 'Women and the Political Debate', *Guardian*, 19 May 1986.

7. Emeka Omeruah, speech (see note 1).

8. I had three entries from Nigerian television broadcasts about women's protests in my field notes for this period. In January 1987, in Benin, Bendel state, 5,000 market women clashed with police as they marched on the streets for the third time in a month, protesting increases in high school fees. Sixty-three policemen had prevented their meeting from taking place as planned at Urhokpota Hall, firing tear-gas canisters into the hall. The women regrouped about 500 metres away at Ekenwan Road, chanting songs denouncing the increases in fees. More tear-gas was fired at women in the hall who refused to disperse until they had been heard by government officials. The chief superintendent of police later invited the women for a dialogue. The women sent two representatives – one from each market. As they spoke, more tear-gas was fired at the women.

In February 1987, there was a series of protests by women over school fees. I also noted that the professional women were more concerned about performing their jobs, making speeches and presenting gifts. At a meeting of the state's education commissioner and nineteen women local government councillors to discuss the protests, the woman commissioner, also a university professor, said, 'As members of the third-tier government system, you have the onerous responsibility to enlighten the womenfolk in rural areas on the policies and objectives of the government.'

In February 1987, in Ibadan, market women protested against a 50 kobo daily levy by the Ibadan municipal council. It was the Olubadan, Oba Oloyede Asanike, who persuaded the women to return to their stalls.

9. See my political debate papers cited in note 1 of Chapter 8.

10. The Nnobi reply was published in *Weekly Star*, Sunday 20 April 1986, under the title 'A Rejoinder to an Article Titled "Youth Important as the Nation"' – *Weekly Star* of 23 March 1986.

Sources

Afigbo, A. E., 1972, *The Warrant Chiefs: Indirect Rule in South-Eastern Nigeria, 1891–1928*. London: Longman.

Akinyemi, A. B., P. Cole and W. I. Ofonagoro (eds), 1979, *Readings on Federalism*. Lagos: Nigerian Institute of International Affairs.

Awa, E. O., 1976, *Issues in Federalism*. Benin City: Ethiope Publishing House.

Bello-Imam, I. B., 1983, *Local Government Structure in Britain and Nigeria – A Study of Structural Evolution*. Lagos: Nigeria Institute of Social and Economic Research (NISER).

Cohen, A., 1959, *British Policy in Changing Africa*. London: Routledge and Kegan Paul.

Gavin, R. J. and J. A. Betley, 1983, *The Scramble for Africa*. Ibadan, Nigeria: Ibadan University Press.

Heussler, Robert, 1968, *The British in Northern Nigeria*. Oxford: Oxford University Press.

Kirk-Greene, A. H. M. (ed.), 1965, *The Principle of Native Administration in Nigeria: Selected Documents*, 1900‑47. London: Oxford University Press.

Morris, H. P. and M. Read, 1964, *Indirect Rule and the Search for Justice*. Oxford: Oxford University Press.

Nwabara, N., 1977, *Iboland: A Century of Contact with Britain, 1860–1960*. London: Hodder and Stoughton.

Nwoso, E. J. (ed.), *Achieving Even Development in Nigeria: Problems and Prospects*. Enugu, Nigeria: Fourth Dimension.

Ogot, B. A. (ed.), 1972, *War and Society in Africa*. London: Frank Cass.

Perham, M., 1962, *The Colonial Reckonings*. New York: Knopf.

Webb, S. and B. Klebb, 1963, *The Development of English Local Government*. Oxford: Oxford University Press.

10. Gendering grassroots democracy in the women's committee system

I have already pointed out (in Chapter 3) the difference between the National Committee on Women and Development and other women's organizations and how the committee, through direct consultation and fact-finding visits, effectively highlighted the social and economic conditions and the needs of rural women. Its first tours of some women's projects in Anambra state in February 1986[1] saw what women's groups were doing in a few communities, the assistance they received from government, and some of their problems, enabling the committee to recommend areas where the government could assist.

Apart from the fact that every Igbo woman belongs to a women's organization by kinship rights, as a daughter, wife or village female citizen, information which I received from the social welfare division of the Anambra State Ministry of Information, Social Development, Youth, Sports, and Culture in 1987 indicated that there were 136 registered women's organizations in Anambra state which included: women's patriotic unions, women's improvement unions, associations of wives of professional men, church women's organizations, such as mothers' unions and Christian mothers, women's trade organizations, market women, organizations of women contractors and women in industry, women's people's clubs, *okwesilieze* women's clubs (women who are fit to be kings) of very wealthy and independent business women. It is therefore obvious that visits by the committee were made only to a very select few. The visits were formal and included members of the committee, a staff member from the State Ministry of Agriculture, and a press representative from the State Ministry of Information.

One project noted in the committee's report was the Ojoto health centre, built by the Njikoka Women's Organization in 1956 and turned over to the state government in 1972. The compound and building continued to be maintained by the Njikoka Women's Organization who did the painting, wiring and cleaning, although the State Department of Rural Development supplied the electricity-generating plant used at the health centre. The state water board provided two water boreholes, and the Federal Ministry of Health supplied the freezer for vaccines. Drugs were supplied by the State Ministry of Health and the World Health Organization, but patients had to pay for them. A village health volunteer ran the small pharmacy, while a trained government health officer controlled the dispensary. The maternity section was run by a nursing sister, a staff nurse and twelve volunteer health aides. Services at the centre included immunization and general treatment for the public. Problems at the health centre included lack of money for paying health workers and lack of co-operation between government staff, village health workers and the community. There was also no resident doctor.

In addition to the health centre, Njikoka Women's Organization ran a farm which had not done well because of infertile soil and poor-quality seedlings. They hoped to start a fish pond and a poultry farm. The women had to seek approval from the government before the fish pond project could begin, however, and they needed veterinary extension staff to assist with the poultry farm. They also needed the government-subsidized rate for the purchase of fertilizers, equipment and seedlings, and improved training for their personnel.

Another project was the Oba multipurpose centre and home, which had been built by the Federal Ministry of Agriculture and handed over to the Oba Women Patriotic Union, which actually ran the centre. It was a vocational centre for training young girls and women in handicrafts, agriculture and home economics. It included a daycare centre, a nutrition unit with kitchen, gas cooker, refrigerator, freezer, basins and cooking utensils, and a home-management unit with knitting and sewing machines and other materials. The machines were supposed to be maintained by the Federal Ministry of Agriculture, but most machines had packed up because of lack of maintenance. Teachers were paid by the women's organization from the sale of products.

The committee saw a need for personnel who could train teachers on the use of some of the machines. The women themselves requested that the government take over payment of teachers and workers at the centre and asked that it assist in building a hostel for visitors. They also wanted the government to assist them in setting up money-yielding ventures and in supplying agricultural extension staff and fertilizer at the government-subsidized rate.

In Enugu-Ngwuo there were two sister organizations, the United Soul Sisters of Ngwuo and the Nightingale Sisters of Ngwuo. The Nightingale Sisters ran a home-economics centre and received equipment from the Federal Department of Rural Development. Some women trained in their centre found jobs in schools and hospitals as cooks, while others became self-employed. The United Sisters had evening home-economics and adult-education programmes. Its first group graduated in 1979. In 1982, they introduced courses at the secondary school level. They also hoped to build a multipurpose centre which would include adult primary and secondary schools, a nursery school, and a home-economics hall. They had acquired land to start a vegetable garden as an income-generating project and a demonstration farm for students. Their problems included lack of suitable accommodation and financing for the multipurpose centre, teachers' salaries and utilities such as electricity bills. Since much of their money was spent on renting typewriters, they had requested a supply of type-writers from government, as well as home-economics teachers, teaching aides for the nursery school and home-economics equipment.

The committee expressed disapproval over the age of children who attended the evening primary school which ran from 6.00 to 9.00 p.m., arguing that the children should be in bed. The Soul Sisters pointed out that most of the children were housemaids and that the adult education unit of the Ministry of Education had approved the scheme. The committee's objection shows the hypocrisy of the bourgeoisie, since they knew full well that housemaids were often kept busy by elite women until much later at night.[2] The Sisters, however, promised to reschedule the time.

The Nachi Women's Group was sponsored by Ezinne[3] Women's Association and was jointly run with the State Ministry of Agriculture and the Federal Department of Rural Development, which supplied teaching equipment. The women's group offered classes in food and nutrition, home management, dress-making, backyard poultry production and small-scale vegetable gardening. They aimed at income-generating skills to help rural women improve their standard of living and to foster unity among women in the town. The products they made included soaps, pomades and snacks.

They too had a number of problems. One was the need for a place of instruction, as they were sharing a church hall with many other groups. They also lacked transportation, both for themselves and for ministry officials who were willing to come and teach. The growing numbers of participants meant a need for more equipment, and other commitments, such as paying school fees for their children, made it impossible for the women to make regular contributions towards the purchase of equipment.

The women wanted an adult-education programme so they could learn to read and write. They wanted assistance in setting up a poultry farm. They requested a supply of fertilizer at the government rate, improved seedlings and agricultural equipment. They also wanted the government to equip their health centre, which was not in use. This meant that they had to travel far away to Oji or Udi for medical treatment. Lastly, they requested electrification, water, a resident home-economics supervisor and more home-economics centres in the town.

I have used these examples to show how the picture of African women's involvement in development is distorted and incomplete when listed as projects in this way. When compared with the case of women in Nnobi, we realize that rural women are more occupied with their busy lives around daily farming or other commercial activities, and that projects as described above are part-time activities which are externally motivated. Women had better access to government ministries the nearer their location to the state capital, but only if they 'knew someone inside'. As such, projects have a corrupting influence in creating favoured groups or individuals in new class hierarchies because of structural defects in the mechanisms of implementation of government policies.

Structural defects of the Committee on Women and Development

Given the stated aims and objectives of the Committee on Women and Development and its specific focus on rural women, the elitist composition of the committee was questionable. The women on the committee were drawn from top positions in the civil service. The committee itself was located in the federal capital and the states' capitals. In addition, it lacked the funding and staff necessary to set up an effective system of linkages and contact with women at the grassroots level. In Anambra state, for example, a women's unit was set up in the social welfare division of the Ministry of Information, Social Development, Youth, Sports, and Culture. Its entire staff was one female welfare officer, who was also secretary to the Committee on Women and Development. Her budget for the fiscal year 1987 was 1,000 naira.

In Britain, where all basic infrastructural amenities are provided by local government and where local government concerns itself with the provision of social services, from inside knowledge as a women's officer, I know that a women's unit usually employs several officers. They serve a women's committee, which has a budget of thousands – and sometimes millions – of pounds, a figure based on a percentage of the total local government council capital budget. A women's committee with the aims and objectives of the Committee on Women and Development would normally be an integral part of a local government council. The Anambra state commissioner, who set up the committee in his ministry, stressed the importance of promoting measures designed to integrate women in development. He should have created the women's unit and its committee as part of the local government council.

When we look at the function of a local government women's unit in the British system, from which the Nigerian model is derived, we find it serves the women's committee, which consists of elected councillors, co-opted representatives of local women's organizations and local residents. The women's unit functions as an administrative arm of the women's committee, which is a policy-making body. If this structure is applied effectively to develop a gendered local government democracy in Nigeria, both organizations would consult effectively with rural women. Such a committee would provide first-hand information, guidance and 'enlightenment' to those rural women who are illiterate, uninformed and marginalized and thus integrate all women into governmental development plans and strategies through democratic processes – that is, through local or community self-government. The powerful meetings of the women's committee would provide a forum for different classes of women to discuss and argue issues, policies, budget allocations, grants and funding as a matter of civil rights. Here then is a possible link connecting the lone female councillor, the women's unit, the women's committee and local women.

Under such a democratic arrangement, Nnobi women's council would bring its cultural traditions of orature and organizational skills into a contemporary political forum. Women would debate policies about market development. They would approach the women's committee to fund their projects, so would Njikoka women, Oba women, Enugu-Ngwuo women, Nachi women, and numerous local women's groups and organizations in other Nigerian communities. Such a unitary system would encourage inter-community and regional exchanges and alliances among women from different local communities; and structurally linking women to government would encourage the decentralization of state power and a more regionally balanced democracy. It would enable women and their communities and local governments to negotiate the degree of access they wish to grant international development agencies. Most of all, local women would be better placed to respond to the corruption that tempts elite women as agents of donor agencies.

Under such a system, how would international development agencies argue the right to intervene in democratic communities in Africa? I will look briefly at a few such agencies functioning in Nigeria, how they are structured, what they say they are doing, and the real effects of their presence as an instrument of class reproduction.

Developmentalism, corruption and class reproduction

I pointed out that Nnobi women and women of the other Igbo communities whose projects were visited in 1986 by the Committee on Women and Development saw their daily economic and social activities as integrated in the development of their towns. The idea of development as itemized projects was externally imposed. When women were told to submit a list of their projects, we find that the list involved part-time concerns or activities outside their daily duties. It is sad, therefore, that more attention and money go to these projects rather than building up local government infrastructures. In 1986, the United Nations Development Programme (UNDP) approved grants totalling US$1 million for developing the skills of rural women in Nigeria. The scheme was to be set up within the home economics division of the Federal Ministry of Agriculture, Water Resources and Rural Development. The grant also provided for a teacher-training project in Gongola state.

When we look at the activities of the UNDP scheme, they are exactly the same as the projects described by women at the beginning of this chapter. When women say that they receive equipment and so on from the Ministry of Agriculture, we see how women's demands have been influenced by dictates of the UNDP. At the time, other activities of the scheme were limited to Enugu, Ibadan and Jos. The home economics division was mandated to train women in various work skills to increase the production of processed farm, semi-agricultural and craft products, using appropriate technology and local resources. Uneven development can be seen in its policy to identify specific women's groups and their needs, provide food-processing, preservation and storage equipment to ten select village women's groups, and to train women in basic business management skills, including the formation and operation of co-operatives. We saw that women's access to these resources depended on their having someone inside the establishment. This would therefore breed corruption and inequality.

While the UNDP worked through a government ministry, there are other independent international organizations such as the Centre for Applied Religion and Education/Christian Association of Nigeria (CARE/CANS) also claiming to work on development. Western cultural imperialism has continued recently in the religious arms of development under bodies set up by the Christian establishment. Between August and September 1986, for example, Women in Church and Society, a sub-unit of the World Council of Churches, organized a seminar in Harare for rural and peripheral urban women leaders in Africa involved in development work. Its aims were to bring the leaders together in order to develop an awareness of their role in effecting positive change in society and in the lives of people, to enable them to evaluate development as practised in church and government programmes, to encourage leadership skills and innovative methods of work, to visit project sites, to share experiences and to make recommendations.

Out of this seminar grew the idea for a workshop on 'training women group leaders as agents of social change'. I attended the workshop which took place in January 1987 and was sponsored by the Centre for Applied Religion and Education (CARE), Eastern Area office, Enugu, in co-operation with the sub-unit on Women in Church and Society of the World Council of Churches, Geneva, and the Catholic Organization on Development Education and Leadership (CODEL) in New York. The workshop included women group leaders of parishes, circuits and local churches, dioceses and presbyteries; self-help association leaders (e.g. *Esusu*, indigenous co-operative club leaders); women co-operative society leaders; representatives of town development unions (women's wings); local government area women councillors; community development officers in LGAs and adult-education officers in LGA headquarters.

The workshop's aim was to motivate group leaders in the churches and communities, through discussion and dialogue on the main issues obstructing women's active participation in their own development. It also hoped to enable women group leaders to discover the role that a committed sharing group can play in the development of women themselves and their community. To achieve this, it hoped to enable women's groups involved in rural development in Africa to create a network for sharing problems and gains with women from other parts of the world as a way of learning from one another, thereby improving their situations.

Each Centre of Applied Religion and Education has a co-ordinator who takes charge of its women's programme and projects. Their projects rely on shared funding for setting up self-help projects, with the goal that the projects eventually become self-reliant. This frankly is tautological, since they give funding to on-going projects. I learned from an application form distributed at the workshop that prospective grantees are required to answer the following questions: How is this programme arrived at by your group? (By feasibility study. By executive committee decision. By sampling opinion of women in local meetings and carrying out a survey of the people concerned.) Who plans the programme or project when identified? (Your group members. The executive committee. The accredited representatives of the programme or project beneficiary. Those sponsoring the project/programme from outside your group or community.) How are your group's programmes funded? (By levy of members. Fund-raising activities. Fanfare ceremonies.)

Other questions include: Does your group at all consider the issue of development education for women in your communities? Name and describe two of your group's programmes or projects geared towards women's development education and training. (Formation of co-operatives. Saving and loans schemes. Farmers' forums. Support aid group. Vocational training centres for women. Domestic science centres. Skill-training work-shops. Fish-smoking project.) What are the problems that hinder your group's programme or project from becoming self-reliant after some period? (Lack of proper leadership and management. Lack of technical know-how. Lack of new strategies to keep up with the times. Lack of adequate funding.) The last question, number 21 on this complex form, which is designed for illiterate rural women, asks: 'What do you think your group can be helped to do in order to surmount these problems militating against your group's mapped out development programme becoming self-reliant in the distant time? Explain your concrete proposals herewith.'

CARE/CANS in its sectional interest obviously mixes church moral training with development interests, and is likely to have more success reaching rural Christian women to the exclusion of other women. This is hardly the desired objectives of national development. This example further exposes problems arising from lack of effective government and local government infrastructure. All these cases prove that African women have continued to build traditional women's organizations, while bourgeois women and agents of development agencies are capitalizing on their knowledge of the existence of these organizations. Like capitalist entre-preneurs, they use a select list to solicit external funding and they use externally determined development policies not only to fragment women's gender solidarity organizations and councils, but also to distract women from their traditional commitment to the development of their towns and villages.

Gender and class consequences of external interventions

In our criticisms of the role of the United Nations and its development agencies in Africa, we tend to stress economic and policy issues, and do not place sufficient emphasis on the role of these agencies in gender and class reproduction in the formations of elite movements and leadership. Every development strategy devised by the Economic Commission for Africa of the United Nations (ECA) – modernization theory and its variants from the 1950s to the 1970s, to SAPs from the 1980s – in reality, has translated into punishment of the poor for the corruption of their governments. Under the earlier strategies before SAPs, we at least had strong gov-ernments, even though the operators were corrupt. We also witnessed imaginative opposition in left-wing intellectuals and activists denouncing corrupt politicians. They condemned imperialism and external capitalist intervention, whether economic, political or cultural, pointing out that the presence of these forces leads to underdevelopment. These discourses had a radicalizing influence on African feminists and radical women's groups. But it all took place in a climate of stong feelings about the sovereignty of the state.

As I argued in Chapter 1, SAPs weakened the state in Africa and the concept of sovereignty. They introduced a diferent kind of corruption with its formalized global rhetoric of rights. This has had a negative and corrupting effect on African feminists and women's groups, as they become development entrepreneurs and approach donor agencies using fixed language and a begging bowl mentality. This is not the language of revolution taught by the daughters of the Goddess or the 1960s and 1970s activists.

The African Training and Research Centre for Women (ATRCW) of the United Nations EC for Africa is one of the major instruments for achieving this development agency mentality at a continental level. ATRCW grew out of the ECA women's programme and claims to lay its emphases on building women's resources and women's participation in policy and planning. Like the other agencies, it too works through local women's groups. From what we have seen of African women's local activities, only the control of US dollars enables ECA and its ATRCW to claim pioneer ideas of development, as Margaret Snyder and Mary Tadesse (1995) would have us believe.

Development isssues are everyday activities everywhere, whether in Africa or Europe or America. Institutionalized intervention in the name of development is a continuation of colonialism and modernization with daughters of imperialism as agents. The defensive history of women's development in Africa, written by Snyder and Tadesse, would have us believe that ATRCW pioneered the human resource development approach. Nnobi women have never heard about ATRCW or been part of an ATRCW programme, yet they combine a number of approaches in their personal, kinship and community efforts in welfare, human resources, moral ethics, rights and social justice, and empowerment. The major difference is that they do not command so many dollars and do not think up development approaches for women in Europe or America. They do not tell women elsewhere how to live their lives.

The International Research and Training Institute for the Advancement of Women (INSTRAW) is a co-operator with ATRCW. During field work in 1986, women's groups in Nigeria who knew about INSTRAW said that it was set up by the Economic and Social Council of the United Nations to promote full participation of women in all aspects of development through research, training and exchange of information. It works through existing networks of women's organizations and research institutes.

The board of trustees of INSTRAW consisted of eleven members, only one of whom was African: Mrs V. N. Okobi, a Nigerian, from the Federal Ministry of Social Development, Youth, and Sports. INSTRAW conducts research on current development problems related to women; monitors and analyses research findings and methodology on the role of women in development processes; organizes seminars, workshops and meetings to provide training for women; and provides advisory and consultancy services to governmental and non-governmental women's organizations. Among its goals are the incorporation of women in development planning and programming processes, especially with regard to the role of women in the international drinking water supply and sanitation decade; the role of women in industrial development; and strengthening the role of women in agricultural and food systems. INSTRAW is funded by voluntary contributions from governments, non-governmental organizations, philanthropic institutions and individuals. It is based in Santo Domingo, Dominican Republic.

My argument is not that African communities should not receive assistance. I am arguing against the patterns of development strategies that have undermined the state in Africa and fragmented communities. I am also arguing against the development interventions that have undermined community self-reliance and encouraged dependency. I am arguing against the development mentality that has accepted refugee camps as permanent homes for millions of Africans.

There is good sense in the welfare approach of UNICEF which aims to give limited assistance and not to build governments or organize anyone; as such, it must approach the communities via governments. The new governor of Anambra state appears to recognize the importance of community initiative in its own development. Dr Chinwoke Mbadinuju is promising a new programme called Joint Action on Development (JAD), described as an articulated, consistent and systematic development of every town in the state. This would involve a consultative process whereby every town in the 177 communities in Anambra state is a centre of development. He dubbed the existing development strategy 'epileptic' – 'some governments come, and put water there, put light here and they build roads. It is epileptic. They just choose where to site these things' (*The News*, 6 September 1999).

Productive and community activities are national issues for government policy and civic groups to negotiate contextually as local forces play themselves out and reach an equilibrium. External intervention disrupts these local contestations and creates terrible imbalance in the system. In contemporary times, it has created dictatorships, as, for example, the case of military regimes in Nigeria and the emergence of a cult of 'First Lady' under the Ibrahim Babangida regime, reproduced in the Abacha successor regime.

Notes

1. Interview and reports given to me by Mrs Chikodi J. Amobi, secretary, women's unit of Anambra State Women and Development Committee. She was also a senior social welfare officer at the state's Ministry of Information, Social Development, Youth, Sports, and Culture.

2. Most elite women got around the problem of education for their maids by having at least two, sending one to morning school and the other to afternoon classes so that there was always one maid in the house.

3. *Ezinne* in Igbo means beautiful-good mother, a heritage from the Goddess and a name popular with daughters of the Goddess.

Source

Snyder, Margaret C. and Mary Tadesse, 1995, *African Women and Development: A History.* Johannesburg and London: Witwaterstrand University Press and Zed Books.

11. Class corruption and women's mobilization: the cults of first lady

Nigeria women's organizations and Maryam Babangida

In Nigeria, the strong governments of the 1960s and 1970s also produced corrupt bureaucrats and technocrats, who grew rich through embezzlement. They became well established in business and were powerful enough to form alliances with other power groups to finance successful military coups and military dictators. Before the regime of General Sani Abacha, the regime of General Ibrahim Babangida (August 1985 to August 1993) was seen as one of the most brutal and destabilizing that Nigerians have ever experienced. This same regime and its well-developed state instruments of coercion also institutionalized corruption. Babangida's wife, Maryam, emerged from this culture of corruption into a formidable political figure in Nigerian politics, thanks to the rhetoric of women's development projects.

Such a background explains why Maryam Babangida and other senior wives of the establishment have one view of their roles and achievements; other Nigerians, including members of the military, have a different opinion of the role of wives' associations. In Chapter 4, I showed how the Nigerian Army Officers' Wives' Association (NAOWA) grew in importance as the military entrenched itself in national politics and monopolized the state. Over the years this association has emerged as the most powerful women's organization in the country as it became an instrument of class reproduction. I have also shown how Maryam Babangida came to prominence as president of NAOWA.

As Nigerians debated how to rid themselves of 'the military menace' from government and politics, some of them saw NAOWA as the potential source of a coup due to the publicity-seeking culture of army wives.[1] They did not see the association as a philanthropic organization but as political partners of the military rulers. Maryam Babangida was certainly a daughter of imperialism who sought credibility as a champion of women's emancipation. News items such as 'first lady seeks equal opportunity for women' and 'first lady campaigns against inflation' gave the impression of a liberal agenda. The truth is that it was her husband who implemented the SAP, and Maryam Babangida who played a key role in deceiving women in accepting the introduction of the World Bank-prescribed Second-tier Foreign Exchange Market (SFEM) in 1986.

SFEM, which was a means of devaluing and externally fixing the value of the Nigerian currency, was a component of the SAP already referred to in Chapter 1 in relation to its devastating effect on African women. The SAP was a condition laid down by the World Bank through the International Monetary Fund (IMF) to debt-ridden African and Third World countries. This was supposedly designed to effect economic reform and economic recovery through financial loans with interest repayment. The stringent measures in this package included currency devaluation, removal of certain state subsidies, de-indigenization, and privatization of state-owned enterprises, reduction in state expenditure, and trade liberalization. These measures, in effect, spelt general economic and social hardship, particularly weakening the autonomy of the state. As many have claimed, this was the single most effective means of multilateral recolonization of Africa in order to serve western capitalist economic interests.

In this case, this self-interest placed more value on budget balancing than on people's basic needs. Women as food producers, family carers, farmers and subsistence economy workers, dominant in the informal sector, would suffer directly from loss of government subsidy of imported goods, food, health care and education. One cannot help but wonder if this result was intended to keep Africa dependent on development agencies.

The Babangida regime introduced SFEM after the majority of Nigerians had rejected the loan option, following a state-sponsored debate in 1985 on the theme, 'To take or not to take'. SFEM was consequently very controversial and unpopular and met with widespread resistance. Nigerian market women held the power to frustrate SFEM from its outset, since they control marketplaces and the prices of certain commodities (they can, for example, hoard goods, thereby precipitating a price hike). The government therefore used Maryam Babangida, as patron of the National Council of Women's Societies (NCWS), and the council itself, to check the opposition from market women by calling a meeting and ensuring their co-operation.

At the meeting between the NCWS and the traders, Maryam Babangida explained the proposed SFEM system and outlined the deleterious effect that price hikes and hoarding of scarce goods by market women and distributors would have. Indeed, she spoke on behalf of the establishment and against the general interest of market women. Invoking the myth of unity, she said, 'Our collective strength is in mutual support', and proposed that consumers organize within the law to fight for fair play, perhaps through the establishment of consumer-protection societies to act as watchdogs on market misbehaviour and as pressure groups on behalf of ordinary consumers.

The president of the NCWS claimed that the purpose of the meeting was to give market women an opportunity to defend the accusation that they were hoarding commodities. She did admit, however, that the problem of hoarding and inflation lay with middlemen and not with market women, which suggests that the purpose of the meeting was to intimidate the women. Since the market spokeswoman gave her promise that they would co-operate with the government on SFEM, the tactic seems to have succeeded. Market women must today regret that compromise, since SFEM marked the beginning of the fall of the naira, and unprecedented mass poverty and general economic decline.

Maryam Babangida was a performer who knew her role; having succeeded in disarming the women, as a daughter of the establishment, she stepped aside and introduced the men for whom she had prepared the ground. The director of budget, Federal Ministry of Finance, explained the modalities of SFEM to the market women, as did the director of exchange control at the Central Bank. They were men who had previously never taken the trouble to explain monetary matters to women. The irony at the time was that market women would never enter the Central Bank to bid for SFEM, which was open only to banks and large businesses through the banks.

External agency gave Maryam Babangida enormous influence and power and she proceeded to change the traditional role of the consorts of heads of state and build a powerful cult of 'first lady' in a most corrupt government. In an article that examined Babangida a year after her husband's military coup, the language is flattering, and she is compared with wives of elected presidents of civilian governments. She is 'as dazzling and elusive as Jackie Kennedy Onassis, yet is as active as Rosalyn Carter',[2] in contrast with the image of wives of former heads of state: Mrs S. Buhari is described as 'taciturn' and an appendage to her husband; Ajoke Mohammed was not seen in public except at the funeral of her husband; Elizabeth Ironsi is described as 'tense'; and Victoria Gowon is 'a money-guzzling, fashion-conscious woman'. Flora Azikiwe, the only civilian wife listed, is 'different entirely'. None of these women reached the eminence of Maryam Babangida.

While most Nigerians believe that the wife of the head of state should be 'a back-bencher', Maryam Babangida, after only a year, was not seen in this way, even though she did not give a press interview until August 1988 when she spoke with Eddie Iroh and Ada Momah in the London-based *Chic* magazine. In that interview, Maryam Babangida presented herself as a private and family woman who shunned publicity, saying she did not like being in the limelight. The facts tell another story, for, as president of NAOWA and as first lady, she claimed that she saw her role as an opportunity to mobilize Nigerian women in the service of the country. One reporter said of her: 'She is not exactly averse to the flattering dazzle of the klieg light and the flash cubes, yet not much is really known about Maryam Babangida ... No formal bio-data or curriculum vitae on her is known to exist.' At this stage, the first lady's curriculum vitae contained only statements about marriage and motherhood; she was pretty and a good wife, but 'the amount of clout she wields behind the throne' was unknown.[3]

In the absence of an official curriculum vitae, which is normal in western democracies, Nigerian journalists teased out her beliefs from her speeches. She saw women's roles as stemming from their roles as mothers and wives. She urged women to use their 'feminine attributes of sympathy, intuition and tact to influence our menfolk and the entire nation'. Some columnists berated her:

> Perhaps Mrs. Babangida shouldn't have allowed her fashion consciousness to over-shadow her genuine concern for the progress and unity of the country, which she strives to achieve through her involvement with the different women's organizations. She seems caught between playing the stunningly exciting part of Jackie Kennedy Onassis or the practical down-to-earth part of Rosalyn Carter.

She was, however, given credit for her use of locally-made fabrics.

Using Maryam Babangida's speeches aired in the media, we too can gain some insight into the issues she has identified herself with: 'Mrs Babangida advises youths to be disciplined', 'The President's wife calls for the instillation of our cultural values and norms into our youth'. At a function organized by the Federation of Muslim Women's Associations, she called on fathers to devote quality time in the home to the upbringing of their children. On another occasion, she called for the adoption of birth-control measures to reduce 'the huge burden of dependency arising from too many children'. Deviants and misfits, she said, tend to come from 'large families where parents pay too little attention to their children's up-bringing'.[4] Both Maryam Babangida and the National Council of Population Activities took up the crusade against population growth following a visit by a delegation of the British All-Party Parliamentary Group in January 1987. Nigeria, the delegation said, should check its population growth.[5] Gradually, Maryam Babangida learnt the formalized rhetoric of rights mixed with conservative politics.

After three years in office, Maryam Babangida was described as 'Nigeria's most visible First Lady', 'an effective mobilizer', and 'an asset to the President'. While some viewed her role as a welcome departure from the traditional ceremonial and informal office of the first lady, others saw her as cutting too radical an image, championing causes 'with a messianic zeal, using the appropriate state structures. In one breath, she [was] into campaigns against drug abuse; in another, she [was] engaged in charity work for orphans and handicapped children; and still more importantly, she has taken on full-blast the daunting task of a "Better Life For Rural Women".'[6] Although Maryam Babangida was commended for her unusual role, she was often also reminded of her position and the connections which made it possible for her to carry out her wishes. Her tenure, of course, was transitory, and she was advised to work within existing state structures. However, for the structures that she herself set up, there was 'a more comprehensive approach to make the structure succeed and endure'.[7]

How genuinely concerned were Maryam Babangida and other daughters of the establishment about the lives of the poor or the improvement of conditions for rural women? Popular language, which dubbed her programme 'Better Life for Better Women', believed that she was acting out of self-interest. The launchings of these programmes provided occasions for society women to show off their wealth and privileges – in their clothes, in the amount of money they were able to raise, and in the calibre of dignitaries who attended. Maryam Babangida's book launching was aptly captioned 'Maryam's Day of Glory' in *Newswatch*.[8] A caption of 'Dazzling the Countryside' launched her Better Life Fair for Rural Women held in Lagos. Maryam Babangida was chief hostess, and her husband, President Ibrahim Babangida, and other notables paid visits. Although it was a trade exhibition, rural women were objects acted upon. The president told women that they 'have the creative potential that no nation can ignore'. The dignitaries spoke in English, and the ladies were 'gorgeously clad' in white designer chiffon. An unemployed female graduate remarked,

> The expensive wrapper and hair-do one sees here leaves no-one in doubt that these are women who have travelled far and wide and have seen the light. It is only the urban visiting the urban. The real rural woman tills the soil all day long with a child strapped on her back. She is the wife, mother, and confidante who is always bothered by her husband. I don't see any of these here.[9]

At the end of her first year in power, journalists had searched for a curriculum vitae for the first lady.[10] Two years later they had it: Maryam

Babangida, Nigeria's first lady, author of *Home Front* and prime mover of the better life for rural women programme.[11] At the end of four years, it was said:

> She has toppled a whole volume of political assumptions and reinvented the idea of a Nigerian first lady: a first lady not just contented with her routine honorary status and boring titular functions. . . . She has used her proximity to power to ensure not only the allocation of substantial resources to women's development programs, but also the establishment by the Armed Forces Ruling Council, AFRC, of the Commission for Women and Development. She is currently spearheading the construction of the multimillion naira Center for Women's Development in Ajuba. The foundation stone for the centre was laid November 5 by the president. In the five days that followed, she sponsored and hosted the conference by the United Nation's Economic Commission for Africa (ECA) on the Integration of Women In Development ... She has donated more than a million naira yet accruing to the launching and sale of her book, *The Home Front*, to disabled children's homes.[12]

This prominent role assumed by the consort of a military ruler and some facts revealed in Babangida's book seem to give weight to the view that the ambition of army wives was a potential source of a *coup d'état*. Wives of the military establishment appear to have had a lust for power within their own hierarchical organizations. According to Babangida: 'Quite a good number of officers' wives have consequently invented for themselves the military rank a step ahead of their husbands' (Babangida 1988: 15).

Corruption and dictatorship or the women's committee system

In the introduction to this book, I had Chief Bankole and Mrs Establishment to illustrate the contrast between daughters of the Goddess and daughters of imperialism. The major difference centred on the question of legitimate authority and the structural position that the women held in relation to the grassroots women's organizations, local and state political systems. I saw Chief Bankole as the one who held a structural position of legitimate authority and accountability in relation to her local women's groups. I obviously laid more emphasis on organic leadership and formal and informal organized structures of local women. It is for the same reason that I argued in Chapter 3 that the National Committee on Women and Development had the potential to empower women because, as part of government structure, it was a fact-finding and policy-implementing body. Of all the women's organizations, the Committee on Women and Development had the legitimate authority to implement government's policy on women and rural development. It had the potential to be structured into a developed local government system.

I showed in Chapter 10 that, in a strong local government, the women's committee would function as a discussion forum for different classes of women, and provide a link between female councillors, the women's unit, the women's committee and local women.

Better life for rural women and Mrs Maryam Babangida

The possibility of developing the potential of local self-government was sabotaged by the wives and daughters of imperialism through the co-optation of individual elite women and the appropriation of the role of state-instituted organs of development. Maryam Babangida bypassed the Committee on Women and Development to set up her own structure for the management of women and development in her office in the presidential building. Claiming to be interested in taking up women's issues, Mrs Babangida established a group of women known as the 'M' team, with M standing for Maryam. This was a group of twenty-seven women who have been described as 'educated, influential, and respectable, but city-bound women'.[13]

In setting up a women and development group in the presidential building, Mrs Babangida could point to a precedence in the structure of the Directorate of Food, Roads, and Rural Infrastructure (DFRRI). Instead of focusing on building strong local governments, DFRRI was created in the 1986 budget speech and set up in 1987 by the Babangida federal military government to work with specific ministries on rural development, including projects for rural women. In this scheme, rural development was conceived as a high command or task force issue of increased productivity necessitating mass mobilization rather than a slow generative process of building and democratization of a strong local government. Resources were diverted from local government structures into a separate network that communities were told to utilize for access to basic infrastructural amenities.

The DFRRI plan (see Appendix I to this chapter) was the most detailed ever on rural development in Nigerian history. One of its major weaknesses was this 'appointment' mentality which inevitably led to a system of patronage and corruption, as rural development became a commodity up for grabs, and importers and contract seekers bypassed lesser DFRRI officials and went straight to the governors or even to the very top. The directorate under a military chairman was part of the presidency. Each state was accountable to the state governor as its chairman. The governors were under the chief of general staff, who was directly under the president. The chairman of DFRRI rejected the idea of the directorate being converted into a ministry on the excuse of cost efficiency – fewer than 300 staff in place of thousands of personnel in a ministry, the paying of salaries, purchase of vehicles, paying of rent, furnishing of houses. In his opinion, it was better to sink money into projects than into the overheads and staff. He did not want files going backwards and forwards.

DFRRI became a money-guzzling venture. An assessment of its progress by a monitoring team after two years found that, by 1989, the directorate had deployed 1.2 billion naira: 200 million naira on phase 1 of rural feeder roads; 99 million naira on phase 2; 100 million naira on phase 1 of the water scheme; 43 million naira on phase 1 of rural electrification. Figures were not given for spending on rural housing, food, engineering and technological development, organization and mobilization. There were figures on achievements in one area of the DFRRI programme – the provision of rural water and VIP latrines for which five million naira had been allocated to each state. In the first phase of this scheme, billed for five years, DFRRI had planned to provide potable water to 250 communities in each of Nigeria's thirty states which consist of about 90,000 communities. In Katsina state, 163 water points were built to serve 187 communities, and only 153 of these wells contained potable water. Only fifty blocks of VIP latrines had been built. In Kaduna state, only 150 of the 234 water points contained potable water. In Bendel state, only eighty water points were built. Three hundred million naira were spent on building 90,000 kilometres of earth or laterite roads which proved to be seasonal, as they were washed away by rain and erosion.

Given the poor quality of what was actually built and the low percentage of target achievement, Chuks Iloegbunam voiced the general disappointment with DFRRI:

> Gaps such as this create doubts in the minds of people who keep asking if rural development in Nigeria has felt a 1.2 billion naira impact since 1986. DFRRI is the main plank of IBB's [General Ibrahim Babangida] thrust in the rural area. Government ambition is to open up these areas where 75 percent of the populace live, to stimulate commerce and social interaction. It was launched with fanfare … DFRRI was the programme that raised national hope. That hope appears to have been dashed. Riddled with corruption and incompetence, the directorate has failed to sustain the hope it awakened in the rural populace. If it ends belly up, it would be a national tragedy.[14]

DFRRI did end in disgrace following the fall of the Babangida regime when the directorate became defunct, and individual states in turn took over its assets. In many cases, private contractors were not paid for jobs done for the states, or contractors did not repay bank loans.[15]

The DFRRI plan allowed the formation of development associations and clubs, and DFRRI was also part of the presidency and therefore an encouragement to bypass democratic processes. The DFRRI example was emulated by Mrs Babangida, for what began for the wife of the president as an informal, elite women's equivalent of a 'boys' club' took on official status and grew into a national network for managing women and development. It was called Better Life for Rural Women, again an echo of DFRRI rhetoric of improving the quality of life of rural people.

In a publicity exercise report, it is claimed that, at the inception of the Better Life programme in September 1987, its objectives were:

a. To stimulate and motivate rural women towards achieving better living standards, and sensitize the rest of Nigerians to their problem.
b. To educate rural women on simple hygiene, family planning, the importance of child care and increased literacy rates.
c. To mobilize women collectively, in order to improve their general lot and for them to seek and achieve leadership roles in all spheres of society.
d. To raise consciousness about their rights, the availability of opportunities and facilities and the social political and economic responsibilities.
e. To inculcate the spirit of self-development particularly in the fields of education, business, the arts, craft and agriculture.[16]

The programme covered areas such as agriculture, co-operatives, cottage industries, trade fairs and exhibitions. In agriculture, the programme claims to have succeeded in increasing land acreage for use by women, with the result of increased agricultural activities and productivity. Another claim was that it facilitated women's access to credit facilities through revolving loan and research institutions such as agricultural development projects (ADPs), the Federal Agricultural Co-ordinating Unit (FACU) and the International Fund for Agricultural Development (IFAD). Vegetable gardening and livestock farming were claimed as special successes, as the Better Life programme had 1,531 farms, 253 vegetable gardens and 136 fish/livestock farms throughout the country. The programme also claimed success in co-operatives as a mobilizing force for rural women, encouraging team work, increasing women's status, thus reducing discrimination against women in access to credit facilities and federal financial assistance. In 1993, Better Life had 9,492 co-operatives, as against 3,778 in 1987. The co-operatives were involved in farming, livestock rearing, production of art and craft and trade items. By December 1992, Better Life also had 1,435 cottage industries in cassava processing, rice milling, palm oil and palm fruit threshers, grain-shelling, pomade and soap-making.

The Better Life programme claimed successes not only in increased productivity, efficiency and growth, but also in creating sales outlets through its shops and markets in every state and local government, and more markets for export, all with the assistance of the Nigerian Export Promotion Council. The programme had 308 shops and 138 markets in all the states and Abuja.

To show how women's issues are manipulated, in another publicity exercise, this time in the women's page of the British *Guardian*, it is not the above-mentioned economic productivity achievements that were advertised, but all the negative issues that satisfy western racism. The article starts by saying:

> Nigeria is a difficult country in which to fight for women's rights: sexism is deeply embedded in tribal and religious tradition, and rivalries and tensions between the three leading tribes and two major religious groupings make social change difficult, not to say dangerous, to engineer. Against that background, Nigerian first lady Maryam Babangida has made amazing progress with Better Life for Rural Women, the movement she created two years ago to fight for better conditions and greater political influence for women in Nigeria.[17]

According to this article, key issues for Mrs Babangida were health and education: birth control, 'rampant polygamy', female circumcision. The article concludes:

> If General Babangida succeeds in his ambitious plan to return Nigeria to democratic rule by 1992, he will owe thanks to his wife for helping to keep the country united behind him with her evident concern for the plight of Nigeria's poor. 'We have a saying in Nigeria that if you educate a woman, you educate a nation,' said the first lady, with a smile.

In a special *TimesWeek* report in 1991 in honour of the achievements of Better Life, after Maryam Babangida was given the 1991 $100,000 award of the African Prize for Leadership for Sustainable End of Hunger by the World Hunger Project, Maryam Babangida was asked if there was a link between the Better Life programme and the creation of her office, to which she replied, 'No. Why?' *TimesWeek* reminded her that the office was new and unprecedented, and asked the first lady if there was no conflict between the objectives of DFRRI and those of the Better Life programme. Maryam Babangida replied, 'Why did DFRRI not state in its objective that women are the target of its activities?' This is not strictly correct, since we saw in the DFRRI plan that the Ministry of Social Development, Youth, and Sports was to provide the core of an integrated rural development support team; one of its programmes was the mobilization of rural youth and women for increased productive activities. We also saw that national women's organizations and the Committee on Women and Development had already embarked on that task. But Maryam Babangida said: 'On behalf of the president, I can choose any subject matter I think wise to embark upon because he knows my capabilities.'[18]

In Mrs Babangida's opinion, she could have chosen to work on any number of issues such as children's, men's, the disabled, but she chose women's issues:

> I knew that the woman is the issue because of her triple roles. And being a woman, I know where the shoe pinches. I got the message to target the rural woman as my concern first and foremost because she is the one that is disadvantaged and baseless. So, they needed somebody to fish them out to the limelight by giving them all the necessary enlightenment, guidance and support. So I picked at the rural women in particular. I think the first meeting I had with women group, DFRRI was invited to table out its aims and objectives and in the process we discovered that there was nothing for women and I came to the conclusion that I have to fashion out a programme. That was how we started.[19]

Yet, what is at issue here is not anyone's capabilities but the question of democracy and power; the question of the direction of state funds to concerns of elite women, presented in generalized terms as issues of public interest. Mrs Babangida commanded the services of the female elite, including university professors and lecturers, for this state- and foreign aid-sponsored project, although she claimed that the project took off through fund-raising since allocation to women's issues by the states was, in her own words, 'chicken feed'. The corrupting influence of donor agencies in class reproduction also assisted the programme in gaining international recognition, so that it was not only that Mrs Babangida received a prestigious award, but the Better Life model was also sold to other African countries by the Rome-based International Fund for Agricultural Development (IFAD) which in 1992 organized a summit of African first ladies in Brussels, supposedly 'to discuss the economic advancement of poor rural women in developing countries in order to give recognition to the latter's role in promoting household and national food security'.[20] But a report of the summit in the British *Guardian* claimed that the first ladies were really after foreign aid: 'As each representative took the platform, however, to talk about work being done – usually due to programmes they had initiated at home – it became clear that the first ladies, as one later confessed, "were using the forum largely to attract more foreign aid to their countries".[21]

Like the DFRRI programme whose weaknesses were embedded in an 'appointment' mentality, the Better Life model also bred a system of patronage and corruption, since women's issues and the enlightenment of rural women were made into a commodity for power conversion for first ladies and wives of top executives.

In 1990, the Kwara state implementation committee on the Better Life for Rural Women project publicized its activities and organizational structure.[22] The national secretariat of the programme was directly headed by Maryam Babangida herself. The state committees, on the other hand, had a chairperson, a co-ordinator, a director of women's affairs, and appointed members. It ran on what was described as a three-tier structure of organization – namely, the state organizing committee, headed by the wife of the military governor, with members appointed from 'all relevant agencies/ ministries'; the local government committee, headed by the wives of the local government 'chairmen'; and the community/village level committee, consisting of 'recognized opinion leaders within the community'.

One of the main activities of the project was holding annual fairs, where the emphasis was on local crafts, methods of food-processing/ packaging and preservation, and local entertainment with traditional music. Among other things, it acted as a liaison to all relevant ministries/ departments in implementing income-generating activities for rural dwellers. It also claimed to have identified prospective beneficiaries of loans in the forms of cash and materials. The rare commodities that this clientele controlled included cash and farm fertilizers.

Kwara Better Life committee listed its area of emphasis as:

1. *Agriculture*: Dry-season market gardening; backyard mini-orchard; rabbitry and snail-raising; oil palm plantations and small-scale industries such as food-processing, black soap/pomade/oil-processing, and local crafts, including textiles.
2. *Literacy Programme*: A market centre daycare programme; a farmstead daycare centre; adult literacy/vocational centres.
3. *Fertilizer Procurement/Distribution*: The Better Life Programme has made the distribution and procurement of fertilizers easier through the Kwara Agricultural Development Project. This provides an opportunity for women to have direct access to fertilizers. Kwara State is grateful to Her Excellency Mrs Maryam Babangida for the supply of 272 bags of fertilizers to the state some time in July 1989. These fertilizers have been distributed to all the existing Local Government Areas of Kwara State.

4. *Seminars/Workshops*: The Better Life Programme has organised seminars/workshops for women on topics related to family planning, income generation, use of soya beans to improve protein intake, leadership role in community mobilisation, storage and preservation of consumable items in the home, a political awareness/transitional programme, regular television/radio programmes on specific items of the Better Life Programme.[23]

Contrary to Mrs Babangida's claim that the DFRRI did not include women in its objectives, the Kwara state Better Life committee stated that the DFRRI had released its first instalment of 100,000 naira to women beneficiaries and that the state government also made a budgetary allocation of 500,000 naira to the programme in 1989. In a full-page advertisement, the Better Life women's committee congratulated the Kwara state military governor 'for successfully piloting the affairs of the state throughout his first 100 days. We wish the governor and the state more dynamic, purposeful and result oriented days.'[24] A photograph of the governor's wife, state chair of the committee, was placed next to that of her husband.

In this way, elite women, in the name of service to the rural poor, undermine democratic processes and gain prestige, status and power for themselves. At the opening of the seven-day Better Life fair in March 1990, which cost several million naira, Mrs Babangida was described as

> a Roman empress on a throne, regal and resplendent in a stone-studded flowing outfit that defied description. Her head-gear, a rose-pink and white creation perched coquettishly on her head, was a statement of extravagant opulence. She took in the official ceremony with a permanent smile on her face. [Each day,] accompanied by a winding entourage, [she visited the stands.] Dressed in captivating outfits, she clearly stole the show from the rural women. But they loved it, as most of them look up to her as their motivator. In apparent appreciation of her contribution, some wore outfits with her portrait printed on them and turned the popular gospel chorus, 'I have decided to follow Jesus' into 'I have decided to follow Maryam'.[25]

Other voices of local opposition to the Better Life programme included Nigeria's often imprisoned radical lawyer Gani Fawehinmi who has continued to fight a legal guerrilla war on Nigeria's military dictatorships. Fawehinmi saw the programme as 'a bottomless pit project', and repeatedly sued the Babangidas, husband and wife, seeking a court restraint on them from spending public funds on what he saw as an unviable project. He particularly attacked the millions of naira of tax-payers' money spent on the first national Better Life fair in September 1989 and the second in March 1990. He argued that this wasteful spending meant that government could not meet social reponsibilities like free education, payment of students' bursaries, a good transport system and so on. Fawehinmi's suit was thrown out by government lawyers.[26]

Other international trade fairs and exhibitions followed: in Atlanta, Houston, Mali, Burkina Faso, Berlin, Dubai, Senegal; the Universal Exposition Seville, Spain, 1992; the fourth United Nations Economic Commission for Africa's Regional Conference on the Integration of Women in Development, Abuja, 1989; the Joint Assembly of member-states of the ACP and EEC in Luxembourg; twenty-seventh summit of the OAU in Abuja; the ECOWAS summit in Abuja and in London. The sum of 4.4 million naira earmarked for the sixth anniversary of the Better Life programme was cancelled following the submission of a proposal by the committee appointed by Mrs Babangida's successor, Maryam Abacha, to review the Better Life programme.[27] The Central Bank's report of government spending shows that five years of Better Life used up 400 million naira, not including running costs and overheads.[28] Apart from the claim that, at the end of her eight years in power, Maryam Babangida's net worth was about US$2 billion,[29] a considerable amount of money was also spent in her efforts to convert financial accumulation into power and prestige through honorary titles: Cambridge University received an unsolicited gift of £500,000 to name a women's studies centre after her. This gift was rejected following protests by pro-democracy activists. However, the University of Nigeria, Nsukka, went ahead and gave Mrs Babangida an honorary doctorate degree for the payment of 7.5 million naira. During her visit to London to receive the 1991 African Prize for Leadership award, Maryam Babangida donated £250,000 to the Africa Centre in London, with a promise of a further £50,000.[30]

Analysing Mrs Maryam Babangida's role in a paper where some of these data were presented, I again raised the question of a dual gender political system and the possibility of her role being seen as a continuation of the traditional matriarchal power wielded by African women (Amadiume 1996).[31] Although she was operating in a different context – an unauthorized and illegitimate political dictatorship to be precise – and was not herself directly involved in the local women's production processes, in the *Times Week* interview, her response to the question of sharing of the role of the wives of the service chiefs in the programme to accommodate rural women, borrowed from traditional matriarchal thinking. She saw the whole project as a chieftaincy system, with wives of service chiefs as mothers of the people and she as the senior female chief who packages the programme which was then handed down to those below:

We have a system, in line with government structure. We have myself here as the national chairperson. I work out the modalities, package this to the states to guide them in their work. The state governors' wives are the state chairpersons because they are wives of top executives, they are in position to assist in the programme in that their husbands are the chief executives and so, the governors' wives would visit the rural areas in the states. Because the programme is so broad, not funded and because it started like a voluntary exercise, the governor's wife being assigned the role of mother, I would say, going to the rural areas, seeing to the problems of the people, coming back to her husband to inform him correctly on the situation on the ground, you might say we have a fact-finding movement. The man would want to make success of his stay, so the problems identified are reported to the governor who would then invite officials so concerned in the various areas. He would assign his officials to assist in the programme. Each state chairperson has a committee – that is on the state level. On the local government areas, we have the wife of the chairman as our co-ordinator who has her own committee members working in the grassroot level. So we have a good system. That is why we've been able to succeed.[31]

I have argued that contextual issues and organized forces of resistance by far outweigh and outlive personality or identity politics. On 26 August 1993, her husband's regime was overthrown by a popular mass movement. As such, Maryam Babangida's show ended, but the issue of women's development remained.

The Beijing Women's Conference and Mrs Maryam Abacha

In keeping with the personality cult of the first lady, the 4-billion-naira centre for women's development in Abuja was named the Maryam Babangida International Centre for Women's Development. This personalization laid the question of women's development open to criticism when other institutions created by Ibrahim Babangida were subjected to public condemnation and probed for corruption following his removal from office. Scheduled projects of the centre were reported to have been abandoned for lack of patronage.[32] The class orientation of the centre can be seen in the nature of the scheduled projects: a cookery course for baking cakes, rolls, biscuits and pies; the preparation of juices, jams, jellies and marmalades, continental and indigenous desserts; a frying course; a sewing and fashion designing course; pomade-making; the making of hair-pins, lace chair covers, baby shawls and throw pillows; a course on tie and dye and batik; food preservation and storage; decorative fabric-printing for wall hangings, table covers, napkins, shirts, bou bou, bedsheets and pillows. The media questioned the continued relevance of the centre to Nigerian women and national development, and portrayed it as being in poor financial shape and disoriented. This negative representation can be seen as a preparation for its takeover by Mrs Abacha.

The fact that the Better Life programme was an instrument of patronage meant that, when one military dictatorship was replaced with another, it became a hostage in the jealousies and rivalry for power between the wives of different regimes. When Mrs Babangida's Better Life was criticized, preparing the basis for a change of orientation, the corruption and dictatorship of the previous regime were not mentioned. The progress of women was set back when Hajiya Hannatu Fika, acting director-general of the National Commission for Women, claimed that Better Life promoted women's progress in opposition to men, and that men had felt threatened 'that their wives could get out of their control in the name of the programme'.[33] It was also claimed that active members of the programme neglected their homes and children.

On 17 May 1994, Mrs Abacha went ahead to dismantle officially the Better Life programme, notifying all local government councils, women's groups and organizations of the changes. The official letter (ref. no. 1907/S. 7/C. 98) issued by her aide, Alhaji Abubakar Abdullahi, states:

> Sequel to critical examination and careful analysis of the Better Life Programme as well as the general public outcry against the programme for its elitist, theoretical and flamboyant outlook, the need to redefine the scope and objectives of the programme to conform with the political realities and the mood of the nation cannot be overemphasized ... Accordingly, Her Excellency, the First Lady, Mrs Maryam Abacha, has approved with immediate effect the redesignation of Better Life Programme to Family Support Programme.[34]

This change of name was criticized by Nigerians, who are experts at reading the minds and actions of their authoritarian leaders. Maryam Abacha with her intended 'social crusade' was reminded of the fact that the Better Life for Rural Women Programme which she had condemned had already received a critical analysis since its

> master-minds garnered an international award jointly with a Kenyan lady for the thorough-paced, grassroots appeal of the venture ... the new first lady should chart out her own course, beat out her own track, instead of tinkering with another person's initiative. By changing the name and not the letter (i.e. the spirit of the venture) of BLP this can draw murmurs from discerning minds. It is indefensible to say the least. It is funny how we keep nibbling at the fringes of our national life, leaving the rotten interior uncleansed.[35]

Mrs Abacha took over the Maryam Babangida International Centre, dismissed its chairperson, Mrs Eno Irukwu, and dissolved its board of directors. It was renamed the Maryam Abacha Centre, even though this was strictly illegal. In 1992, the centre, a public project, had been registered as Maryam Babangida's private corporate business owned by MIB Foundation (meaning Maryam Ibrahim Babangida). The certificate of occupancy and the land occupied by the centre are all privately registered in the name of the MIB Foundation. Its trustees for life were Maryam Babangida and Hadiza. This legal provision allowed Mrs Babangida to continue to control the centre and issue decrees after she and her husband were forced out of government.

In November 1994, Mrs Abacha lauched her 500-million-naira Family Support Fund. I have shown how the establishment turned out to support the launching of Mrs Babangida's book, *The Home Front*. The list of attendees shows old collaborators who are now deadly enemies, for Abiola, Abacha and Babangida were all there together. Mrs Abacha closed Better Life as a result of claims of elitism and flamboyance. How does her own launch compare with that of Mrs Babangida? It reveals how government funds go into private enterprise and the depth of the corruption of the Nigerian ruling class and their wives. Unfortunately, it is all done in the name of women's development.

The ceremony in Abuja is reported to have cost 150 million naira. All hotels and airlines were fully booked, as all federal, state and local government top officials, traditional rulers and contractors were required to attend. At the ceremony, Mrs Abacha, in asking for donations, described the intentions of her Family Support Fund: to establish a multipurpose international children's complex, with a recreational and educational centre, equipped with computer facilities, a 600-seat theatre, classes, hostels, gymnasium, an art gallery, conference rooms and facilities for the disabled; a comprehensive 200-bed referral hospital with complete diagnostic services; an international shopping complex to accommodate wholesale and retail shops, department stores and community banks.

Donations receiving applause had to exceed 100,000 naira. In official donations, Chief Don Etiebet, the oil minister, gave 100 million naira; Kano state gave 42.9 million naira; Borno state gave 20 million naira; Kaduna state gave 11 million naira; the Federal Ministry of Transport gave 22.4 million naira; the Federal Ministry of Works and Housing gave 20 million naira; and the federal capital territory, Abuja, gave 15 million naira. In personal donations, Chief Emmanuel Iwuanyanwu, publisher of Champion Newspapers, gave 5 million naira; Chief Gabriel Igbinedion, the Esama of Benin, gave 1 million naira, including free use of his Okada aircraft for the ceremony; Chief Pere Ajuwa, a former presidential candidate, gave 5 million naira, and pledged 40 million naira from Rivers state. Donations were announced and recorded, so that when the Abachas had to leave and the master of ceremony, Ikenna Ndaguba, temporarily called a halt, more than 400 million naira had been collected. Donations continued later.[36]

I am arguing here for genuine democratization and not token concessions from corrupt military dictators to promote their wives. Like the Better Life programme, the Family Support Fund is also a personal instrument of patronage. Individuals and directors of other programmes pay 'a courtesy visit to the First Lady, Mrs Maryam Abacha' to offer their services, curry favour or seek co-operation. For example, in March 1995, following the creation of the Ministry of Women's Affairs by Sani Abacha, it was reported in the *Daily Times* that Colonel Soyemi A. Sofoluwe, director-general of the National Youth Service Corps (NYSC), offered assistance to the Family Support Programme (FSP) in the areas of health and health education for the family, literacy, child welfare and programmes for the disabled and destitute. He actually led a team of officials to Abuja to make this offer. He commended Mrs Abacha for what he termed her consistent dedication to the cause of the Nigerian woman and family, and her unrelenting pursuit of this cause.[37] On the same page of this newspaper, there were reports of university students protesting the election annulment, promises that justice will be done to coup suspects, and news that the police had ordered tight security in the states.

This chaos and violence is a reminder that an illegitimate and repressive government had overthrown the democratically elected president and imprisoned him and many others, had crushed all opposition and silenced civil discourse. The first lady as wife of the leader of such a regime has, in truth, no social base on which to assume leadership over Nigerian women. For the first few months following her husband's seizure of government, Mrs Maryam Abacha was in fact constantly attacked by the press as an invisible first lady with no public duties to perform, since the flamboyant Maryam Babangida was seen as the embodiment of the Better Life programme. Here we see the role of international donor agencies in class reproduction and corruption, for it was the iodine immunization programme which provided Mrs Abacha with an excuse for public duty.

If the immunization programme gave her a chance to appear in front of the cameras, the Beijing conference legitimized her leadership over Nigerian women, for she saw in it an excuse to call a national conference at which she gave the opening address and laid down rules for national participation.[38] To control the events surrounding Beijing, she had to take over the formal administrative structures set up by Maryam Babangida and quickly launch her Family Support Fund.

Two years after her husband grabbed state power, the once modest and invisible Maryam Abacha, a wonderful mother of ten children who had asked for a 'de-emphasized' offfice of first lady, was seen to have greatly extended her reach and influence into government ministries. Odia Ofeimun confirms:

> [Maryam Abacha's] brief ... has become progressively wider than that of Babangida's Maryam who, in spite of her cocksureness, overtook only the social welfare departments and others, tangentially. Now, the immunization of children, a formal zone of the Ministry of Health, has become part of the Family Support Programme. Maryam Abacha can find a haven for her pet schemes beyond the formal Ministry of Women's Affairs.[39]

The problems of this kind of 'turf-control' not only include patronage and corruption, they also include vindictiveness. Again Ofeimun expresses this well when he writes in the same article: 'people in her good books tend to prosper, and outsiders to it capsize. Nothing has given her better opportunity for showing this than her out-reach for the famous Beijing Conference. God helped those whom she did not give a nod. For those who enjoyed her grace, the conference still reverberates in every move that she makes or is made on her behalf.'

Institutions, projects and schemes created for the advancement of women have served as instruments of patronage for wives of military dictators. At the time, the press had its day describing how women were fighting to get seats on Maryam Abacha's presidential jet to the Beijing women's conference, simply because Mrs Abacha had tampered with the official list to add her choice of women. Nigeria ended up with 450 delegates at the cost of 4.5 billion naira, the largest delegation at the conference.[40] Professor Wangari Muta Maathai and her group of concerned African women condemned the exhibitionist attitudes of the official Nigerian delegates at a press conference, bemoaning the 'take-over tendencies' of African first ladies; yet Maathai had shared the 1991 Africa Prize for Leadership with Mrs Babangida on an equal footing.[41] Had Maathai refused to share the prize with the wife of a coup-maker and used the platform to expose how these corrupt dictators were appropriating and silencing autonomous women's organizations, her action at Beijing would have carried more weight. We have seen how a Nigerian commentator cited the prize as international approval of Maryam Babangida's Better Life programme. Today Stella Obasanjo is Nigeria's first lady. What will be her legacy?

Using case studies of two first ladies, this chapter has shown how women's development has become an instrument of class advancement and class reproduction in the hands of elite women. In the name of service to rural women, democratic processes are undermined, and the rights of autonomous and even formal women's organizations are appropriated as corrupt bourgeois women gain prestige, status and power for themselves. Class corruption in gender politics is not uniquely Nigerian or African, as is shown in the next chapter which looks at the politics around women's empowerment in Britain. There is, however, a difference in the fact that, unlike in African countries, Britain has a highly developed local government with checks and balance mechanisms built into the system. Corruption assumes a different guise where organized groups and citizens have formal institutional platforms where abuse of office and public funds can be detected, challenged and even punished. In addition, we shall see that the British government does not adopt a projects-approach to the improvement of women's lives, but concentrates on the building of infrastructure and the provision of jobs, social services and leisure.

Appendix I: The DFRRI plan – a summary

The DFRRI plan is set out in a government document titled *Proposed Organisation of our Rural Communities for Increased Productivity and Development*, Federal Republic of Nigeria, 13 August 1986, signed Air Commodore I. D. Koinyan, Chairman. This plan was endorsed by the president, Major-General Ibrahim Babangida, in a speech titled, 'Mobilizing popular participation for rural development', Tuesday, 14 October 1986, at the Nigerian Institute of International Affairs, during a seminar on integrated rural development organized by DFRRI, office of the president.

The following is a summary of some relevant clauses in the document. In the DFRRI plan, the aim of rural development is stated:

a) To improve the quality of life and standard of living of the majority of the people in the rural areas, for example:

- by substantially improving the quality, value and nutritional balance of their food intake
- by raising the quality of rural housing, as well as the general living and working environment in the rural areas
- by improving the health conditions of the rural peoples
- by creating greater opportunities for human development and employment, particularly self-employment, and consequently enhancing rural income levels
- by making it possible to have a progressively wide range and variety of goods and services to be produced and consumed by the rural people themselves as well as for exchange

b) To use the enormous resources of the rural areas to lay a solid foundation for the security, socio-cultural, political and economic growth and
development of the nation by linking the growth and development
activities of the rural areas to those of the Local Government Areas,
the States and the Nation (p. 5).

This means that the rural areas were not seen in self-development, but
as objects of exploitation. To this effect, rural communities within each
Local Government Area were divided conceptually in territorial space
'along modern organizational lines for greater productivity and real development' into primary production centres/units; higher production/
development centres; and development areas. Within these spaces, communities were ordered to form into community development associations
or unions for increased productive effort (p. 10).

Below the community development associations, other groups, societies,
clubs, etc., can be formed for productive tasks such as farming, fishing,
handicrafts, cottage and small-scale industries; other development tasks
such as moral development, cultural development, educational development, sports and physical development, political development, provision
of infrastructures, etc. with organizations like farming and fishing co-
operatives, age-grade groups, youth leagues, radio and television viewers'
clubs, handicraft associations, artisans' groups, etc.

States were supposed to inaugurate their own DFRRI. State ministries,
particularly those of local government, agriculture, works, education,
health, etc., were also expected to play their role. It was the responsibility
of states to identify all rural communities in all the LGAs, and, in collaboration with local government councils and the people, establish the suggested
three tiers of production organization below the local government level.
The state was really the mobilizing and supervisory force that would work
with local governments to help communities form development unions and
associations to pursue DFRRI programmes, including the organization of
land. In this plan, instead of empowerment through the strengthening of
the local government councils, more power went to state governments:

Local Government Level:

For the masses of the people, the local government system is supposed to
be the most important tier of government because this is the level at which
government is supposed to relate most immediately with them. For rural
development particularly, the local government system is the fulcrum as
well as the major facilitator for success. Operators of the Local Government system must themselves, therefore, be aware of these expectations
of the system they operate.

To be successful, the local government system must be

- staffed with highly motivated and knowledgeable people
- adequately funded and equipped
- extremely responsive to the needs and aspirations of the people at the grassroots whom they are supposed to serve.

States have a crucial role to play here particularly as regards the staffing, equipping and funding of the local government system. (pp. 27–8.)

On the important issue of the funding of local government, the DFRRI plan accepted the Revenue Act of 1981 which gave a 10 per cent share of the federation account directly to local government, and 10 per cent of states' total revenue. With a twinge of conscience, perhaps, about the disempowerment of local government, the plan goes on to state:

Indeed, a critical look needs to be taken now at the relationship between the States and their constituent Local Governments as regards Local Government funds and functions. States should also give back to the Local Governments their traditional internal revenue sources. The local government system operators must themselves exhibit the highest degree of financial prudence, civic responsibility and public accountability. The need, therefore, in the first instance, for state governments to appoint people of proven integrity into local government systems cannot be over-emphasised. (p. 28)

Notes

1. Paul Nwabuikwu, 'Will they ever go?: Nigerians wonder if the military will ever let go', *African Guardian*, 12 September 1988, p. 24.

2. 'Maryam Babangida, the Power Behind the Throne', *Guardian*, 27 August 1986.

3. Kelechi Onyemaobi, 'The Radiance of the Queen', *Guardian Sunday*, 15 March 1987.

4. *Daily Star*, 16 June 1986.

5. *Guardian*, 14 January 1987.

6. *African Guardian*, 26 September 1988.

7. Ibid.

8. Special edition on the 'Changing Lifestyle of Nigerians', *Newswatch*, 3 October 1988. The article journeyed through the lives of Nigerians in different social classes, painting a vivid picture of 'hard times, hard luck, sins of the few and visionless shepherds of state [that] have turned the wheel of fortune away from most Nigerians'.

9. Ibid.

10. Kelechi Onyemaobi, 'Who is the real Maryam?', *African Guardian*, 15 August 1988.

11. *Newswatch*, 13 November 1989.

12. *Newswatch*, 8 January 1990.

13. Chuks Iloegbunam, 'Progress with small "p": DFRRI awakened hopes in the rural populace but two years later, only few chages', *Newswatch*, 4 September 1989.

14. Ibid.

15. In a notorious case in Kwara state, four DFRRI contractors were reported to have died of heart attacks due to harassment by credit banks. Unpaid contractors also demanded that they should be paid by the government, since the government took over the assets of DFRRI worth 45 million naira. Kwara state closed DFRRI in January 1994 and sent its employees to various ministries and parastatals. ('4 DFRRI contractors die of heart attack', *Daily Times*, 15 March 1995.)

16. Julie Alumonah, 'Better Life Programme: A Success Story (1987–1992)', Special Report, *African Economic Digest*, vol. 14, no. 3, 8–21 February 1993, pp. 17–20.

17. 'Jeffrey Ferry meets Nigeria's feisty first lady: Fighting for a better life', *Guardian* (London), 24 May 1990.

18. Dapo Thomas with Fola Ayedun and Uchenna Kanu, 'Special Report: Honour for Better Life', *TimesWeek*, 30 September 1991.

19. 'I know what I wanted ... ', Maryam Babangida, ibid.

20. Dapo Thomas with Fola Ayedun and Uchenna Kanu, ibid.

21. 'Angella Johnson reports from Geneva on how the wives of United Nations heads of state are working to put poverty on the political map: leading ladies', *Guardian* (London), 27 February 1992.

22. *Newswatch*, 14 May 1990. Mrs Babangida confirmed this hierarchical structure of the Better Life programme in her interview, 'I know what I wanted ... ', *TimesWeek*, 30 September 1991.

23. *Newswatch*, 14 May 1990.

24. Ibid.

25. *Newswatch*, 26 March 1990.

26. Dapo Thomas with Fola Ayedun and Uchenna Kanu, 'Special Report'.

27. Seye Kehinde, 'A Lady Called Maryam', *The News*, 12 August 1996, p. 11.

28. Dapo Olurunyomi, 'The Maryam Phenomenon', *The News*, 4 October 1993, p. 13.

29. Ibid. The above article carried detailed revelations of Maryam Babangida's business transactions and exercise of power by former friends and associates.

30. Dan Akpovwa, 'What happened to the 250,000 pounds Maryam Babangida donated to the African Center [*sic*] in London?', *Quality*, vol. 9, no. 26, 25 June 1992.

31. 'I know what I wanted ... ', Maryam Babangida.

32. 'Blueprint needed for Maryam Babangida Centre', *Daily Champion*, 17 February 1994.

33. 'Better Life stays, but modified', *Daily Times*, 13 April 1994.

34. Seye Kehinde, 'A Lady Called Maryam', p. 12.

35. Davey Ozurumba, 'Leave Better Life Programme', *Daily Champion*, 21 July 1994.

36. Seye Kehinde, 'A Lady Called Maryam', p. 13.

37. 'NYSC offers assistance to FSP', *Daily Times*, 13 March 1995, p. 33.

38. See her photo under the caption, 'First Lady, Mrs Maryam Abacha opening the National Finalization workshop for the Beijing Conference', *Sunday Star*, 7 August 1994.

39. Odia Ofeimun, 'Peace and the First Lady', *The News*, 12 August 1996.

40. Seye Kehinde, 'A Lady Called Maryam', p. 15.

41. Established in 1987, the Africa Prize for Leadership is an annual award by the Hunger Project. Chester Crocker, former United States Under-secretary of State for Africa, is chair of the Africa Prize international jury. The prize is given to a distinguished African for exceptional leadership bringing about the sustainable end of hunger at a national, regional or continental level. Mrs Babangida was praised as a visionary and effective organizer, while Maathai was praised for bravery and imagination. The winner receives a cash award of $100,000 and a sculpture by Takenobu Igarashi. 'Honour for Better Life', *TimesWeek*, Special Report, 30 September 1991; 'Her Crown, Her Glory', *Newswatch*, 7 October 1991.

Sources

Amadiume, Ifi, 1996, 'Beyond Cultural Performance: Women, Culture and the State in Contemporary Nigerian Politics', in David Parkin, Lionel Caplan and Humphrey Fisher (eds), *The Politics of Cultural Performance*. Providence, RI: Berghahn Books.

Babangida, Maryam, 1988, *The Home Front*. Ibadan, Nigeria: Fountain Publications.

12. The politics of women's committees: lessons from Britain and lessons for South Africa

Lessons from Britain

There are parallels in the patterns of class reproduction and elite politics between Nigeria, a former British colony, and Britain, the colonizer. In Nigeria, we saw how women's issues have been transformed into an instrument of power by elite women and the wives of military dictators. The 1980s witnessed a period of class consolidation and the institution of corruption under the Babangida regime. With a multiethnic and multi-cultural power group, united by economic and political interests, in-dividuals could rationalize choices and alliances which were determined by greed, as bourgeois men and women slipped in and out of different cultures, using a multiplicity of symbolic forms and identities. Thus, the 1980s had reduced early post-independence ideals and euphoria to the politics of petty private interests couched in generalized terms of public service.

My experiences of British social history, as a women's communications officer in local government in one London borough and a community education worker in another, led me to the analysis that, by the 1980s, the British Labour Party had become a classic example of elite opportunism in peasant and workers' movements. A new bourgeoisie had emerged in the struggle of the working class, and it finally took over the leadership. The new structures which it set up were exclusive, benefiting primarily the highly educated elites. For example, the women's committees set up by Labour-controlled local government councils in the early 1980s, with the well-meaning intention to encourage women's participation, ended up being affected by this elitism, which was built into their structure and made it difficult for grassroots women to attend, participate in, or follow the committees' proceedings. Thus the majority of women had little say in their local councils, and the women's committees were not accountable to women in general.

The Paradise Women's Committee in 1984   When the Paradise
Women's Committee was set up in 1982, it consisted of seven Labour
councillors and four Tory councillors. They were all white and mostly
young, trendy feminists, even though black and ethnic minority women
formed a substantial portion of the local populace. To convince itself and
the general public that it was democratic and representative, it decided
also to include seven additional members: three were to represent black
and other ethnic minorities women; one was to be a trade unionist; one
a lesbian woman; one a disabled woman; and the last an elderly woman.
The committee instituted eleven working groups on topics such as housing,
jobs, two on prostitution, lesbian women, women with disabilities, health
care, child care, black and ethnic minorities women, arts and leisure, and
safety. Each working group took its ideas and decisions to the co-ordinating
group, which met every six weeks, to discuss ideas and draw up proposals
for the women's committee to consider. Public meetings were held every
two or three months to generate ideas. Decisions reached at the women's
committee meetings still had to be taken to the Labour group, which
might accept or reject them.

These arrangements required a great deal of reading and paperwork
as well as the confidence to speak in public meetings which were usually
very formal. Many women, unused to speaking in formal public meetings,
were too shy to speak. The design of the huge council chamber served
further to intimidate the average woman; indeed it inhibited even some
of the most daring women I knew who would heave a sigh of relief
whenever they managed to get through a whole sentence, let alone a
speech in the council chamber. Each chair had a microphone and the
mayor's chair, a traditional male seat, reached nearly to the ceiling, dom-
inating the hall.

When issues of representation and consultation arose in the women's
unit, white women argued that decisions on the structure of the women's
committee had been reached at open public meetings. When asked to
give figures, they conceded that, usually, between 50 and 200 women
attended. There was no breakdown by interest groups, class or colour. In
fact, those who attended these open meetings were articulate, middle-
class, activists, mostly single women, who continued to dominate the
various meetings and the working groups of the women's committee.

The women's unit   The women's unit was the bureaucratic arm of
the women's committee. It was supposed to function as a collective. The
women who served as principal officers received high salaries. The elite
women who created the structure argued that they needed women with
'clout' whose authority would be heeded. They felt that women should

begin to get accustomed to earning the same high wages as men, and they made the salaries high so that women sharing jobs could live comfortably on their half-pay. The contradiction is that it was not the women cited in the arguments for this policy who benefited. Those who received the high-salaried, full-time jobs were single women with no child-care or family responsibilities. Those who job-shared were either married women or single-parent mothers.

The married women were not heads of families. Most had fully salaried husbands. Most worked part-time to get out of the house, so their salaries were 'pocket money'. These women, and the fully salaried single women, took weekend trips abroad. The single-parent women, who really needed fully salaried jobs, were forced to job-share. They found it very difficult to live a decent life on half-pay and, in most cases, were usually no better off than when they were on the dole. Single women with no children, on the other hand, were able to hold two part-time jobs. In a callous and materialistic society, these facts obviously affected power relations among women, and this was certainly true of the women's unit.

Class, gender, and sexuality   Serious issues ripped the Paradise Women's Unit apart in 1984 and nearly led to its disintegration. The issues were nepotism, lesbianism, racism and elitism. Nepotism and lesbianism do not usually have a close relationship, but the function of these factors in structuring the women's committee and the unit, which handled the committee's administrative work, compels me to link them.

Single women with no children somehow dominated the women's committee, the women's unit, and the lesbian working group of the women's committee. The general trend – which seemed to apply to the structure of all the women's committees – was for the women who set up the structures to have attended the same universities, and have a common political history. They dominated and controlled everything. Important issues – the structure of the committee, rules of voting, various policy papers – were usually discussed and written up by the lesbian working group, which was under the leadership of these single, middle-class women.

It is not surprising, perhaps, that the women's committee had a policy of not funding nurseries. These middle-class women believed that if the committee took on the responsibility for funding nurseries, it would reinforce the stereotyped image of women as mothers. It would also be seen as accepting the conventional gender division of labour, which leaves the responsibility of caring to women. The women's committee would therefore not fund nurseries directly. It acted as a watchdog, monitoring the work and activities of other council departments, making sure that women's interests were taken into consideration, and called for a policy statement from the social services department as to what it was doing about nurseries.[1]

In taking this decision, there was no proper consultation with the broad mass of local women. In my own communications with local women, white and black, the issue of nursery provision kept cropping up. Women believed strongly that the women's committee should provide and fund nurseries. That duty, as far as they were concerned, should be the main work of a women's committee that claimed to represent their interests. As a working mother, I was in agreement.

Since the women's committee had the power to allocate grants, I believed that money for the provision of nurseries – which usually went into the budget of the social services committee – should be redirected to the women's committee, thus increasing its capital budget. The women's committee could then allocate the money appropriately to the different types of nurseries required in the borough, since it was in the best position to know the arguments and reasons for the provision of nurseries. Had the funding of nurseries been made a priority, this basic need would have been met within a few years. Women would have had real choice about getting out of their homes to work or to take part in politics or do whatever else they wished. Once actively involved in public life, local women could then call for the reversion of the responsibility for nursery provision to other departments of the council, since it would be only a matter of maintenance and development.

The concerns and priorities of the middle-class women who ran the women's unit centred more on the provision of leisure activities for women. The highest percentage of grants consequently went to the creation of women's centres, women's groups, a women's bus, a safe-women's-transport scheme, and so on. It did not occur to them that only single, free, mobile and literate middle-class women would benefit. Working-class women and the majority of black women and those from other ethnic minorities were not in the habit of visiting or using women's centres, since routine household chores left them with little time. Many ethnic minority women did not even speak English, and Muslim women were not accustomed to leaving their homes unaccompanied. The elitist concerns of the women who ran the centres alienated the majority of local working-class women.

Educated and single women also found it easier to organize around their various interests because they were free from family and child-care responsibilities. Their literacy enabled them to take full advantage of council provisions. Consequently, the most productive and active organizations were those of white lesbian women. The idea of free and safe women's transport was to enable women to go out safely at night. From

7.00 p.m. to 7.00 a.m., women could pick up a phone and dial a ride. The assumption behind this scheme was that women could go to theatres and visit friends and relatives. I could see that the majority of black and other ethnic minorities women would not be in a position to benefit. They did not have the money to go to theatres, which in any case catered to a white audience. They had too many family responsibilities to find the time for an evening out, and when they did go out, it was with their families. Many worked early morning shifts or did evening or early morning clean-ing. Muslim women did not even venture out at night. After church or after lunch on Sundays was the time for most black people's outings. The bourgeois white women did not even know the habits or constraints of their black sisters.

For similar reasons, the women's bus project, intended to disseminate information about the council, was as far as I was concerned, a failure and a waste of money. The old non-power-steering, double-decker bus cost more to maintain than it had cost to purchase. The white and black women who drove the bus, as well as suffering racism, were breaking down with backaches. The black and other ethnic minorities women, including working-class women, the information was aimed at, were not interested in the brightly coloured bus. Even though it was parked outside their council estates, most women did not come out of their flats. The few who did, often abandoned their toddlers on the bus and quickly sneaked out to do some shopping (suggesting that the main need of the average mother was for child care). The bus attracted only little boys, who were interested in vandalizing it, as they had little else to do on a depressed council estate.

There was a deep gulf between the non-mothers who ran the women's committee and the grassroots local women, who were mostly mothers. The anti-motherhood position of elitist middle-class white feminists per-vaded the policies and orientation of the women's committee and the women's unit.

There is no doubt that the structure required a basic demasculinization of models, infrastructure and ideas to encourage the participation of ordinary local women. One solution would have been to take the com-mittee out of the town hall and to hold meetings in rotation around the wards of the local borough in more familiar surroundings. Under this kind of arrangement, women who brought complaints to the committee would have been able to point to concrete problems. A quick familiar-ization walk around the council estates would have been more productive than a twenty-page report that no one bothered to read. The bourgeois women would also see the homes of their poorer sisters and have this picture in mind when making policy. Another suggestion was that the committee produce simplified fact leaflets giving women all the information they needed, translated into the appropriate ethnic languages.

Voting system   Given the prevailing structure, it is not surprising that a handful of militant black women from a local women's group monopolized the general affairs of the council and the women's committee. Their uncompromising position on racism made them a thorn in the flesh of white women. At the same time as the women's unit was disintegrating, some of its members and some elected councillors in the women's committee determined to hasten the death of this controversial group by stopping the women's grant and changing the voting pattern of the women's committee.

Before this incident, the women's committee had not considered it a priority to adopt a rigid rule on voting at co-ordinating group meetings or at meetings of the committee itself. All women present had been able to vote on an individual basis. Since white women always outnumbered black women – indeed, at times there were no black women present at all – the white women were satisfied with this voting system. Objections arose from white women when black women were able to work out a strategy of inviting support at meetings where specific issues of interest to them were to be discussed, and thus they were able to counter the voting power of the majority white women. As soon as this strategy began to work in favour of black women, there was a huge outcry from white women who began to ask, 'Who controls the women's committee?' The committee suspended its voting system and decided to work out new voting rules on the grounds that it was trying to ensure that it was more accountable to and worked for all the local women. Consequently, it wished to ensure that decisions were not made by only one or two groups of strong or active women in the borough, hoping that all women would work together truthfully and in a sisterly manner.

Individual views in the Paradise Women's Unit   The structure of the women's unit barely tolerated the presence of a few black women for a year, and then lines of cleavage began to crack wide open. In the resulting power struggle there were several factors at work: racism, lesbianism, ambition and power. The women had to decide if they could continue to work together and agree on the nature of the work of the unit, before working out an equitable voting system for the committee. They decided to find out what had motivated them to apply for their jobs, how they saw those jobs, and how they saw the unit and the committee *vis-à-vis* local women.

Grace, a black woman, applied for the job because she had experience in the council bureaucracy and felt she could move on to a more responsible job. She did not see her job as political or requiring any special convictions. She hoped to effect policy and changes from within the existing structure of the council. She did not see the women's unit as directly accountable to local women because she felt that responsibility lay with the elected councillors of the various wards. She felt that the council had an effective system of checks and balances in its structure: local people had access to the committees of the council, which directed the policies and work of its various departments and units.

Grace's position made Zinzi, another black woman, ask why a women's unit was necessary. As far as Grace was concerned, its only function was to do paperwork. Grace did not feel that unit members needed to go into the local communities for consultation meetings, and argued that others could do that. Zinzi argued that it would be none the less necessary for officers to follow up on whatever meetings or discussions she and her co-worker Mandy had with local women. This was because each women's officer in the unit had a particular area of responsibility and was therefore in a position to give detailed information on her area and could follow up on issues raised by local women. Grace felt that that could be done through elected councillors. Unfortunately, there were no black councillors, yet Grace still failed to see her job as political.

On how to improve the work of the unit, Grace insisted that the women's unit had not taken on board the issue of racism. Maria said that no one took consideration of her as a lesbian woman; what it meant to her working in an all-women collective. Lucy suggested inviting a counsellor to come and talk over their problems in the unit, but Grace dismissed that idea outright. They were all articulate, strong women who had no problems with talking to people or lobbying or campaigning. No one would be invited, she said; they would only talk and talk and talk!

Ada and Agnes were very educated women. Ada had an Oxford doctorate and lived in a house in a trendy part of London. Agnes had been a high-powered barrister before joining the unit. She understood bureaucracy and worked within it. She was very diplomatic. Lucy, a black woman, had been a teacher and then worked in the civil service. This job was the next step up her career ladder. She was simply doing the job set before her. Somehow, she dreaded meeting local women, especially black women.

The two women with strong political convictions, Mandy and Maria, were truly dedicated to working for women. Zinzi worked closely with both of them. Unfortunately, both women had a problem with racism, and Zinzi found it intolerable.

Mandy and Maria had attended the same university and had been involved with the same political organizations, although they came from different backgrounds: Maria had a middle-class background and Mandy a working-class one. This meant that, in situations of conflict, Mandy was not always loyal to Maria, especially in situations having to do with race. Mandy usually exposed something of Maria's past or private life – that she had been living with a darkish woman, who probably had 'coloured' ancestry, for example – which might account for Maria's tendency to 'side with' black people. Zinzi would just stare at Mandy, not believing her ears.

Mandy and Maria hoped to effect real political change in the situation of women when they took on their jobs. Unlike the other women, they had a good knowledge of the history of the western women's movement, and they were dedicated feminists. They were also active unionists and members of the Labour Party. Both had been teachers. Both were innovative.

Mandy and Maria felt that the women's unit should be accountable to the elected councillors who sat on the women's committee. They believed that they should consult local women in the course of their work, but the final direction for their work should come from the councillors. Zinzi disagreed. She felt that they should provide information to the councillors but that they were accountable to local women from whom they should take directions.

Zinzi's background made her something of an oddity in the women's unit. She had spent the previous five years consulting with and working in women's organizations in Britain and Africa, and she held strong views and had high expectations when she joined the women's unit. She saw her role as political, since they were dealing with underprivileged groups and campaigning for better and equal rights and opportunities for women. She was also a black woman working within a white establishment, bridging the gap between local women, elected councillors and council departments.

Zinzi felt that both the women's unit and the elected councillors should be accountable to local women. They had a duty to support local women who exposed any councillor who did not live up to her election promises. Because there were no black councillors, she believed that the women's unit had a special responsibility to consult local black women. Thus she saw their role as one of service to local women, providing advice and information on council services, without necessarily allowing themselves to be bullied, harassed or controlled by local women. She did not see the women's unit as part of the 'establishment' but as fighting for women's rights.

Candid discussions in Paradise Women's Unit made it clear that in-dividual members were separated by huge gulfs, and they decided to review the past work and achievements of the women's committee to see exactly how black women fitted into the picture.

Achievements of the women's committee   There were areas where several inroads were made towards bettering the situation of local women, even if it was primarily white women who benefited. The women's committee, through its advisory role and effective lobbying of the other eleven standing committees of the council, succeeded in getting some council departments to increase spending on improving services for women.

The women's committee's annual budget was approximately £580,000. It represented some 0.5 per cent of the council's total budget, despite the fact that women make up more than 53 per cent of the population. With this comparatively small budget (but a lot when compared with the financial situation of Nigerian women and Third World women), the committee funded community groups, drop-in women's centres which provided advice and information for women, a women's bus which was also a mobile advice and information centre, a telephone contact system for women with disabilities, funds for outings, young women's projects, arts and leisure projects such as festivals, a sign-on campaign for unemployed women, a women's aid refuge for battered women, and homeless action which provided research on housing for homeless women. A worker was employed to set up a lesbian centre, and the National Association for Carers (for elderly women) was also funded.

All these services and those provided by other council departments primarily benefited white women. Racism and discrimination constituted a large stumbling block to the use of council services by other women. Food provided for the elderly, for example, did not include items favoured by Asian, Chinese, Greek, Arab or African peoples. People who came to them for home help were white women who spoke only English.[2]

The lesbian working group of the women's committee had been the most articulate participants in committee meetings and had made a lot of gains. They succeeded, for example, in compelling the council to state fully its equal opportunities policy in job advertisements, making it clear that there were equal opportunities for lesbian women and homosexual men in the council. The group also fought the harassment of women living together on estates. They lobbied the social services committee to change its policy on lesbian custody and taking children into care. Although there was not a single black woman in the group meetings or its working group, it was this working group which received the grant for the creation of a lesbian centre. The decision to fund the project prompted an angry reaction and petitions from local black lesbian women who accused this group of white women of racism.

The all-white professional women who met in the housing working group of the women's committee concerned themselves more with issues of housing allocations, design and transfers rather than homelessness or racial harassment. The last two issues affected large numbers of blacks. Only the occupation of the town hall by desperate homeless families, burnt out of their homes by racial attacks, forced the council to agree to prioritize the housing of homeless families. At the same time, the scandalous case of three black women who had been waiting eleven years for housing transfers (while all their white neighbours were getting transfers) was exposed. This case finally forced a major review of housing policies and practices, with a special focus on hidden sexism and racism within council policies. Money for making a video on racial harassment and vandalism on council estates went to an Asian group. Although the group was asked to include Afro-Caribbean families, the final film showed only Asian families as victims of racial harassment and vandalism on council estates. In the reviews of the film, the group which made it was advised to include Afro-Caribbeans.

In the area of child care, the black community came to realize that fostering and adoption were specifically black problems which they could no longer leave to white people to tackle on their behalf. Figures showed that 33 per cent of the children 'voluntarily' received into care and 60 per cent of the children compulsorily taken into care were black, mostly African and Afro-Caribbean. The local black community began to question why nearly all the social workers were white and asked how the workers' middle-class values affected their assessments and decisions. What about their racial prejudices? How did they relate to black families? Were cultural differences taken into account in assessment and decision-making? What efforts were directed towards prevention rather than cure? Why were black children placed with white families but not the reverse? Was any consideration given to the importance of one's individual cultural identity, especially in a racist society like Britain?

A strong and sustained campaign by black groups – not the women's committee – prompted a review of social services' adoption and fostering policies. It became clear with adoption procedures, for example, that discrimination was not discouraged: white parents preferred lighter-skinned black children. (One can imagine the problems of hundreds of such children raised in racist families.) In 1985, as a result of the initiative by black groups, a national guideline for council policy on child care was adopted, requiring that every child, as much as possible, should be brought up by a family of the same race and ethnic group.[3]

On the question of women's safety, the committee concentrated work on street lighting, the lowering of kerbs, and self-defence classes. Black women probably need self-defence classes more than most because they are usually involved in manual and shift work and go home at odd times, especially late at night and early in the morning. Unfortunately, they have neither the time nor the energy to attend. Of the 12,500 reported attacks on women in London each year, the highest percentage involve black women. There is also some reason to believe that black women have been assaulted and killed by the police: the death of two such mothers sparked off riots in London and prompted unidentified rioters to batter a police-man to death.[4]

Most of the gains made by the women's committee on equal oppor-tunities and challenging discrimination have been within the council. Despite its equal opportunities policy and the fact that 47 per cent of its work-force was female, there were almost no women holding higher positions. Most women served in the traditional low-pay, low-status jobs in administration, cleaning and cooking. Those at the bottom and in dead-end jobs were black women. The affirmative action scheme was therefore aimed at developing training for women. Unless black women received more education, those gaining from the scheme would be daring white feminists who are now beginning to undertake non-traditional occupations as technical assistants, carpenters, plumbers, street-sweepers, gardeners, electricians and bus drivers.

A self-review of the achievements of the women's committee proved beyond any doubt that the committee had not tackled the problem of racism. It had not assessed the participation of black and other ethnic minorities women, and their interests had not been reflected in the achieve-ments of the women's committee. It was therefore decided that the next phase of work should prioritize the needs of black women. To that end, the remainder of the grant for that financial year was set aside for the fulfilment of these needs. The decision was to work on two main issues: simplifying grant forms and procedures and setting up a black women's centre to give local black women's groups more formally guaranteed access to council funds and resources.

Grants It was obvious that ethnic minorities, especially black women, had not benefited from the council's standard grant. Most minority in-dividuals were unfamiliar with the procedures for obtaining the grant, and those who knew the procedures found the form too complex and difficult to complete. There were also complaints that grant investigation officers sent to women's groups were all upper-middle-class white women who were, consciously or subconsciously, racist. Possessing more than their share of material things, they could not understand that lower-class women lacked very basic things such as toys and books for their children. The sad irony was that black women were faced with severe obstacles in applying for a grant of £200 or less, while white women (and men) easily applied for, and received, grants of up to £100,000.

It was no surprise to find that only about 8 per cent of the women's committee grant budget had been awarded to black women. Setting aside the remainder of the grant allocation for the year to fund applications from black women seemed justifiable. The white women agreed because the figures were indisputable.

Once the forms and the procedures for obtaining grants had been simplified, it was important to give priority to black women who wished to set up new women's groups, and thus encourage black women to organize. They would also be able to get the money in a matter of weeks instead of the many months they had to wait for the standard grant. To balance this sudden advantage for black women, however, the white women simplified the procedures for obtaining publicity grants; because there were more white women's groups, they were in a position to exhaust the publicity funding before black women could organize and agree to apply for a publicity grant. It was a vicious circle.

Black women, space and autonomy   The issue of setting up a black women's centre was a real testing point for the unit. It was necessary to set up something where black women could be in control, a place that would give them a point of reference. The unit agreed that this was a viable proposition and put the case to local black women.

The first consultation was with the black and ethnic minorities working group. Most members welcomed the idea. One member of the militant black women's group was not enthusiastic, however, as she thought the unit might be using the proposal as a ploy to marginalize or obliterate the militant group. It was explained that the role of the centre would be complementary: some women might prefer to participate in the centre, where they could organize cultural activities rather than political ones, and the centre itself could provide a much-needed forum for black women, and a co-ordinating centre outside the structure and control of the council. It was suggested that the black women apply for a large grant, which could include funding for the militant black women's group.

At about the same time, it was learned that some local black women were already planning a black women's refuge project. The proposal was presented at their next meeting. Mulatto women dominated the group and the meeting, even though they were few in number. There were also glaring differences between the attitudes of mulatto women and those of African and Afro-Caribbean women to the objectives of black women's organizations, funding and their relationship to the council. While African and Afro-Caribbean women were practical and realistic; the mulatto women had a theoretical approach.

In writing their constitution, the two mulatto women who prepared it concentrated on the theoretical analysis of socialism, class and sexuality. They felt that, as a socialist-oriented group, they should not accept a grant from the council, since it would only sabotage, compromise and direct their group. The African and Afro-Caribbean women believed that they should take the money from the council and use it purposefully, and still concentrate efforts on fund-raising as well. They believed that a council grant would ensure continuity of the group and enable it to take on useful projects, involving other members of the black community, including a project for young women and girls. The working of the council was explained in detail, and also that the council was not supposed to control local groups. Funding money was derived from rates paid by local residents. All the council required was an account of how the grant was spent as it was publicly accountable for its spending. Whether or not to accept a council grant turned out, in fact, to be a very difficult issue, although those who were against the grant were very much in the minority. In the end, the view of the majority prevailed. Whether becoming grant-aided changed the orientation and dynamics within the group and corrupted individual women is an open question.

As we have seen, corruption and interest group politics are not peculiar to contemporary African nations. These are issues in local politics in Britain. The major difference is that Britian has a highly developed local government system which has provided a civil space over and above civic group interests based on all the different 'isms', including tribalism, which some would understand better as ethnicity. Civic groups can be constituted along one or several interests, but must compete for resources that are allocated as of right and not on patronage. Other competing groups can go to council meetings and table a motion of allegation of corruption, or even racism, and demand an investigation.[5] Women's groups do not go to the British queen or the wife of the prime minister for directives.

Checks and balances are also implied in the public nature of the civil space, precisely by the nature of its composition, which is based on representation, and the structure of council proceedings which compels accountability. Periodic and annual accounts of budget spending are given to committee members, and residents receive annual accounts of council expenditure.[6] Working groups discuss public issues, decisions go to the co-ordinating group meeting, and proposals from this meeting go to the women's committee for public discussion. Decisions are then taken to the working group of the political party, and the political party is subject to public sanction or approval through the ballot box. These are the real democratic institutions that the West should share with African communities, rather than setting Africans back with the superficial pretexts of 'developmentalism'.

In many ways, African women would be more adept at operating a women's committee in an effective local government system, due to the fact that they are articulate meeting-going veterans. My experience of the village is of endless series and layers of meetings, roll calls, minute readings, agendas, haggling and amendments, levies and fines. African village culture is one of oratorial public discourse, even if that space is gender-informed. African women are confident speakers in their meetings, as is clear from the report of the National Political Debate in Chapter 8. When women grabbed a microphone, it was difficult to stop them, simply because they had a lot to say and, like bourgeois women, they too wanted to claim the public space, including the publicity that entailed. A democratic civil space is therefore an ideal place for class contestations. Most importantly, a formal civil forum will extend rights to non-kinship-based group identities in the villages, as village populations expand and transform in a movement to absorb strangers. This is why there are lessons applicable to the transformation going on in South Africa.

Lessons for South Africa

Since the release of Nelson Mandela in February 1990, after twenty-seven years in apartheid prison, talks have been conducted about policies and programmes for a gradual negotiated transition to full democracy, with no retribution against whites by blacks who have endured centuries of systemic racism under European settler colonialism since 1652. The Amnesty Committee of the Truth and Reconciliation Commission headed by Archbishop Desmond Tutu was designed to prevent retribution against perpetrators.[7] On the surface, therefore, post-apartheid national politics in South Africa would seem to offer a unique opportunity for change and transformation with a political model based on open debate and extensive consultation. The South African 1993 Constitution, finally signed on 10 December 1996, guarantees equality before the law and equal protection of the law, including on matters of gender and sexual orientation.[8] The fact that the government is seeking women's voices and input in matters of policy would also suggest official approval and encouragement of gender-equality work.

In 1992, South Africa lauched a fact-finding mission, led by the ANC Women's League, with the National Commission for the Emancipation of Women, under the new umbrella organization, the Women's National Coalition, which embraced women of all backgrounds, including an Afrikaans women's group, the Black Sash, Inkatha, and the Rural Women's Movement. More than seventy groups participated. By 1994, the Women's National Coalition was made up of seventy-nine women's organizations. Its specific task was to ensure that women's rights were written into the new constitution, but the women took a different approach, seeing the task not simply as a women's project, but as a project in participatory democracy which would involve a long period of research by field workers covering the whole nation. The easy route of conference-based theorizing for an 'immediate, legally and theoretically constructed document' was rejected. Claire Messud reported in the *Guardian* that members of the ANC did not regard Europe as a model of 'an egalitarian society', particularly in matters of equality of the sexes.[9] Frene Ginwala, deputy head of the Emancipation Commission, did not think that mere policy statements on gender issues would eradicate negative attitudes to women overnight, but it was important to get a correct framework. That framework could not come from western feminism which, as Messud reported, 'ANC members argue, has been about women blaming men rather than working with them; about trying to change the symptoms of women's oppression without examining the socio-economic inequalities at the root.'

Others in the coalition saw policy documents as mere rhetoric and preferred to think of the fact-finding mission as a process of education and consciousness-raising that would produce an inspirational document. Consequently, when, in 1994, the Women's Coalition issued a 'Women's Charter for Effective Equality', it could be claimed to be one of the most liberal in the world. It was achieved after wide consultation and differences were set aside for the enrichment of diversity, as it was expressed at the time. The charter sets out the desired changes in many aspects of life which include measures to deal with poverty in order to improve women's economic and social status; no taxation on basic foodstuffs; recognition of the need to increase government allocation and spending in order to improve women's access to resources, such as a right to land. In response to the demands articulated by women, a working group on women's rights was instituted in the Department of Land Affairs to investigate methods for improving women's position in respect of their rights within a land reform programme. To cap it all, in the first democratic election held in South Africa, 26–29 April 1994, of the 400 members of the National Assembly, 101 were women. By 1995, South Africa had a high score of 25 per cent of women in parliament, thus beating most countries in the world by its seventh position (see Chapter 1). Are these simply token concessions, only good for cultural performance at the national level?

Civil discourse and the rhetoric of rights pose a dilemma in the South African context due to the unique character of the anti-apartheid movement. The South African anti-apartheid liberation struggle was a global movement, even though those who laid their lives on the line were local South African youths, African women, the black working class and grass-roots people. As such, the world has maintained an unusually intrusive interest in the processes of democratization in the new South Africa. It would seem that the government of Nelson Mandela reacted to this gaze by promising 'all things to all men'. Yet, the rhetoric of the anti-apartheid movement, borrowing heavily from communist, socialist, trade union and leftist movements from all over the world, was clear at the time in its support of black majority rule in South Africa. There was some continuity of this social and economic commitment to the masses in the policy set out by the African National Congress (ANC) campaign objectives in the Reconstruction and Development Programme (RDP). According to the ANC, 'Democracy means more than just the vote. It is measured by the quality of life of ordinary people – men, women, young and old, rural and urban. It means giving all South Africans the opportunity to share in the country's wealth, to contribute to its development and to improve their own lives.'[10]

The RDP under the Government of National Unity is a five-year development plan, promising social reconstruction with one million new houses; the redistribution of 30 per cent of farm land and a land reform guaranteeing victims of forced removals restitution through a lands claims court; the creation of 300,000 to 500,000 non-farm jobs a year through the public works programme; the provision of drinking water for 12 million people; the provision of adequate sanitation for 21 million people; the supply of electricity to 19,000 black schools, 4,000 clinics and two-thirds of South African homes; the provision of a specific number of telephone lines; a ten-year transition to compulsory schooling; and the restriction of class sizes to no more than forty by the year 2000; a doubling of the number of free textbooks within one year; and the provision of a national bursary and loan system. These promises were at the same time contained by the rhetoric of a non-racial social democracy and economic orthodoxy promising growth and redistribution, to the delight of private business and white South Africa.[11] By 1995, it was already clear that black expectations of liberation victory were not being met, as emphasis shifted to crime control and the creation of 'a stable macroeconomic environment 'for sustained growth – measures that were more pleasing to whites. The strength of ethnicity and race in the new South Africa is such that some Africans are demanding that the ANC take a more Africanist line and stop worrying about 'the anxieties of affluent whites'; and Mandela's cabinet members were also criticized for being overdependent on whites, Indians and people of mixed race appointed to top policy jobs.[12] In December 1994, at the ANC's 49th national conference – the first since it came to power – Mandela conceded mistakes, and defended efforts to meet the expectations of the country's poor. With restrictions on spending, both the housing project and the RDP were criticized for failure to deliver.[13]

During Mandela's celebrated state visit to London in July 1996, it was evident that his government had embraced capitalism; he met with bankers and the CBI (Confederation of British Industry) to solicit loans and invite businessmen into South Africa. On the claims of accepting contemporary capitalism, Anthony Sampson, Mandela's official biographer, quotes Mandela: 'I don't expect businessmen to come running before we address our own problems, like crime or union pressures … I'll be meeting Cosatu to make it clear that we are going ahead with privatising companies – some completely, some partly, others not, according to their state of efficiency.' Sampson comments: 'All this makes especially absurd the attacks of the British right-wing critics who accuse the ANC of being secretly communist and "begging for investment".'[14] Charges of corruption in government intensified in 1996 and have continued under Thabo Mbeki who succeeded Mandela on 26 June 1999 after the ANC again won elections in early June 1999 with about two-thirds parliamentary majority.

In terms of gender, under this global gaze, to what extent does the national rhetoric of rights – non-racial and non-sexist new South Africa – affirm the concrete material reality of most South African women? Is what we are seeing from South Africa an example of formalized international language rights reproduced in national discourse? On several controversial issues, such as abortion and gay rights, ANC liberal reforms are claimed to come from the top down and to be ahead of the masses.[15] It is easy to think that it is because of its stated commitment to the enjoyment of all human rights by women, that the South African submission to the Fourth World Conference on Women covered so meticulously nearly all aspects of women's lives, and would seem to present a good model of fundamental areas of importance on issues of women's rights – how to enable women to overcome poverty by instituting equality in productive activity, how to institute equal access to education and easy access to health services, how to eliminate violence against women, how the advancement of peace can reduce the effects of conflict and war on women, the importance of a healthy environment and basic infrastructure to women's lives and survival, the wholesome development of the girl child. Recognizing the importance of access to and participation in communication systems, information and easily accessible services are seen to be crucial.[16]

When we learn that South Africa has a free health service for pregnant women and children under six, it is easy to reach the conclusion that this shows that government and community organizations are working together on matters of policy to institute mechanisms to promote the advancement of women and to eliminate inequality between men and women in decision-making processes. Yet in reality this is not so, for South Africa is still a very divided society. The danger of the formalized post-apartheid rhetoric of the non-racial and non-sexist new South Africa is that boiling issues of differences may be suppressed, leading to the silencing of the traditionally oppressed African masses, and the worsening of their conditions.

If we compare the laundry-list approach to women's rights adopted by African women at Beijing with the discursive exchanges of pre-transition South Africa which continuously pointed out the marginalization of rural African women and those in squatter settlements, we can easily identify those areas where there are silences, even though not much has changed in reality. In an important article, Pethu Serote reported in detail on conflicts of race, gender and class differences between South African women at three major international conferences in 1991–92: women and gender in South Africa; gender and development; international perspectives on gender and popular education.[17]

All three conferences shared a common problem of power hierarchy between classes of women: academic women versus activists; middle-class academic women versus grassroots women; white women's participation versus black women in which the issue was the marginalization or objectification of black women, by white academics; and intellectual versus grassroots women. These differences meant that it was false to see women as constituting a homogeneous category. Unity could not be taken for granted, least of all the assumption that women's problems are the same everywhere, as the United Nations planners of Beijing wanted women to believe.

Serote points out the fact that there are now excellent analyses of the triple oppression of black women and the intersection of gender, race and class. Yet these conferences continue to reproduce the same forms of domination and oppression. The meetings stagnate and the debate does not move forward:

> In all three cases, the issues were dealt with in a superficial manner, just enough for the meeting to proceed with its business. If our intention is to build a strong women's movement that will effectively challenge the exclusion of women in decision-making organs of our organisations and country, we need to confront the issue of power seriously. This would mean examining the power we have as individuals and as groups, the power we want and the way we want to seize and wield it.

She goes on to state the advantages of a starting point, such as having an analysis of 'our situation as women, epecially with regard to our history', involvement in a national liberation struggle, and experiences from other countries. In her opinion, race was a primary issue because of the South African context of apartheid. The idea is not to give power to those whom apartheid has already empowered above others. South Africans can not therefore ignore the hierarchy of apartheid. The place of gender in national liberation is of course also important, and it informed Serote's suggested ways of empowering women in South Africa: skills training and confidence-building as a priority; devoting time in seminars/conferences to anti-racism work; and a separate black women's caucus acting as a support group and formulating gender theories based on their specific experiences.

It is discourses from these specific histories which should inform women's development choices in South Africa. In this, I am informed by the position taken by Oshadi Mangena who puts human survival at the centre – what she calls 'sustaining sustainable life'.[18] After studying sub-Saharan Africa in the context of the UN development strategy for women, Mangena condemns the constant denigration of the African mode of thought by the European, insisting that Africans can depend on 'existing legacies of the African systems together with the prevailing knowledge about them' to formulate an authentic development theory. Her argument is for an alternative case of 'holism in terms of African philosophy', in relevant and empowering ideas generated by indigenous African societies for their philosophical merit in a 'search for an alternative theory of human development for the emancipation of African women'. Mangena's holism is 'African understanding of nature and human life as an indivisible wholeness'. As a mature daughter of the Goddess and one who made personal sacrifices and suffered tragic losses in the anti-apartheid liberation struggle, her theory is an informed contribution to the global debate on human development and feminist methodology.

Critiquing the whole UN project, she uses the example of Kaswanga Women's Group in Kenya who build houses together with men to challenge the idea of 'women's integration into development' independently and exclusive of men. In short, in her opinion, the European capitalist approach to technology is fragmented and destructive, and the socio-economic relations promoted by the UN in the name of development is Eurocentric. By linking underdevelopment only to the new nations, thus removing these peoples from history, development became an agent of imperialism of the key European powers, including the USA and Canada. This translated into neo-colonialism and the protection of the economic interests of the former colonial powers. The World Bank and the International Monetary Fund play a key role in enabling and facilitating development programmes – the same UN efforts set up the World Bank and the IMF at a UN monetary and financial conference held at Bretton Woods, New Hampshire, USA, in July 1944, where the 'Articles of Agreement' for both agencies were drafted. These agencies were supposed to have come into existence in 1945 as independent bodies, but were brought under the aegis of the the UN in 1947. The colonies had nothing to do with these moves.

The World Bank as an instrument of capitalism had as its main aim 'to promote economic and social progress in developing nations by helping raise productivity'. Other objectives were to facilitate industrial construction and restructuring programmes. In this venture, priority is given to private investors, hence its role in encouraging foreign investment and allocating loans and grants for such projects. In contrast to African traditional modes of production, this is understood only in terms of industrial production under the free enterprise system or capitalism. Furthermore, in this partnership, the World Bank synchronizes its policies with the IMF, and the main aim of the IMF is to promote international currency stability, hence it lends to governments. Only countries that are members of the IMF are considered for membership of the World Bank.

In other words, be a debtor first, before you can have access to development programmes. Put simply, the ideological war continues, and for many African countries external intervention through developmentalism has resulted in class reproduction and loss of national sovereignty. How independent of external pressures and capitalist interests, in terms of policy, and how gendered is South Africa's main organ of development, the Reconstruction and Development Programme? The RDP should resist bad advice which might seek to snare South Africa in the IMF trap. The focus on basic needs to abolish economic enslavement, and building strong local authorities as an instrument of meeting popular expectations, are for the black masses of South Africa what the achievement of the first and thirteenth amendments to the US Constitution, guaranteeing personal freedoms and abolishing enslavement, are for black Americans.

South Africa, like Nigeria and other African countries, also manifests the tensions and conflicts between daughters of the Goddess and daughters of imperialism. In such a multiethnic and multicultural society, which of these groups will determine choices of legal, constitutional, customary and cultural advancements? Which of these groups will favour the building of democratic state institutions, particularly a strong and effective local government system in rural South Africa that will truly provide structures of checks and balances, and make a difference in people's daily lives? As I have shown, there are precedents elsewhere showing the importance of structurally-instituted democratic platforms in local government systems where citizens and civic groups can contest rights and resources. History should serve as a lesson in making or contesting these choices.

Notes

1. Thanks to this policy, nursery provision in Britain today has remained the most neglected area of social services. In Camden, for example, the social services

department has a policy of not catering to children under age two, as it believes that children this young should remain at home with their mothers. The current Labour government's answer to criticisms of mass closures of pre-school play centres and nurseries appears to be an effort to lower the school age, which is how the Pre-school Learning Alliance describes a new limited number of free nursery school places for three-year-olds in select inner-city areas (*Guardian* (London), 6 September 1999).

2. The women's committee revealed that 75 per cent of carers are women, and their unpaid labour saves the nation £3.7–5.3 billion annually.

3. In 1989, there was a heated public debate on the adoption of a child of mixed race, following a court ruling on 23 August 1989 by Lord Glidwell and Lord Justice Balcombe which ordered a child of mixed race to be removed from white foster parents and placed in a black family. See Law Report, 'Adoption of a child of mixed race', *Guardian* (London), 8 September 1989; letters to the editor: 'why love not colour must be route to happiness', *Guardian* (London), 28 August 1989; 'colour "was not issue" in adoption row' and 'my unwitting white foster parents, by woman of mixed race', *Guardian* (London), 28 August 1989; 'the crucial issues behind mixed race adoption' *Guardian* (London), 31 August 1989; 'a history of racism behind today's adoption problems', *Guardian* (London), 1 September 1989; 'theory adds up to racism' and 'mixed blessing' and 'racial policy puts future of "happy" child in jeopardy' and 'revealed: new mixed-race baby row', *Observer* (London), 3 September 1989; 'adding unnecessary risk to adoption complexities', *Guardian* (London), 4 September 1989; 'black children "kept waiting for months" in the adoption queue', *Observer* (London), 10 September 1989; 'sixty years of legal adoption is a short time to get it right, argues Una Cottingham. and there's still the vexed question of race getting under the skin (this article reveals that up to the 1960s, black or mixed children were simply not placed, and were reared in children's homes), *Guardian* (London), 19 September 1989; 'Mellor steps into "racial" fostering row' (attacking 'a prescriptive and dogmatic approach' to trans-racial adoption) *Guardian* (London), 23 September 1989): revealed private foster arrangements in which children, mostly West African and particularly Nigerian, were placed with unsuitable foster parents, usually white, who had criminal records for violence and indecent assault. The report went on to reveal: 'Local authorites were concerned at the potential cultural confusion for Nigerian children being fostered by whites. "Some of the foster parents hold racist views but have no appreciation of the impact this might have on the children they foster", wrote one department', *Guardian* (London), 23 October 1989; 'race should be factor in adoption, reports government inquiry', *Observer* (London), 21 January 1990; 'minister backs adoption by race' (the debate was clinched when according to this article, 'social service departments are right to try to place ethnic minority children with parents of the same race in adoption and fostering cases, a government report said'), *Guardian* (London), 30 January 1990. Unsuitable private arrangements continued and were again exposed in 1996 when illegal networks fostering Nigerian children were discovered: 'Up to 9,000 are at risk of abuse as private arrangements bypass social services and foster parents are not vetted', wrote Stuart Miller, *Guardian* (London), 16 July 1996; *Observer* (London), 18 August 1996, described an abused Nigerian girl, left with unregistered foster parents on an estate in Warwickshire: 'She was like a slave. She was lying on a filthy mattress,

in a room with two broken windows, in the middle of winter. She had been there four years.' Those who resorted to private fostering were mostly students, workers and illegal immigrants. About 98 per cent of those who put their children in private fostering were Yoruba, the article reveals, and this includes success stories such as footballers John and Justin Fashanu and Olympic medallist, Kriss Akabusi, while at least 11,500 have disappeared, lost through abandonment by parents or illegal dealing by foster parents and paedophiles.

4. Police harassment of young black men in Britain is a well-known fact. What was not widely known until the death of two black mothers, as the police raided their homes accusing their sons of theft, was that black women could not be separated from their sons. On 28 September 1985, the police shot Cherry Groce during a raid on her home in Brixton; this was followed by a riot. On 5 October 1985, the police broke into the home of Cynthia Jarrett on Broadwater Farm estate in Tottenham, north London, without showing a search warrant, claiming they were searching for stolen goods, after having arrested her son on suspicion of theft. With racial insults and abuses, they pushed Cynthia who fell and died of a heart attack during the police raid. The following day, people gathered outside Tottenham police station and community leaders asked that the officers involved in the search of Cynthia Jarrett's home be suspended, pending a full public inquiry. This request was refused and hostile and provocative police behaviour during the public demonstration which followed led to an uprising during which PC Keith Blakelock was killed by a mob. Three youths, Winston Silcott, Mark Braithwaite and Engin Raghip, who came to be known as the Tottenham Three, were imprisoned for life without evidence of their involvement in the death of PC Blakelock, as pointed out by an independent commission of inquiry led by Lord Tony Gifford. Christina Dunhill's *Boys in Blue: Women's Challenge to the Police* (Virago, 1988), which deals with policing crimes against women, the criminal justice system and police powers, includes a chapter on the women of Broadwater Farm and shows that the stopping and searching of young black men is commonplace, as is the questioning of black women, while a traffic violation can easily lead to an immigration inquiry. On 1 August 1993, Mrs Joy Gardner, a single mother, died in Whittington Hospital, north London, as a result of injuries sustained on 28 July from a police attempt to arrest and deport her to Jamaica. Her mother, Mrs Myrna Simpson, who had lived in Britain for thirty-three years, said: 'The police killed my daughter. They said she collapsed but she was a healthy woman. They had no need to treat her with such force. They went in with vengeance in their hearts. It's one law for black and another for white' (*Guardian* [London], 3 August 1993). Mrs Gardner's son, aged five and born in Britain, was the only witness to what took place when five police officers and an immigration official burst in, hand-cuffed and attached tape to his mother's mouth and legs. It was later reported that she may have asphyxiated or had a heart attack, and was already in a coma by the time they reached the hospital, and never recovered consciousness, ('Black woman's death after arrest reopens community's old wounds', *Guardian* [London], 7 August 1993); it was later revealed that Joy Gardener 'was dead on arrival' to the hospital. She suffocated because of being restrained.

On 18 September 1993, Mr Derek Beackon, an avowed racist, won a seat on the Tower Hamlets council. This first ever election of a neo-Nazi member of the British National Party to any level of government resulted in the focusing of public attention on racial attacks in Britain. It was revealed that, in 1992, there were 7,734 reported incidents in England and Wales, up by 76 per cent since 1988. Racial discrimination remains institutionalized.

5. In 1984, an internal inquiry found the Greater London Council (GLC) women's unit ineffective and institutionally racist. The panel of inquiry was made up of senior GLC officers and trade unionists. The GLC women's unit was set up in 1982 with three women's officers, and expanded to a staff of over forty, which was responsible for an annual budget of £8 million. David Hearst wrote that the panel of inquiry 'claimed that the unit's staff were inexperienced at taking management decisions and upheld a claim that they suffered from "institutional racism" in the composition of their staff and in their choice of women's groups to fund … The question of how to secure relevant applications from wider sections of the black community had not been effectively addressed … The panel concluded: "We are satisfied that as time went on institutional racism became embedded in the unit's methods of working and actions taken by individuals have been racist in their efforts." The inquiry said that many of the managerial problems stemmed from the GLC's own failure to anticipate the level of demand for the unit's services from women in London' (*Guardian* [London], 30 April 1984). In 1983, the unit received 900 applications for grants of which 300 were successful; £6.2 million was awarded in grants, while £1.8 million accounted for staff costs and conferences.

Women's units were a Labour Party invention set up without a blueprint for local authorities to follow, with the result that there was a variety in their types of work. No doubt, many women's units were doing valuable equality work, in spite of structural problems which could be corrected. When, therefore, the Conservatives began to use the excuse of 'efficiency and cost-saving' to close down race, police, lesbian and gay, and women's units, this action must be seen in terms of ideological differences between the main political parties. It highlights the fact that the Conservative Party has been opposed to the use of 'positive action' to combat and eliminate discrimination.

6. In 1990, for example, as a resident of Islington, I received, as a matter of right, a booklet entitled, *Want to know how we used your money … ? Look inside – it's all here*, giving a detailed account of Islington Council's expenditure for 1990/91. Specific services provided and costs were listed for education, environmental health, highways, housing, planning and economic developement, recreation and tourism, refuse collection and disposal, social services, street cleaning, other services, contingencies, and contributions to or from reserves.

7. See Ifi Amadiume and Abdullahi An-Na'im (eds), *The Politics of Memory: Truth, Healing and Social Justice*, Zed Books, spring 2000.

8. The *African Guardian* (vol. 9, no. 18, 9 May 1994) published a special edition following the election victory of the ANC and Nelson Mandela in April 1994. It covers the following topics: 'The beginning of history'; 'Colour of a new day: Nelson Mandela and the ANC set to chart a new course for South Africa'; 'The struggle is my life'; 'The man who dared' (on De Klerk); 'The rise and fall and rise of Winnie Mandela'; 'Religion and apartheid'; 'The many lives of the ANC'; 'Battles of Freedom'; 'Blow down the walls': 'Struggles on the literary front'; and 'Africa's new giant'.

9. Claire Messud, 'Doing it for themselves', *Guardian* (London), 16 December 1992.

10. 'The race for power: Barbara Akakpo highlights some of the main proposals of the African National Congress and ruling National Party manifestos', *West Africa*, 28 February–6 March 1994, p. 351.

11. *Financial Times*, 7 May 1994; 'Survey on South Africa', *Financial Times*, 18 July 1994.

12. Bill Keller, 'For Mandela, polls show honeymoon isn't over', *New York Times*, 18 December 1994.

13. 'Survey on South Africa', *Financial Times*, 18 July 1994; *Weekly Mail and Guardian*, 31 March 1995; 'Survey on South Africa', *Financial Times*, 21 November 1995; *Weekly Mail and Guardian*, 21 April 1995.

14. 'Mandela has embraced capitalism so why is British business so timid about backing his vision with investment?', *Observer* (London), 14 July 1996; 'Will whites return to Johannesburg?', *Independent on Sunday* (London), 21 July 1996.

15. David Beresford, 'ANC liberal reform stuns South Africa: New legislation on gay rights is proving unpopular', *Observer* (London), 21 July 1996.

16. The South African Beijing Conference Report, 1995.

17. Pethu Serote, 'Issue of race and power expressed during gender conferences in South Africa', *Agenda*, no. 14, 1992.

18. J. M. Oshadi Mangena, 'Eurocentric Development and the Imperative of Women's Emancipation in Sub-Saharan Africa: An Introduction to and Alternative', PhD thesis, University of Amsterdam, 1996.

Conclusion

This study has argued strongly against the commoditization of women's issues in the name of development and the external intervention in the sovereignty of African nations and in the lives of ordinary folks as a result of this developmentalism. It has also shown how this mode of development is a monopoly of the elites who have turned it into an instrument of cults of elitism for class reproduction. The commoditization of development and the formalization of the rhetoric of women's issues and rights have therefore bred corruption. I have instead emphasized the building of public democratic institutions through a strong local government system, the contextual recognition of the rights of local grassroots women's organizations for political self-expression, a more equitable allocation of the budget to support self-generated rural social and economic development, and the respect for national sovereignty. It is a perspective with a focus on basic needs which is informed by the pre-IMF/SAPs progressive discourse in Africa.

Using facts and figures, I have shown that the effects of the World Bank and the IMF-instituted SAPs in the 1980s have been devastating on African women, resulting in poverty-related maldevelopment, and that people are worse off today than they were a decade ago before SAPs. Worse still, cyclical debt dependency has weakened the effectiveness of the state in Africa. The promises of SAPs have not been realized: there are no increased investment and savings rates; no improved export performance; debts have not diminished; unemployment has increased; there has been no sustained growth; the poor have grown poorer, as the majority of African women are locked in a cycle of poverty; and women's autonomous economic sectors have been exposed to the profit interests of market forces. Instead of 'macro-economic stability' and economic growth and development, we have the weakening of civil rights and the abuse of human rights under weakened African states that are monopolized by brutal dictatorships, which cannot even pay salaries to their workers. Even a 1991 report by the Economic and Social Council of the UN in Addis Ababa maintained that the restrictive economic climate of the 1980s, following World Bank-imposed neo-classical economics, limited the ability of government to mobilize the public sector for social and economic change.

In view of these glaring facts, the United Nations Development Programme's (UNDP) new policy decision is to move away from crisis management to long-term strategic thinking and planning in African countries. Called the National Long-term Perspective Studies (NLTPS) policy, it is to be achieved through its research and business management consultancy project, African Futures, located in Abidjan, Ivory Coast.[1] The shift implies a strong criticism of the neo-classical macro-economic policy of the World Bank which has weakened African states while unleashing capitalism on Africa. As we have seen, whatever has been achieved in democratization in South Africa so far is due to a strong but open and consultative state promising support for gender-equality work. African Futures' advice in Mauritius and Ivory Coast indicates the undermining of agriculture in favour of agri-based industrialization. Yet, as we have seen throughout this study, in most communities in African, subsistence agriculture, food processing and marketing are dominated by women. African Futures also recommended to Mauritius a shift from the textile industry to information technology, electronics, printing, publishing and engineering; all of which requires dependency on imports and foreign exchange. In both countries all the suggested alternative scenarios are in the male domain.

Under this new development direction also, it looks as if grassroots African women, who are mostly illiterate, will fare the worst. Rwanda, however, presents to the UNDP a test case. Following barbaric mass killings, in the new Rwanda women make up 70 per cent of the population compared to 51 per cent previously.[2] Meanwhile, legislation is under way to enable women to own land, and the international community, through the UNDP, had agreed to contribute $627 million to rehabilitation and reconstruction. With a high rate of illiteracy, lack of access to property, unequal education and lack of representation in government, Rwandese women present an excellent test case for UNDP's NLTPS. Women of Rwanda are hard working and, prior to the war, the rate of activity of women in agricultural and pastoral work was 97.9 per cent. This is a golden opportunity for the NLTPS process to produce the first country of women engineers, scientists and agro-business industrialists in the year 2020.

A solution for crisis-worn Rwanda would not be applicable to the rest of Africa, since this development direction is still within the interventionist mode. Yet, further proposals for solutions to maldevelopment continue to come from the same agencies that have been planning national developments in Africa. The UN has come up with what it calls the System-wide

Special Initiative on Africa which is expected to consume an estimated $25 billion over the next ten years.[3] When the initiative was launched on 15 March 1996, the then UN Secretary-General Boutros Boutros-Ghali announced that the plan would be carried out through collaborative efforts between the UN and 'specialized agencies and the Bretton Woods institutions', as each of the fourteen projects will be led by a UN agency.

It is claimed that the Organization of African Unity (OAU) endorsed the plan. Margaret Novicki writes:

> Providing a response on behalf of Africa via satellite from Addis Ababa, the seat of the Organization of African Unity (OAU) and headquarters of the UN Economic Commission for Africa (ECA), Ethiopian Prime Minister Meles Zenawi, the current OAU chairman, told the audience that the Special Initiative 'holds great promise of success' because it is 'firmly based on priorities for development that we in Africa have identified for ourselves' – basic education, primary health care and the advancement of women, among others.

But why should this be the responsibility of UN agencies rather than local governments in Africa? The plan claims its objective is to strengthen governance:

> African leaders' efforts to improve governance will be bolstered under the initiative by supporting Africa's civil service to better manage development, helping build independent judicial systems, supporting the functioning of parliaments and electoral processes, and making public administration more accountable. The Initiative will also seek to strengthen the capacities of civil society to be more active in development and policy-making, including peace-building and conflict resolution.[4]

Reading this well itemized list of aims and objectives, particularly its focus on the basic education of all children, with a special focus on girls, literacy and numeracy for women, it would seem that is after all what Africans have been recommending, until we realize who and what are involved in the plan. Eighty-five per cent of the required resources will come from the good old World Bank, while $2.5 billion a year of the financing, which is 20 per cent of official development assistance to Africa, will be provided through 'reallocations of existing resources at the national and international levels'. The IMF would help to establish the macro-economic framework that will underpin the implementation of the programmes. With all this loan money available at high interest rates for budget management, encouraged by the mentality of growth accounting, the renewed interest in Africa is hardly surprising. In 1996 the UN embarked on a year's campaign to raise Africa's priority status and gain the partnership of donor countries and institutions.[5] Those present at the launching in New York included senior executives of the World Bank, UNDP, IMF, UNICEF and UNFPA. The plan was also launched in Paris, Geneva, Rome, Nairobi, Vienna, Accra, Dakar, Pretoria and Addis Ababa.

Boutros-Ghali had claimed that the special initiative was intended as an encouragement and support for recent African efforts; as such, it was not a matter of generosity to Africa on the part the of international community, but a question of conscience and giving Africa 'its due' for peace and prosperity. I leave the debate open as to whether or not this plan could be seen as neo-colonial developmentalism.[6] In Chapter 10, I pointed out the role of development agencies in gender and class reproduction in elite movements in contemporary African countries.[7] In this context, I argued that development strategies of the Economic Commission for Africa (ECA), ranging from modernization to SAPs, have made the poor bear the burden of the corruption of their governments. The period pre-1980 seemed more optimistic since, in spite of corrupt operators, governments were strong and under criticism by progressive and imaginative intellectuals and activists. There were powerful discourses on decolonization in politics, development and gender that we ought to revisit to inform contemporary discourses on Africa's crises.

Even as some were celebrating independence, there were those for whom it was not an occasion for euphoria as they saw through this ritual of musical chairs, fearing the violence of cultural reproduction. Those who dreamed of an African personality or a united Africa in the Pan-African Movement, like Ghana's Kwame Nkrumah, soon saw their dreams killed, as they witnessed the destabilization of his economic plans for Africa's industrialization and the killing of Patrice Lumumba supposedly for harbouring communist ideals. The principled and idealistic young revolutionaries of Congo Kinshasa were replaced by Mobutu Seso Seko, the 'darling' of the capitalists. There were therefore ideological differences in the Pan-African Movement. The radicals in the Paris-based *Présence Africaine* were also split. Frantz Fanon even split with a section of the Africans. Cheikh Anta Diop also went a different way to pursue African meaning in ancient history. The South Africans were split in their Pan-African Congress, hence the birth of the ANC and its alliance with the communist movement. All these tendencies were contesting the notion of freedom and the necessary alliance that would enable Africa to achieve its goal of sovereignty, which is what was meant by decolonization and liberation.

No matter the tendency, the question of the revolutionary level of the consciousness of the peasantry has remained problematic because of that age-old assumption by the inspired elites that the peasantry wants to make a revolution. Yet, before the intrusion of developmentalism, there were thousands of African villages which knew nothing about the national capitals and did not identify with the nation-state. Their concern about the peasantry exposes the neo-elites as always seeking a role or relevance *vis-à-vis* the peasantry. Consequently, pre-IMF/SAPs discourse on self-reliant development and empowerment was a welcome departure from the imperialism of the modernization theory.

Since discourse on leadership for change or revolution got stuck on the the mobilization of the peasantry, it made sense to go back to basics and focus on equity in order to counter the post-Second World War model of economic growth in development theory, which assumed that growth also meant development and redistribution. Growth accounting and budget management do not address social issues; if anything, they encourage and hide gross social inequalities and human rights abuses. The focus on rural development meant a recognition of inequalities in the rural–urban divide with more than 80 per cent of the population in rural villages and towns. It also enabled researchers to observe the destructive effects of capitalism on the domestic mode of production, as it generated inequalities among regions, communities and socio-economic classes. Inequalities are manifested in the deprivation of rural areas, income inequalities, differences in physical resources, differences in development of the work-force and differences in access to political power. Researchers were able to acknowledge that the poor and the the rural communities constitute the vast majority of the deprived. Uneven regional devlopment is a result of the national urban-biased investment pattern, the so-called modern sector of the national economy, which had made African towns parasitic rather than generative. Thus, attention has to be paid to agriculture, local trading networks and patterns, small-scale industries and small enterprises which make up the informal sector. No doubt, as women throughout this study affirmed, they need training and improved skills. The objective therefore is an indigenized, people-oriented, self-reliant development in an integrated participatory government. As A. L. Mabogunje (1981) put it: 'Rural development implies a broad re-organization and mobilization of the rural masses so as to enhance their capacity to cope effectively with the daily tasks of their lives and with changes consequent upon this.'

Rural focus meant that the question of gender in development had to be addressed because of the visible presence of women in economic and social production in rural society. This shift enabled researchers to move away from over-romanticization of the peasantry and face both class and gender contestations in the rural communities, as we have indeed seen in this study.

Government rural development programmes thus gained attention as researchers exposed enormous waste and corruption. For example, in the case of Nigeria, the 1981–85 National Development Plan gave rural development independent recognition for the first time, but, due to corruption from the top, rural farmers found themselves marginalized by heavily financed government agricultural projects. As shown by Ukwu I. Ukwu, money allocated to three projects immediately swallowed up 58.7 per cent of 4,490 million naira allocated to the agricultural sector.[8] Agricultural inputs and extension services programmes received 972 million naira that went to fertilizer supply projects in which mostly big-time farmers benefited, thanks to 'Operation Finish the Naira'. This means that the potential of the small-scale farmers was underutilized. The River Basin Development, which involved the building of dams and the supply of water, feeder roads, electricity and agricultural services for the rural areas, received 924 million naira, but has yielded a negative result due to high development costs that have resulted in the high cost of produce. The scheme has also resulted in the marginalization or displacement of small farmers, in waste or mismanagement of land, with its intensive use of foreign technology and personnel. Worse still, its remoteness alienated the local populace.

The integrated agricultural/rural development projects concerned with the improvement of agricultural output by the supply of fertilizers, improved seeds, pesticides, credit schemes, co-operatives, and infrastructural amenities, were allocated 741 million naira. A standard rhetoric which went with this scheme was the stated intention to generate income and improve the standard of living of rural dwellers. In the Nnobi case used in this study to show what was actually going on in one rural community, we saw that there was no government support for people's self-help efforts. Not surprisingly, the integrated agricultural/rural development projects had all the negative results of the River Basin project. Its first project cost 90.2 million naira and involved 133,000 project farmers, with each farmer getting 678 naira. Like the other schemes, there was no local government involvement, and the local population was not involved. The allocation of budget was in their name, but not for them: Ukwu writes, 'A scaled-down, more self-reliant, more community-oriented version would do much to transform the rural environment in a much larger number of localities than is now possible.'

From the money allocated to these schemes, we can see that the Nigerian government targeted agricultural production as the main focus of rural development planning. The largest number of small-scale farmers are women, and they almost control subsistence farming and marketing; as such, women should have been directly involved in the planning and running of the schemes. All these schemes also have World Bank financing in terms of loans. With effective full local government and a women's committee system in its formal structure, local women's organizations would be able to negotiate their role in the acceptance and implementation of the government-funded projects on the basis of equal opportunity or proportional gender representation. Women would also have a monitoring system to ensure that rules are kept.

In industrial planning for rural development, the emphasis on improving linkages with technology and manufacturing continues to pose a danger to women's traditional areas of expertise such as food processing, as the bulk of support goes to the industrial manufacturing of beer and soft drinks. Government-backed agencies and the network of first ladies distribute or import certain essential commodities and thereby take business away from women in the marketplace. Women are also being displaced from their traditional hold on markets, as the drive for new sources of revenue forces villagers to transform markets to lock-up shops, as we saw in Nnobi. Daughters of imperialism and wealthy businessmen are also those who are gaining the benefits of heavy government financial support for co-operatives, a traditional women's invention, whose present bureaucratic procedures now alienate grassroots women. Where it was thought that the new ideas of rural banking, community or village banking would facilitate loans for villagers, we find that these banks take money from the rural people and give it to urban dwellers who have ready collateral.

Women need to be aware of these new threats and organize to maintain control of their traditional spaces. As women's organizations and advocacy groups have pointed out, only a free education system can benefit the huge need for mass education in the rural areas.

Influenced by 1970s' discourse on development alternatives, at its 1982 Dakar seminar on 'Another Development with Women', the Association of African Women for Research and Development (AAWORD), focusing specifically on women's needs, also laid emphasis on the eradication of poverty, local self-reliance, environmental harmony, structural transformation and the necessary immediate action.[9] Even though they recognized the complexity of women's issues, and the dialectical relationship between economics and culture, they acknowledged the national character of women's struggles and the choice of methods used in the struggle. They were in favour of another development which permits the release of new creativity, that is, the development of favourable endogenous culture, just like the endogenous and self-reliant development in which women must play a decisive role to change world development.

They were concerned with a more profound analysis of women's subordination in society, the nature of male–female relationships in society, and the effects of economic systems on these relationships – all of which pointed to a focus on rural development and industrialization in Africa. The discourse highlighted women's needs, such as: access to resources, especially land; legal safeguards to land; credit; extension services; access to seeds and technology; and marketing possibilities. Heavy financing and advanced technology poured into the transnationalization of the male-dominated industrial production processes means occupational segregation in which women have the lowest production cost in home industries, thus explaining their low wages. Women's domesticity in home and agriculture were also seen as reasons for immobility and marginalization in decision-making; consequently, women must be recognized as individuals and citizens with rights to own and control their output. There was therefore a need for diversification of women's work by broadening their access to education and training.

In those days, these women were still discussing capitalism, socialism and imperialism, and they saw culture and religion as ideologies of oppression; westernization and religious fundamentalism were seen to be the same, as one leads to the other. In their analysis, fundamentalism and traditionalism were self-defensive reflexes against westernization. On feminism, the position was that concerns and priorities vary in North–South relations, for Third World feminists were still caught between women's issues or more comprehensive political struggle on the one hand, and autonomous women's organizations or integration within political parties or structures on the other. What shaped the consciousness of these women was their knowledge of the international division of labour which placed the Third World on the lowest rung on the industrial ladder, as a result of the collective poverty of Third World countries within the pattern of world economic development.

All this was before SAPs weakened the state in Africa and the concept of sovereignty, a formalized global rhetoric of rights, introduced corruption through intense participation in international conferences. The result was a negative and corrupting effect on African feminists and women's groups which are now development entrepreneurs, and dependent on donor empowerment. As daughters of imperialism, their rhetoric contrasts strongly with the language of revolution taught by the daughters of the Goddess or the progressive thinkers and activists of the 1960s and 1970s.

Progressive pre-IMF/SAPs discourse condemned imperialism and external capitalist intervention, whether economic, political or cultural, pointing out that the presence of these forces leads to underdevelopment. These discourses had a radicalizing influence on African feminists and radical women's groups, but they took place in a climate of a stong belief in the sovereignty of the state and the capacity of the state to effect radical transformation and total liberation. Differences centre on the form in which the state is most effective – centralized or decentralized? – and the ideological implications of this in terms of gender, race and class (see Amadiume 1997).

Summary of recommendations

1. A major shift in ideas of development from pure market interests to the ideals of state sovereignty and inclusive gendered democracy in effective local governments.
2. Structural linkages with local women's groups, advocacy groups, women's units and committees or ministries, research institutions, etc., to build up a support network of checks and balances.
3. Shared management of development projects with women and the encouragement of institutionalizing systems of accountability to women participants in development projects.
4. The legal right of women to control their own incomes, and to become unionized.
5. Access to property and land title as assets in order to qualify for credit to improve and expand women's economic activities.
6. Information and training to enable women to use new technologies and improved seeds and crops.
7. Gender balancing in recruitment of more female staff and gender training and sensitization of agricultural field agents and development workers and managers.
8. Improvement in women's technical skills, education and training in science and technology, and supportive policy and legal measures.
9. Gender-disaggregated data to guide improvement and change.
10. Men must be legally made to support their children and contribute to family maintenance.

Notes

1. 'Africa strives to move from crisis management to strategic thinking', *Africa Recovery* (Special Issue on UNDP project to revive long-term planning in African countries), United Nations, vol. 9, no. 3, November 1995.

2. *Detailed Report on Situation of Raped, Widowed, Landless and Otherwise Traumatized Women in Rwanda Presented to Anti-Discrimination Committee*, Committee on Elimination of Discrimination Against Women, WOM/896, 1 February 1996, Fifteenth Session 306th Meeting (PM).

3. Margaret A. Novicki, 'UN System Launches Special Initiative to Spur Africa's Development', *Africa Recovery* (Special Report: Global Coalition for Africa Conference in Maastricht) United Nations, vol. 10, no. 1, May 1996.

4. Margaret A. Novicki, 'A new impetus for African development: the Special

Initiative aims to improve access to basic education and primary health care', *Africa Recovery*, ibid.

5. The United Nations itself is in financial crisis, since the United States publicly refused to pay the almost $2 billion it owed in dues, and stood alone in its insistence in refusing Boutros Boutros-Ghali a second term as UN Secretary General, for which the award-winning professor of environmental studies, Donella Meadows, has dubbed her country 'a deadbeat, muscle-bound but lily-livered, self-centered bully' in her weekly column, *Global Citizen* (Donella Meadows, 'Rest of the world realizes there's a jerk in the neighborhood', *Valley News*, Saturday, 7 December 1996).

As part of its response to increasing pressure to restructure itself and make radical reforms, the UN was also reorganizing the ECA and its staff of 800 in Addis Ababa, to meet the new developments, and to serve Africa better. In this regard, the ECA executive secretary, Dr K. Y. Amoako, described ECA's three guiding principles and core mandate – 'first, the need for excellence; second, greater cost-effectiveness; and third, more effective partnerships. ECA's core mandate – to provide intellectual leadership and technical support to African countries – demands excellence in performance' (Desmond Davies, 'Shake-up at the ECA', *West Africa*, 1–7 July 1996). In view of this renewal programme and the drive for 'high-calibre staff', ECA staff union also reported that the talks of change, the private sector, and downsizing have been a source of anxiety and worries. The staff would be facing a wage freeze, transfers, early retirements, no promotions. ECA was founded by the United Nations Economic and Social Council in 1958, and receives $45 million annual funding (ibid.). As a kind of think tank for Africa, ECA set up the African Development Bank, founded sub-regional economic grouping, e.g., ECOWAS and the Preferential Trade Area, and drew up major plans of action. The second of its five programme areas of work between 1996 and the year 2001 is in ensuring food security and sustainable development. Women's issues come under this programme, described thus: 'The second programme will focus on the link between food security, population and the environment, known as the nexus. The ECA will concentrate on six issues: enhancing national capacity to manage the nexus issues; strengthening population policies; increasing water supply for food production; supporting regional efforts to enhance food security; furthering the advancement of women; and keeping an overview of science and technology developments, particularly relating to the nexus issues' ('Of changes and reforms: what the ECA's renewal programme is all about', *West Africa*, 1–7 July 1996). Strengthening development management comes under the third programme area, which 'is aimed at developing an efficient public sector, a robust private sector and enhanced popular participation through civil society' (ibid).

6. We are hearing that the present UN Secretary-General, Kofi Annan, an African, is very angry. Annan sees the call for a 'big movement to save Africa' in terms of aid. Thirty-three of the 41 poorest contries in the world are in Africa. Together they owe a so-called debt of $230 billion, only one-third of which the G7, the leaders of the seven most industrialized countries, proposed to reduce at a meeting in Cologne on 18 June 1999. Discussions on proposals to reduce or even cancel these 'debts' had been going on since the summit in Naples in 1994. This

one-third reduction amounts to between $20 billion and $70 billion. It took not years but only a few weeks to decide to commit $50 billion to rebuild Kosovo, inhabited by only two million people. This difference in commitment to Africa's development is nothing new.

Does Africa's crisis call for aid or a rekindling of the spirit of liberation against corrupt African leaders, and a renewed sense of sovereignty?

7. Events during the Rwandan refugees crisis support this theory. Michael Hill reports that in Kigali, apart from the conflict between the government of Rwanda and refugees/militias, there was a major conflict going on between the government and foreign aid agencies, including the UN High Commission on Refugees. The Rwandan government felt that the $1 million a day spent on refugees in camps should have been used to rebuild Rwanda, while aid workers saw their responsibility as feeding and clothing the African refugees. The Rwandan government saw the refugees as people returning to their villages, and aid trucks were being commandeered to drive the refugees to their homes as quickly as possible. The government did not want transit centres or anything resembling a camp, and insisted their home villages were where the refugees could start re-building their lives. Here is a direct contrast made between camp and home, which is a surprise since it shows that aid workers are not able to help refugees in their home villages. (Michael Hill writes, 'The claim is that the Tutsi-led government, if it does not want to mete out punishment to the Hutus, at least wants them to know who is in charge now. Fred Kasozi, who also works with Save the Children in Nkamira, had a more prosaic explanation for the rift between the government and the aid organizations: "I was a civil servant in Uganda so I have been on both sides," he said. "If you work for an NGO, usually you are better paid, you dress better, you have a better car than you do if you work for the government. Yet the government people are supposed to be in charge. So it is not surprising that friction develops." But others criticize the aid organizations for using crises like this one to build their status. At times the aid groups seemed to be trying to outdo one another in giving dire predictions on the refugees' status' (Michael Hill, 'Rwanda's Tutsi-led government clashes with aid agencies over Hutu refugees' treatment', *Valley News*, Sunday, 1 December 1996).

8. Ukwu I. Ukwu, 'Planning and Rural Development: The Nigerian Experience', *Nigerian Journal of Development Studies*, vol. 3, nos 1 & 2, April & October 1983.

9. 'Another Development with Women', *Development Dialogue*, 21–25 June 1982.

Sources

Amadiume, Ifi, 1997, *Reinventing Africa: Matriarchy, Religion and Culture*. London and New York: Zed Books.

Mabogunje, A. L., 1981, *The Development Process: A Spatial Perspective*. New York: Holmes and Meier.

Index

Aba Riot (1929), 84
Abacha, Maryam, 100, 247; and Beijing
  Conference, 248–53
Abacha, Lt.-Gen. Sani, 100, 191, 232, 234,
  251
Abayomi, Lady Oyinkan, 39, 40–1, 52, 57
Abdul Azeez, Ladi, 76, 77, 78
Abdullahi, Alhaji Abubakar, 249
Abdullahi, Ango, 75
Abeokuta Resistance (1948), 84
Abeokuta Women's Union (AWU), 46
Abiola, Dr Hamidat Doyinsola, 95, 96
Abiola, M.K.O., 191
Abisoye Commission of Enquiry, 73–5
abortion, 13, 131–2, 135, 143, 144, 148–9,
  151, 156, 274; protest killings in USA,
  144; self-inflicted, 144
Abubakar, Malam, 125
accountability, 33, 61, 64, 265, 290
Achalonu, Rose, 173
Achebe, Chinua, 37
Ada, a grassroots woman, 165
Ada, of the Paradise Women's Unit, 264
Adams, M.U., 44
Adefarasin, Mrs Hilda, 55, 66, 72, 126, 127
Adekogbe, Elizabeth Adeyemi, 50, 51, 52
Ademola, Lady, 45, 52, 57
Adesioye, Dupe, 11
African National Congress (ANC), 271, 272,
  273, 274, 285; Reconstruction and
  Development Programme (RDP), 273;
  Women's League, 271
Agbroko, Godwin, 99
Agnes, a market woman, 166
Agnes, of the Paradise Women's Unit, 264
agriculture: child labour in, 27; subsistence,
  283; women in, 24, 27, 67, 71, 283, 287
Agugua, N.E.N., 152
Aguiyi-Ironsi, Victoria, 100
Agwu, Confort, 173
Agwuna, Igwe Osita, 138
Ahmadu Bello University (ABU), 67, 70;
  closure of road, 69; massacre of
  students, 73–5; rape cases at, 142

Aids, 23, 29, 98, 138, 142; holistic approach
  to, 29; prevention of, 30
Aig-Imoukhuede, Emily, 59, 61
Aiyedun, Mrs, 51
Ajasa, Sir Kitoye, 40
Ajuwa, Chief Pere, 250
Akande, Professor Jadesola, 97
Akinkugbe, Mrs Adefunke, 95
Akinrinade, Chief Mrs J., 59, 60
Akintunde-Ighodalo, Chief Mrs Fola, 12
Akran, Mrs, 52
Alakija, Mrs Aduke, 94–5
Alice, a schoolteacher, 165–6
Alkali, Zaynab, 119
Amina, Queen, of Zaria, 110
Aminu, Jibril, 107, 146
Amucheazi, Dr, 179
Anne, Princess, 42
anti-apartheid movement, 272–3
Anyanwu, Chief Mrs Ada, 170, 175
armed forces of Nigeria, 185–6; changes in,
  100 see also Nigerian Army Officers'
  Wives' Association
Arusha Strategies for the Advancement of
  Women Beyond the United Nations
  Decade (1984), 14
assaults on black women, 268
Association of African Women for
  Research and Development
  (AAWORD), 288
Awka-Eti village, dispute with Inyom
  Nnobi, 217–18
Awkwa Ibom State Better Life Programme,
  7–9
Awolowo, Hannah Idowu, 51, 100
Awolowo, Obafemi, 100
Azikiwe, Flora, 236
Azikiwe, Dr Nnamdi, 44, 164

Babangida, Major-General Ibrahim, 6, 69,
  162, 170, 191, 197, 202, 219, 232, 234,
  238, 241, 243, 253, 258
Babangida, Maryam, 56–7, 100, 102, 174;
  African Prize for Leadership, 243; and

293